Semantic Interpretation in Generative Grammar

Studies in Linguistics Series
edited by Samuel Jay Keyser

RAY S. JACKENDOFF

Semantic Interpretation in Generative Grammar

The MIT Press
Cambridge, Massachusetts, and London, England

Library of Congress Cataloging in Publication Data

Jackendoff, Ray S
    Semantic interpretation in generative grammar.

    (Studies in linguistics series, v. 2)
    Bibliography: p.
    1. Semantics. 2. Generative grammar. I. Title.
P325.J3   425   72-4210
ISBN 0-262-10013-4

I think I'd like to dedicate this book to Sparky and Sim.

CONTENTS

FOREWORD

We are pleased to present this book as the second volume in the series Studies in Linguistics.

As we have defined it, the series will offer book length studies in linguistics and neighboring fields that further the exploration of man's ability to manipulate symbols. It will pursue the same editorial goals as its companion journal, *Linguistic Inquiry*, and will complement it by providing a format for in-depth studies beyond the scope of the professional article.

By publishing such studies the series will, we hope, answer a need for intensive and detailed research that sheds new light on current theoretical issues and provides a new dimension for their resolution. Toward this end it will present books dealing with the widest range of languages and addressing the widest range of theoretical topics. From time to time and with the same ends in view, the series will include collections of significant articles covering single and selected subject areas and works primarily for use as textbooks.

Like *Linguistic Inquiry*, Studies in Linguistics will seek to publish work of theoretical interest and excellence.

Samuel Jay Keyser

PREFACE

The research reported in this book is an attempt to meet semantics on its own terms and assess the contribution it makes to the overt syntactic patterns of English. Like much other recent work in linguistics, it developed out of a realization that many current problems cannot be solved insightfully within the linguistic theory provided by Chomsky's *Aspects of the Theory of Syntax*, because they involve semantics too deeply.

Most people working on these problems seem to have taken the approach of allowing more semantic factors to enter into the formulation of transformational rules. This approach has developed into the theory of generative semantics, which claims that syntax and semantics are inseparable and homogeneous. However, a small group of linguists, myself included, have adopted a different hypothesis—that if rules of semantic interpretation can be formulated properly, their properties and the properties of the semantic representations they derive can be used to account for these semantic phenomena, leaving the syntactic component as free of semantic intervention as it was in *Syntactic Structures*.

This book is a consolidation of about five years of research on such an interpretive approach to semantics. While it is hardly a complete formulation of a grammar of English, work has progressed far enough that the outlines of the theory are clear, and enough interesting problems have been dealt with to demonstrate the viability of the approach. It is my hope that the publication of this material will stimulate further research and bring about a more widespread understanding of the interpretive theory.

Portions of this book have previously appeared in earlier form in my doctoral dissertation, "Some Rules of Semantic Interpretation for English" (Massachusetts Institute of Technology, 1969), and in my papers "An Interpretive Theory of Negation" (*Foundations of Language*, 1969) and "An Interpretive Theory of Pronouns and Reflexives" (Indiana University Linguistics Club, 1968). However, the analyses presented here differ substantially in many respects from the earlier versions, partially to meet criticisms of unclarity and empirical error, and partially to make possible a more generally coherent theory.

During the writing of this book and the dissertation that was its predecessor, many people have helped me clarify issues and work out problems, linguistic and otherwise. Here are some that stand out in my mind: Adrian Akmajian, Steve Anderson, John Bowers, Peter Culicover, Joe Emonds, Janet Fodor, Dollie Meyers, Jerry Katz, Martin Kay, Howard Lasnik, Gary Martins, Dick Stanley, and Bill Watt. To each of them, many thanks.

I think it only fair also to acknowledge Haj Ross, George Lakoff, and Paul Postal. Much of the material in this book is due to my being in sufficiently violent disagreement with their work to want to do something about it. Without their opposition, the book would have been considerably less comprehensive.

Particular thanks must go to Vicki Fromkin, Carlos Otero, and Jay Keyser. Not only did they read through the entire manuscript and offer detailed comments on both substance and manner of presentation; they lent much-needed encouragement during those blackest days when it seemed the book would never be finished. In addition, I must thank Jay, in his role as editor of the MIT Press series Studies in Linguistics, for much help in getting me through the traumas of publication.

Finally, my deepest gratitude goes to Noam Chomsky and Edward Klima; and my debt to Morris Halle, as he will be the first to acknowledge, is infinite: these three taught me how to do linguistics.

And now, ladies and gentlemen, on with the show.

R.S.J.
Cambridge, Massachusetts

Semantic Interpretation in Generative Grammar

CHAPTER ONE

Outline of the Theory

This study will address itself to the question, How is a generative grammar organized? In particular, how do the rules that deal with meaning interact with those that determine syntactic form? Katz and Postal's *An Integrated Theory of Linguistic Descriptions* (1964) presents an extremely appealing approach to this question that has had far-reaching consequences for linguistic theory. It is the contention of the present study, however, that their approach is incorrect, and that the vast amount of linguistic research that has taken place since 1964 can be accommodated more adequately within a rather different view of the role of semantics in grammar, to be proposed here.

1.1 The Problem of Semantics

In the early days of generative grammar, the nature of the rules relating syntactic structures to meaning was not discussed. Chomsky's *Syntactic Structures* (1957) shows that a linguistic theory in which meaning is determined at least in part by a level of underlying structure can capture important generalizations. But Chomsky does not propose explicit mechanisms for representing or deriving meaning; his main concern is with the formal syntactic devices of the language. With the publication of Katz and Fodor's "The Structure of a Semantic Theory" (1963), the picture changed. Katz and Fodor argue that a grammar should be thought of as a system of rules relating the externalized form of the sentences of a language to their meanings. Hence a complete linguistic description must contain an account of meaning.

   Katz and Fodor suggest that meanings are to be expressed in a universal semantic representation, just as sounds are expressed in a universal phonetic representation. Universality is necessary so that representations are language-independent; we must be able to compare meanings of sentences across languages. Put more strongly, to suppose a universal semantic representation is to make an important claim about the innateness of semantic structure. The semantic representation, it is reasonable to hope, is very tightly integrated into the cognitive system of the human mind.

Of course, compared to phonetic representations, semantic representations are only very indirectly accessible. It is fairly easy to talk about sameness and difference of meaning, but meaning itself, as generations of philosophers have known, is elusive. Thus the study of semantics has always been somewhat derivative, indirect, and fuzzy. It was Katz and Fodor's hope that by making semantics an explicit part of generative grammar, more incisive studies of meaning would be possible. And to some extent their hope has been realized, in that generative grammar has permitted the construction of more highly structured hypotheses about meaning.

It has generally been assumed that semantic representations are not formally similar to syntactic structures (the theory of generative semantics, however, denies this). A complete linguistic description, therefore, must include a new set of rules, a semantic component, to relate meanings to syntactic and/or phonological structure. This is the content of Katz and Fodor's slogan, "linguistic description minus grammar equals semantics" (where "grammar" is used to mean "syntax and phonology"). Katz and Fodor's phraseology, however, is unfortunate: their slogan seems rapidly to have acquired the negative connotation "Semantics is whatever you have to shove under the rug." This interpretation was perhaps a predictable outcome of the relative availability of syntactic and semantic formalisms; it is always less troublesome to defend a syntactic solution to a problem where the formalism is taken for granted than to solve it by developing a new semantic formalism that may not appear independently motivated. Thus research has been biased heavily in favor of syntactic solutions to problems.

It is the intent of this investigation to begin to right this imbalance. By now, many more grammatical phenomena have been studied in detail than in 1963, and much more is known about the criteria that must be met by a system of semantic representation and the rules relating it to syntactic structure. We will approach a number of these phenomena with the possibility of a semantic solution in mind. Insofar as possible, concrete semantic solutions will be proposed and defended with a rigor at least equal to that generally accepted for current transformational formulations. The variety of phenomena covered will permit an integration of the solutions into a more comprehensive and precise theory of the semantic component than has heretofore been proposed.

1.2 Semantic Representation and the Semantic Component

Katz and Fodor characterize semantic representation as a structured bundle of "semantic markers." From their relatively primitive model, a model of semantic representation has evolved in common use that treats semantic representation as something structured like a phrase-marker that is rather similar to syntactic representations, with perhaps some additional information added on somehow. What is taken for granted is that there is basically a single hierarchical structure into which the semantic material of the lexical items in the sentence is arranged.

We will take a fundamentally different approach here. In an attempt to account for a large range of semantic phenomena, we will find that these phenomena divide themselves into a number of independent groups for which rather different analyses are required (see section 1.5). To make clear the independence of these different aspects of semantic representation, we will separate semantic representation into four parts, including two hierarchical structures. Very crudely, the first hierarchical structure, the *functional structure*, represents relations in the sentence induced by the verbs, including such notions as agency, motion, and direction. The *modal structure*, the second hierarchical structure, specifies the conditions under which a sentence purports to correspond to situations in the real world. The *table of coreference* indicates whether pairs of noun phrases in the sentence are intended to be coreferential or not. The *focus and presupposition* designate what information in the sentence is intended to be new and what is intended to be old. The failure of earlier studies to properly distinguish these semantic substructures, particularly the two hierarchical structures, has been the source of much difficulty and confusion.

The commonly accepted view of the semantic component, proposed by Katz and Postal (1964), is that the only syntactic information used in determining semantic representation is the underlying (deep) structure. The motivation of this view, some objections to it, and some of its consequences will be discussed more thoroughly in section 1.3. What is noteworthy here is that this view is based on the assumption that functional structure is the sole source of semantic information. From the beginning of generative grammar, the idea that functional structure is preserved by transformations has been fundamental. In fact, one of the original arguments for the explanatory adequacy of a level of underlying syntactic structure, related to the surface by transformations, was that this underlying level expresses necessary generalizations about understood subjects and objects of verbs—for example the active-passive relationship or the ambiguity of sentences like *I found the boy studying in the library.*

The present study will propose a different view of semantic interpretation, namely, that various parts of semantic representation are related by the semantic component to various levels of the syntactic derivation. The difference between the two theories of the semantic component can be illustrated by the schematic diagrams (1.1), a grammar incorporating Katz and Postal's proposal, and (1.2), the alternative to be argued for here.

(1.1)

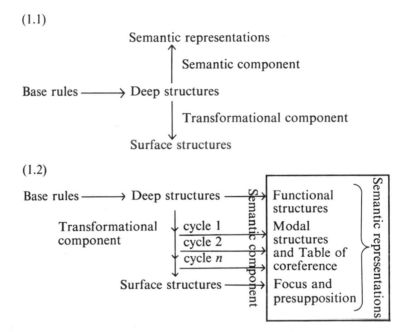

(1.2)

In the most recent variant of (1.1), generative semantics, it is claimed that the semantic component consists of at most an isomorphism, so that the base rules essentially generate semantic representations directly. In this case, given the nature of structures generated by the base within that theory, it can be said that there is no independent level of deep structure that is of any interest. But if (1.2) represents the organization of the grammar, one cannot claim that the "deep structures" we have been searching for are actually semantic representations, and that the level of deep structure can therefore be dispensed with. Such a claim is incomprehensible, since the output of the base rules can represent only one of the aspects of semantic representation. On the contrary, in model (1.2) we must retain the conception of deep structure as representing a level of *syntactic* generality, the conception that originally motivated its existence.

Before going on to some of the basic issues involved in the decision to pursue (1.2) as a linguistic theory, it might be well to remark on one non-issue. To many people, (1.2) intuitively seems to be a repugnant way to organize the grammar. To some extent this feeling is natural, since (1.2) is more complex than (1.1). But it must be emphasized that the choice of a linguistic theory must be made empirically, not on the basis of intuition or personal preference. The reader is enjoined to weigh the considerable empirical evidence presented in this study before making his decision.

One particular point where intuition may be misleading is the question of performance models. The straight-line model of grammar (1.1) is admittedly very appealing in that it makes a performance model look easier to construct, particularly if we (pointlessly) reverse the direction of the upper arrow in (1.1). The performance model that comes to mind, however—one in which the language user actually performs derivations in his head—is open to serious doubt in any event (see for example, Fodor and Garrett 1966 and 1967, and Bever 1970). On the other hand, (1.2) requires a performance model in which some sort of parallel processing is taking place in the construction or interpretation of a sentence. It is hard to see immediately how such a performance model could work. But one must not let a lack of imagination dictate what are truly empirical decisions. From what is known about performance even in the temptingly easy-looking domain of phonetics, it is clear that the correct performance model will involve as yet undreamed-of subtleties. So much more should we expect nonobvious solutions in areas as abstract as syntax and semantics. The conceptual difference between (1.1) and (1.2) is undoubtedly trivial compared to the complexity of an adequate theory of performance.

1.3 The Katz-Postal Hypothesis

Because theory (1.1) has won such general acceptance, it is important to examine the reasoning that led to its adoption. Katz and Fodor (1963) suggest that semantic interpretation is performed by a set of *projection rules*. These rules add to the semantic representation of a sentence those parts of its content and organization not due to the lexical items, that is, the part of the interpretation traceable to the syntactic structure.

The syntactic structure of a sentence is generated by the application of a sequence of rules—first phrase-structure rules, then transformations. The differences in structure between two sentences are produced by differences in the sequences of rules which generate the sentences. Since two sentences containing the same lexical items can differ in meaning only if different sequences of rules have applied, it seemed natural to Katz and Fodor to attribute the meaning contributed by the structure to the operations of the rules themselves; that is, for each phrase structure rule and transformation in the grammar, there would be an associated projection rule telling how the phrase structure rule or transformation contributes to the meaning of sentences in which it operates. Thus projection rules can be divided into two classes, those that are associated with phrase structure rules (called type 1 projection rules or P1) and those associated with transformations (called type 2 projection rules or P2).

The type 1 projection rules create readings for a tree by starting at the lowest constituents in the tree and successively amalgamating readings of sister constituents to produce a reading for the mother constituent. Eventually, when the readings of all constituents have been amalgamated, there is a reading associated with the highest node, S. For each phrase structure rule telling how to expand a node into its constituents, there is a projection rule telling how to amalgamate the readings of the constituents to form a reading for the higher node. There are two examples of P1 rules in Katz and Fodor: a rule of attribution accounting for modifier-head relationships, and a rule combining the interpretation of a verb with the interpretation of its subject or object.

Type 2 projection rules are much less substantively discussed. Presumably a P2 rule shows how a given transformation changes meaning. When Katz and Fodor wrote their paper, P2 rules were absolutely essential, because the combining of kernel sentences into complex structures was regarded as a transformational operation: full interpretation of a complex sentence thus required projection rules to interpret the effect of the embedding transformations. Since then, however, recursion has come to be regarded as a property of the base component, so this particular type of P2 rule is no longer necessary.

Katz and Postal's *An Integrated Theory of Linguistic Descriptions* (1964) set out to show that no P2 rules are necessary, that is, that no changes of meaning are induced by transformations. First, let us consider obligatory transformations. Under the Katz-Fodor conception of projection rules, differences in meaning must be associated with choice-points in the derivation. Since there is no choice whether or not to perform an obligatory transformation, there can never be two sentences differing in meaning solely because of the application of the transformation. Therefore there cannot be P2 rules associated with obligatory transformations. This leaves two cases: optional singulary transformations and generalized, or embedding transformations.

Embedding transformations have already been disposed of by assigning their recursive properties to the base. Optional singularies fall into three types: deletion, insertion, and order-changing rules. Deletion rules can be kept from changing meaning if we adopt *recoverability of deletion* as a condition on transformations (Katz and Postal, p. 81). The known insertion rules all insert meaningless particles such as *do* and inflectional markers, so they do not change meaning. Order-changing rules preserve understood grammatical relations. Since the Katz-Fodor theory tacitly assumes that grammatical relations (as generated by phrase-structure rules and interpreted by P1) are the only kind of structural information relevant in semantic interpretation, order-changing transformations preserve meaning as well.

Thus under Katz and Postal's assumptions about semantics, no P2 rules appear necessary. Furthermore, Katz and Postal show that stating a P2 rule is tantamount to restating the operation of the transformation with which it is associated, so that the whole concept of P2 is suspect. Therefore, the whole burden of semantic interpretation falls on P1, which are associated with the phrase-structure rules of the base component.

Katz and Postal's argument hence leads to the following conclusion:

Katz-Postal Hypothesis, weak form (KP1):
Semantic projection rules operate exclusively on underlying phrase-markers; hence transformations do not change meaning.

From the conclusion that all information required for the operation of projection rules is present in underlying structure, it is a simple rhetorical step to

Katz-Postal Hypothesis, strong form (KP2):
All semantic information is represented in underlying structure.

Given the Katz-Fodor conception of projection rules associated with the choice-points in derivations, and given the limited power proposed for projection rules, Katz and Postal make a very good case for even the strong form of their hypothesis. The Katz-Postal Hypothesis is, of course, theory (1.1) of section 1.2.

KP2 makes a very strong claim. Just how strong it is can be seen from the following paraphrase: every nonlexical semantic difference must be represented as a deep structure difference. But even this strong a claim seems to have been accepted nearly universally.

KP2 follows from KP1 if the semantic component is composed entirely of simple combinatorial rules like those given by Katz and Fodor. But suppose that some projection rule actually *adds* meaning, that is, it adds semantic markers to an interpretation other than those contained in the lexical items in the sentence. Suppose further that this rule is optional, and that the information it adds is not essential for a well-formed interpretation. Then it is possible for there to be two interpretations for a single sentence, differing only in whether this optional projection rule has applied. The logical possibility of such a situation shows that KP2 and KP1 are not equivalent: projection rules may operate exclusively on underlying phrase-markers without all semantic information being represented there. Hence KP2, the universally accepted form of the hypothesis, does not follow from KP1, the form Katz and Postal state and claim to prove.

KP1 itself is open to question as well. Katz and Postal's treatment of apparent counterexamples is largely correct, but there is at least one serious error, and subsequent research has uncovered a great many more areas of the grammar where KP1 cannot be justified on independent syntactic grounds. Much of this book will be devoted to discussing these areas.

The error in Katz and Postal's analysis is in their discussion of negation. In the grammar of *Syntactic Structures*, negation was simply added by an optional transformation, which obviously changed meaning. Katz and Postal point out (p. 74) that the analyses of Lees (1960) and Klima (1964) independently motivate a negative morpheme in underlying structure, so that no transformation which changes negative sentences to positive sentences is necessary. However Katz and Postal overlook the fact that even with the negative morpheme, Klima's system of rules is not meaning-preserving: he derives from the same underlying structure the nonsynonymous sentences *Not much shrapnel hit the soldier* and *much shrapnel didn't hit the soldier*. We will discuss examples of this sort and attempts to preserve KP1 in spite of them in Chapter 8.

How can we simultaneously reject KP1 and accept Katz and Postal's arguments against type 2 projection rules? It turns out that in fact there is no consistent way to characterize the way the passive, for example, changes meaning, so there cannot be a projection rule for the passive. Rather, the generalizations that we will observe concern derived structure configurations, regardless of what transformations are involved in the derivation. Hence the semantic rules we propose here will be of a type not envisioned by Katz and Fodor—rules that interpret derived structure rather than derivations.

It is important to notice the significance of deep structure in a theory incorporating KP2. KP2 claims that all meaning differences are represented in deep structure. Since projection rules therefore cannot add or change any elements of meaning, deep structures must in fact represent logical structure rather than syntactic structure if any conflict between the two arises, regardless of complexities thereby incurred in the transformational component. The need for "abstract" deep structures exemplified in G. Lakoff (1968a, 1970a, 1971), Ross (1969a, 1970), Bach (1968), R. Lakoff (1968), and McCawley (1970) is a natural consequence of KP2.

As deep structures become more and more "abstract," they gradually become denuded of syntactic significance. Distributional facts that can be captured naturally by a relatively "shallowly" conceived base must instead be explained by somewhat arbitrary restrictions on transformations. Thus aspects of linguistic description that can be accomplished within the relatively limited power of a context-free phrase-structure grammar must instead be delegated to a much more powerful transformational component, complete with a full and extremely powerful theory of exceptions. The concomitant limitation of the base is hardly commensurate. An oft-repeated argument that the semantic component is simplified by the use of abstract deep structures is not justified: the transformational component, it can be argued, would be correspondingly simplified by writing certain processes as rules in the semantic component. And in fact, we will show that for many grammatical processes a semantic account adds less total machinery to the grammar than does a syntactic account. Without formulating serious proposals in both frameworks, no such decision can be made.

Following the tendency toward abstract deep structure to its logical conclusion, the deep structures grow closer and closer to one's intuitive notion of "semantic representation." This has to be the case, since the power of the semantic component is so severely constrained by KP2. One is thus led rather persuasively to the idea of dispensing altogether with the autonomous level of deep structure, generating instead semantic representations, and proceeding directly to surface structures by means of transformations. Such a proposal is made in McCawley (1968a, 1968b, 1970) and discussed further in G. Lakoff (1970b) and Postal (1970).

Implementation of such a theory of "generative semantics," however, seems to lead to an extremely unconstrained conception of transformations. Furthermore, G. Lakoff (1969, 1970b) has argued that even less constrained devices, derivational constraints, must be widely used in a grammar based on generative semantic principles. The conceptual generality of a grammar containing only base rules, transformations, and derivational constraints has been claimed (for example, by Postal, to appear) as a great advantage over the theory proposed here, which contains several types of semantic rules in addition to phrase-structure rules and transformations. Lakoff (1970b) points out that semantic rules operating on derived structure are expressible as special cases of derivational constraints, concluding that they do not form part of a substantively different linguistic theory.

However, these arguments miss the point. To see why, we must consider more carefully what factors enter into the choice between two competing theories.

1.4 On Choosing Between Two Theories

Let us now make clear what empirical issues are involved in deciding between models (1.1) and (1.2). I take a linguistic theory to be an abstract representation of human language ability.[1] It defines a set of grammars of individual languages, each of which is claimed to be a possible human language. Therefore the adequacy of a linguistic theory is measured by how well the class of grammars it defines matches the class of human languages.

If it were shown that the class of grammars defined by theory (1.1) were identical to the class defined by theory (1.2), we would of course decide in favor of (1.1) on aesthetic grounds. Similarly, if the set of grammars de-

[1]The possible degree of abstraction of linguistic theory is easily underestimated. Kepler's laws of interplanetary motion are certainly abstract in that they are mathematical relations relating position and velocity to time; they do not describe the inertial and gravitational mechanisms governing the motion. Yet they constitute a strong explanatory theory relative to other theories of Kepler's time. It may well be that the present stage of linguistic theory is equally abstract. This does not make the theory less interesting.

fined by a theory incorporating only phrase-structure rules and no transformations were identical to the set of grammars defined by the theory of transformational grammar, we would decide in favor of the former. When defending a structurally complex theory against a structurally simple one, one must show that the two theories do not define the same set of grammars, and that the complex theory proves a more accurate model of the data. To defend the simpler theory, one need only show that the two theories are empirically equivalent.

There are three kinds of differences that we will adduce in favor of theory (1.2) (corresponding to Chomsky's (1965) levels of observational, descriptive, and explanatory adequacy). First, if it can be shown that theory (1.1) cannot define a grammar that generates the full range of English sentences, theory (1.2) may include such a grammar. That alone would justify the more complex theory. In practice, however, this argument is not so easy to advance, because of the nearly unlimited ability of any theory of this scope to accommodate awkward points. For example, Chomsky (1970b) points out that one can always simulate derived structure rules of semantic interpretation in a theory of the form (1.1), by generating constituents of arbitrary structure in the base, filtering them in the base for the desired semantic property, then using a filtering transformation at the desired point of the derivation to match these arbitrary structures with the derived structure. In the course of this study, we will see many examples of such attempts to save theory (1.1).

A second difference we may find between the two theories is in their ability to express significant generalizations about the language. When applying the alternative theories to simple cases, it often turns out that they require virtually the same amount of machinery. When we dig deeper, however, it often turns out that they make slightly different but crucial predictions. For example, it will be shown in Chapters 4 and 5 that in theory (1.2), the three fundamental rules Pronominalization, Reflexivization, and Complement Subject Interpretation can be ordered together, enabling us to capture the substantial similarity in their environments. This generalization cannot be captured in theory (1.1) without additional constraints of a brute force nature. Many such differences arise in the course of this investigation. They may be relatively small points in the entire description of the language, but given two theories as sophisticated as those we are comparing, it may often be the small points of generality that decide between them.

The third and perhaps most important difference we may find between the theories concerns the classes of possible grammars defined by the theories. A linguistic theory claims that the grammars it defines all correspond to possible human languages. Hence a theory can be defective in that it defines grammars which, insofar as we can determine, do not correspond to any human language. To clarify terminology that is often misinterpreted, such a theory can be said to be "too powerful" in that it defines too large a set of grammars, or "too weak" in that it fails to constrain the class of possible grammars sufficiently. The addition of several new kinds of semantic interpretation rules in theory (1.2) appears superficially to make (1.2) a more powerful, or less constrained, theory. But it will turn out that we will be able to place substantial limitations on the power of each type of rule in the grammar, including transformations, so that the end result will be a smaller class of possible grammars, or a less powerful theory, than theory (1.1).

I will illustrate first a very specific example of a heavier constraint possible in theory (1.2), then go on to somewhat more general and speculative discussion. In the standard theory of pronominalization, perhaps the most natural under theory (1.1), it is claimed that pronouns are transformationally reduced forms of fully specified NPs. Transformations producing pronouns must, among other things, verify that a potential pronoun is coreferential with its antecedent. Therefore this theory must specify that coreferentiality of two NPs is a possible condition on transformations. What is not explained is why only pronominalization-like rules ever make use of this kind of condition. Why, for example, is there no rule that moves an NP if it is coreferential with an NP elsewhere in the sentence? In the interpretive theory of pronominalization developed in Chapter 4, where pronouns are generated by the base and semantic rules determine their antecedents, there is no need for transformations ever to refer to coreference conditions. Hence we can deprive transformations of the ability to refer to coreference and construct a weaker theory in which a movement rule dependent on coreference cannot be stated. Thus the interpretive theory, while it has an extra conceptual device, that is, semantic rules which establish coreference on the basis of derived structure, describes a more constrained set of grammars.

A more general constraint on transformations permitted by theory (1.2) concerns the integrity of lexical items. Chomsky (1970a) proposes the Lexicalist Hypothesis, roughly, that transformations do not perform derivational morphology. This hypothesis in turn leads to constraints on the form of the base and to generalizations about certain transformations (see also Bowers 1969a and Jackendoff 1968c and 1971a for generalizations expressible under the Lexicalist Hypothesis). Theory (1.2) is consistent with the Lexicalist Hypothesis, and perhaps with a stronger position: transformations cannot change node labels, and they cannot delete under identity or positive absolute exception (see sections 5.2 and 6.9–10). This means that the only changes that transformations can make to lexical items is to add inflectional affixes such as number, gender, case, person, and tense. Transformations will thus be restricted to movement rules and insertion and deletion of constants and closed sets of items. We will refer to this set of constraints as the Extended Lexical Hypothesis.

Another heavy constraint on the power of transformations is proposed by Emonds (1970). Roughly, he proposes that with a certain specifiable class of exceptions, the output of a transformation must be a structure that can be independently produced by a base rule. Thus, for example, he claims that it is no accident that the deep object of a passive sentence comes to occupy subject position rather than perhaps a position between the auxiliary and the main verb, where no noun phrase can be generated in the base. Likewise, it is no accident that the deep subject of a passive ends up in a prepositional phrase which is like all other prepositional phrases, rather than in some altogether new kind of constituent. The exceptions to Emonds's generalization are transformations that operate only in a special class of clauses, primarily main clauses; these transformations each perform one of a very small class of possible operations. Clearly this hypothesis puts very strong constraints on the notion "possible transformation." It seems much more likely to be true of the transformations needed by the theory proposed here than it is of those needed by a theory incorporating the Katz-Postal Hypothesis.

Of course, these heavy restrictions on transformations must be accompanied with concomitant restrictions on possible semantic rules, if the number of possible grammars is to be reduced. But the rules to be proposed here fall into a small number of very restricted types, and places where they apply in the syntactic derivation are similarly restricted. One would hope that the rule types and their orderings would be universal, for example that the coreference rules, whatever their exact form in a given language, would be rules of semantic interpretation operating at the end of each transformational cycle, as theory (1.2) suggests they are in English. If this claim is correct, the number of possible grammars is greatly reduced, since all the ordering problems of the standard transformations dealing with coreference are no longer open to question.

Thus it appears quite possible that the addition to linguistic theory of semantic rules applying to derived structure, though it produces conceptually more complex grammars, results in fewer possible grammars, and grammars that capture more generalizations. These are the empirical criteria that measure linguistic theories.

The remainder of this chapter will lay the groundwork for the development of a semantic component.

1.5 Elements of Semantic Interpretation

Let me sketch some of the things which must appear in semantic representations. Katz and Fodor are interested in such properties of readings as synonymy, analyticity, anomaly, and truth conditions, as well as the actual content of the reading. Here we will be primarily interested in the content of the reading, and how it is derived.

First, to strike a discouraging note, it is not even clear that one can construct a formal object which corresponds to the intuitive notion "semantic interpretation of a sentence," because of the infinite divisibility of many semantic properties and the (perhaps undecidable) problem of choosing what information is part of the reading and what information merely follows from the reading (see for example Wittgenstein 1958 and Quine 1960). Much of the difficulty in defining semantic readings arises in trying to represent the meanings of lexical items. Here, however, we will be more concerned with how the meanings of lexical items are combined to form meanings of sentences on the basis of syntactic structures, in other words, the contribution of structure to the meanings of sentences. And within this domain, I think it is possible to separate out certain discrete aspects of meaning and deal with them coherently. This is not to imply that specifying the meanings of lexical items is any less important. It is just a separate and perhaps more difficult problem.

The aspect of semantic representation that is perhaps most closely linked to syntactic structure is the *functional structure* of a semantic reading. We can think of verbs as semantic functions of one or more variables, the readings of syntactically associated noun phrases providing semantic values for the variables. Under this assumption, each verb in the deep structure of a sentence presumably corresponds to a function in the semantic representation. The embedding relations of functions in the semantic representation will presumably mirror the embedding relations of verbs (and other functional words) in the deep structure. This part of semantic representation was recognized by Katz and Fodor; in subsequent work it was assumed to be the only contribution of syntactic structure to semantic representation.

A refinement of this aspect of meaning might provide for a partial analysis of verbs into semantic subfunctions such as *causative, directional,* and so forth, giving the semantic representation of a verb some internal functional structure. Such an analysis can provide a way of grouping verbs into natural semantic (and syntactic) classes and thus explain certain similarities in behavior. The proposals of Katz (1966) and Gruber (1965, 1967a, 1967b) are attempts to analyze verbs in this fashion. The "higher pro-verbs" of G. Lakoff (1971) and McCawley (1968b) and the case grammar of Fillmore (1968) are attempts to represent this internal structure externally, as a part of syntax. But basically there is no disagreement on the claim that these semantic properties can be represented structurally, and that it is the deep structure which determines them. In Chapter 2 we will discuss further this aspect of meaning.

Other elements of semantic representation do not lend themselves to being represented in trees or functional form. One example is coreference relations among noun phrases. Although the determination of coreference relations does depend on syntactic structure, the semantic notion "NP^1 is (non)coreferential with NP^2" has nothing to do with the functional structure of sentences. For example, to say that *John* is the subject of *knew,* that *you wouldn't believe him* is the object of *knew* and that *him* is the object of *believe* in the sentence *John knew you wouldn't believe him* is to say nothing about whether *John* and *him* are to be understood as the same individual. Rather, an independent device is necessary to express coreference relations. Referential indices, introduced in *Aspects of the Theory of Syntax,* are one such device. Here we will use a different formalism, a *table of coreference* independent of the functional structure. Each entry in the table will contain a pair of NPs and a relation "coreferential" or "noncoreferential" obtaining between them. For certain formal reasons which will appear in Chapter 4, this notation has additional advantages. What is important to observe for the present is that however coreference is marked, it is clearly not the same kind of semantic information as functional structure. Chapters 4 and 5 will develop the rules deriving the table of coreference.

Another element of semantic interpretation which has nothing to do with the functional structure is *focus and presupposition*. Various concepts have been discussed under these names and also under such names as *topic-comment* or *thematic structure*.[2] Here we will use *focus of a sentence* to mean "the information in the sentence that is assumed by the speaker not to be shared by him and the hearer"; *presupposition of a sentence* will mean "the information in the sentence that is assumed by the speaker to be shared by him and the hearer." Changing the focus and presupposition of a sentence, for example by introducing emphatic stress, does not change the understood functional relationships between verbs and their arguments: *JOHN saw Bill*, *John SAW Bill*, and *John saw BILL* differ in focus and presupposition, but John is performing the same action with respect to Bill in each case. Chapter 6 will discuss the rules which determine this element of the interpretation.

The scope of negation and quantifiers is another independent aspect of semantic interpretation. Negation and quantifiers may appear to be part of the functional structure, since we can set up expressions in the predicate calculus in which negation and quantifiers appear to have function-like behavior. Such an approach has been taken in Carden (1968) and G. Lakoff (1971). However, the syntactic and semantic behavior of negation and quantifiers is sufficiently different from that of verbs that this claim cannot be made lightly. Chapter 7 will argue that this aspect of interpretation is more adequately represented in a second hierarchical semantic structure, the *modal structure*, which has considerably different properties than the functional structure.

Three semantic properties having to do specifically with reference must appear in semantic representations. The first is specificity of indefinite NPs (see Baker 1966 and Dean 1968): *Fred wants to meet a voluptuous blonde* is ambiguous as to whether or not the speaker can point out the girl Fred wants to meet. The second is genericity: *A unicorn is a dangerous beast* expresses properties of the species *unicorn*, not of some individual. The third is referential opacity: *John thinks that the book that was burned was not burned* is ambiguous in that it can ascribe to John either an inconsistent or an incorrect belief, depending on whether he is to be responsible for the

---

[2]See Halliday (1967). Halliday's use of the term *theme* is emphatically not to be confused with the use to be introduced in Chapter 2 as an expression of functional structure.

correctness of the description *the book that was burned.*[3] Attempts to treat
these properties in terms of functional structure (for example Baker 1966
and Bach 1968) have inevitably required deep structures far removed from
the surface and powerful transformational apparatus. Chapter 7 will suggest that the formalisms of the modal structure are well adapted to express
the first two of these properties of semantic representation.

Finally, the illocutionary force of a sentence is an aspect of semantic
interpretation that has recently been open to heated discussion. It has been
argued, most comprehensively by J. R. Ross (1970a) and R. Lakoff (1968)
that whether a sentence is a declarative, an imperative, or an interrogative
should be represented explicitly in the functional structure. Anderson
(1968b), Fraser (1970), and Culicover (1970) argue against this position in
several ways; Culicover goes on to propose an approach that treats them
as independent from the functional structure, thereby gaining several important generalizations in the transformations. In Chapter 7, we will see a
number of indications that illocutionary force is a further element of
interpretation that can be represented in the modal structure.

The semantic interpretation of a sentence, then, is to be viewed as a
collection of information of various sorts about different aspects of the
meaning. To say that because of its complexity, this view is inferior to a
position claiming that all meaning can be represented as functional structure is only to assert prejudice. Again it must be emphasized that the decision is empirical; it must be based on the relative adequacy of the linguistic theories which entail these views of semantic representation.

1.6 Well-Formedness Conditions on Semantic Interpretations

The box on the right-hand side of diagram (1.2) represents the collection of
elements of meaning assigned to a sentence by the semantic interpretation
rules of the grammar. What is not necessarily determined by the grammar
is whether this collection of disparate elements actually forms a sensible
meaning. To determine this there must be a set of well-formedness conditions on semantic interpretation. Some of these conditions are parts of
the grammar, but others shade off into pragmatics or knowledge of the
real world. At this point I will present only two examples of well-formedness conditions, both fairly obvious, and mention a few more to be
developed later on.

---

[3]Referential opacity has been discussed by many philosophers, including Frege,
Russell, Carnap, and Quine. Janet Fodor (1970) discusses it in the framework of
generative grammar.

A first example of semantic well-formedness conditions might be *selectional restrictions*. Under this hypothesis, (1.3), for example, would be generated by the grammar and receive an interpretation, but the interpretation it receives would be nonsensical.

(1.3) Colorless green ideas sleep furiously.

This position is taken by Chomsky in *Syntactic Structures*, but not in *Aspects*. Jackendoff (1966a) and McCawley (1968a) argue for a return to Chomsky's earlier position. (Ironically, G. Lakoff (1968a) points out that his arguments for the "abstract" source for instrumental adverbs hold only if one accepts the position of *Aspects*, which Lakoff has since given up in favor of the position taken here.)

There are a number of reasons for taking this position. To claim that sentences with selectional violations are not generated by the syntax makes it impossible to produce perfectly acceptable sentences like (1.4).

(1.4) It's crazy to talk of rocks eating.

If, instead, sentences with selectional violations were generated by the syntax but received no reading, (1.4) could not be interpreted. If they were interpreted, but the interpretation they received were simply ANOMALY, containing no information of the lexical items and their semantic relations to each other, then we would predict (1.4) and (1.5) to be synonymous: both would mean "It's crazy to talk of ANOMALY."

(1.5) It's crazy to talk of Bill elapsing.

We see therefore that sentences with selectional violations must receive interpretations; hence they cannot be filtered out before readings are completed.

Furthermore, there are cases where selectional restrictions cannot be applied until the readings of an indefinite number of constituents have been amalgamated to form a reading. Compare (1.6) and (1.7):

(1.6)   I ate something that was the result of what Bill acknowledged to be a new baking process.

(1.7) *I ate something that was the result of what Bill acknowledged to be a syntactic transformation.

The selection in these sentences is between *eat* and the final NP in the sentence, which is deeply embedded. To capture this at the stage of lexical insertion, as proposed in *Aspects*, would involve duplicating all the machinery of the semantic component. Sometimes the selection is based on semantic properties that can be identified in general only with an entire sentence, not with some particular formative. For example, it will be argued in Chapter 5 that *shout* in (1.8) requires the complement sentence to be something that *Bill* can cause to happen.

(1.8) I shouted to Bill for Harry to leave.

It has often been noticed that this selection imposes a constraint on possible verbs in the complement:

(1.9) *I shouted to Bill for Harry to $\begin{cases} \text{know the answer.} \\ \text{be tall.} \\ \text{have black hair.} \end{cases}$

What has been overlooked is that choice of complement subject is relevant. By changing the complement subject in (1.9) appropriately, the sentence is acceptable.

(1.10) I shouted to Bill for the next recruit to $\begin{cases} \text{know the answer.} \\ \text{be tall.} \\ \text{have black hair.} \end{cases}$

Thus the selection must be dependent on the reading of the entire sentence, not just the verb or subject. This is a further argument that it must be performed on completed semantic readings.

Finally, violation of selection restrictions can occur either on the basis of knowledge of the language or on knowledge of the real world. (1.11), if uttered while pointing to a man, seems to be the same sort of violation as (1.12), even though (1.11) depends on facts external to the language and (1.12) does not.

(1.11) That person over there is pregnant.
(1.12) *That man over there is pregnant.

And as with the analytic-synthetic distinction, it is impossible to tell where linguistic knowledge leaves off and extralinguistic knowledge takes over.

(1.13) is presumably ruled out on the basis of one's knowledge of the language (although even this is open to question). On the other hand, the very similar (1.14) can be ruled out only on the basis of a mathematical theorem.

(1.13) Irving drew a circular square.
(1.14) Irving constructed a five-sided regular polyhedron.

The only level of derivation at which linguistic and extralinguistic facts can be brought to bear on sentences in identical fashion, as appears necessary in (1.11)–(1.14), is the level of semantic representation. Thus the most general solution to the problem of selection seems to be a well-formedness condition on semantic representation.

Another well-formedness condition will be used extensively in Chapters 4 and 5: the Consistency Condition on coreferents. This condition states simply that if two noun phrases are marked coreferential by the grammar, they must in fact be able to represent the same individual. (1.15) is an obvious case of its application.

(1.15) *The old man saw herself.

The only possible antecedent for *herself* is *the old man*; we will assume that the semantic component actually produces this interpretation. But since the two noun phrases differ in gender, they cannot denote the same individual, so the Consistency Condition rules out this interpretation of the sentence. Since it is the only possible interpretation, the sentence is rejected as unacceptable.

By adopting well-formedness conditions on interpretations, it will often be possible to avoid complex constraints on interactions between various rules. In this way the rules of the grammar will be able to apply freely, producing readings without regard to their acceptability. For example, in Chapter 3 we will show that the rules generating and moving adverbs, which have generally been treated as extremely idiosyncratic, can be made perfectly general by subjecting the resulting semantic interpretations to independently motivated well-formedness conditions: if an adverb occurs in an incorrect position, it will be integrated into the interpretation of the sentence in a way incompatible with its possible range of meanings. Another well-formedness condition, the Thematic Hierarchy Condition developed in Chapters 2 and 4, explains a number of exceptions to the passive and replaces complex constraints on the application of transformations (the Crossover Condition). The interaction of two independent well-formedness conditions developed in Chapter 5 constrains the selection of coreferents for complement subjects in a way that eliminates a complex system of constraints on transformations. The result in each of these cases is that the transformations can be permitted to apply without constraint because the resulting semantic interpretation can readily be ruled out. Thus the rules already necessary for semantic interpretation can replace constraints whose only motivation is the need to rule sentences out.

1.7 Assumptions about the Syntax and the Lexicon

We will assume a base component of the usual form, a context-free phrase-structure grammar whose initial symbol is *S*. However, there are two important differences between the base component we will use here and that of *Aspects of the Theory of Syntax.*

The first difference concerns the process of lexical insertion. In *Aspects,* category nodes such as *N* and *V* are expanded into *complex symbols* which express subcategorization and selectional restrictions. Then lexical items are inserted by context-sensitive rules which prevent deep structures from violating these restrictions. Inasmuch as we have argued that these restrictions are properly implemented in the semantic component, a simpler lexical insertion process is possible. We will assume that lexical insertion rules insert lexical items freely under category symbols, eliminating the notion *complex symbol* altogether. In other words, we will assume that *Colorless green ideas sleep furiously* does have a well-formed deep structure.

The second difference concerns the use of node symbols. One of the consequences of the Lexicalist Hypothesis of Chomsky (1970a) is that syntactic nodes are to be represented as matrices of distinctive features. This change in the conception of syntactic nodes is parallel to the replacement of the IPA alphabet by matrices of distinctive features in phonological theory; the arguments are of similar form, based on cross-classification of categories with respect to rules of the grammar. We will make particular use of the concept of syntactic nodes as distinctive feature matrices in dealing with the analysis of adverbs and reflexives in Chapters 3 and 4 respectively. Hence we will assume that the base component and all other rules which refer to phrase-markers have the distinctive feature mechanism available as a means of capturing generalizations; such symbols as *NP* and *VP* will be considered as abbreviations of feature matrices, just as *ü* and *č* are treated as abbreviations of feature matrices in phonology.

Aside from the introduction of syntactic distinctive features, the transformational component will be assumed to be substantially the same as proposed in *Aspects*. Transformations will be assumed to be strictly ordered and applied according to the principle of the transformational cycle: the complete sequence of transformations is applied to the most deeply embedded *S*, then repeated, each time applying to the next most deeply embedded *S*. In Chapter 4 we will show that at least some NP nodes govern a cycle as well.

Finally, a little attention must be given to the internal structure of the lexicon. Under the Extended Lexical Hypothesis, transformations cannot perform derivational morphology. How then can we capture the semiproductivity of morphological processes? At the time of Lees's *Grammar of English Nominalizations* (1960) there was no possibility but a transformational solution, since the concept of a lexicon had not been proposed. But as with semantics, the potentialities of a lexicon were not explored even after the theoretical framework was available. Thus at present most well-known proposals about derivational morphology are couched in transformational formalisms, for example, G. Lakoff (1971) and Chapin (1967). One notable exception is Gruber (1967b).

Such solutions are not available to us. Rather, it is necessary to list, for example, both a verb and its nominalization in the lexicon. To capture the relation between them, there must be a way to express the fact that there is less independent information in a pair of lexical items consisting of a verb and its nominalization than in a pair consisting of a random verb and noun. One way to capture this redundancy is to consider the measure of information a simple counting of features, but to eliminate all or some of the features of the nominalization to capture the generality; this method, however, is not consistent with our assumption that both the verb and the nominalization are fully specified in the lexicon. Alternatively, one could propose that the regularities are expressed within the measure of information itself, as *redundancy rules* that say that certain shared features of the nominalization do not count as independent information. Such a solution will be assumed here.

We will suppose, then, that part of the lexicon (or information measure for the lexicon) is a set of morphological and semantic redundancy rules, parallel in function to the morpheme structure rules, that specify independent phonological information content. These redundancy rules will enable us to express the concept "separate but related lexical items" without the use of transformations. Jackendoff (to appear) explores this assumption in some detail, with application to a wide range of word-formation processes; it is shown that these redundancy rules make somewhat different and more satisfactory predictions than transformations in a number of cases.

1.8 A Remark on Motivating Rules

In a theory of grammar that minimizes the power of the semantic component, the base, and the lexicon, such as the theory of generative semantics, there is only one way in which similarity in meaning or co-occurrence restrictions between two constructions can be captured: a transformation. In a theory permitting a number of different kinds of rules, such as the theory to be explored here, there are many ways of capturing generalizations. In addition to transformations, there are all the different kinds of semantic rules operating at different levels of the derivation. Generalizations can also be captured within the lexicon, by means of the redundancy rules mentioned in section 1.7. Furthermore, certain generalizations can be expressed by treating the nodes for lexical categories as feature complexes, then stating base rules, transformations, and semantic rules so as to refer to more than one major category at a time.

With all these different kinds of rules at our disposal, several very different analyses will often come to mind for the same phenomenon, each of which seems equally capable of expressing the proper generalization. How do we decide which account is to be preferred? There can be no sort of principle that says, "Always choose an X rule if you have a chance": it is not difficult to construct algorithms to reduce all rules to any chosen type, given exception machinery of sufficient power, such as G. Lakoff's (1971). Rather the decision will be made on the basis of how the rules interact with each other most naturally and how appropriate the power already proposed for a particular type of rule is for handling something new. In general, similar processes should be handled by similar kinds of rules, to limit the total power of the theory.

Also of prime importance in motivating a particular treatment of a phenomenon is how it is reflected in the lexicon. If a process takes place only for certain lexical items, or varies over several classes of lexical items, we should choose the way out of handling the process that least increases the independent information content of the lexicon. The use of exception features is the worst possible solution, in that it represents an arbitrary bifurcation of the lexicon, and so every marked feature represents independent information. Interpreted another way, the use of exception features makes the claim that each exceptional lexical item must be learned individually. On the other hand, if the difference in grammatical behavior has something to do with the meaning of the items in question, then that is the best possible case, since the rule has only to refer to the properties already present—if the meaning of the item is learned, its behavior is known automatically.

Unfortunately, this latter case is also the least formalizable, since we often do not have a principled way of expressing the meaning. For the sake of stating a rule, however, it seems to me perfectly adequate to provisionally adopt an arbitrary feature, if we have clear intuitions about when this feature is present, and if it is fully understood that it has no life independent of the complete reading in which it is embedded.

Our investigation will be organized as follows: Chapter 2 introduces a formalism for expressing functional structure and defends it with respect to other current proposals. Chapter 3 is a detailed investigation of adverbs and adverbial phrases, a demonstration of the efficacy of a theory employing projection rules and syntactic distinctive features to capture generalizations. Chapters 4 and 5 are concerned with coreference. The former develops an interpretive theory of pronouns and reflexives; the latter extends this analysis to the deleted complement subject and explores its extensive consequences on the complement system as a whole. Chapter 6 discusses focus and presupposition, with a systematic semantic analysis of some intonation contours. Chapter 7 introduces the modal structure as a representation of specificity and extends it to several other phenomena. Chapter 8 is a detailed study of negation and its interaction with modal structure and focus and presupposition. Chapters 9 and 10 present conclusions and consequences of the proposed semantic theory for the transformational component.

CHAPTER TWO

Grammatical Relations and Functional Structure

2.1 The Semantic Insufficiency of Grammatical Relations

Chapter 1 claimed that one aspect of semantic representation, the functional structure, is determined on the basis of underlying phrase-markers, and that other aspects of readings are determined at other levels. In this chapter we will briefly sketch an approach to functional structure that will be of use in succeeding chapters.

The feature of underlying syntactic structure that presumably relates to functional structure is the system of *grammatical relations*, that is, the structural relations obtaining between verbs and the noun phrases, adjective phrases, prepositional phrases, and sentence complements that they strictly subcategorize. Much of the justification of transformations involves arguments about understood grammatical relations and their representation in deep structure. Yet the "natural" grammatical relations such as subject and object do not correspond in any simple fashion to the understood semantic relations. Consider these well-known examples:

(2.1) The door opened.
(2.2) Charlie opened the door.

(2.3) Fred bought some hashish from Reuben.
(2.4) Reuben sold some hashish to Fred.

In the traditional sense of grammatical relations, (2.1)–(2.4) have their underlying grammatical relations expressed in the surface as well; the sentences have undergone no movement transformations that would alter the underlying positions. But the grammatical relations do not express certain obvious semantic facts. *The door* has the same semantic function in (2.1) and (2.2), although it is the subject in one and the object in the other. In both (2.3) and (2.4) the relation between *Fred* and *Reuben* is *recipient-donor*. Yet in (2.3) *Fred* is subject and *Reuben* is in a prepositional phrase; and the reverse holds in (2.4).

The existence of numerous examples like (2.1)–(2.4) has led many grammarians to feel that something is seriously wrong with the traditional notion of grammatical relations. Their feeling is substantiated in a theory of grammar which includes the strong form of the Katz-Postal Hypothesis. For if all semantic information is contained in deep structure, the "natural" deep structures of (2.1)–(2.4) cannot be the "real" deep structures. In the "real" deep structures, *the door* would occupy the same position in (2.1) and (2.2), and *Fred* and *Reuben* would occupy the same respective positions in (2.3) and (2.4).

If we assume the strong Katz-Postal Hypothesis, then, we are forced to give up the "natural" deep structures of (2.1)–(2.4) in favor of some more "abstract" representation. The original notion of deep structure as a representation of syntactic distributional patterns must thus be rejected in favor of a more semantically based conception.

Alternatively, one could retain a notion of deep structure in the spirit of *Syntactic Structures*, adopting the "natural" deep structures for (2.1)–(2.4), and give up the strong Katz-Postal Hypothesis. Thus deep structures and semantic representations will not be isomorphic; we will have to find a mapping relating them. The problem, then, is to decide which of these alternatives to choose in order to arrive at an adequate description of (2.1)–(2.4).

There have been two rather different lines of approach within the constraints of the strong Katz-Postal Hypothesis. One approach, proposed in Lakoff (1971) and taken up and developed by the generative semanticists, is to break off parts of the semantic reading and express them as higher pro-verbs that must eventually be deleted. For example, the similarity of (2.1) and (2.2) would be represented by the deep structures (2.5) and (2.6).

In (2.6), a transformation raises *open* into the position of the causative pro-verb, leaving no trace of the pro-verb; then various nodes are deleted, leaving the "natural" surface structure for (2.2). The presence of the clause *the door open* in (2.5) and (2.6) explains the semantic relation between (2.1) and (2.2).

A number of objections can be made to this approach, mostly concerned with the nature of the proposed pro-verbs. First, it should be noticed that it is a substantial increase of power in the syntax to allow lexical items which never appear in the surface, and which always must be deleted by a particular transformation (which in turn is used only to delete pro-verbs). Lakoff presents other, more precedented, cases of lexical items which must undergo particular transformations, then proposes a formalism to handle them called a *positive absolute exception*. But in each of these other cases,

(2.5)

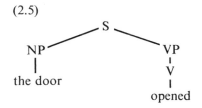

(2.6)

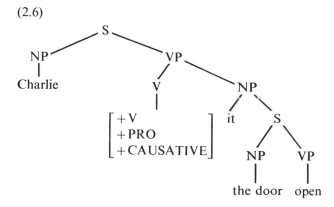

two other conditions hold: the lexical items do not delete, and the transformations they must undergo also apply to other lexical items, optionally.
Hence these cases differ significantly from the hypothetical pro-verbs. In
applying the notion of positive absolute exception to hypothetical pro-
verbs, Lakoff shows that he has chosen a device far more powerful than is
necessary to handle his original data. (For discussion of Lakoff's other
examples of positive absolute exceptions, see section 5.9.) This is the kind
of power the Extended Lexical Hypothesis seeks to exclude.

One might attempt to meet this objection in part by claiming that the
main verb in (2.6) is not a hypothetical pro-verb, but the real verb *cause* (or
bring about). It would thus be claimed that *Charlie opened the door* and
Charlie caused the door to open have the same deep structure, that is, are
synonymous. But this cannot in general be the case. (This point is due to
Katz, among others.) In (2.7) and (2.8), *drop* has a paradigm similar to
open:

(2.7) The glass dropped to the floor.
(2.8) Floyd dropped the glass to the floor.

Thus we would incorrectly predict that (2.9) and (2.10) are synonymous:

(2.9)   Floyd caused the glass to drop to the floor by tickling Sally, who
         was holding it.
(2.10) *Floyd dropped the glass to the floor by tickling Sally, who was
         holding it.

The causation implied in (2.2) and (2.8) is of a more direct nature than
seems to be expressible by any verb in English. Therefore it cannot be due
to the deletion of any real item; the verb must be the hypothetical form that
Lakoff posits, and the original objection stands (see Jerry Fodor 1970 for
other relevant points).

   Another way of expressing the semantic relations of (2.1)–(2.4) in deep
structure has been discussed by Fillmore (1968); a somewhat different
version of the same theory is given in Matthews (1968). Instead of expand-
ing deep structures of sentences into additional clauses, Fillmore puts more
deep structure information into the clause itself, in the form of a system of
case relations. The deep structures of (2.1) and (2.2) are (2.11) and (2.12),
respectively.

(2.11)

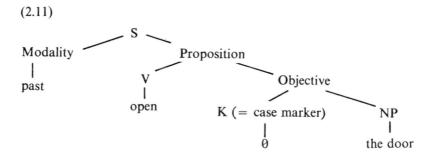

(2.12)

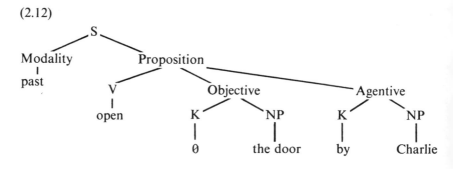

The surface forms are created by transformations which move exactly one
NP into subject position and delete its case marker. The semantic similarity
of (2.1) and (2.2) is expressed in the case relations; the surface disparity is
explained by the application of the transformations that create subjects.
As in Lakoff's approach, the traditional notion of underlying grammatical
relations is of no importance.

Fillmore's approach makes the interesting claim that there is a relatively
small class of case relations, and that they are universal. One extremely
interesting question that it poses, then, is what the right case relations are
for expressing the observed semantic and syntactic generalizations.

I will propose here a third way of accounting for (2.1)–(2.4). It is based
on a system of semantic relations developed by Jeffrey S. Gruber in his
dissertation and other work (Gruber 1965, 1967a). This system of semantic
relations looks superficially like a possible realization of Fillmore's case
system. However, section 2.3 will demonstrate that they differ in an important way, and that Gruber's system is preferable. In section 2.4 we will
relate this system to deep structure by developing a general framework for
the lexical entries of verbs and for deep structure projection rules. Section
2.5 will show that this system enables us to make some interesting predictions about the applicability of the passive transformation.

2.2 Thematic Relations
The fundamental semantic notion in Gruber's analysis is the *Theme* of a
sentence. The centrality of the Theme accounts for the term *thematic relations* with which I will refer to the entire system. (The term is due to
Richard Stanley.) In every sentence there is a noun phrase functioning as
Theme. Gruber does not give totally explicit criteria for determining in
every sentence which NP is the Theme, but some overall considerations
emerge from his work.

With verbs of motion the Theme is defined as the NP understood as
undergoing the motion.

(2.13) The rock moved away.
(2.14) John rolled the rock from the dump to the house.
(2.15) Bill forced the rock into the hole.
(2.16) Harry gave the book away.
(2.17) Will inherited a million dollars.
(2.18) Charlie bought the lamp from Max.
(2.19) Dave explained the proof to his students.

In the first three examples, involving physical motion, *the rock* is obviously the Theme. Note that depending on the main verb and the presence of other NPs, the Theme can be either subject or direct object. The other four examples illustrate nonconcrete types of motion, to which the definition of Theme is extended by analogy. *The book*, *a million dollars*, and *the lamp* are Themes undergoing change in possession rather than physical position. *The proof*, or rather information about it, is undergoing change in some sort of abstract position. This last kind of motion is the least conceptually transparent, but it is important because it will be of great interest in subsequent discussion here (see sections 2.5 and 4.11).

With verbs of location, the Theme is defined as the NP whose location is being asserted:

(2.20) The rock stood in the corner.
(2.21) John clung to the window sill.
(2.22) Herman kept the book on the shelf.
(2.23) Herman kept the book.
(2.24) The book belongs to Herman.
(2.25) Max owns the book.
(2.26) Max knows the answer.

In (2.20)–(2.22), we are dealing with physical location, and *the rock*, *John* and *the book* are Theme. (2.23)–(2.25) involve possessional location, and *the book* is Theme in each case.[1] (2.26) is an abstract analogue of possession, so *the answer* is Theme.

An important principle for the extension of the notion *Theme* to abstract verbs is that when a verb can be used to express motion or location in different domains, the Theme occupies the same syntactic position. For example, *kept* in (2.22) expresses physical location, and in (2.23) possessional location, but *the book* is Theme in both cases. This principle follows from the belief that a verb is fundamentally the same in its different uses. A large number of such correspondences are discussed in Gruber's thesis.

A further principle that emerges from Gruber's work is that the Themes of morphologically related words are in semantically parallel positions. For example, consider the following two sentences:

[1]There is not time in the present discussion to motivate the analogy of possessional to physical location in these examples. Gruber goes through a lengthy discussion (1965, Chapter 4) to establish such an analysis, based on correspondences in prepositional patterns.

(2.27) The circle contains the dot.
(2.28) The dot is contained in the circle.

In (2.27) it is not clear which NP is the Theme and which is the Location. But (2.28) has the preposition *in*, an unmistakable mark of a Location phrase, so *the dot* must be Theme. Therefore we conclude that *the dot* is the Theme in (2.27). Arguments similar to this are used throughout Gruber's work.

Besides the Theme, Gruber works with several other thematic relations. I will discuss only four more here. The first three of these are the expressions of Location, Source, and Goal. *Location* is defined as the thematic relation associated with the NP expressing the location, in a sentence with a verb of location. It is often, but not always in a PP: (2.20), (2.21), (2.22), and (2.24) have a preposition, and (2.23) (*Herman*), (2.25), and (2.26) (*Max*) have none. Adjectives can function as abstract locations, as if they meant "in the abstract domain (of 'quality space') containing those things which are *Adj*." For example, *stay* can express either a physical or an abstract location:

(2.29) John stayed in the room.
(2.30) John stayed angry.

Corresponding to Location with verbs of location, we have the thematic relations *Source* and *Goal* with verbs of motion. Like Location, these are often expressed with a PP, but not always. Consider again (2.13)–(2.19). *The dump* in (2.14) and *Max* in (2.18) are clearly expressions of Source. *The house* in (2.14), *the hole* in (2.15), and *his students* in (2.19) are expressions of Goal marked by a PP. *Away* in (2.13) and (2.16) is analyzed by Gruber (section 5.3) to mean something like "to another place," so that it is also an expression of Goal. *Will* in (2.17) and *Charlie* in (2.18) are expressions of Goal in subject position. As with abstract Location, abstract Source and Goal may also be filled by an adjective: compare the following examples:

(2.31) George got to Philadelphia.
(2.32) George got angry.
(2.33) Harry went from Bloomington to Boston.
(2.34) Harry went from elated to depressed.

The last thematic relation I will discuss is Agent. The Agent NP is identified by a semantic reading which attributes to the NP will or volition toward the action expressed by the sentence. Hence only animate NPs can function as Agents (or perhaps the other way around, i.e. the semantic relation "potential agent" is a defining criterion for the feature +*animate*). The Agent is generally in the subject, but the subject can simultaneously bear other thematic relations. For example, in (2.13) there is no Agent, but if we change *the rock* to *John*, there is a reading in which John deliberately moved away, so *John* is functioning both as Agent and Theme. In (2.14), *John* is only the Agent, and in (2.15), *Bill*, since in both cases it is *the rock* that moves, that is, is Theme. In (2.16) and possibly (2.19) the subject is functioning as both Source and Agent, whereas in (2.18) the subject is Goal and Agent. In (2.17) however, there is no Agent: an act of volition is not being attributed to Will since one cannot say, for example, *Will inherited the money intentionally*. Gruber notes, by the way, that "causative" sentences are sentences like (2.14), where the subject is only Agent.

The presence of an Agentive subject correlates in part with the possibility of using purposive constructions like *in order to* and *so that* and purposive adverbials like *intentionally*, *accidentally*, or *on purpose*.

(2.35) *The rock deliberately rolled down the hill.
(2.36)   John deliberately rolled down the hill.

(2.37) *John received the book from Bill in order to read it.
(2.38)   John took the book from Bill in order to read it.

(2.39) ?John lost the money so that he could get sympathy.
(2.40)   John gave the money away so that he could win his friends' admiration.

(2.41) ?John intentionally struck Bill as funny.
(2.42)   John intentionally made Bill think of him as funny.

The first two of these examples show the difference between an inanimate object acting as Theme only and an animate subject functioning both as Theme and Agent. (2.37) is an example of an animate subject which is not an Agent. Contrast this with (2.38), which expresses the same semantic content but with the added proviso that the subject is Agent, permitting the *in order to* phrase. (2.39) and (2.40) form a similar pair. Finally, (2.41) is a type of example we will return to in sections 2.5 and 4.11; the inappropriateness of the adverb indicates that the subject is not an Agent. In (2.42), however, the volition on John's part is expressed explicitly, and so the adverb is permissible.

Likewise, imperatives are permissible only for Agent subjects:

(2.43) *Receive the book from Bill.
     ?Lose the money.
     ?Strike Bill as funny.

This follows naturally from the fact that the possibility of successfully carrying out an order depends on the order requiring volition (i.e. agent-hood) on the part of the hearer.

The *lack* of an Agent subject in a sentence generally correlates with the possibility of embedding it as a gerund under such verbs as *resent* and *accept*:

(2.44) John resented $\begin{cases} \text{inheriting the money.} \\ \text{*hitting Bill.} \\ \text{having to hit Bill.} \end{cases}$

Obviously, I am only giving a skeleton of Gruber's lengthy analysis.

One might well ask in what sense this system of thematic relations is more than a way of describing certain facts about semantic interpretations and the distribution of prepositions. From what has been said so far, there is little evidence that some other set of relations cannot do just as well. There are two reasons, however, why I think this system is of more than usual theoretical interest. First, it provides a way of unifying various uses of the same morphological verb. One does not, for example, have to say that the *keep* in *Herman kept the book on the shelf* and *Herman kept the book* are different verbs; rather one can say that *keep* is a single verb, indifferent with respect to positional and possessional location. Thus Gruber's system is capable of expressing not only the semantic data, but some important generalizations in the lexicon.

A second reason to prefer Gruber's system of thematic relations to other possible systems will become apparent in section 2.5 and in Chapters 4 and 5. It turns out that some very crucial generalizations about the distribution of reflexives, the possibility of performing the passive, and the position of antecedents for deleted complement subjects can be stated quite naturally in terms of thematic relations. These generalizations have no a priori connection with thematic relations, and in fact radically different solutions, such as Postal's Crossover Condition and Rosenbaum's Distance Principle, have been proposed in the literature. It will be shown, however, that a solution involving thematic relations is more satisfactory. The fact that they are of crucial use in describing independent aspects of the language is strong indication of their validity.

2.3 Thematic Relations vs. Case Grammar

Can thematic relations be thought of as simply one possible set of cases for a case grammar of Fillmore's type? It seems to me that there is one crucial difference between the two that makes this impossible; this difference argues that case grammar cannot be altogether correct.

In proposals on case grammar with which I am familiar, the deep structures differ from surface structures in word order and in the addition of case nodes and case markers. However, the number of noun phrases in the deep and surface structures is the same: each surface structure noun phrase is assumed to have exactly one deep structure case. On the other hand, in Gruber's system of thematic relations, noun phrases can function in more than one thematic role within the same sentence. For example, in (2.45), *the rock* is Theme; the semantic similarity of Max's action in (2.46) shows that *Max* is also Theme.

(2.45) The rock rolled down the hill.
(2.46) Max rolled down the hill.

However, (2.46) is ambiguous. On one reading Max may be asleep and not even be aware of his motion. On the other reading he is rolling under his own volition; for this reading he must be an Agent. However, to say simply that the ambiguity of (2.46) is between the two functions Theme and Agent misses the fact that on the Agent reading, Max still undergoes the motion implied by the Theme reading. Therefore the similarity between the two readings can be captured only if we allow *Max* to be both Theme and Agent on the second reading. The only way to express this in a case grammar would be to introduce *Max* in two different places in deep structure, once under each case, then add a transformation to delete one of them—obviously an undesirable complication of the grammar.

Or consider the pair of verbs *buy* and *sell*.

(2.3) Fred bought some hashish from Reuben.
(2.4) Reuben sold some hashish to Fred.

On one hand, there is a similarity in the action in these two sentences: the hashish is passing from Reuben's possession to Fred's. This can be expressed by saying that *some hashish* is Theme, *Reuben* is Source, and *Fred* is Goal in both sentences. On the other hand, the sentences differ with respect to who is designated as taking initiative—*Fred* in (2.3) and *Reuben* in (2.4). To see this, append *on purpose* to both sentences. Note especially that if *Fred* is moved into surface subject position by the passive applying to (2.4), *on purpose* still applies to *Reuben*, if the sentence is acceptable at all.

(2.47) Fred was sold some hashish by Reuben on purpose.

These facts can be captured by specifying that with both *buy* and *sell*, the subject is Agent, but with *buy* it is also Goal and with *sell* it is also Source. There is no convenient way in a case grammar to simultaneously express the reciprocity of the Source-Goal patterns and the Agent status of the subject.

To show that *Agent* is not the only relation which can combine with others, we turn to a more complicated example, which involves some semantic relations not discussed by Gruber. Consider the verb *trade*, which takes a direct object, an optional phrase with *to*, and an obligatory phrase with *for*.

(2.48) Esau traded his birthright (to Jacob) for a mess of pottage.

This sentence describes two related actions. The first is the change of hands of the birthright from Esau to Jacob. The direct object is Theme, the subject is Source, and the *to*-object is Goal. Also there is what I will call the *secondary action*, the changing of hands of the mess of pottage in the other direction. In this action, the *for*-phrase is Secondary Theme, the subject is Secondary Goal, and the *to*-phrase is Secondary Source.

The *for*-phrase indicating Secondary Theme is not restricted to the verb *trade*. It appears as an optional element in the complements of, for example, *buy*, *sell*, and *pay*.

(2.49) Harriet bought a pig from Zelda for $5.98.
(2.50) Zelda sold a pig to Harriet for $5.98.
(2.51) Harriet paid $5.98 to Zelda for a pig.

All of these sentences describe the same transaction. They differ in which of the transfers is primary and which is secondary, as well as in the identity of the Agent, which we have already discussed. With *buy* and *sell* the transfer of the pig is primary; with *pay* the transfer of money. There does not seem to be a verb in English expressing a transaction in which the transfer of money is primary and the person receiving the money is Agent. *Collect* might be close.

(2.52) The agency collected $79.50 from Max for back taxes.

Rent is interesting in that the transfer of the thing being rented is primary and the transfer of money is secondary, but the direction of the transfer is left open. The direction of the secondary action is, as usual, opposite to the primary action.[2]

(2.53) Max rented an apartment to Harry for $197 a month.
(2.54) Harry rented an apartment from Max for $197 a month.

Any adequate semantic representation must express secondary actions, since they are indeed part of the meaning, and important semantic differences between verbs hinge on them. But when there is a secondary action, the primary Source is also the Secondary Goal, and the primary Goal is the Secondary Source. A theory of case grammar in which each noun phrase has exactly one semantic function in deep structure therefore cannot provide deep structures which satisfy the strong Katz-Postal Hypothesis, that is, which provide all semantic information about the sentence. Since the motive for adopting case grammar as a theory of deep structure is to enable deep structures to satisfy the strong Katz-Postal Hypothesis, its plausibility is weakened by these examples.

2.4 Correlating Thematic Relations with Deep Structure
Section 2.3 showed that the strong Katz-Postal Hypothesis cannot be implemented without considerably increasing the power of transformations

[2]One might speculate on another possible use of the *for*-phrase of Secondary Theme. A well-known problem has been to characterize the difference between *ask a question* and *ask for a book*. If we recognize this *for*-phrase as a Secondary Theme, we see that the primary action expressed by *ask* is always verbal, just as with *say* and *tell*. But unlike *say* and *tell*, a secondary action can be implied, an action in which something returns to the speaker. What is peculiar about *ask*, in comparison with the other verbs with secondary actions we have discussed, is that it can express overtly only one of the Themes at a time.

and at the same time losing generalizations about syntactic distribution. Therefore there is little reason for trying to implement thematic relations in deep structure by some enlargement of the theory of case grammar, unless there is considerable syntactic evidence that such a step is necessary. Much of the purely syntactic evidence for case grammar comes from the analysis of surface case inflections. Surely it would be an important generalization if the surface cases in some way mirrored the deep cases. Since I am not making any proposals at all on how to handle inflectional morphology in the theory proposed here, this particular advantage of case grammar must stand unchallenged.

On the other hand, the deep structures used in case grammar are sufficiently different from surface structures to require careful consideration. The particular point open to question is the claim that surface subjects always must arise through the application of transformations. For English there would be a number of different transformations that move NPs into subject position from case positions in the Proposition constituent. Thus grammars incorporating case grammar-type deep structures violate Emonds's structure-preserving constraint (see section 1.4). The movement of NPs into subject position cannot take place unless an NP node in subject position can occur in deep structure, which is exactly what case grammar denies. If something like Emonds's constraint proves useful in otherwise constraining transformations in the correct way, we should be suspicious of case-grammar deep structures.

Since we are not adopting the strong Katz-Postal Hypothesis here, semantic considerations do not force us into adopting a case grammar formulation of deep structure. Instead we will choose a more traditional deep structure, in an effort to constrain the transformational component as much as possible. The base rules are then to be conceived of, in the spirit of *Syntactic Structures*, as describing "basic" sentence forms in the language, while the transformations describe the distortions applicable to these forms.

It will be left to the semantic component to derive the thematic relations of a sentence from the deep structure. Clearly the verb of the sentence is what determines the relationship: the lexical entry of a verb must correlate grammatical and thematic relations. For a first approximation, the strict subcategorization features of the verb can effect this correlation. For example, given the representation (2.55) for the general form of lexical items,

(2.55) $\begin{bmatrix} \textit{phonological properties} \\ \text{syntactic properties} \\ \text{SEMANTIC PROPERTIES} \end{bmatrix}$

(2.56) and (2.57) could be the entries for *buy* and *sell*.[3]

(2.56)

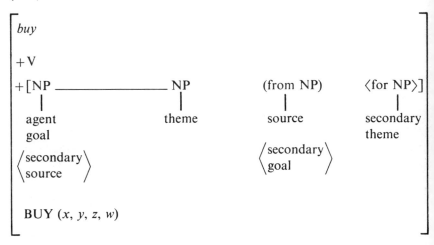

(2.57)

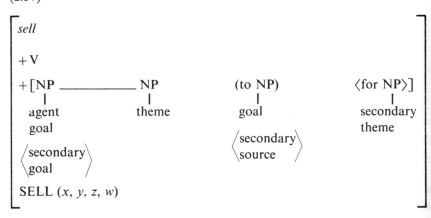

[3]The angled brackets ⟨ ⟩ in (2.56)–(2.57) denote co-occurring portions of the semantic interpretation: in (2.56) for example, the subject NP is Secondary Source and the *from*-phrase is Secondary Goal in case the *for*-phrase is present.

This first approximation gives us the thematic relations from the deep structure position, but nothing else. It does not show that the thematic relations play an integral part in the semantic relationship between *buy* and *sell*.

The two semantic functions that are relevant for the present discussion can be referred to as CAUSE and CHANGE. CAUSE will be a semantic function that takes two arguments, an individual and an event; its meaning will be that the individual causes the event, in the special direct sense of "cause" which is not accurately conveyed by the lexical item *cause*. We may be able to regard CAUSE as a universal possible constituent of semantic readings, and quite possibly as a semantic primitive. CHANGE takes three arguments, an individual, an initial state, and a final state; presumably it will also be semantically primitive. By expressing these concepts as purely semantic functions, we can avoid any commitment as to whether there should be a lexical item carrying their particular meanings.

The thematic relations can now be defined in terms of these semantic subfunctions. Agent is the argument of CAUSE that is an individual; Theme is the argument of CHANGE that is an individual; Source and Goal are the initial and final state arguments of CHANGE. Location will be defined in terms of a further semantic function BE that takes an individual (the Theme) and a state (the Location).

Of course, these three semantic functions alone are insufficient to characterize the semantic readings of verbs. For example, CHANGE can have other semantic information added on to restrict the nature of the change to locational, possessional, or abstract. More precise information as to manner, for instance the difference between *break* and *smash*, can also be specified in terms of additional semantic specification on the subfunctions. Presumably, the projection rules incorporate the readings of constituents like manner adverbs into the readings of sentences by attaching them as additional specifications of some semantic function, without disturbing the embeddings of functions and arguments. This would explain the semantic similarity of, for example, *smash* and *break violently* (see section 3.7). Perhaps instrumental phrases are incorporated as modifications of CAUSE; this would account for their relationship to Agent phrases (cf. Chapter 8 of Gruber 1965 for extensive documentation of this relationship).

Given this conception of a lexical item's semantic reading, the similarity of *buy* and *sell* might be expressed more accurately with these approximations to their lexical structure:

(2.58)

$$\begin{bmatrix} buy \\ +V \\ +[NP^1 \underline{\hspace{1cm}} NP^2 \text{ (from } NP^3)(\text{for } NP^4)] \\ \text{CAUSE } (NP^1, \begin{bmatrix} \text{CHANGE} \\ \text{possession} \\ \begin{bmatrix} \text{accompanied by} \\ \text{CHANGE } (\begin{bmatrix} NP^4 \\ \text{money} \end{bmatrix}, NP^1, NP^3) \end{bmatrix} \\ Y \end{bmatrix} (NP^2, NP^3, NP^1)) \end{bmatrix}$$

(2.59)

$$\begin{bmatrix} sell \\ +V \\ +[NP^1 \underline{\hspace{1cm}} NP^2 \text{ (to } NP^3)(\text{for } NP^4)] \\ \text{CAUSE } (NP^1, \begin{bmatrix} \text{CHANGE} \\ \text{possession} \\ \begin{bmatrix} \text{accompanied by} \\ \text{CHANGE } (\begin{bmatrix} NP^4 \\ \text{money} \end{bmatrix}, NP^3, NP^1) \end{bmatrix} \\ Y \end{bmatrix} (NP^2, NP^1, NP^3)) \end{bmatrix}$$

The superscripts in the strict subcategorization feature correlate with those in the semantic representation so that semantic functions can be properly derived from grammatical relations. The fact that a grammatical argument can appear more than once as a semantic argument accounts for the possible multiplicity of thematic relations associated with a particular syntactic position. If an optional syntactic position is not filled, the projection rules will fill its semantic position automatically with an indefinite reference. If an obligatory syntactic position is not filled, a well-formed reading cannot be generated.

I have somewhat arbitrarily chosen to represent the secondary action as a condition modifying CHANGE of the primary action. The selectional restriction on NP^4 is represented, again arbitrarily, by the expression "money" beneath NP^4; it is to be regarded as a presupposition about NP^4

placed on it by the verbs *buy* and *sell*, which *trade* (for example) does not put on its secondary theme. *Y* represents simply any semantic residue that has not yet been expressed; presumably it will be more or less the same for *buy* and *sell*.

The lexical entries for *open* as an adjective, as an intransitive verb, and as a transitive verb can be represented as (2.60)–(2.62), respectively.

(2.60)

$$\begin{bmatrix} open \\ +A \\ +[NP^1\ be\ \rule{1cm}{0.4pt}] \\ OPEN\ (NP^1) \end{bmatrix}$$

(2.61)

$$\begin{bmatrix} open \\ +V \\ +[NP^1\ \rule{1cm}{0.4pt}] \\ \begin{bmatrix} CHANGE \\ physical \end{bmatrix} (NP^1,\ NOT\ OPEN,\ OPEN) \end{bmatrix}$$

(2.62)

$$\begin{bmatrix} open \\ +V \\ +[NP^1\ \rule{1cm}{0.4pt}\ NP^2] \\ CAUSE\ (NP^1,\ \begin{bmatrix} CHANGE \\ physical \end{bmatrix} (NP^2,\ NOT\ OPEN,\ OPEN)) \end{bmatrix}$$

The semantic information represented here as OPEN will of course be more enlighteningly specified in a real lexical entry. Redundancy rules in the lexicon will make the amount of independent information in the lexicon less than if (2.61) and (2.62) were entirely different from each other and from (2.60).

This approach to the structure of lexical entries is not particularly novel: the actual semantic representations resemble Gruber's "pre-lexical" structure, the lexical entries of Katz (1966), and the deep structures of generative semantics. The projection rules for relating deep structure to functional structure are not especially complex; since the lexical entries make all the important decisions, a simple algorithm referring to superscripts of arguments can construct a semantic representation from deep structure. For example, in *Charlie opened a pistachio nut*, *Charlie* is identified as NP^1 and *a pistachio nut* as NP^2 in the strict subcategorization feature of (2.62). The projection rule therefore substitutes the interpretations of *Charlie* and *a pistachio nut* for NP^1 and NP^2, respectively, in the semantic interpretation of (2.62) in order to form the functional structure (2.63) for the sentence.

$$(2.63)\ \text{CAUSE (CHARLIE,} \begin{bmatrix} \text{CHANGE} \\ \text{physical state} \end{bmatrix} \text{(A PISTACHIO NUT, NOT}$$

OPEN, OPEN))

Such a simple process can hardly be cause for worry about excessively complicating the semantic component.

Likewise, the considerations that motivated the choice of the form of (2.58)–(2.62) for lexical entries are not new: the conclusion that syntactic and semantic generality cannot both be captured by a single level of deep structure has been the motivation for generative semantics and case grammar. Where we differ from these two schools of thought is in trying to preserve the traditional notion of deep structure for the sake of syntactic generality, and in trying to state the semantic generalizations directly at the semantic level, independent of deep structure considerations.

Of course, the material presented here should be considered as only a crude sketch of this section of the grammar. In addition to the need for more specific and highly structured semantic representations, there are at least two important mechanisms that must be built in. The first is a set of rules describing generalities among the lexical correlations of thematic and grammatical relations. For example, Agents are invariably found in subject position. The apparent solution in our framework would be to state a redundancy rule in the lexicon that would make lexical items contain less independent information if they conform to such generalizations. The redundancy could be expressed in terms of not needing to specify superscripts in the lexical entry. The other mechanism needed is a consistent way of handling prepositions in some way conceptually parallel to Gruber's (which we have not discussed here). More specifically, one would sometimes like to be able to avoid stating the permitted prepositions in the subcategorization of the verb, allowing the meaning of the preposition itself to specify whether the phrase in question is a Source or a Goal or an Instrument. For example, the meaning of *away* should tell the grammar that it is a possible expression of Goal, without listing *away* as a possible complement of every verb taking a Goal. For another example, *put* subcategorizes a locative phrase, but many different prepositions are possible. The formalism I have given does not have a way to take into account the meaning of the preposition.

These shortcomings aside, this approach seems to me to be able to reflect the insights about functional structure discussed in the literature on case grammar and generative semantics without having to put deep structures in a form only remotely related to the surface. The more conservative deep structures permit us to state heavier restrictions on transformations, and the projection rules required are relatively trivial. Moreover, the internal structure of lexical entries does not seem any more complex than would be required in the other theories. Thus it appears that this approach may permit an overall reduction in the class of possible grammars, without any loss of generality.

2.5 The Thematic Hierarchy Condition

Set up the following hierarchy of thematic relations:

(2.64) (The Thematic Hierarchy)
  1. Agent
  2. Location, Source, Goal
  3. Theme

The following condition seems to hold on the application of the passive transformation:

(2.65) (Thematic Hierarchy Condition)
  The passive *by*-phrase must be higher on the Thematic Hierarchy than the derived subject.

Exactly how (2.65) is applied to a derivation will be discussed in a moment. Let us first verify its claim.

First, consider sentences with verbs that optionally mark the subject as Agent. Take, for example, *touch* or *hit*, which mark Theme in the subject and Location or Goal in the object, but only optionally mark Agent in the subject.

(2.66) John was touching the bookcase.
(2.67) John hit the car with a crash.

(2.66) and (2.67) are ambiguous between an agentive and nonagentive reading of *John*. However, let us form the passives of (2.66)–(2.67).

(2.68) The bookcase was being touched by John.
(2.69) The car was hit by John (?with a crash).

Only the agentive readings are present in (2.68)–(2.69). The absence of the nonagentive reading is predicted by the Thematic Hierarchy Condition: if *John* were only Theme, it would be lower on the hierarchy than the derived subject, which is Location or Goal. However, if *John* is also Agent, it bears a thematic relation higher than that of the derived subject, so an acceptable passive can be produced.

Next consider verbs of measurement, whose inability to undergo the passive has been remarked upon many times.

(2.70) *Five dollars are cost by the book.
(2.71) *Two hundred pounds are weighed by Bill.

With these verbs, the measure phrase is an expression of Location on the scale of value being measured. The (deep) subject is Theme, and the sentence specifies its location on the scale denoted by the measure phrase. This analysis is confirmed by the use of the locational preposition *at* with measure phrases in expressions like (2.72)–(2.73).

(2.72) The champ weighed in at 654 pounds.
(2.73) I wouldn't buy oranges at 25 cents apiece.

Also note the use of the locational words *high* and *low* to refer to relative measures. Given this thematic analysis of verbs of measurement, observe that the (2.70)–(2.71) violate the Thematic Hierarchy Condition: the *by*-phrase, being Theme, is lower on the hierarchy than the derived subject, which is Location.

Finally consider so-called psychological predicates, such as *impress*, *strike*, and *regard*.

(2.74) Bill $\begin{Bmatrix} \text{strikes} \\ \text{impresses} \end{Bmatrix}$ Harry as pompous.

(2.75) Harry regards Bill as pompous.

The adjective, functioning as an abstract Location, is attributed to the subject in (2.74) and to the object in (2.75). This means that the subject is Theme with *strike* and *impress*, but the object is Theme with *regard*. Further, (2.74) has the alternative form (2.76):

(2.76) Harry is $\begin{Bmatrix} \text{striking} \\ \text{impressive} \end{Bmatrix}$ to Bill.

The presence of *to* here shows that the object of *strike* and *impress* is a Goal. From the semantic parallelism of (2.74) and (2.75), we can infer that the subject of *regard* is also a Goal.

Now notice what this thematic analysis predicts about the passives of these verbs. *Regard* should passivize, since the *by*-phrase will be Goal and the derived subject Theme, meeting the Thematic Hierarchy Condition. But *strike* and *impress* should not, since the *by*-phrase will be Theme and the derived subject Goal. And this prediction is borne out:

(2.77) *Harry is $\begin{Bmatrix} \text{struck} \\ \text{impressed} \end{Bmatrix}$ by Bill as pompous.

(2.78)   Bill is regarded by Harry as pompous.

We see then that three apparently unrelated exceptions to the passive can be united under the generalization expressed by the Thematic Hierarchy Condition. There are three possible ways in which this condition could be applied within the grammar. The first incorporates the condition as part of the passive transformation, specifying the Thematic Hierarchy within the structural description that must be met before the rule can apply. The second uses the Thematic Hierarchy Condition as a redundancy rule in the lexicon, marking exceptions to the passive on the basis of thematic relations expressed in a verb's lexical entry. The third claims that the passive transformation has various effects on semantic interpretation, one of which is the assertion that the Thematic Hierarchy Condition holds; if a passive sentence violates the THC, its interpretation will then make contrary claims about thematic relations and hence it will be ill-formed.

While the first of these solutions appears the least problematic, it is inconsistent with the theory of grammar we are pursuing here, in that it permits semantic factors to be mentioned in the structural description of a transformation. Were this permitted in general, grammatical theory would be far less constrained than it is in the theory that transformations can mention only syntactic conditions. The second solution is straightforward but ad hoc; we are trying to eliminate exception features from the lexicon whenever possible. Exceptions automatically specified by a redundancy rule are nevertheless exceptions and to be avoided.

There remains the third solution, which unfortunately is so vague at this point as to be virtually untestable. However, a certain amount of evidence for it will appear in later chapters. The strongest piece of evidence (section 4.10) is that another Thematic Hierarchy Condition governs the distribution of reflexive pronouns in a way that cannot be expressed as a condition on transformations or as lexical exceptions, but only as a well-formedness condition on interpretations. If the two Thematic Hierarchy Conditions are to be related, they must be expressed in the same part of the grammar. Only the third solution leaves this possibility open. Weaker evidence for the third solution arises in sections 3.10 and 8.8, where it is shown that certain exceptions to subject-aux inversion can be expressed only in terms of a solution similar to what we have proposed for the passive—a semantic effect that conflicts with a well-formedness condition on interpretations. The existence of such phenomena with a transformation other than the passive makes the solution less isolated in the theoretical framework; it argues at least for the plausibility of the solution, if not for its correctness.

However the Thematic Hierarchy Condition may be incorporated into the grammar, it provides strong evidence that thematic relations are a valid expression of functional structure; these relations enable us to formulate a significant generalization in an apparently unrelated part of the grammar. Thus thematic relations go beyond pure description and acquire explanatory power.

CHAPTER THREE

Adverbs

3.1 The Approach

In the literature of generative grammar, perhaps the least studied and most maligned part of speech has been the adverb. This is to some extent understandable, considering the variety of semantic and syntactic roles adverbs play in English. The fact that the category "adverb" has traditionally been a catch-all term further confuses the issue.

But adverbs have been maltreated beyond the call of duty. Most studies in generative grammar do not even concede to them the right to be a part of speech. Before the introduction of the semantic component and the lexicon, this tendency could be justified. At that time it was thought necessary to state co-occurrence restrictions at the syntactic level. To make co-occurrence restrictions maximally general, it was important to reduce the number of deep grammatical relations in which a category took part, and to reduce cases of similar co-occurrence relations to identical grammatical relations. Adjectives submit fairly docilely to this reductionist treatment: since there is almost always a paraphrase for an *Adj-N* construction with a relative clause *N which is Adj*, a rather simple set of transformations suffices. Adverbs are more unruly, since the constructions they occur in are less homogeneous, and since their paraphrase relations are much more widely varied. Hence they were neglected in favor of more tractable constructions.

The study of adverbs also suffers from a second assumption held over from early work. The lack of feature mechanisms forced early generative grammarians to subdivide major categories into a multitude of classes. For example, in Lees's *The Grammar of English Nominalizations* (1960), verbs are divided by phrase structure rules into predicative verbs, activity verbs, transitive verbs, intransitive verbs, and middle verbs; these classes are then further subdivided. In such a theory it is only natural to subdivide adverbs into manner adverbs, locatives, time adverbs, means adverbs, degree adverbs, and so forth. However, the treatment of adverbs has not kept up with the times. At least since *Aspects of the Theory of Syntax* (1965), the subdivision of verbs has been expressed in a set of syntactic and semantic lexical features, not by phrase structure rules. Yet the different adverb categories are still usually treated as entirely distinct in the phrase structure.

The result of these two tendencies has been the ready acceptance of quite different underlying structures for similar adverbials, along with the implicit claim that *adverb* is only a surface structure notion with no relevance to "deep" syntax or to semantics. In section 3.3 we will demonstrate the lack of generality entailed by such an approach. A rather different account of adverbs and adverbials will be attempted here. By using the full potential of the lexicon and the semantic component, we will try to bring order to a large segment of the adverbial system. It will be shown that adverbs, prepositional phrases, and (surprisingly) modals make similar contributions to the structure of the semantic reading of sentences, although they are introduced by different phrase structure rules and are treated differently by transformations. The cross-classification of syntactic and semantic functions will be taken as evidence for the need to keep syntax and semantics distinct, as implied by a grammatical theory such as the present one, which incorporates an interpretive semantic component.

It is fairly easy to see how to eliminate the need for a reductionist approach to adverbs. First of all, given that lexical items have semantic interpretations, we can abandon the division of adverbs into syntactic categories. Adjectives are not divided syntactically into adjectives of color, size, quality, degree, frequency, and so forth; it is taken for granted that their semantic representations will automatically account for these properties. We will assume that the same is true of adverbs. For example, the ungrammaticality of *John knew the answer terribly* will require no special consideration in the syntax, any more than *the green idea* does: both will be considered simple violations of selectional restrictions.

How will these selectional restrictions be captured? It has often been observed that adjectives and related adverbs share selectional properties. A common conclusion is that adverbs must be reduced to adjectives so that shared selectional restrictions need not be stated twice. However, under the assumptions of Chapter 1 this argument need not hold. Given the ability to capture the notion "separate but related lexical items" by redundancy rules in the lexicon, as proposed in section 1.7, parallelism of selectional restrictions will follow from the lexical rules relating adjectives to -*ly* adverbs. Furthermore, the assumption that selectional restrictions are defined as well-formedness conditions not on deep structures, but on semantic readings, implies that similarity of semantic structure is sufficient to explain paraphrase relations between adjective and adverb constructions; no deep structure similarity is necessary.

We will assume therefore that the base mentions a category *Adv*. There will be no structural indication such as *AdvManner*: we will regard the specification "manner" as a semantic marking only. We will further assume that the existence or nonexistence of a paraphrase with an adjective construction is more or less fortuitous. However, in case there is a paraphrase, we will assume that it indicates a lexical relationship and that the semantic structure of the paraphrase can tell us something about the semantic structure associated with the adverb. To begin, let us accumulate some data.

3.2 Some Distributional Classes of Adverbs

There are three basic surface positions in a sentence in which a -*ly* adverb can occur: initial position, final position without intervening pause, and auxiliary position, i.e. between the subject and the main verb (but see section 3.6 for more positions). We can distinguish various classes of adverbs by their occurrence in combinations of these three basic positions.

One class can occupy all three positions, but changes meaning according to position, for example, in (3.1)–(3.3).

(3.1) John $\begin{Bmatrix} \text{cleverly} \\ \text{clumsily} \end{Bmatrix}$ dropped his cup of coffee.

(3.2) $\begin{Bmatrix} \text{Cleverly} \\ \text{Clumsily} \end{Bmatrix}$ (,) John dropped his cup of coffee.

(3.3) John dropped his cup of coffee $\begin{Bmatrix} \text{cleverly} \\ \text{clumsily} \end{Bmatrix}$.

(3.1) is ambiguous, meaning either (3.2) or (3.3). These latter two are approximate paraphrases of (3.4) and (3.5), respectively.

(3.4) It was $\begin{Bmatrix} \text{clever} \\ \text{clumsy} \end{Bmatrix}$ of John to drop his cup of coffee.

(3.5) The manner in which John dropped his cup of coffee was $\begin{Bmatrix} \text{clever} \\ \text{clumsy} \end{Bmatrix}$.

Some other adverbs that behave this way are *carefully, carelessly, happily, truthfully, specifically,* and *frankly*.

For other adverbs which can occupy all three positions, there is no discernible change in meaning, for example, *quickly, slowly, reluctantly, sadly, quietly, indolently, frequently, immediately, often, soon*.

There are -*ly* adverbs which can occur only in initial and auxiliary position (3.6)–(3.8); they typically have paraphrases like (3.9).

(3.6) $\begin{Bmatrix} \text{Evidently} \\ \text{Probably} \end{Bmatrix}$ Horatio has lost his mind.

(3.7) Horatio has $\begin{Bmatrix} \text{evidently} \\ \text{probably} \end{Bmatrix}$ lost his mind.

(3.8) *Horatio has lost his mind $\begin{Bmatrix} \text{evidently} \\ \text{probably} \end{Bmatrix}$.

(3.9) It is $\begin{Bmatrix} \text{evident} \\ \text{probable} \end{Bmatrix}$ that Horatio has lost his mind.

Often these adverbs will be acceptable in final position if separated from the rest of the sentence by a pause and accompanied with a drop in pitch, thus:

(3.10) Horatio has lost his mind, $\begin{Bmatrix} \text{evidently} \\ \text{probably} \end{Bmatrix}$.

Some other members of this class are *unbelievably, certainly, understandably, unfortunately, naturally,* and *apparently.*

A fourth class can occur only in auxiliary and final position.

(3.11) *$\begin{Bmatrix} \text{Completely} \\ \text{Easily} \end{Bmatrix}$ Stanley ate his Wheaties.

(3.12) Stanley $\begin{Bmatrix} \text{completely} \\ \text{easily} \end{Bmatrix}$ ate his Wheaties.

(3.13) Stanley ate his Wheaties $\begin{Bmatrix} \text{completely} \\ \text{easily} \end{Bmatrix}$.

Consistent paraphrase relationships for these adverbs with adjective constructions are not evident to me. *Easily* has the paraphrase (3.14), but *completely* has only the lame (3.15).

(3.14)   It was easy for Stanley to eat his Wheaties.
(3.15) ?Stanley's eating (of) his Wheaties was complete.
         ?The degree to which Stanley ate his Wheaties was complete.

Other adverbs that have the paradigm (3.11)–(3.13) are *purposefully, totally, altogether, handily, badly, mortally, tremendously.*

Some adverbs, typically non -*ly* adverbs, occur only in the final position.

(3.16) *Hard John hit Bill.
     *Well Sam did his work.
(3.17) *John hard hit Bill.
     *Sam well did his work.
(3.18) John hit Bill hard.
     Sam did his work well.

Others like this are *more, less, before, early, fast, home, slow, terribly, lengthwise, indoors*, and *downstairs*.
    Finally, there is a class which occurs in auxiliary position only.

(3.19) Albert is $\begin{Bmatrix} \text{merely} \\ \text{truly} \\ \text{simply} \end{Bmatrix}$ being a fool.

(3.20) *$\begin{Bmatrix} \text{Merely} \\ \text{Truly} \\ \text{Simply} \end{Bmatrix}$ Albert is being a fool.   (*Truly* is ok with a different meaning.)

(3.21) *Albert is being a fool $\begin{Bmatrix} \text{merely} \\ \text{truly} \\ \text{simply} \end{Bmatrix}$.

Others in this class are *utterly, virtually, hardly*, and *scarcely*. For these adverbs it is typically the case that there is no appropriate adjective paraphrase.

(3.22) It is $\begin{Bmatrix} \text{*mere} \\ \text{true (\textit{wrong meaning})} \\ \text{*simple} \end{Bmatrix}$ that Albert is a fool.

The next two sections will show the difficulties inherent in a transformational account of adverbs.

3.3 Problems for a Syntactic Resolution of Adverb Classes

The general approach of a transformational account of adverbs is to claim that they originate from deep structure sources similar to available paraphrases which do not contain the adverbs. Even from the scanty literature on adverbs in a generative framework, it is evident that one can expect no generality in the underlying forms of surface adverbials. Deep-surface pairs as disparate as the following have been proposed.

(3.23) Seymour used a knife to slice the salami ⇒
    Seymour sliced the salami with a knife (G. Lakoff 1968a)
(3.24) It is certain that the *Pueblo* entered the territorial waters of North
    Korea ⇒
    The *Pueblo* certainly entered the territorial waters of North Korea
    (Ruwet 1968)
(3.25) John is careless at driving his car ⇒
    John drives his car carelessly (G. Lakoff 1965)
(3.26) The manner in which John disappeared was elegant ⇒
    John disappeared elegantly (Kuroda 1968; Katz and Postal 1964)

The reason that so few possible sources have been proposed is that there is so little literature on adverbs. One can discover many examples like (3.27)–(3.31) for which more curious paraphrases are necessary. (Some of the following examples were pointed out to me by R. Weeks.)

(3.27) Stanley easily won the race ⇐ it was easy for Stanley to win the race
(3.28) Frankly, there is no reason for it ⇐
    I am being frank in saying that there is no reason for it
(3.29) Assuredly John can't do it ⇐ I assure you that John can't do it
    (*It is assured that John can't do it* means something else)
(3.30) Harry was formerly known as "The Red Death." ⇐
    The time at which Harry was known as "The Red Death" was a
    former time.
(3.31) This new development doubly complicates matters ⇐
    The extent to which this new development complicates matters is
    double the extent to which matters were complicated before.

There are many more cases where a related adjective exists but cannot be used to form a convincing paraphrase.

(3.32) The men were individually asked to leave.
    *It was individual that the men were asked to leave.
    *The manner in which the men were asked to leave was individual.

(3.33)   Ira readily accepted the offer.
          Ira was ready to accept the offer. (different meaning)
          *The manner in which Ira accepted the offer was ready.
(3.34)   Stanley completely ate his Wheaties.
          ?*Stanley's eating of his Wheaties was complete.
          ? The degree to which Stanley ate his Wheaties was complete.
(3.35)   Irving finally broke down and proposed to Daisy.
          *It was final that Irving broke down and proposed to Daisy.
          *The event in which Irving broke down and proposed to Daisy was
          final.
(3.36)   Tom absolutely refuses to give up.
          *The degree to which Tom refuses to give up is absolute.
          *Tom is absolute in refusing to give up.
(3.37)   The job paid handsomely.
          *The manner in which the job paid was handsome.
          *The degree to which the job paid was handsome.
          *The job was handsome in paying.
(3.38)   Actually, John can't lose.
          *It is actual that John can't lose.

Examples (3.27)–(3.38) hardly appear to be isolated exceptions; such behavior is typical of adverbs.

Now consider the machinery involved in a transformational account of
these adverbs. Take *frankly*, for example. The adjective *frank* will have to
be listed in the lexicon as optionally undergoing a minor transformational
rule which is peculiar to *frank*, *truthful*, and a small number of other adjectives. This transformation will reduce the imposing paraphrase to the
surface form, changing the adjective to an adverb in the process.

There will be a large number of such transformations, one for each tiny
class of adverbs, each governed by an exception feature. Each transformation will have the power to destroy the main clause and insert lexical material (i.e. the adverb) into a lower clause. Among the traditional repertoire
of transformations, none such is known.[1] It would clearly be desirable to

[1]All the other examples of transformations that delete a higher clause, such as quantifier lowering (cf. Carden 1968) and performative deletion (cf. Ross 1970a), are intimately tied up with attempts to preserve the strong Katz-Postal Hypothesis, so to
cite them as counterexamples to the present argument would be begging the question.

restrict the power of transformations to prohibit such drastic changes, especially when the transformations for which this power is needed are so limited in generality.

For the adverbs in (3.32)–(3.38), there is not even a plausible adjectival source. For these adverbs, some otherwise unmotivated source must be proposed, and the adverb must be marked as obligatorily undergoing a (probably complex) transformation that creates the surface form. Again, for each small class of adverbs, there must be a different transformation.

By proposing all this transformational machinery, we seem still not to have gained any new insight into the nature of adverbs. In examples (3.23)–(3.31) certain similarities in co-occurrence restrictions have been captured. In (3.32)–(3.38) even this is missing, since it is impossible to relate the co-occurrence restrictions of the surface adverbs and adjectives in any useful way at all. In fact, this approach to adverbs actually loses one important insight. If one claims that each class of adverbs is inserted into a sentence by a different transformation, there is no obvious explanation of why there are any surface similarities at all among adverbs. In particular, the division of adverbs into a fairly small number of different distributional classes is purely accidental. It might of course be possible to capture these facts by suitably restricting adverb-creating transformations or by adding some surface structure constraint. But since I know of no discussion of this problem in the literature, and since there is no point in creating additional straw men, I will pursue this particular argument no further.

The only other possible advantages that could be claimed for a trans-formational source for adverbs are (1) that the category *Adv* could be elim-inated from the base rules and the lexicon, or (2) that other simplifications of the base could be possible. Note that the first of these is a very strong claim: if there is any class of adverbs that must be introduced as such into base structures, the category *Adv* is necessary in the lexicon and in the base. Also note that both claims are interesting for the grammar of English only if they have strong syntactic motivation. And, in turn, they are interesting for universal grammar only if they are interesting for the grammar of English.

Some of the proposed sources for adverbs do permit a simplification of the base, for example (3.24) and (3.25). (3.23), the *use* source for instru-mentals, appears to eliminate the need for instrumental in the base. But, as Bresnan (1969) points out, this analysis leaves no way to generate (3.39).

(3.39) Seymour used a knife to slice the salami with.

(3.39) seems to be the result of a more general deletion process that yields constructions like (3.40)–(3.41):

(3.40) Seymour used the pole to hang his clothes on.
(3.41) Seymour used the house to lean the ladder against.

This being the case, *with* in (3.39) must be an underlying instrumental phrase, since it cannot be in turn derived from

(3.42) *Seymour used a knife to use a knife to slice the salami.

The example without *with* (3.23) can then be derived from (3.39) by a simple optional *with* deletion.

Likewise, the other adverbials in the VP require at least some uneliminable PP in the base rules. In the derivation (3.26), for example, there is no way to eliminate *in wh-some manner* from the deep structure of the constituent sentence without losing the semantic interpretation. Thus the only simplification in the base afforded by a derivation like (3.26) is that the expansion of VP will mention only PP, not $\left\{\begin{array}{c} \text{PP} \\ \text{Adv} \end{array}\right\}$. This simplification seems hardly worth the extra transformational power it requires.

Furthermore, adverbs such as *merely*, *utterly*, and *virtually* are counterexamples to the claim that the category *Adv* can be eliminated entirely. These have parallel adjectives *mere*, *utter*, and *virtual*, but the adverbial uses do not seem even remotely derivable from the adjectival uses within the syntactic component. The adjectives occur only in prenominal position, in NPs which either are indefinite or have a relative clause.

(3.43) He is $\left\{\begin{array}{l} \text{a mere boy.} \\ \text{*the mere boy.} \\ \text{the mere boy we expected him to be.} \end{array}\right.$

(3.44) The play turned out to be $\left\{\begin{array}{l} \text{an utter disaster.} \\ \text{*the utter disaster (of the year).} \\ \text{the utter disaster I predicted.} \end{array}\right.$

(3.45) The war caused $\left\{\begin{array}{l} \text{a virtual collapse of the economy.} \\ \text{?the virtual collapse of the economy.} \\ \text{?the virtual collapse of the economy that had been} \\ \quad \text{predicted.} \end{array}\right.$

If anything, these adjectives must be derived from their corresponding adverbs, not the other way round. But if this class of adverbs must be generated in the base, there is no gain in deriving all the other adverbs from adjectives by transformations: they can just as well be introduced by the base rule that introduces *merely*, *utterly*, and *virtually*. Their distribution in the sentence can at worst be accomplished with exception features on movement transformations, features that will be needed in any case.

To summarize the argument, then, the semantic motivation for a transformational source of adverbs is some similarity in co-occurrence restrictions between adverbs and related adjectives. However, the considerable increase in power of transformations necessary to implement the transformational position is compensated only by negligible simplifications in the base component. Thus, on the grounds of simplicity of the syntactic component of the grammar, it seems highly preferable for the base to introduce adverbs into the clauses in which they appear on the surface, assuming some other way can be found to account for the semantic evidence.

3.4 The Orientation of Sentence Adverbs

In this section we will show that some of the apparent semantic evidence for a transformational theory of adverbs, when examined carefully, actually disconfirms the theory.

Consider the adverbs that have a reading in initial and auxiliary position. Some of them are understood as relating the speaker's attitude toward the event expressed by the sentence, and some somehow comment on the subject of the sentence. The adverbs that can occur only in initial and aux position, such as *evidently* and *unfortunately*, all seem to be speaker-oriented. Thus they often have a paraphrase *it is Adj (to me) that S* or *I consider it Adj that S*. In the class of the adverbs which have different readings depending on position, such as *cleverly* and *clumsily*, one reading is usually a manner adverb. In the other reading, some are speaker-oriented:

(3.46) Happily (,) John won the game.

(3.47) $\begin{Bmatrix} \text{Truthfully (,)} \\ \text{Frankly (,)} \end{Bmatrix}$ John lied to Bill.

Note that the last two in their other reading are anomalous in this particular sentence, though they are not generally bad.

(3.48) *John lied to Bill $\begin{cases} \text{truthfully.} \\ \text{frankly.} \end{cases}$

(3.49) John told the story to Bill $\begin{cases} \text{truthfully.} \\ \text{frankly.} \end{cases}$

Others in this class of adverbs are subject-oriented—they express some additional information about the subject, as can be seen by their adjectival paraphrases.

(3.50) $\begin{pmatrix} \text{Carefully} \\ \text{Clumsily} \\ \text{Cleverly} \end{pmatrix}$ (,) John spilled the beans.

(3.51) John was $\begin{Bmatrix} \text{careful} \\ \text{?clumsy} \\ \text{clever} \end{Bmatrix}$ to spill the beans.

(3.52) It was $\begin{Bmatrix} \text{*careful} \\ \text{clumsy} \\ \text{clever} \end{Bmatrix}$ of John to spill the beans.

A strong version of the transformationalist position, in which the orientation is predictable from the exact form of the paraphrase, is clearly untenable: the paraphrases are hopelessly varied. *It is Adj (to me) that S*, which works for many of the speaker-oriented adverbs, does not work for those in (3.46)–(3.47). (3.46) might come from *I am happy that S*; (3.28) has been suggested as a possible source for (3.47).

(3.28) Frankly, there is no reason for it $\Leftarrow$
       I am being frank in saying that there is no reason for it

(3.51)–(3.52) show that a consistent source for subject-oriented adverbs is out of the question too.

One might take a weaker transformationalist position, in which the orientation is predictable from the presence of *I* or the subject somewhere in the paraphrase. This would be consistent with the data presented so far, and it could be said at least to explain the difference in interpretation between subject-oriented and speaker-oriented adverbs.

But even this weak hypothesis cannot be maintained if we examine a

wider class of adverbials, including clauses and prepositional phrases which
function as sentence adverbials. There is an incredibly wide variety of these.

(3.53)

In all probability,
In my opinion,
According to Albert,
In spite of his mother's admonitions,
In order to kill his mother,
By going to Cincinnati,
(Being) sick at heart,
Having lost the game,
Now that he is married to Sally,
To tell the truth,
Taking all things into consideration,

Bill has ruined his chances
of an inheritance.

Observe that these adverbials can be divided by orientation. In particular,
the orientation is revealed by the reference of deleted subjects. *In order to*
clauses, *by* (*means of*) clauses, and nominative absolutes (*-ing* clauses) all
have deleted subjects understood to be subjects of the main clause. However, *to tell the truth* and *taking all things into consideration* certainly do not
have subjects coreferential with the subject of the main clause: the understood subject is *I* or *one* or something more obscure—these are speaker-
oriented adverbials. There is no possibility of deriving the adverbials in
(2.53) from adjectival paraphrases; yet they exhibit the same semantic
range as *-ly* adverbs in initial position. Orientation of adverbials thus seems
to be a much wider semantic phenomenon than can be predicted by a
transformational theory of adverbs; hence it would be a *loss* of generality
to account for adverb orientation transformationally.

It seems advisable, then, to give up the transformational theory and
generate adverbs directly in the base. In the next two sections we will discuss the syntax of adverbs under a phrase structure theory; in sections
3.7–3.8 we will discuss possible ways to account for their semantic behavior
and for whatever semantic similarity they may bear to adjectives.

Incidentally, we should note that manner adverbs also exhibit differences
of orientation. For example, *John opened the door slowly* asserts that the
motion of the door is slow (contrast with *Slowly John opened the door*); but
John opened the door enthusiastically attributes enthusiasm to John. The
orientation seems to be tied to the deep structure grammatical relations in

the sentence, hence to the thematic relations. In section 3.9 we will show how this contrasts with the orientation of sentence adverbs.

3.5 Some Syntax

Given the assumption that adverbs are generated in the base, we must decide which surface positions are generated in the base, which positions are transformationally derived, and what transformations are necessary. A paramount consideration will be the ability to distinguish various adverb classes. Section 3.7 will show that the different distributional classes of *-ly* adverbs can be distinguished on semantic grounds. The syntactic component must therefore be set up in such a way that the semantic rules can make the relevant distinctions.

3.5.1 Auxiliary Position

Let us start with auxiliary position. There is fairly good evidence that this should be an underlying position for *-ly* adverbs. All of the *-ly* adverbs can occur there, and there are some, such as *merely* and *utterly*, that can appear only there. Thus this aspect of distribution can be captured without difficulty with a phrase-structure rule. But there is a more interesting reason than this.

Chomsky (1970a) develops a generalized set of base rules that accounts for the fact that nouns and verbs take similar complement structures. This, combined with a lexicon incorporating morphological and semantic redundancy rules (see section 1.7), enables us to express the fact that verbs and their nominalizations behave alike in some ways. We are assuming similar relations between adjectives and adverbs; the nature of some will be suggested in section 3.7. Can we use base rule and transformation schemata to relate them syntactically? The answer is yes, if we are willing to give up the long-standing assumption that all adjectives in noun phrases are derived from reduced relative clauses. We will justify giving up this assumption in a moment. But first let us see what there is to be gained.

We would like to capture the traditional intuition that adverbs are related to sentences (or verb phrases) as adjectives are to noun phrases. With this intuition in mind, it seems no accident that the surface position of adjectives in noun phrases is between the determiner and the head, exactly parallel to auxiliary position of adverbs in sentences. In particular, the parallelism between adjectives in derived nominals and adverbs in gerunds is striking.

(3.54) John's rapid reading of the letter

(3.55) John's rapidly reading the letter

Furthermore, those adjectives that can appear only prenominally, such as *mere*, are paralleled by adverbs that can appear only preverbally, such as *merely*. In a grammar that derives adjectives from reduced relatives and adverbs from higher clauses, this parallelism is unexpressed. However, a base rule schema which generates these positions directly can capture the generalization.

To write this rule, assume that X is the set of syntactic features common to nouns and verbs and that the feature $[\pm \text{Verb}]$ distinguishes nouns from verbs. Assume that Y is the set of syntactic features common to adjectives and adverbs, and that the feature $[\pm \text{Adverb}]$ distinguishes them. Adopting the convention for the feature analysis of phrase nodes suggested in Chomsky (1970a), we use $\overline{\text{X}}$ to mean the node directly dominating a lexical head X, and $\overline{\overline{\text{X}}}$ to mean the node directly dominating $\overline{\text{X}}$. We can use these features to abbreviate the two base rules (3.56)–(3.57) into the schema (3.58). (The use of α notation in (3.58) parallels its use in phonology: it means that if $+ \text{Verb}$ is chosen on a particular application of the rule, $+ \text{Adverb}$ must be chosen as well, and likewise for $- \text{Verb}$ and $- \text{Adverb}$.)

(3.56) $\overline{\text{N}} \rightarrow (\text{Adj}) - \text{N} - \text{Complement}$

(3.57) $\overline{\text{V}} (= \text{VP}) \rightarrow (\text{Adv}) - \text{V} - \text{Complement}$

(3.58) $\begin{bmatrix} \overline{\text{X}} \\ \alpha \text{ Verb} \end{bmatrix} \rightarrow \left(\begin{bmatrix} \text{Y} \\ \alpha \text{ Adverb} \end{bmatrix} \right) - \text{X} - \text{Complement}$

Therefore, if we must generate *-ly* adverbs at some position in the base, the choice of auxiliary position lets us get adjectives in noun phrases at no extra cost to the syntax.[2]

How plausible is it that at least some adjectives are not derived from reduced relative clauses? From a syntactic point of view, the issue is simply whether the addition of a node *Adj* in the phrase structure rules for NP has any additional motivation or permits other syntactic simplification. Again it can be argued that the parallelism between (3.54) and (3.55) must be expressed, and that some adjectives can appear only in this position and

---

[2]Bowers (1969a) points out some striking parallels in the syntax of adverb and adjective phrases, some of which can be expressed only by means of feature notation. His work thus supports the present analysis.

not in the copula, for example, *mere, utter, virtual, former, present*, and one sense of *poor*.[3] Given the base rule (3.58), they can be generated directly in their surface position. Their exceptional behavior then will not have to be expressed as a positive absolute exception to the relative clause reduction rule; rather, it can be expressed as a strict subcategorization condition. As we are trying to eliminate positive absolute exceptions from grammatical theory (see section 1.8), this change would be an advantage. If the relative clause reduction rule could be eliminated by adding (3.58), the case for (3.58) would of course be strengthened. Unfortunately, this does not appear feasible: there seems to be no way to avoid Chomsky's argument (*Syntactic Structures*, pp. 72–75) that relative clause reduction is needed independently to derive *the sleeping child*, in which *sleeping* is a verb, not an adjective. Thus it may be necessary under a proposal involving (3.58) to distinguish surface adjectives that derive from reduced relative clauses from those that do not.

If there are two different syntactic sources for adjectives in noun phrases, we must account for the similarity in semantic interpretation. It should not be totally fortuitous that *a sick horse* and *a horse which is sick* are synonymous. To get a reading for a base-generated adjective-noun combination, we will need a projection rule of attribution, more or less like the one Katz and Fodor (1963) discuss for this construction. This rule essentially takes the union of the semantic markers of the adjective and the noun to produce a reading for the $\overline{\text{N}}$. Will this projection rule be needed for anything else? There are two possibilities for making it part of a more general process of semantic interpretation. First, it may generalize, exactly as the base rule (3.56) does, to handle the interpretation of adverbs in VPs as well (see section 3.7), adding no complexity. This is an intriguing proposal, but I will not test it here.

More important is the nature of the projection rule that determines the meaning of relative clauses in noun phrases. A relative clause can be thought of as a syntactic device that enables the language to express new

---

[3]Quang Phuc Dong (1969) points out that certain derivatives of the category "quasi-verb" can also appear in this surface position, although no relative clause form is possible.

Drown that $\begin{Bmatrix} \text{fucking} \\ \text{goddamn} \end{Bmatrix}$ cat.

*Drown that cat which (is) $\begin{Bmatrix} \text{fucking. (wrong meaning)} \\ \text{goddamn.} \end{Bmatrix}$

and complex properties, properties for which there may be no single lexical item. From this point of view, the projection rule for relative clauses must in fact be the same rule of attribution, so extending the relative clause projection rule to adjectives adds virtually no complexity to the grammar.

So far, then, we have shown that it will be no problem to interpret adjectives generated prenominally in the base. We still have to contend with the fact that there are two structural configurations with identical co-occurrence relations: *Det-N is Adj* and *Det-Adj-N*. The desire to reduce these to a single co-occurrence relation is the semantic motivation for deriving *Adj-N* constructions from *N-Relative Clause* constructions. Thus we seem to be playing off description and generalization of syntactic position of adjectives against a corresponding loss of generality in co-occurrence.

A conceivable way out, though at present unformalizable, might be to argue that the projection rules for these two constructions create very similar semantic readings. The relation between the noun and the adjective is the same in both cases, that is, the property denoted by the adjective is attributed to the members of the set denoted by the noun. But in the case of the copula, the resulting expression is a proposition; in the case of $\overline{\text{N}}$, the result is a more restricted set. The difference is intuitively illustrated by the contrast of (3.59) and (3.60):

(3.59) N has the property Adj (copula)
(3.60) N having the property Adj ($\overline{\text{N}}$)

That is, the only difference between the two projection rules is some sort of formal operator. This renders the similarity of co-occurrence relations more understandable, since we are maintaining that co-occurrence relations are well-formedness conditions on semantic readings (see section 1.6).

To sum up the preceding argument, it seems plausible on distributional grounds to generate adverbs in auxiliary position. Furthermore, the generalization between adverb position in sentences and adjective position in noun phrases can be expressed by the use of a distinctive feature analysis of syntactic nodes if we allow at least some adjectives to be generated in their surface position in noun phrases and not as reduced relative clauses. Again, on distributional grounds this seems plausible. The main obstacle to such an analysis is accounting for the similar semantics of the two adjective positions; one approach to this problem has been sketched.

3.5.2 Final Position

Let us deal first with the non -*ly* adverbs, such as *hard, before,* and *early,* which occur only in final position. Klima (1965) analyzes these adverbs as intransitive prepositions, which can be generated by the base in the same positions as normal prepositional phrases. His evidence is essentially that they often substitute semantically for prepositional phrases, and that in addition, many of them can act as normal prepositions or are morphologically related to prepositions. The following examples illustrate these similarities.

(3.61) Johnny ran $\begin{cases} \text{home.} \\ \text{into the house.} \\ \text{downstairs.} \\ \text{down the stairs.} \end{cases}$

(3.62) Tommy didn't do amusing things like that $\begin{cases} \text{alone.} \\ \text{by himself.} \\ \text{afterward.} \\ \text{after that.} \\ \text{before.} \\ \text{before his tenth birth-} \\ \text{\quad day.} \\ \text{long.} \\ \text{for many years.} \end{cases}$

Klima suggests, therefore, that the base rule for prepositional phrases, like the base rules for noun phrases and verb phrases, contains an *optional* NP following the head:

(3.63) PP → P − (NP)

This way, at no extra cost we can generate intransitive prepositions in the base, and we can use the same projection rules to account for their semantic relationships to the sentence as we use for prepositional phrases. It is not clear to me, however, why adjectives such as *hard* and *fast* should be in this category. Perhaps a more enlightened feature analysis of the lexical categories will shed some light on this question.

For the -*ly* adverbs in final position, there appear to be two possibilities.

We can either extend the base rule for intransitive prepositions to include
-*ly* adverbs, perhaps using a feature analysis; or we can add a transformation to move them into the VP from auxiliary position. I will argue that we
must choose the former possibility.

The argument hinges on the assumption that the functional structure of
a semantic reading is determined on the basis of deep structure. Chapter 2
showed the correspondence between the strict subcategorization restrictions induced by a verb on its sentence and the functional structure of the
semantic representation: for every constituent strictly subcategorized by
the verb, there is a variable to be filled in the functional structure. Part of
the role of deep structure in the grammar is to explicitly represent all the
strictly subcategorized arguments of a verb in identifiable positions, so that
they can be correlated by the projection rules with the functional structure
of the semantic interpretation. (Note that I have so far made no commitment as to how the nonstrictly subcategorized arguments are interpreted.)

Most instances of -*ly* adverbs are not strictly subcategorized by the verb
of the sentence. However, there are certain verbs which require an adverbial
of some sort to be present. (This argument was suggested to me by
J. Emonds.)

(3.64)   John worded the letter carefully.
(3.65)   John worded the letter in such a way as to confuse everyone.
(3.66) *John worded the letter.

(3.67)   The job paid us handsomely.
(3.68)   The job paid us enough that we could knock off work for a few
         months.
(3.69) *The job paid us.

(3.70)   Steve dresses elegantly.
(3.71)   Steve dresses in such a way as to attract no attention.
(3.72) *Steve dresses.

Although *handsomely* can normally appear in auxiliary position (*They
handsomely rewarded him*), and the manner senses of *carefully* and *elegantly*
can appear in auxiliary position, in these contexts only final position is
possible.

(3.73) *John carefully worded the letter.

(3.74) *The job handsomely paid us.
(3.75) *Steve elegantly dresses.

Note that these verbs do allow adverbs in other positions, just as long as there is an appropriate adverb in final position:

(3.76) John specifically worded the letter obscurely.
(3.77) The job evidently paid us handsomely.
(3.78) Steve typically dresses elegantly.

Consider how these facts might be accounted for under our two hypotheses about the source of final position -*ly* adverbs. Assume first that the adverbs are produced by a transformation, moving them in from auxiliary position. Verbs such as *word* and this sense of *pay* and *dress* would require one of the following syntactic specifications:

(3.79) Either a semantically appropriate non-*ly* adverbial must appear
       postverbally in deep structure, or a semantically appropriate -*ly*
       adverb must appear preverbally and obligatorily undergo the post-
       posing transformation.
(3.80) A semantically appropriate adverbial must appear postverbally in
       surface structure.

(3.79) involves syntactic features already discussed in the literature: the disjunction of a strict subcategorization restriction with the conjunction of a strict subcategorization restriction and a rule feature. But the combination looks implausibly unwieldy. The second alternative, (3.80), although simpler, involves a new kind of condition—a surface structure strict subcategorization restriction. Since strict subcategorization restrictions are intimately tied up with deep structure, such an addition to grammatical theory also looks implausible.

  If, however, we enlarge the base instead of the transformational component, by allowing adverbs to be generated postverbally, the properties of *word*, *pay*, and *dress* look like perfectly normal cases of strict subcategorization restrictions: just as other verbs specify obligatory objects in their deep structures, these verbs require an adverbial. The convention on application of projection rules to adverbs must then be that if a verb strictly subcategorizes an adverb, the adverb must fulfill that function; otherwise it is free to fulfill any other semantic function that it can. This convention follows from the general well-formedness condition on semantic readings (section 2.4) that all obligatory functional arguments must be semantically filled.

We conclude, then, that the grammar is simpler if postverbal adverbs are generated by the base rules rather than by a postposing transformation. Note that this part of the base will not generalize to adjective constructions in NPs as aux position did.

3.5.3 Initial Position
Again in the case of initial position we are faced with the choice of a phrase structure source and a transformational source. This time the facts seem to favor a transformational source, since adverbs do not always occur in initial position in subordinate clauses.

(3.81) ?George says that evidently Bob has disappeared.
(3.82) George says that Bob has evidently disappeared.

(3.83) *For apparently Bob to be sick would worry Harriet.
(3.84) For Bob to apparently be sick would worry Harriet.

(3.85) *Charley was scared by stupidly Violet's driving the car off the cliff.
(3.86) Charley was scared by Violet's stupidly driving the car off the cliff.

(3.87) ?I won't come because probably my mother is sick.
(3.88) I won't come because my mother is probably sick.

As there are many well-known transformations that apply only in main clauses, while the base is supposed to be context-free, the addition of a preposing transformation adds less complication to the grammar.

To account for the three adverb positions, we therefore need the base rule (3.58) for preverbal adverbs and the base rule (3.63) for intransitive prepositions, which we have argued constitute generalizations of base rules already necessary for other constructions. In addition, we must extend the base rule for VP to permit -ly adverbs to be generated postverbally, and we need a preposing rule to generate initial position adverbs. Now how do we prevent all -ly adverbs from occupying all three positions? The worst possible solution would be to restrict the applicability of the base rules and the preposing transformation by means of arbitrary exception features. In sections 3.7–3.8 we will see that a motivated separation of surface distri-

butional classes is possible on semantic grounds. This is a far superior
solution, since it claims that knowing the meaning of an adverb is sufficient
to predict in what positions it can occur.

3.6 Transportability—An Aside

We have been somewhat oversimplifying the account of -*ly* adverb distribution up to this point. -*Ly* adverbs can occur in the VP in positions other
than at the end, and they can occur between elements of the auxiliary.

(3.89)   John will send the money immediately back to the girl.
(3.90)   John immediately will send the money back to the girl.
(3.91)   John will probably have sent the money back to the girl.
(3.92)   ?John will have probably been getting upset by now.

Also, we have not yet accounted for final position with pause, as in (3.10).

(3.10) Horatio has lost his mind, $\begin{Bmatrix} \text{evidently} \\ \text{probably} \end{Bmatrix}$.

It would be unfortunate if we had to state a special transformation for each
of these positions. Keyser (1968) proposes an addition to the theory of
grammar, called the *transportability convention*, designed to handle these
cases, in the hope that it will prove useful generally in the description of
free word-order phenomena.

Keyser observes that the positions in which adverbs occur correspond to
major syntactic breaks in the derived structure. The transportability convention expresses this by permitting a constituent marked specially, say
[+ transportable], to occupy any position in a derived tree so long as the
sister relationships with all other nodes in the tree are maintained, that is,
as long as it is dominated by the same node. In English, -*ly* adverbs are
transportable; in languages with freer word order, such as Latin, other
nodes will hopefully be characterized as transportable.

By the transportability convention, we would expect adverbs dominated
by S to occur initially, before the auxiliary, and finally: these are the three
possible sister positions to the subject and the VP. All three of these positions actually occur. Presumably final position dominated by S is the position with a pause seen in (3.10); at least this is consistent with the analysis
to be presented in the next section.

Adverbs dominated by VP should occur before the verb, finally (this time without pause), and at various places in between. Also, under the fairly reasonable assumption that the aspectual markers *have* and *be* are daughters of the VP, transportability will account for (3.90)–(3.92). The one place where adverbs sound particularly bad is between the verb and the following NP.

(3.93) *?John sent immediately the money back to the girl.

To take care of this, Keyser appeals to a "surface-structure tendency to prevent anything from intervening between a Verb and the following Noun Phrase" (p. 371). This constraint is only scantily justified, but it is not unreasonable.

Keyser does not discuss the formal nature of the transportability convention. I can see two possibilities but no clear way to decide between them. First, it could be a new kind of transformation that says essentially, "Transport transportable nodes." Second, transportable nodes could be marked in the base with the interpretation "Choose any position for this node."

Actually, under the analysis of section 3.5 it may be necessary to restrict transportability to adverbs dominated by S. Otherwise, we would expect strictly subcategorized adverbs in the VP to move freely, creating ungrammatical examples like (3.73)–(3.75).

(3.73) *John carefully worded the letter.
(3.74) *The job handsomely paid us.
(3.75) *Steve elegantly dresses.

The freedom in VP position may be due to the base rules for VP, which allow adverbs and PPs to be randomly interspersed. The ungrammaticality of (3.93) would then follow from the fact that NP directly follows VP in the base rule:

$$(3.94)\ \mathrm{VP} \to (\mathrm{Adv}) - \mathrm{V} - (\mathrm{NP}) - \left(\left\{ \begin{matrix} \mathrm{PP} \\ \mathrm{Adv} \end{matrix} \right\}^* \right)$$

Nothing very crucial in the present analysis of adverbs hangs on the viability of Keyser's proposal. However, it is useful in that it makes the freedom of word order more convenient to state, so it deserves mention here.

We have now laid the syntactic groundwork for studying the semantics of adverbs. The rest of the chapter will study the projection rules for adverbs. Section 3.7 will give a preliminary statement of the rules. Sections 3.8–3.11 will discuss various refinements in the rules. Sections 3.12–3.13 will present other phenomena for which the projection rules generalize.

3.7 Projection Rules for Nonstrictly Subcategorized Adverbs

Let us try to get a rough idea of the structure of semantic interpretations associated with nonstrictly subcategorized adverbs. Since we want to account for the existence of adjective paraphrases, when they in fact exist, we will use the semantic structure of the adjective paraphrases to help establish plausible semantic structures for adverb constructions.

For convenience, we shall adhere to the following terminology. Let S be a sentence containing *Adv*, a nonstrictly subcategorized adverb. $f(NP^1, \ldots, NP^n)$ will be the part of its reading representing its functional structure, that is, the relation between the verb and the strictly subcategorized arguments $NP^1, \ldots, NP^n$. Let S$'$ denote the sentence resulting from removing *Adv* from S. S$'$ will have the same functional structure as S, since *Adv* does not contribute to the functional structure. Finally, let *Adj* be the adjectival counterpart of *Adv*, and ADJ its semantic content.

The semantic structures of sentences containing adverbs fall into several major types. The first often has a paraphrase for S in which S$'$ is embedded as a sentential complement of a copula clause containing *Adj*, and either there is no other argument in the main clause or there is an NP referring to the speaker. *Adv* in this case is what we referred to in section 3.4 as a neutral or speaker-oriented adverb. For convenience, we will henceforth refer to both neutral and speaker-oriented adverbs as speaker-oriented, except where a distinction is necessary. The paraphrases differ syntactically among the following forms:

(3.95) It is evident (to me) that Frank is avoiding us.

(3.96) It is certain (*to me) that Frank is avoiding us. (Note that *Frank* is not a deep structure subject in the main clause of *Frank is certain to be avoiding us*.)

(3.97) I am happy that Frank is avoiding us. (Paraphrases *Happily, Frank is avoiding us*.)

Though the syntactic structures vary, the semantic structure can in each case be represented by something like (3.98) or (3.99), semantic structures predicating *Adj* of S$'$ and possibly the speaker. For the sake of projection rules, (3.99) is effectively a one-place predicate.

(3.98) ADJ $(f(NP^1, \ldots, NP^n))$

(3.99) ADJ $(SPEAKER, f(NP^1, \ldots, NP^n))$

The second major type of interpretation often has a paraphrase in which S′ is embedded as a sentential complement of a main clause containing *Adj*, but one of the NPs of S must also appear in the main clause, usually the surface subject (see section 3.9). The adverbs requiring this kind of paraphrase were called subject-oriented in section 3.4.

(3.100) John was careful to spill the beans.

(3.101) It was clumsy of John to spill the beans.

(3.102) John was clumsy in spilling the beans.

For these, (3.103) is the minimal semantic structure (where $1 \leq i \leq n$).

(3.103) $ADJ(NP^i, f(NP^1, \ldots, NP^n))$

A third semantic structure is indicated by the paraphrases of manner, degree, and time adverbs. To paraphrase these, a prepositional phrase must be added to S′, which then forms a relative clause on the subject of the main copula clause containing *Adj*.

(3.104)   The manner in which Dave speaks is eloquent.

(3.105)   The times at which Bob walks his pet giraffe are infrequent.

(3.106) ?The extent to which Ted ate his Wheaties was complete.

The relationship of (3.104)–(3.106) to the corresponding sentences with adverbs (3.107)–(3.109)

(3.107) Dave speaks eloquently.

(3.108) Bob walks his pet giraffe infrequently.

(3.109) Ted ate his Wheaties completely.

is exactly the same as the relationship between (3.110) and (3.111).

(3.110) The person whom I met was John.

(3.111) I met John.

Examples (3.110) and (3.111) (aside from presuppositions) seem to mean the same, yet from what has been said so far, they would appear to have different functional structures, since (3.110) contains two verbs and (3.111) contains only one. However, the two structures differ only by the presence in the reading of (3.110) of an identity function and two variables corresponding to *whom* and *person*—formal operators used to combine more meaningful structures. (Akmajian (1970b) discusses the semantic relation of (3.110) and (3.111) in more detail.) Therefore it seems reasonable to assume that the similarity in meaning between (3.110) and (3.111) is due not to formal identity of the structures but rather to logical equivalence.

The same explanation can be offered for the adjective-adverb pairs as well. The prepositional phrases in (3.104)–(3.106) are semantically pro-adverbials, and they presumably fit into the interpretation of the relative clauses in the same way as the adverbs fit into the interpretation of (3.107)–(3.109). Section 2.4 has suggested one way of incorporating their interpretation: they can be attached as additional specification on the function corresponding to the verb, without changing the number or method of incorporation of strictly subcategorized arguments. Thus the similarity in meaning between *break violently* and *smash* will be a result of similar semantic structures, the former having semantic markers about violence added to *break* by projection rules, the latter having these markers already incorporated in its lexical entry. The semantic structure can be represented roughly as

$$(3.112) \begin{bmatrix} f \\ \text{ADV} \end{bmatrix} (NP^1, \ldots, NP^n)$$

A fourth semantic structure is that associated with the *merely* class of adverbs. None of the structures already proposed will do, but I have no suggestions for the proper structure. (See section 6.4 for more discussion of this class.)

The semantic component of the grammar must relate the syntactic structure of sentences containing an adverb to the appropriate semantic structure. Adverbs will be marked in the lexicon as to which of the possible semantic structures they can enter into. For example, *certainly* will be a predicate over an S; the reading of *happily* in (3.97) will be a predicate over an S and the argument SPEAKER; the nonmanner reading of *carefully* will be a predicate over an S and an unspecified NP; *eloquently, frequently*, and *completely* will be semantic markers appropriate to modify functions. For each semantic structure, there will be an associated projection rule. The rule appropriate to *certainly* and *happily* (call it $P_{speaker}$) embeds the functional structure of the sentence as the single unspecified argument of the adverb. The projection rule appropriate to *carefully* ($P_{subject}$) embeds the functional structure as the S argument of the adverb and the subject of the sentence as the NP argument. The projection rule appropriate to *eloquently*, *frequently*, and *happily* (P_{manner}) adds the adverb as an additional set of semantic markers on the function. This rule may generalize to interpret many prenominal adjectives, as suggested in section 3.5.1. There will be a fourth projection rule (P_{merely}) creating the structure for *merely*, whatever that may be. This rule may generalize to interpret adjectives like *mere* in NPs.

Since a projection rule assigns a partial semantic interpretation to a sentence on the basis of its syntactic structure, the rule must include a structural description that says to what trees it applies. The difference in the structural descriptions of the four adverb projection rules can be used to account for the distributional differences between adverb classes. As a first approximation, $P_{speaker}$ and $P_{subject}$ apply to adverbs in initial and auxiliary position, P_{manner} applies to adverbs in auxiliary and final position, and P_{merely} applies only to adverbs in auxiliary position. If an adverb is in a position where the wrong projection rule applies, an interpretation cannot be found.

For example, if *evidently*, a speaker-oriented adverb, is in final position, as in *John walked in evidently*, only P_{manner} will be applicable. P_{manner} adjoins the adverb as an additional semantic marker on the semantic function denoted by the verb, but *evidently* contains a variable that must be filled by the functional structure of the sentence. Thus the interpretation is $\begin{bmatrix} \text{WALK} \\ \text{EVIDENT (S)} \end{bmatrix}$ (JOHN, IN), which is ill formed because of the unfilled variable S. With *evidently* in initial position, $P_{speaker}$ applies, yielding the correct interpretation EVIDENT (WALK (JOHN, IN)).

By making use of the semantic properties of adverbs, which must be stated in any event, we thus can free the syntax of much of the burden of distinguishing adverb classes. The only syntactic classification necessary is the division into "true" adverbs, which can occur in the auxiliary (primarily -*ly* adverbs) and intransitive prepositions, which cannot occur in the auxiliary. The adverbs which occur only in initial and auxiliary position, we claim, must have speaker-oriented or subject-oriented semantic structure. Those that occur in auxiliary and final position must enter only into manner adverb-like semantic structure. Those that occur in all three positions allow more than one projection rule to apply. The fact that many adverbs that occur in all three positions have two distinct meanings and are ambiguous precisely in auxiliary position is thus predicted by this analysis.

Yet to be accounted for is the fact that strictly subcategorized adverbs must occur postverbally. There are two possible ways to account for this. First, strictly subcategorized adverbs might undergo a different projection rule, resembling P_{manner} but used for strictly subcategorized arguments and applying only to postverbal adverbs. Second, the syntactic mechanisms associated with strict subcategorization (e.g., lexical insertion rules) could require that strictly subcategorized arguments of verbs (other than the subject) be postverbal. Either of these proposals will work, but I have no way of deciding between them at present.

Also yet to be decided is at what level of syntactic derivation adverbs are interpreted. Since we are giving up the Katz-Postal Hypothesis, it is logically possible that some or all of the projection rules for adverbs are applied to some level other than deep structure. This question will be investigated in sections 3.9 and 3.10. First, however, let us try to state the structural descriptions of the projection rules more precisely.

3.8 Refining the Projection Rules

We will show next that a certain account of the syntax of English auxiliaries, to be motivated independently, enables us to define $P_{speaker}$, $P_{subject}$, and P_{manner} not in terms of the position the adverb occupies in the tree but simply in terms of the node to which the adverb is attached. From the evidence given so far, it is plausible that $P_{speaker}$ and $P_{subject}$ apply to adverbs attached to S, and P_{manner} to adverbs attached to VP. Initial position (3.113), final position with pause (3.114), and auxiliary position (3.115) can all be characterized by attachment to S:

3.113)

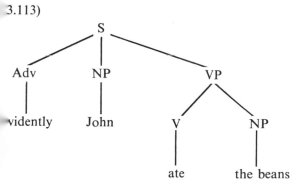

(3.114)

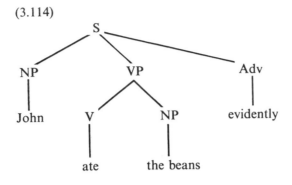

(3.115)

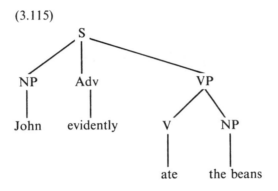

Final position without pause (3.116) can be characterized by attachment to VP, as can auxiliary position (3.117). The ambiguity in auxiliary position can thus be traced to a structural ambiguity.

(3.116)

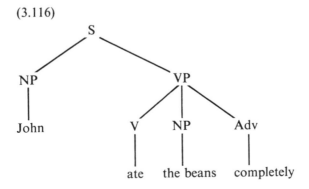

(3.117)

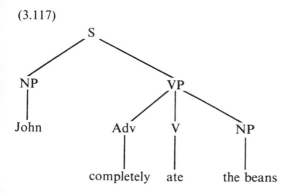

However, there are some interesting complications when the auxiliary contains more than just Tense. Before aspect, a modal, or even emphatic *do*, only S adverbs are possible.

(3.118) George $\left\{\begin{array}{l} \text{probably} \\ \text{*completely} \end{array}\right\}$ $\left\{\begin{array}{l} \text{has read the book.} \\ \text{is finishing his carrots.} \\ \text{was ruined by the tornado.} \\ \text{will lose his mind.} \\ \textit{did} \text{ eat up the cabbage.} \end{array}\right.$

After any one of these auxiliaries alone, either kind of adverb is possible.

(3.119) George $\left\{\begin{array}{l} \text{has} \\ \text{is} \\ \text{was} \\ \text{will} \\ \textit{did} \end{array}\right.$ $\left\{\begin{array}{l} \text{probably} \\ \text{completely} \end{array}\right\}$ $\begin{array}{l} \text{read the book.} \\ \text{finishing his carrots.} \\ \text{ruined by the tornado.} \\ \text{lose his mind.} \\ \text{eat up the cabbage.} \end{array}$

If there are two auxiliaries, and the adverb is between them, the S adverb is highly preferred.

(3.120) George $\left\{\begin{array}{l} \text{will} \\ \text{has} \\ \text{is} \end{array}\right.$ $\left\{\begin{array}{l} \text{probably} \\ \text{?*completely} \end{array}\right\}$ $\left\{\begin{array}{l} \text{have read the book.} \\ \text{be finishing his carrots by now.} \\ \text{be ruined by the tornado.} \\ \text{been finishing his carrots.} \\ \text{been ruined by the tornado.} \\ \text{being ruined by the tornado.} \end{array}\right.$

If the adverb is after two auxiliaries, only the VP adverb is possible.

(3.121) George
$\begin{cases} \text{will have} & \text{read the book.} \\ \text{will be} & \begin{cases} \text{finishing his carrots.} \\ \text{ruined by the tornado.} \end{cases} \\ \begin{cases} \text{*probably} \\ \text{completely} \end{cases} & \\ \text{has been} & \begin{cases} \text{finishing his carrots.} \\ \text{ruined by the tornado.} \end{cases} \\ \text{is being} & \text{ruined by the tornado.} \end{cases}$

There seems to be no principled semantic factor on which these differences can be based, since the results are independent of the auxiliary elements chosen. They must therefore be based on syntactic differences. Let us find what the syntactic differences might be.

One of the basic problems in accounting for the English auxiliary is that a number of different transformations refer to the configuration $\begin{Bmatrix} \text{Modal} \\ \text{have} \\ \text{be} \end{Bmatrix}$ occurring as the first verbal element, including all uses of the verb *be* and the auxiliary and certain other uses of *have* (cf. *Syntactic Structures*). In particular, the subject-aux inversion rule in questions and various other contexts inverts the configuration Tense- $\begin{Bmatrix} \text{Modal} \\ \text{have} \\ \text{be} \end{Bmatrix}$, and the rule for placement of *not* (or *n't*) in finite clauses places them after $\begin{Bmatrix} \text{Modal} \\ \text{have} \\ \text{be} \end{Bmatrix}$. As Ross (1967d) points out, the repetition of this configuration in a number of rules misses an obvious generalization. How can it be captured?

One rather elegant solution has been proposed, in two somewhat different forms, by Klima (1966) and Emonds (1970). I will present here a version free of the particular frameworks they were working in, but still preserving the essential character of the argument. The base rules in this proposal split up the traditional auxiliary in a rather unorthodox fashion:

(3.122) S → NP − Aux − VP
(3.123) Aux → Tense − (Modal)
(3.124) VP → (*have* − *en*) (*be* − *ing*) − V − (NP) . . .

As initial motivation for this division of the auxiliary, note than *have-en* and *be-ing* can occur in infinitives and gerunds but *Tense* and *Modal* cannot.

(3.125)   Max believed Bill to $\begin{cases} \text{have left.} \\ \text{be leaving.} \end{cases}$

          *Max expected Bill to $\begin{cases} \text{might leave} \\ \text{left} \end{cases}$

(3.126)   Having been buying Wheaties all these years, Max resents the
          price increase.
       *Willing leave soon, I'll take you home.
       *Wasing out of town, John couldn't come.

The base rules (3.122)–(3.124) provide an attractive way to account for this by saying that infinitives and gerunds lack an Aux (or, alternatively, that the Aux is expanded into the complementizer *for-to* or *ing*).

   The essence of the Klima-Emonds proposal is a transformation which will be stated here as *Have-Be* raising.

(3.127) *Have-Be* raising

      X $-$ Tense $- \begin{cases} \text{have} \\ \text{be} \end{cases} -$ Y

      1   2   3   4

      $\Rightarrow 1 - 2 + 3 - 4$

      Obligatory

This changes the underlying structure (3.128), for example, into (3.129):

(3.128)

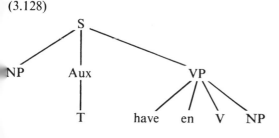

(3.129)

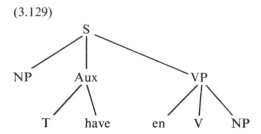

If the underlying structure contains a Modal, *Have-Be* raising will not take place since the structural description will not be met. Thus, after the application of this transformation, the Aux will contain one of the four configurations Tense, Tense-Modal, Tense-*have*, or Tense-*be*. Subject-aux inversion then need move only the node Aux, and *not* placement can simply place *not* in front of VP. *N't*, which inverts with the Aux, can be placed at the end of the Aux node. Thus *Have-Be* raising captures the generalization missed by the rules referring to $\left\{\begin{array}{l}\text{Modal}\\ \text{have}\\ \text{be}\end{array}\right\}$, by isolating in one rule the peculiarity of the verb *be* in all its uses, and *have* in some of its uses.

As further confirmation of the rule, consider the position of negation in infinitives.

(3.130) For John $\left\{\begin{array}{l}\text{not to have}\\ \text{?*to have not}\end{array}\right\}$ left disturbs me.

(3.131) For John $\left\{\begin{array}{l}\text{not to be}\\ \text{*to be not}\end{array}\right\}$ the man I'm looking for disturbs me.

In infinitives the negation precedes the first auxiliary, whereas in finite clauses it follows the first auxiliary. The rule *Have-Be* raising accounts for these facts simply. Under our assumption that infinitive clauses do not contain Tense, the structural description of *Have-Be* raising is not met in infinitives, so the first auxiliary remains under VP. Hence when *not* is positioned before VP, it will fall in front of the first aux.

With this account of the auxiliary, consider the various adverb positions. If Tense is the only auxiliary element, the rule of Affix Attachment (*Syntactic Structures*, p. 39) will attach it under the VP. A preverbal adverb can be attached to either S or VP, yielding ambiguity.

(3.132)

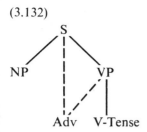

If as in (3.133) there is some auxiliary verb, either *M*, *have*, or *be*, it will be dominated by Aux at the surface. Hence an adverb preceding it must be dominated by S, correctly predicting the possibility of only one sense in (3.118).

(3.133)

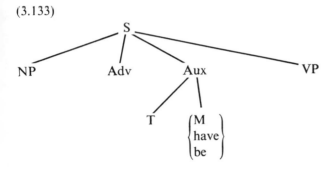

But an adverb following a single auxiliary as in (3.134) (or the main verb *be* when there is no auxiliary verb) can be attached to either VP or S, predicting the ambiguity of (3.119).

(3.134)

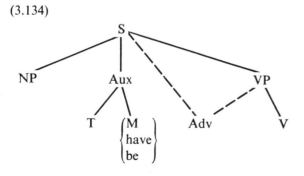

If there are two auxiliary verbs, the second must be under VP, since *Have-Be* raising guarantees at most one auxiliary verb under Aux. Hence an adverb following the second auxiliary, as in (3.135), must also be dominated by VP, predicting the single sense of (3.121):

(3.135)

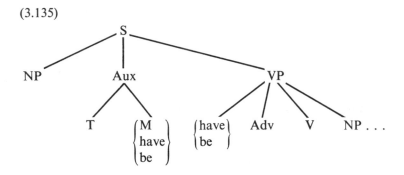

Finally, there is the case of an adverb between two auxiliaries (3.120), where the S adverb is highly preferred. From the structural considerations so far, it would appear that either interpretation should be possible:

(3.136)

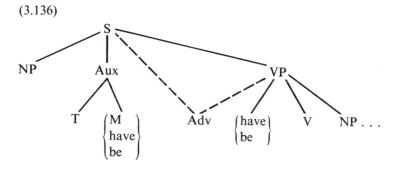

However, the discussion of sections 3.5–3.6 provides a possible way out of this difficulty. Recall that transportability was suggested as a means of moving adverbs about freely. However, it was necessary to restrict transportability to adverbs dominated by S, since strictly subcategorized adverbs, which are under VP, cannot move to the front of the VP. Hence the predicted positions for adverbs dominated by S are initial, before the auxiliary, after the first auxiliary, and final with pause, that is, all possible constituent breaks under S. Under VP, however, the position of adverbs is restricted to wherever the base generates them, since we have proposed no adverb movement rules within VP. Thus we could prevent the VP attachment of Adv in (3.136) by extending the base rule (3.124) to the form (3.137), generating adverbs only after the aspectual verbs.

(3.137) VP → (*have* − *en*) (*be* − *ing*) (Adv) − V − (NP) . . .

This rule is consistent with VP attachment of Adv in (3.134) and (3.135) but not with that in (3.136), since a VP adverb must follow all the auxiliaries. This analysis would give a single reading for (3.120).

Given the base rule (3.137) and transportability only under S, we would expect that no adverbs at all would be possible between a second and a third auxiliary: the permissible positions are indicated in (3.138).

(3.138)

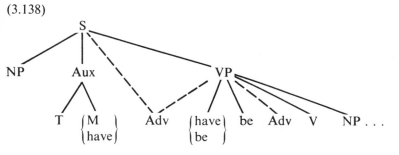

The data seem to bear this prediction out moderately well.

(3.139) John will have $\begin{Bmatrix} ?probably \\ *rapidly \end{Bmatrix}$ $\begin{Bmatrix} been\ beaten\ by\ Bill. \\ been\ finishing\ the\ job. \end{Bmatrix}$

(3.140) John $\begin{Bmatrix} will\ be \\ has\ been \end{Bmatrix}$ $\begin{Bmatrix} *probably \\ *rapidly \end{Bmatrix}$ being beaten by Bill.

In both these examples, the S adverb *probably* sounds much better following at most one auxiliary, and the VP adverb *rapidly* sounds better following the last auxiliary. I have no secure explanation for why *probably* should sound as good as it does in (3.139). There may be a transformation that optionally incorporates perfect aspect into the Aux even when there is a modal. This would explain tag questions such as *Will he have?* as opposed to the less acceptable *Will he be?*

It seems likely, then, that the projection rules $P_{speaker}$ and P_{manner} can be defined in terms of adverbs dominated by S and VP, respectively. $P_{subject}$ can be defined on adverbs dominated by S too: the nonmanner reading of a subject-oriented adverb such as *cleverly* is good in just the places where *probably* is good in (3.118)–(3.121). On the other hand, the structure to which P_{merely} applies cannot be defined in terms of domination; *merely* is acceptable between any pair of auxiliary elements:

(3.141) John $\begin{cases} \text{merely will have been} \\ \text{will merely have been} \\ \text{?will have merely been} \\ \text{will have been merely} \\ \text{merely has been being} \\ \text{has merely been being} \\ \text{?has been merely being} \\ \text{has been being merely} \end{cases}$ beaten by Bill.

Perhaps it is less acceptable between the second and third auxiliary. But either S or VP domination is satisfactory, as long as it is between the subject and the main verb.

3.9 Subject Orientation, the Passive, and the Cycle

As evidence that at least some aspects of the interpretation of adverbs are dependent on surface structure, consider the difference in meaning between the actives and passives of sentences containing subject-oriented adverbs. (The examples all contain perfect aspect to preclude a manner interpretation.)

(3.142) The doctor cleverly has examined John.
(3.143) John cleverly has been examined by the doctor.

(3.144) The police carelessly have arrested Fred.
(3.145) Fred carelessly has been arrested by the police.

(3.146) Joe intentionally has seduced Mary.
(3.147) Mary intentionally has been seduced by Joe.

In these examples, the preferred (and perhaps only) interpretation attributes the cleverness or carelessness or intention to the surface subject.

Many of the same adverbs, functioning as manner adverbs, do not exhibit a change of meaning under the passive.

(3.148) The doctor examined John carefully.
(3.149) John was examined carefully by the doctor.

(3.150) The police arrested Fred carelessly.
(3.151) Fred was arrested carelessly by the police.

(3.152) Joe seduced Mary intentionally.
(3.153) Mary was seduced intentionally by Joe.

Thus we get ambiguities of orientation if the adverb is in auxiliary position.

(3.154) John was carefully examined by the doctor.
(3.155) Fred was carelessly arrested by the police.
(3.156) Mary was intentionally seduced by Joe.

We can explain these readings by saying that the interpretation of these subject-oriented S adverbs is based on the derived subject, but that these manner adverbs attribute a manner to the deep subject (or possibly to the noun phrase functioning as thematic agent). In other words, $P_{subject}$ applies to surface structure, but P_{manner} applies to deep structure.

To further refine the analysis of subject-oriented adverbs, consider the following examples:

(3.157) John is believed $\left\{\begin{array}{l}\text{cleverly to have been}\\\text{to have cleverly been}\end{array}\right\}$ examined by the doctor.

(3.158) Max expected Mary intentionally to be seduced by Joe.

(Unfortunately, examples of this type are somewhat inconsistent in acceptability, for reasons I do not understand. To some extent, this weakens the force of the argument to follow.) The adverb in these examples has the S adverb interpretation, that is, the NP argument of *cleverly* is *John* and the NP argument of *intentionally* is *Mary*. But in these examples, *John* and *Mary* are not subjects of the clauses containing the adverbs: they have undergone subject raising (see Chapter 5) into the main clause. Nor are they deep subjects, because the passive has taken place in the complements.

If the structural description of $P_{subject}$ is to be able to mention the derived subject of the clause, the rule must apply at a point in the derivation where *John* and *Mary* are still within the complement. One such point is at the end of the transformational cycle, whose domain is the complement clause. At this point, (3.157) has the form (3.159).

(3.159) Someone believes [$_S$ for John cleverly to have been examined by the doctor]

$P_{subject}$ can apply here in the usual way, giving the interpretation of *cleverly* before *John* is raised on the second cycle. Thus these examples give evidence for the cyclic application of some of the semantic rules that apply to derived structure. Much more evidence will be accumulated in Chapters 4 and 5.

3.10 S Adverbs and Subject-Aux Inversion

Next we examine some facts for which I have no explanation but which seem to show that other factors of interpretation based on surface structure play a part in the acceptability of S adverbs. We notice first that many S adverbs do not feel comfortable in questions.

(3.160) *Did Frank probably beat all his opponents?
(3.161) *Who certainly finished eating dinner?
(3.162) ?What has Charley evidently discovered?

VP adverbs in these contexts are often better.

(3.163) Did Frank easily beat all his opponents?
(3.164) Who completely finished eating dinner?
(3.156) What has Charley suddenly discovered?

Note first that (3.160)–(3.162) constitute evidence against the transformational theory of adverbs. According to that theory, they should be synonymous with the acceptable (3.166)–(3.168).

(3.166) Is it probable that Frank beat all his opponents?
(3.167) ?Who is it certain finished eating dinner?
         (This sounds odd because *who* has been moved from an embedded subject.)

(3.168)   What is it evident that Charley has discovered?

One might be able to preserve deep structure interpretation for (3.160)–(3.162) by claiming that the incompatibility is due to a question morpheme present in deep structure which is incompatible with sentence adverbs. But the story is not that simple. Although yes-no questions generally prohibit S adverbs, tag questions do not.

(3.169) Frank probably beat all his opponents, didn't he?
(3.170) Max certainly has finished eating dinner, hasn't he?
(3.171) Charley evidently discovered a flaw in my argument, didn't he?

These examples are best with the falling intonation of a rhetorical question, which does not solicit information. This supports the explanation that S adverbs are semantically incompatible with the soliciting of information. On the other hand, with rising intonation, (3.169)–(3.171) seem at least marginal, and certainly better than the corresponding yes-no questions.

The additional margin of unacceptability in (3.160)–(3.162) comes, it appears, from the application of subject-aux inversion. As evidence for this claim, consider two other constructions in which subject-aux inversion is conditioned by an optionally preposed constituent.

(3.172) Never has Bill seen anything to compare with that.
(3.173) So fast did Tom run that he got to Texas in ten minutes.

These presumably are derived by preposing and inversion from

(3.174) Bill has never seen anything to compare with that.
(3.175) Tom ran so fast that he got to Texas in ten minutes.

But note that while (3.174)–(3.175) accept S adverbs comfortably, (3.172)–(3.173) do not.

(3.176)   Bill apparently has never seen anything to compare with that.
(3.177)   Tom probably ran so fast that he got to Texas in ten minutes.

(3.178) ??Never has Bill apparently seen anything to compare with that.
(3.179) ??So fast did Tom probably run that he got to Texas in ten minutes.

How are these restrictions to be stated? We presumably do not want to state identical restrictions on *wh*-preposing, negative adverb preposing, and *so*-Adv preposing, prohibiting them just if there is an S adverb present: the generalization has to do with inversion. We cannot require the absence of an S adverb in the structural description of subject-aux inversion: that would predict that inversion would simply not take place with S adverbs in the sentence. But suppressing the inversion in (3.178)–(3.179) makes the sentences worse.

(3.180) *Never Bill apparently has seen anything to compare with that.
(3.181) *So fast Tom probably ran that he got to Texas in ten minutes.

To state the restriction as a purely syntactic one, still capturing the generalization about inversion (including yes-no questions), one would have to propose a filter on the inversion rule that rejected any derivation containing both an S adverb and an obligatory inversion context. No such conditions are known on transformations.[4] Thus the filter on inversion would stand as an entirely unprecedented addition to the theory of grammar.

But any of these purely syntactic approaches miss the point. Why should there be a restriction on preposing or inversion having to do with totally unrelated constituents? Under this interpretation the grammar would be simpler if this condition were eliminated. A more semantically based analysis is called for, in which there is a reason for these facts.

Although I have no explanation, I will propose a possible approach. As with the passive in section 2.5, inversion would introduce some semantic factor not present in noninverted forms, and this factor would be incompatible with the readings of S adverbs. This semantic effect could be produced in either of two ways. First, it could be produced solely by the presence of certain constituents at the front of the sentence; its presence would in turn be a condition on inversion. However, this solution sup-

---

[4]The filter is similar in operation to Lakoff's positive absolute exceptions, but it must be imposed on an ungoverned rule, which makes it a still more powerful device than Lakoff's. As shown in sections 2.1 and 5.9, even Lakoff's device is far too powerful. The only transformation I know of that requires a similar filter is relative clause formation, which is blocked if nonidentity obtains between the relativized word and the head of the NP containing the relative clause. This case may be eliminable under the interpretive theory of coreference proposed in Chapters 4 and 5 by generating relative pronouns in the base, and in any case, it is much more intuitively appealing than the case under discussion.

poses that derived structure semantic information can affect transformations; we would like to do without such an assumption. Alternatively, the inversion transformation itself could be claimed to have a semantic effect which has co-occurrence relations with the semantic effects of the fronting rules and with those of S adverbs. Some evidence for this alternative will be presented in section 8.8.

The conclusion, in any event, is that a principled explanation of the examples of this section will involve semantic information present because of the operation of optional transformations.

3.11 Order of S Adverbs

In this section we will show that the surface order of S adverbs has an effect on interpretation. We will not establish whether surface order corresponds exactly to deep order; hence these facts alone do not determine whether the interpretation should take place at deep structure or surface structure.

So far we have dealt only with sentences containing a single adverbial phrase. When there is more than one S adverb in a sentence, some interesting constraints appear. The most obvious of these is that two adverbs cannot usually be adjacent. It is not clear to me whether this is a stylistic or a syntactic constraint, or perhaps partly both.

(3.182) *Evidently carefully John left the room.
(3.183)   Evidently John carefully has left the room.
(3.184) ?*John evidently carefully has left the room.
(3.185)   John evidently has carefully been concealing the truth.
(3.186) *John has left the room, evidently, carefully.

The best-sounding of the bad sentences above is (3.184), which can be made plausible with elaborate intonation. Perhaps this indicates that auxiliary position is fundamental for sentence adverbs.

A second obvious constraint is that there cannot be two sentence adverbs of the same semantic class, just as there cannot be two color or size adjectives modifying a noun:

(3.187) *Evidently John probably left.
(3.188) *Usually John frequently leaves Mary at home.

But there is a more interesting constraint involving subject-oriented adverbs: there cannot be more than one of them, and that one must be the last S adverb in the sentence (excluding final position with pause). We will demonstrate this using a few speaker-oriented adverbs of various semantic types (*probably, happily, often, evidently*) and a few subject-oriented adverbs (*carefully, cleverly, quickly, stealthily*). All of these can occur either initially or before or after the first auxiliary.

(3.189)
$$
\left\{
\begin{array}{l}
\text{Probably,}\\
\text{Happily,}\\
\text{Often,}\\
\text{Evidently,}\\
\text{Carefully,}\\
\text{Cleverly,}\\
\text{Quickly,}\\
\text{Stealthily,}
\end{array}
\right\}
\text{Max was climbing the walls of the garden.}
$$

(3.190) Max
$$
\left\{
\begin{array}{l}
\text{probably}\\
\text{happily}\\
\text{often}\\
\text{evidently}\\
\text{carefully}\\
\text{cleverly}\\
\text{quickly}\\
\text{stealthily}
\end{array}
\right\}
\text{was climbing the walls of the garden.}
$$

(speaker-oriented sense)

(3.191) Max has
$$
\left\{
\begin{array}{l}
\text{probably}\\
\text{happily}\\
\text{often}\\
\text{evidently}\\
\text{carefully}\\
\text{cleverly}\\
\text{quickly}\\
\text{stealthily}
\end{array}
\right\}
\text{been trying to decide whether to climb the walls of the garden.}
$$

Combinations of two speaker-oriented adverbs are often acceptable.

(3.192) Probably, Max often was climbing the walls.

(3.193) Happily, Max has evidently been trying to decide whether to climb the walls.

(3.194) Max happily has often been trying to climb the walls.

There are even constraints among ordering of these adverbs, for example *Evidently, Max has happily been climbing the walls*, in the speaker-oriented sense of *happily*. If a subject-oriented adverb follows a speaker-oriented adverb, the sentence is acceptable. (The examples all have an auxiliary following the last adverb, so as to preclude manner interpretations.)

(3.195) $\begin{Bmatrix} \text{Probably,} \\ \text{Happily,} \\ \text{Often,} \\ \text{Evidently,} \end{Bmatrix}$ Max $\begin{Bmatrix} \text{carefully} \\ \text{cleverly} \\ \text{quickly} \\ \text{stealthily} \end{Bmatrix}$ was climbing the walls of the garden.

(3.196) $\begin{Bmatrix} \text{Probably,} \\ \text{Happily,} \\ \text{Often,} \\ \text{Evidently,} \end{Bmatrix}$ Max has $\begin{Bmatrix} \text{carefully} \\ \text{cleverly} \\ \text{quickly} \\ \text{stealthily} \end{Bmatrix}$ been trying to decide whether to climb the walls.

(3.197) Max $\begin{Bmatrix} \text{probably} \\ \text{happily} \\ \text{often} \\ \text{evidently} \end{Bmatrix}$ has $\begin{Bmatrix} \text{carefully} \\ \text{cleverly} \\ \text{quickly} \\ \text{stealthily} \end{Bmatrix}$ been trying to decide whether to climb the walls.

But the opposite order does not work, for any combination of preverbal positions.

(3.198) *$\begin{Bmatrix} \text{Carefully,} \\ \text{Cleverly,} \\ \text{Quickly,} \\ \text{Stealthily,} \end{Bmatrix}$ Max $\begin{Bmatrix} \text{probably} \\ \text{happily} \\ \text{often} \\ \text{evidently} \end{Bmatrix}$ was climbing the walls of the garden.

(3.199) *$\begin{Bmatrix} \text{Carefully,} \\ \text{Cleverly,} \\ \text{Quickly,} \\ \text{Stealthily,} \end{Bmatrix}$ Max has $\begin{Bmatrix} \text{probably} \\ \text{happily} \\ \text{often} \\ \text{evidently} \end{Bmatrix}$ been trying to decide whether to climb the walls.

(3.200) *Max $\left\{\begin{array}{l}\text{carefully}\\ \text{cleverly}\\ \text{quickly}\\ \text{stealthily}\end{array}\right\}$ has $\left\{\begin{array}{l}\text{probably}\\ \text{happily}\\ \text{often}\\ \text{evidently}\end{array}\right\}$ been trying to decide whether to climb the walls.

Neither can any two of the subject-oriented adverbs co-occur.

(3.201) *Carefully, Max quickly was climbing the walls of the garden.

(3.202) *Quickly, Max has cleverly been trying to decide whether to climb the walls.

(3.203) *Max cleverly has stealthily been trying to decide whether to climb the walls.

One would hope that this constraint is not syntactic. If it were, we would have to admit a syntactic difference between subject-oriented and speaker-oriented adverbs, which we have so far successfully denied. But in fact a semantic explanation seems possible. Recall the projection rules for sentence adverbs. $P_{speaker}$ embeds the reading of the rest of the sentence as an argument to the reading of the adverb. $P_{subject}$ embeds the reading of the rest of the sentence as one argument and the reading of the derived subject as the other argument to the adverb. Now suppose that the "rest of the sentence" includes all adverbs to the right of the adverb currently being interpreted, but not those to the left. Then a particular pair of adverbs in a particular order may produce a bad reading if the reading of the right-hand adverb combined appropriately with the functional structure cannot be embedded as an argument to the left-hand adverb. Thus we could claim that (3.198)–(3.203) are not acceptable because they have interpretations with anomalous embeddings.

To make this proposal more explicit, let us see how the modification of the projection rules applies to two of the examples above. Take first *Probably Max carefully was climbing the walls*. $P_{subject}$ applies to *carefully*, and $P_{speaker}$ applies to *probably*. The arguments of *carefully* are the reading of the subject (MAX) and the reading of S', the "rest of the sentence," which by the convention we have just established will not include *probably*. The reading including *carefully* but excluding *probably* is thus CAREFUL (MAX, CLIMB (MAX, THE WALLS)). In the application of $P_{speaker}$ to *probably*, the argument to be embedded is the reading of the rest of the sentence, including the adverb *carefully*. Hence the reading we derive for the entire sentence is PROBABLE (CAREFUL (MAX, CLIMB (MAX, THE WALLS))).

In *Carefully Max probably was climbing the walls*, the same projection rules apply, but a different reading results. $P_{speaker}$ applying to *probably* takes as argument the reading of the rest of the sentence excluding *carefully*, which is to the left. Thus $P_{speaker}$ produces PROBABLE (CLIMB (MAX, THE WALLS)). $P_{subject}$ applying to *carefully* takes the two arguments *Max* and the reading of the rest of the sentence including *probably*, giving the complete reading CAREFUL (MAX, PROBABLE (CLIMB (MAX, THE WALLS))), which we claim is an ill-formed reading.

The easiest way to test this claim is to try similar sentences with the semantic embeddings explicitly represented in adjective paraphrases. The acceptability correlates exactly.

(3.204) It is probable that Max often was climbing the walls.
   I am happy that it has been evident that Max has been trying to decide whether to climb the walls.

(3.205) $\left\{ \begin{array}{l} \text{It is probable that} \\ \text{It is evident that} \\ \text{I am happy that} \\ \text{It often happened that} \end{array} \right\}$ Max $\left\{ \begin{array}{l} \text{was careful in} \\ \text{was clever in} \\ \text{was quick in} \\ \text{was stealthy in} \end{array} \right\}$ climbing the walls.

(3.206) *Max was $\left\{ \begin{array}{l} \text{careful in} \\ \text{clever in} \\ \text{quick in} \\ \text{stealthy in} \end{array} \right\}$ $\left\{ \begin{array}{l} \text{its being probable} \\ \text{its being evident} \\ \text{my being happy} \\ \text{its happening often} \end{array} \right\}$ that he climbed the walls.

(3.207) *Max was $\left\{ \begin{array}{l} \text{careful in} \\ \text{clever in} \\ \text{quick in} \\ \text{stealthy in} \end{array} \right\}$ $\left\{ \begin{array}{l} \text{being careful} \\ \text{being clever} \\ \text{being quick} \\ \text{being stealthy} \end{array} \right\}$ in climbing the walls.

Thus the claim that the relative semantic embedding of adverbs is reflected in their left-to-right surface order correctly accounts for (3.195)–(3.203).

It is interesting that this account of (3.195)–(3.203) is so far consistent with a transformational theory of sentence adverbs. One might in fact claim that by adopting a transformation derivation of adverbs, including a transformational or derivational constraint (cf. G. Lakoff, 1970b) correlating left-to-right surface order with depth of underlying embedding, one could account for (3.195)–(3.203) simply by knowing the acceptability of (3.204)–(3.207). Even forgetting the difficulties of the transformational hypothesis discussed in section 3.3, this solution does not have any advantages over the interpretive solution proposed here. Both solutions express the generalization that (3.198)–(3.203) and (3.204)–(3.207) are unacceptable for the same reasons, which is the important generalization. In a transformational theory, the generalization is expressed by deriving one construction from the other, subject to a left-to-right constraint on adverb order; in an interpretive theory, it is expressed by assigning them the same (or similarly structured) interpretations, with adverb interpretation mentioning the left-to-right factor.

However, the transformational theory fails again for the same reason that it failed in accounting for orientation. The PPs that serve semantically as speaker-oriented adverbs obey the same ordering constraints.

(3.208)
$\left\{\begin{array}{l}\text{Of course,}\\\text{In my opinion,}\\\text{In all probability,}\\\text{By the way,}\end{array}\right\}$ Max $\left\{\begin{array}{l}\text{carefully}\\\text{cleverly}\\\text{quickly}\\\text{stealthily}\end{array}\right\}$ was climbing the wall.

(3.209)
* $\left\{\begin{array}{l}\text{Carefully}\\\text{Cleverly,}\\\text{Quickly}\\\text{Stealthily,}\end{array}\right\}$ Max was, $\left\{\begin{array}{l}\text{of course,}\\\text{in my opinion,}\\\text{in all probability,}\\\text{by the way,}\end{array}\right\}$ climbing the wall.

Note that at least some speaker-oriented adverbs are permitted in initial position in frames like (3.209), so (3.209) is not simply a syntactic problem (although it obviously is bad stylistically).

(3.210) ?Often Max has, in my opinion, acted like a jackass.
(3.211) ?Happily, Max has, in all probability, reached Texas by now.

The difficulty in (3.210)–(3.211) has to do with breaking up the sentence with too many pauses. But the interpretation of the initial adverb is secure; this is not the case in (3.209), which has semantic problems in addition to the stylistic ones.

In a transformational theory, one would presumably derive *in my opinion* from *it is my opinion that S*. *In all probability* could come from *it is probable that S*, but for the troublesome morpheme *all*—I will hazard no guesses as to what source might be proposed for it. *Of course* and *by the way* have no obvious relationships to any other expressions. Thus the derivations will be highly idiosyncratic and probably unique for each expression. Granting such derivations, though, one could naturally propose doubly embedded deep structures for (3.208)–(3.209) similar to those for (3.198)–(3.203). But there would be no way of assuring that the surface order reflects the deep structure embedding—why should a syntactic constraint applying to adjectives and adverbs constrain these entirely different derivations as well?

In the interpretive theory, on the other hand, we have assumed that prepositional phrases and adverbs, although syntactically distinct, are semantically interchangeable and undergo the same projection rules. Thus the interpretive theory predicts (3.208)–(3.209), while the transformatiional theory must add more unenlightening descriptive machinery.

Incidentally, it appears that final position with pause acts as thought were the leftmost position with respect to some of the ordering constraints: (3.212) seems closer in acceptability to (3.213) than to the doubtful (3.214).

(3.212)   Often John avoids work, evidently.
(3.213)   Evidently John often avoids work.
(3.214) ?Often John evidently avoids work.

Likewise, (3.215) seems less acceptable than (3.212), indicating that it is more closely related to (3.214) than (3.213).

(3.215) ?Evidently John avoids work, often.

But a subject-oriented adverb cannot be in initial position if there is a speaker-oriented adverb finally:

(3.216)* Carefully John avoids work, $\begin{cases} \text{evidently.} \\ \text{often.} \end{cases}$

Also notice that final position with pause is acceptable with only speaker-oriented adverbs. Apparently $P_{subject}$ does not apply to this configuration.

(3.217)   John carefully has avoided work.
(3.218) ?*John has avoided work, carefully.

3.12 Generalization of the Projection Rules to PPs and Parentheticals

We have already pointed out a number of times the similarity in interpretation of adverbs, prepositional phrases, and various adverbial clauses. The prepositional phrases that function as sentence adverbs can occur in all the usual positions for sentence adverbs:

(3.219) $\left\{ \begin{array}{l} \text{Of course,} \\ \text{In all probability,} \\ \text{In my opinion,} \end{array} \right\}$ John has lost the race.

(3.220) John, $\left\{ \begin{array}{l} \text{of course,} \\ \text{in all probability,} \\ \text{in my opinion,} \end{array} \right\}$ has lost the race.

(3.221) John has, $\left\{ \begin{array}{l} \text{of course,} \\ \text{in all probability,} \\ \text{in my opinion,} \end{array} \right\}$ lost the race.

(3.222) John has lost the race, $\left\{ \begin{array}{l} \text{of course.} \\ \text{in all probability.} \\ \text{in my opinion.} \end{array} \right.$

These PPs must be distinguished from time expressions and locatives preposed from the VP, which cannot occupy anything but initial position. Note that VP adverbs do not undergo the PP preposing transformation.

(3.223) $\left\{ \begin{array}{l} \text{At 6:00,} \\ \text{In the garden,} \end{array} \right\}$ John will lose his wallet.

(3.224) *John, $\left\{ \begin{array}{l} \text{at 6:00,} \\ \text{in the garden,} \end{array} \right\}$ will lose his wallet.

(This example may be acceptable with a nominative absolute reading, which has an S adverbial source.)

(3.225) *John will, $\left\{ \begin{array}{l} \text{at 6:00,} \\ \text{in the garden,} \end{array} \right\}$ lose his wallet.

(3.226) ?*John will lose his wallet, $\left\{ \begin{array}{l} \text{at 6:00.} \\ \text{in the garden.} \end{array} \right.$

(This example to be carefully distinguished from the same sentence without comma)

We can describe the difference between these two kinds of PP without much difficulty. In deep structure, the PPs of (3.219)–(3.222) occupy the same positions as S adverbs, but the PPs of (3.223) are dominated by the VP. The surface structure (3.223) is the result of a preposing rule. By ordering the rules which move S adverbs (perhaps transportability) before the rule preposing PPs out of VP, we can prevent locative and time PPs from occupying other than initial position in surface structure.

Two things are to be noted in this analysis. First, it represents a further generalization of the semantic and syntactic roles of PPs and adverbs. In section 3.7, where we discussed the interpretation of the adjective paraphrases for manner adverbs such as *the manner in which Dave speaks is eloquent*, we casually assumed that the PPs *in wh-some manner*, *at wh-some time*, and *to wh-some extent* undergo P_{manner} exactly as adverbs do. Now we have found that PPs that undergo $P_{speaker}$ are to be generated by a base rule again containing the configuration $\left\{ \begin{matrix} PP \\ Adv \end{matrix} \right\}$. Thus this analysis gives us further reason to believe that PPs and adverbs share syntactic and semantic features.

Furthermore, this analysis in no way requires a syntactic distinction between prepositions that can be generated under VP and those that can be generated under S. As with the adverbs, the distinction is a purely semantic one, based on the appropriateness of the meaning of the PP to the semantic structure into which the projection rule inserts it. For example, if *in all probability* were inserted under a VP, it would be interpreted as a locative phrase, which is nonsensical—a close to minimal pair, where the distinction gets fuzzy, might be *in my opinion* (S adverbial) vs. *in my dreams* (VP adverbial—locative).

In section 3.4 a number of adverbial clauses were mentioned which display the same orientation as adverbs; we can conclude that they ought to be interpreted (at least in part) by $P_{speaker}$ and $P_{subject}$. There is in addition another class of clauses which can be enlighteningly described in this framework: the parentheticals (data selected from Rardin 1968).

(3.227) John is, I think, a fink.
(3.228) Susan, we understand, is now in Brazil.
(3.229) This analysis may, I fear, be incorrect.

It is obvious that some relationship must be established between these and (3.230)–(3.232).

(3.230) I think John is a fink.
(3.231) We understand (that) Susan is now in Brazil.
(3.232) I fear (that) this analysis may be incorrect.

However, any transformational derivation leads to trouble. Consider what sort of transformation is required to produce the derived structure (3.234) from (3.233) (dotted lines denote alternative connections).

(3.233)

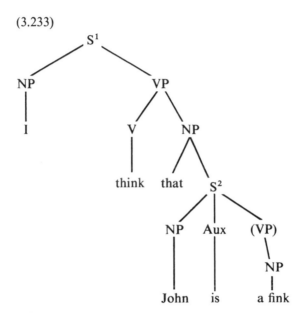

(3.234)

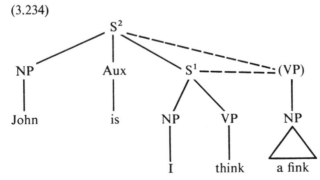

A transformation lowering S^1 into S^2, as suggested by Rardin (1968), moves nonconstituents such as *I think*; a transformation raising (part of) S^2 above

S^1, as suggested by Emonds (1970), also moves nonconstituents such as *John is* in (3.234).

Other difficulties are pointed out by Rardin: the parenthetical must be of "positive" import, and there is no convenient way to state this in the transformation.

$$(3.235) \text{ John is, } \left\{ \begin{array}{l} \text{I think,} \\ \text{*I don't think,} \\ \text{*I doubt,} \\ \text{I don't doubt,} \end{array} \right\} \text{ a fink.}$$

Also, the transformation does not preserve meaning, as the following contrasts show:

(3.236) Helen thinks that John is a fink, but he isn't.
(3.237) Margaret believes that Myrtle will come tomorrow, but she actually came yesterday.

(3.238) John is a fink, Helen thinks (*but he isn't).
(3.239) Myrtle will come tomorrow, Margaret believes (*but she actually came yesterday).

At least some of these difficulties can be solved if the relation of (3.227)–(3.229) to (3.230)–(3.232) is nonsyntactic. Generating the parenthetical clauses as sentence adverbials immediately solves the syntactic problem of accounting for the derived structure (3.234) (with the VP (*be*) *a fink* attached to S^2). Parentheticals can occur in all the positions of sentence adverbials, except possibly initial position (where they either do not exist or are indistinguishable from the normal complement construction). (3.228) illustrates preauxiliary position, (3.227) and (3.229) post-aux position, and (3.240) final position with pause.

(3.240) We must continue to pay taxes, I assume.

Rardin also illustrates positions in the middle of the VP.

(3.241) The President is insane, one suspects, beyond all hope.
(3.242) The painters came, I claim, on Friday.

In these positions S adverbs are also permitted, if surrounded with heavy pauses. I will not speculate on the derived structure.

(3.243) The President is insane, certainly, beyond all hope.
(3.244) The painters came, of course, on Friday.

One totally aberrant position for both S adverbs and parentheticals is between the verb and the direct object.

$$(3.245) \text{ Bill ate, } \begin{cases} ??\text{I think,} \\ ??\text{of course,} \\ *\text{certainly,} \end{cases} \text{ the pumpernickel.}$$

If parentheticals are S adverbials, as their distribution so far indicates, they are obviously speaker-oriented. Therefore we should expect them to occur before but not after subject-oriented adverbs, as predicted by the constraints of section 3.11. And this indeed seems to be the case.

$$(3.246) \text{ John, } \begin{cases} \text{I think,} \\ \text{we suspect,} \end{cases} \text{ has cleverly been examined by the doctor.}$$
     (Note that *cleverly* is subject-oriented and not manner here: cf. section 3.9.)

$$(3.247) *\text{John cleverly has, } \begin{cases} \text{I think,} \\ \text{we suspect,} \end{cases} \text{ been examined by the doctor.}$$

The violation in (3.247) does not merely have to do with the adverb preceding a parenthetical: substituting a speaker-oriented adverb for *cleverly* in (3.247) makes the sentence acceptable.

$$(3.248) \text{ John usually has, } \begin{cases} \text{I think,} \\ \text{we suspect,} \end{cases} \text{ been examined by the doctor.}$$

To further demonstrate the similarity between parentheticals and S adverbs we observe that the constraints illustrated in (3.235)–(3.239) for parentheticals have parallels with S adverbs. Closest in meaning to parentheticals are adverbs like *truthfully*, *honestly*, and *sincerely*. Like parentheticals, they do not have negative counterparts.

$$(3.249) \begin{Bmatrix} \text{Truthfully,} \\ \text{*Falsely,} \\ \text{Honestly,} \\ \text{*Dishonestly,} \\ \text{Sincerely,} \\ \text{*Insincerely,} \end{Bmatrix} \text{I can't tell you the answer.}$$

They certainly cannot occur in contexts like (3.238)–(3.239) either.

(3.250) *Truthfully, John is a fink, but he isn't.

Thus it appears that a semantic explanation of the constraints can generalize with S adverbs as well.

Of course, there still remains the fundamental problem of explaining the relation of *I think John is a fink* to its parenthetical counterpart *John is, I think, a fink*. We must therefore show how a parenthetical receives a semantic interpretation in which the main clause is embedded as an argument of the parenthetical. But this is not difficult. All the parentheticals are semantically one-place predicates: exactly one argument, the complement sentence, is missing from the functional structure. Syntactically, we can think of them as sentences generated with one node missing (or with the sentence complement replaced by an empty node—see section 5.2). Generated alone, they would receive a defective semantic interpretation, since one strictly subcategorized argument would be absent. However, generated as sentence adverbials, they are subject to $P_{speaker}$, which embeds the rest of the sentence as a single argument to the adverb. $P_{speaker}$ will therefore fill the missing argument of the parentheticals with the reading of the main clause, exactly the structure needed to provide semantic similarity to the complement constructions. The difference in meaning between the two constructions, noted in (3.236)–(3.239) and related to presuppositions, is independent of the embedding and is contributed by $P_{speaker}$, as we have seen on independent grounds.

By abandoning a traditionally oriented transformational analysis of parentheticals and treating them as sentence adverbials, then, we have gone a long way toward explaining their peculiarities. We have avoided adding a complex (and perhaps unstatable) transformation to the grammar, but we have still provided a correctly structured semantic interpretation, using already motivated semantic rules. In addition, we have automatically captured a number of important distributional generalizations with sentence adverbs, generalizations that could not even be suspected in a traditional account. Thus parentheticals provide strong evidence for the interpretive theory of adverbs.

3.13 Modals

It has often been observed that some English modals have two distinct senses, called the "root" and "epistemic" senses.

(3.251)

	Root	Epistemic
may	permission	possibility
can	ability	possibility
must	obligation	logical entailment
won't	refusal	future nonoccurrence
should	obligation	supposition

It is clear that the two senses must be distinguished in the lexicon and in semantic interpretation. Should they be distinguished syntactically as well?

Ross (1967d) and Perlmutter (1971) claim that the two senses should arise from two distinct deep structures, both of which represent the modal as the main verb of a higher sentence which embeds the surface main clause as a complement. However, this approach ignores the totally different syntactic behavior of modals and verbs. Consider the differences. Modals do not undergo number agreement, though all verbs do. Modals do not occur together, and they do not appear in gerunds and infinitives.[5] The first of these properties is obviously syntactic. The latter two cannot be explained on semantic grounds either, since the verbal paraphrases of modals are acceptable in these constructions.

(3.252) *I should can use two modals in a row if they are verbs.

(3.253) *I want to may leave the room.

(3.254) *I don't like musting use modals in gerunds.

---

[5]These arguments do not hold for modals in German, which behave much more like normal verbs. Instead of arguing, as Ross does, that this proves on universal grounds that English modals are verbs too, we will take this difference as an indication that English modals have become a separate part of speech through a process of historical change including a syntactic reanalysis. Old English modals were much more like German modals.

(3.255) I should be able to use two modals in a row if they are verbs.
(3.256) I want to be allowed to leave the room.
(3.257) I don't like having to use modals in gerunds.

Modals also differ from all main verbs but *be* and some uses of *have* in that they undergo subject-aux inversion, precede *not*, and block *do*-support.

Furthermore, if the surface main clause in sentences with modals is to be a deep structure complement clause, modals must govern a rule deleting the complementizer, since none shows up at the surface. Again, this is a purely syntactic property, since the verbal paraphrases retain the complementizer *to*, as in (3.255)–(3.257). There is a small class of verbs semantically unrelated to modals (*make, hear, see, feel, watch*) which also delete the complementizer. But there is syntactic evidence that these verbs can occur as main verbs, since they embed freely and do not invert, and since they can occur with a PP replacing the complement clause in closely related, if not identical, senses. The PP and complement cannot co-occur.

(3.258) Harry made John $\begin{cases} \text{wash the dishes every night.} \\ \text{(into) a nervous wreck.} \end{cases}$

(3.259) Betty heard Sue $\begin{cases} \text{walk into the bathroom.} \\ \text{in the bathroom.} \\ \text{*in the bathroom wash her hair.} \end{cases}$

For modals there is no such syntactic evidence that they are main verbs. There are, of course, main verbs which always must occur with a complement clause, including the verbal paraphrases of the modals. But these verbs also embed freely and retain the complementizer *to*, so again there is evidence that they are verbs.

Thus we can treat modals as verbs only if we are willing to concede that they represent a remarkable coincidence of a large number of purely syntactic aberrations. On the other hand, the analysis of the English auxiliary given in *Syntactic Structures* and developed here in section 3.8 captures the syntactic disparity quite accurately, with no use of the notion "exception" at all. The only cost of this analysis is the addition of the node Modal in the base rules.

We will therefore retain the standard analysis of modals and attempt to account for the differences in meaning with rules of semantic interpretation. In an interpretive approach, we need in the lexicon exactly the idiosyncratic semantic features on individual modals that are needed in Ross's and Perlmutter's transformational theory. These idiosyncrasies indicate whether the modal has a root sense or an epistemic sense or both, and what these readings are. We do not, however, need any syntactic exception features.

Corresponding to the addition of the node M in the base, the interpretive theory will require projection rules to integrate the interpretation of the modal into the interpretation of the sentence. At worst, two new projection rules will be needed, one for the root modals and one for the epistemic modals. I will show, however, that epistemic modals are interpreted by the projection rule for speaker-oriented adverbs. Furthermore, Newmeyer (1970) shows that the interpretation of root modals cannot be accounted for in a transformational theory of modals that assumes the Katz-Postal Hypothesis. (His evidence will appear in a moment.) Hence the additional complication in the semantic component will be shown to have independent semantic justification, as well as the syntactic justification already presented.

Consider first the epistemic modals. It is plausible to assume a semantic structure in which the reading of the rest of the sentence is embedded as an argument to the reading of the modal:

$$(3.260) \quad \begin{Bmatrix} \text{WILL} \\ \text{MAY} \end{Bmatrix} \text{(JOHN LEAVE)}$$

This semantic structure is identical to that predicted by the transformational theory, in which the epistemic modal is characterized as an intransitive verb embedding the rest of the sentence as a subject complement. However, it is also similar to the structure associated with speaker-oriented adverbs. The projection rule $P_{speaker}$ could easily be generalized to epistemic modals, since they, like speaker-oriented adverbs, are dominated by S (disregarding the possibly superfluous node Aux).

Is there other evidence to support this generalization? First note that the restrictions on some speaker-oriented adverbs in sentences with subject-aux inversion (section 3.10) seem to hold for some epistemic modals as well. For example, although (3.261)–(3.262) are ambiguous between the two senses of the modals, (3.263)–(3.264) strongly favor the root interpretation.

$$(3.261) \quad \text{Max} \begin{Bmatrix} \text{must} \\ \text{should} \\ \text{may} \end{Bmatrix} \text{leave soon.}$$

(3.262) Max $\begin{Bmatrix} \text{must} \\ \text{should} \\ \text{may} \end{Bmatrix}$ see only three people.

(3.263) $\begin{Bmatrix} \text{Must} \\ \text{Should} \\ \text{May} \end{Bmatrix}$ Max leave?

(3.264) Only three people $\begin{Bmatrix} \text{must} \\ \text{should} \\ \text{may} \end{Bmatrix}$ Max see.

If epistemic modals are treated like speaker-oriented adverbs by the semantic component, this restriction will follow automatically. On the other hand, there is nothing in the transformational approach that can predict these facts. In particular, questioning the verbal paraphrases of epistemic modals produces no anomaly; the transformational theory in fact incorrectly predicts that (3.263) should have a reading similar to (3.265).

(3.265) Is it $\begin{Bmatrix} \text{possible} \\ \text{likely} \end{Bmatrix}$ that Max will leave?

More remarkable evidence is provided by the ordering restrictions of section 3.11. Recall that speaker-oriented adverbs can precede but not follow subject-oriented adverbs. This is true of epistemic modals as well, although the degree of unacceptability is not so great (these facts were pointed out to me by Jay Keyser). Perfect aspect is used in (3.269)–(3.271) to preclude a manner interpretation.

(3.266) ?*Slowly John will open the door.
(3.267) ?*Dave quietly may leave the room.   } (epistemic
(3.268) ?*Carefully Pete should creep out of there soon. } reading)

(3.269)   John will slowly have opened the door.
(3.270)   Dave may quietly have left the room.
(3.271)   Pete should carefully have crept out of there (by now).

On the other hand, combinations of epistemic modals and speaker-oriented adverbs are acceptable in either order, provided that semantic redundancy (e.g. *probably* and *may*) is avoided.

(3.272) John $\begin{Bmatrix} \text{will evidently} \\ \text{evidently will} \end{Bmatrix}$ open the door.

(3.273) Bill $\begin{Bmatrix} \text{probably should} \\ \text{should probably} \end{Bmatrix}$ have left by now.

(3.274) $\begin{matrix} \text{Usually Fred must} \\ \text{Fred must usually} \end{matrix} \Big\}$ get out by climbing the wall.

The claim, then, is that speaker-oriented adverbs and epistemic modals, which are syntactically totally dissimilar except that they are daughters of S, are treated identically by the semantic component, which only makes use of the single syntactic property they have in common. Insofar as earlier sections have shown the constraints of sections 3.10–3.11 to be semantic, the similarity of the constraints illustrated in (3.261)–(3.274) is not accidental, but an automatic consequence of the theory.

Ideally, one would hope that the root senses of modals could be produced by $P_{subject}$, the other projection rule for S adverbs. Unfortunately this seems not to be the case. If it were, we would incorrectly predict that root modals could not precede speaker-oriented adverbs: (3.273) and (3.274) (using the root sense of the modal) are counterexamples to that prediction. Further, root modals behave somewhat differently with respect to the passive than subject-oriented adverbs do. As with adverbs, meaning often changes under the passive:

(3.275) The doctor $\begin{pmatrix} \text{may} \\ \text{must} \\ \text{won't} \end{pmatrix}$ examine John.

(3.276) John $\begin{pmatrix} \text{may} \\ \text{must} \\ \text{won't} \end{pmatrix}$ be examined by the doctor.

In each case, the surface subject is understood as having permission, being under obligation, or refusing. Thus these examples are parallel to (3.142)–(3.147) in section 3.9:

(3.142) The doctor cleverly has examined John.
(3.143) John cleverly has been examined by the doctor.

(3.144) The police carelessly have arrested Fred.
(3.145) Fred carelessly has been arrested by the police.

(3.146) Joe intentionally has seduced Mary.
(3.147) Mary intentionally has been seduced by Joe.

and support a generalization of subject-oriented adverbs and root modals. However, as Newmeyer (1970) points out, there are cases when a root modal does not change meaning (at least in the same way) under passive, particularly when the deep object is inanimate.

(3.277) Visitors may pick flowers.
(3.278) Flowers may be picked by visitors.
(3.279) Sam must shovel the dirt into the hole.
(3.280) The dirt must be shoveled into the hole by Sam.

On the other hand, subject-oriented adverbs in the same contexts yield anomalies with the passive.

(3.281)   Bill carefully has picked some flowers.
(3.282)   *Some flowers carefully have been picked by Bill.
(3.283)   Sam cleverly has shoveled the dirt into the hole.
(3.284) ?*The dirt cleverly has been shoveled into the hole by Sam.

Apparently both $P_{subject}$ and P_{root} (the projection rule for root modals) require a specially designated NP as an argument. For $P_{subject}$ this must always be the derived subject, and if the derived subject cannot satisfy the selectional restrictions, anomaly results. P_{root}, on the other hand, can choose another appropriate NP if the derived subject is unsatisfactory. Thus we have found two significant differences between $P_{subject}$ and P_{root}, and a generalization seems improbable. The generalization of epistemic modals and speaker-oriented adverbs is thereby set off in stronger contrast.

3.14 Summary

We have proposed an analysis of adverbs in which they are generated in their clause in the base and interpreted by a variety of projection rules. This proposal has been shown to have several advantages over a theory in which adverbs are derived from deep structure adjectives, in particular, far greater simplicity in the transformational component and in the system of transformational exceptions. The dependence of adverb interpretation on position in the sentence has been shown to follow from a simple principle of domination by S or VP, given an otherwise attractive analysis of the English auxiliary.

The projection rules for S adverbs, when investigated in more detail, turn out to involve surface structure considerations. Passive, subject-aux inversion, and the relative order of adverbs have effects on the semantic interpretation.

The projection rules for manner adverbs and speaker-oriented S adverbs have been shown to apply also to PPs. In addition, evidence has been given to show that parentheticals and epistemic modals can also be interpreted by the projection rule for speaker-oriented adverbs, and that significant generalizations follow from this assumption.

Here is a summary of the rules involved in the discussion.

Base rules:

$$S \rightarrow NP - Aux - VP - \left(\begin{Bmatrix} Adv \\ PP \\ S \end{Bmatrix}^* \right), \text{ the final nodes perhaps being desig-}$$

nated in the base as transportable, S designating parentheticals.

$$Aux \rightarrow Tense - (Modal)$$

$$VP \rightarrow (\text{have-en})\text{-}(\text{be-ing})\text{-}(Adv) - V - (NP) - \left(\begin{Bmatrix} Adv \\ PP \end{Bmatrix}^* \right)$$

This may undergo generalization, via the base rule schema, with

$$\bar{N} \rightarrow (Adj) - N - (PP^*)$$

Transformations:

Transportability of S adverbials (if this is a transformation)

Passive

Preposing of locative and time PPs, negated constituents, and *wh*-constituents

Have-Be raising

Subject-aux inversion

Affix attachment

Projection rules:

Designate the class $\begin{Bmatrix} \text{Adv} \\ \text{PP} \\ \text{S (at least parentheticals)} \\ \text{Modal} \end{Bmatrix}$ by F.

$P_{speaker}$: If F_1 is a daughter of S, embed the reading of S (including any members of F to the right of F_1) as an argument to the reading of F_1.

$P_{subject}$: If Adv_1 is a daughter of S, embed the reading of S (including any members of F to the right of Adv_1) as one argument to Adv_1, and embed the derived subject of S as the second argument to Adv_1.

P_{manner}: If $\begin{Bmatrix} \text{Adv} \\ \text{PP} \end{Bmatrix}$ is dominated by VP, attach its semantic markers to the reading of the verb without changing the functional structure.

P_{merely}

P_{root}

CHAPTER FOUR

Pronouns and Reflexives

4.1 Introduction

The standard transformational theory of pronouns and reflexives (Lees and Klima 1963, Ross 1967b, Langacker 1969) assumes that pronouns originate as fully specified noun phrases identical with their antecedents in deep structure. Transformations change noun phrases into pronoun or reflexive forms on the basis of morphological identity and intended coreference with other noun phrases in the sentence. This chapter will explore the alternative theory that pronouns and reflexives are present in deep structure and that their antecedents are determined in the semantic component.

In this approach, which I will call the interpretive theory, noun phrases are unmarked for coreference relations in deep structure. Rules of semantic interpretation establish relations between pairs of noun phrases, marking them coreferential or noncoreferential with each other.

In the case of plural noun phrases, additional specification must be made of set coreference versus individual-by-individual coreference, in order to explain, for example, the difference between *themselves* and *each other*. Also, a distinction must be made between type and token coreference, in order to explain the difference between *one* and *it*. We will touch upon these aspects of coreference occasionally here, but we will concentrate upon an account of singular definite pronouns, the simplest and best understood case.

Instead of being produced by transformations, pronouns and reflexives will be generated by the base component as lexical items, marked with the feature [+pro], but like other noun phrases, unmarked for reference. Reflexives, in addition, will be marked with the feature [+refl]. Since pronouns such as *someone* must be generated in the base anyway, the only addition to the inventory of lexical features is the feature *refl*.

As motivation for attempting an interpretive approach, let us recall the brief discussion of coreference in Chapter 1. There it was shown that coreference relations among noun phrases are an aspect of semantic interpretation independent of functional structure. If a transformation produces pronouns, it must be able to make use of coreference relations. However, transformations generally cannot mention coreference relations: there is no rule, for example, that preposes a noun phrase if it is coreferential with some other noun phrase. Thus in stating pronominalization and reflexivization transformations that refer to intended coreference, we are implicitly granting transformations power which they do not in general possess. As part of the consistent effort to reduce the power of transformations, we will construct a theory of grammar in which no transformation can use coreference as a criterion of application.

Adopting an interpretive theory of pronominalization will help us to reduce the power of transformations in another important respect, too. A pronominalization transformation changes a fully specified noun phrase into a pronoun. This is the kind of drastic change in the form of lexical material we would like to eliminate from transformations under the constraints of the Extended Lexical Hypothesis (see section 1.4).

After some preliminary motivation in section 4.2, we will make a first approximation to the pronominalization and reflexivization rules in section 4.3. Sections 4.4 and 4.5 deal in detail with the environment and ordering of pronominalization, and sections 4.6–4.8 do likewise for reflexivization. We will argue that both rules apply at the end of each transformational cycle. Sections 4.9–4.11 deal with some unexpected counterexamples observed by Postal in his monograph *Crossover Phenomena* (1971). Sections 4.12–4.13 discuss some further extensions of reflexivization, and section 4.14 integrates the two rules.

4.2 Conceptual Advantages

An important prediction already arises at this rudimentary stage of the theory. Interpretive rules that mark coreference can as easily mark a pair of noun phrases noncoreferential as coreferential, providing a ready way to handle such phrases as *someone else* and *another*, where the reference is unspecified but different from previous references. A transformational approach to pronouns provides no easy way to account for items like these in a fashion consistent with the general treatment.

Another immediate advantage is that the infinite recursion of deep structures in sentences such as (4.1) (first pointed out in Bach 1970) does not arise.

(4.1) The man who deserves it will get the prize he wants.

If the underlying structure of pronouns is a fully specified NP identical with its coreferent, both *it* and *he* in (4.1) must have infinite deep structures:

(4.2) The man [who deserves the prize [which the man [who . . .] wants]]
will get the prize [which the man [who deserves the prize [which . . .]
wants]]

Other difficulties with underlying morphologically identical antecedents
are discussed in Dougherty (1969).

The drastic way out in the transformational approach to reference is to
generate only referential indices in NP positions, then bring in lexical
material from outside conjoined clauses (see McCawley 1970; Postal 1967;
Bach 1968). Such a solution violates the Extended Lexical Hypothesis, since
it requires deep structure proforms that consist of only a referential index.
But more important, this solution requires the addition of clauses to the
deep structure whose precise syntactic form have no bearing on the surface
structure. As it is one principal objective of the present study to eliminate
the need for precisely this kind of "abstract" deep structure, an alternative
formalization of coreference is necessary.

The interpretive theory provides one such alternative. If the reference of
pronouns is determined by a rule of semantic interpretation, the deep structure of (4.1) contains the pronouns themselves, so there is no recursion.
Furthermore, in the process of semantic interpretation, a pronoun need not
be replaced with a duplicate of the noun phrase with which it is coreferential (which would again bring up the problem of recursion), but rather it
may just be marked coreferential with another noun phrase.

A third piece of evidence for the conceptual attractiveness of an interpretive theory is provided by sentences like (4.3)–(4.5).

(4.3) I wanted Charlie to help me, but the bastard wouldn't do it.
(4.4) Irving was besieged by a horde of bills and the poor guy couldn't pay
them.
(4.5) Although the bum tried to hit me, I can't really get too mad at Harry.

There are many noun phrases such as *the bum, the bastard*, and *the poor guy*
that can be used coreferentially with another noun phrase if they are reduced in stress. These "pronominal epithets" can occur in some subset of
the environments in which pronominalization is possible, and they function
semantically more or less as specialized pronouns. We would obviously

miss a generalization if we did not handle them by a rule of the same kind as pronominalization, hopefully a rule that could collapse with pronominalization.

In a transformational framework, however, the generalization cannot be captured. The pronominalization transformation changes NPs into pronouns. In a consistent treatment, in certain contexts an NP could be turned into a pronominal epithet instead. But then which pronominal epithet should the NP be changed into? The meaning is obviously changed if we substitute an epithet for a pronoun or one epithet for another.

In an interpretive framework, we can mark epithets as special lexical items which may function as pronouns in certain contexts of the pronominalization rule, adding their lexical meaning to the intended attributes of the person they refer to. Thus no change need be made in the nature of the interpretive theory in order to include these cases.

4.3 Preliminary Statement of the Rules

It is important to make clear from the start what it means to apply a semantic rule of coreference. There are three relevant points to keep in mind. First, coreference is an exclusively semantic property that cannot be referred to by transformations. Second, coreference is an aspect of semantic interpretation that has nothing to do with the functional structure of the sentence. Third, coreference is formalized in the present approach as a binary relation holding between two NPs (or their semantic readings). Three or more NPs can be understood as mutually coreferential only if they have been marked pairwise coreferential.

A commonly used device for indicating coreference in generative grammar is the index of coreference, introduced by Chomsky in *Aspects of the Theory of Syntax* (1965). In Chomsky's formalism, each noun phrase has an associated integer (or index), and two NPs are coreferential if they have the same index. However, in order to emphasize the three points above, we will abandon this formalism. Instead, we will express coreference relations explicitly in a *table of coreference*. Each entry in the table will consist of a pair of noun phrases and one of the relations *coreferential* or *noncoreferential*. In a complete semantic interpretation, the table will contain an entry for each pair of noun phrases in the sentence. The table will be built up one entry at a time by the application of semantic rules of coreference. Some of the semantic rules will make reference to already existing entries in the table, but transformations will never refer to it.

After the table is completed, it will be subject to well-formedness conditions that determine whether it is consistent both internally and in relation to the rest of the semantic interpretation. One rather obvious condition we must impose is the Consistency Condition:

(4.6) (Consistency Condition)
       If the table of coreference marks two NPs coreferential, those NPs must in fact be able to describe the same individual.

Several other conditions will be developed in this chapter and the next.

Leaving aside the environments for pronominalization and reflexivization for the moment, let us see what kinds of entries the interpretive rules will make in the table of coreference. First consider the simple cases of reflexivization, two noun phrases in the same simple sentence.

(4.7)   John washed himself.
(4.8)a. John washed him.
       b. John washed John.
       c. John washed Bill.

According to the interpretive theory, (4.7)–(4.8) are all possible deep structures. The noun phrases will not be marked for coreference in the deep structure. The rule for interpretation of reflexives must enter in the table that the object of (4.7) is coreferential with the subject, and it must mark all the other objects noncoreferential with the subject. A plausible way to express this is the rule (4.9). We borrow the notion of an α rule from phonology: α is a variable to be replaced by $+$ or $-$, but both occurrences of α must be replaced with the same sign on any particular application of the rule.

(4.9) (Reflexivization, first approximation)
       Enter in the table:
       $$NP^1 \; \alpha \; coref \begin{bmatrix} NP^2 \\ \alpha \; reflexive \end{bmatrix} \text{ in the environment} \ldots$$
       OBLIGATORY

Rule (4.9) says that in the proper contexts for reflexivization, NP^2 is coreferential with NP^1 if and only if it is reflexive. In (4.7)–(4.8), the subject will qualify as NP^1 and the object as NP^2. Since the object of (4.7) is reflexive, (4.9) will enter (4.10) in the table.

(4.10) *John* coref *himself.*

Since the objects in the other three sentences are nonreflexive, (4.9) will create the entries (4.11) for (4.8).

(4.11)a. *John* −coref *him*
     b. *John* −coref *John*[1]
     c. *John* −coref *Bill*

One convention on the application of (4.9) must be that if two possible environments for interpretation of a reflexive crop up at once, either reading is possible. This convention is necessary in order to derive the ambiguity of (4.12), treating either *Bill* or *John* as NP^1.

(4.12) Bill told John about himself.

Note that (4.9) does not say anything about agreement in person or number. At first glance, this would seem to lead to trouble in sentences such as (4.13) and (4.14).

(4.13) *The boy shot herself.
(4.14) *Finkelstein shot yourself.

However, closer examination shows that these sentences can be blocked. The reflexive rule does indeed mark coreferentiality, creating the readings

(4.15) *the boy*   coref *herself*
(4.16) *Finkelstein* coref *yourself*

[1]The strangeness of the sentence *John washed John* is thus due to the fact that the same proper name is being used to denote two distinct individuals. While there are clearly many people named John, the language does not recognize this fact; and if the discourse contains two such individuals, the name *John* takes on some of the properties of a common noun, being modifiable in a way proper nouns usually are not, for example *The tall John washed the fat John.* Similar facts obtain with definite descriptions. Thus *The dog bit the dog* sounds strange without further modification because use of the definite article implies the individual is sufficiently identified to be unique within the discourse at hand, yet two such individuals are referred to.

But these readings can be rejected by the Consistency Condition. *The boy* describes a male individual, *herself* a female. Obviously, then, they cannot be used to describe the same individual. Yet the table of coreference requires that they do. The conclusion must be that the sentence is deviant. Likewise, since (except for vocatives) noun phrases other than second-person pronouns describe individuals other than the hearer of the sentence, *Finkelstein* cannot be the same individual as *yourself*, so the table (4.16) is deviant.

The Consistency Condition is the first case we have encountered where adopting an interpretive theory compels us to use a purely semantic criterion for rejecting violently deviant sentences. Other such cases will occur. There tends to be a prejudice in generative grammar that semantic violations will not be crashingly unacceptable, that sentences like (4.13) must be syntactic violations. There is no a priori basis for this prejudice. The position to be taken here is that syntactic and semantic violations can each produce the entire range of unacceptability, depending on the centrality of the violation. The decision whether a particular sentence is to be regarded as syntactically or semantically deviant will depend on the relative generality of proposals on how to rule it out. We will account for the deviance of (4.13) and (4.14) with a semantic violation, then, because this solution follows naturally from the independent need for a Consistency Condition and the general form of the rules of coreference, which will be justified in considerable detail in this chapter and the next. The extreme nature of the violation is to be attributed to the fundamental conceptualization of reference, which requires individuals to be discrete and identifiable. This is presumably universal and furthermore a psychological consideration independent of language. (For further discussion of these points, see Chomsky 1964 and his remarks in *Aspects* (1965), p. 29 and footnote 15 to Chapter 1.)

In addition to the Consistency Condition, we need a well-formedness condition on the table of coreference to reject a sentence if it contains a reflexive without an antecedent, for example (4.17).

(4.17) *Himself was sick.

The condition can be stated as (4.18).

(4.18) (Requirement that reflexives have antecedents)
For every reflexive R in a sentence, there must exist an entry in the table of coreference of the form X coref R, where X is some other NP in the sentence.

(4.18) will exclude not only (4.17), for which the table of coreference contains no entries (since there is only one NP), but (4.19), whose table is (4.20).

(4.19) *Himself shot himself.
(4.20)   *himself* coref *himself*

Though both NPs appear in the table, only one appears on the right-hand side of an entry, as required by the condition. The covert assumption is that there is a formal distinction between the left-hand side of the table, containing antecedents (NP^1 in the reflexive rule) and the right-hand side, containing corresponding anaphoric expressions (NP^2 in the rule). This distinction will occur several times again in the discussion of reflexivization, so it is not totally unmotivated here. It will be maintained in stating further rules of coreference.

Condition (4.18) differs from the Consistency Condition in that it appears to be a purely formal requirement on the table. It is not connected with conceptualization of the world since it deals only with the occurrence of the feature *refl* in the table. A more interesting such condition will be stated in section 4.11, the Thematic Hierarchy Condition on Reflexives. If it should turn out that the feature *refl* or the notions "antecedent" and "anaphoric expression" have some semantic significance, these conditions might then be explained as a consequence. In the meantime, however, they must just be accepted as further rules of the grammar.

Turning now to pronominalization, we have the following basic data to consider.

(4.21) John looked at him.	noncoreferential
(4.22) John said that he was sick.	ambiguous
(4.23) John said that John was sick.	noncoreferential
(4.24) John said that Bill was sick.	noncoreferential

Pronouns are at most optionally coreferential with another NP. Any two nonpronominal noun phrases in the same sentence, morphologically identical or not, are always noncoreferential. We can therefore state the pronominalization rule as (4.25).

(4.25) (Pronominalization, first approximation)

Enter in the table: NP^1 coref $\begin{bmatrix} NP^2 \\ +pro \end{bmatrix}$ in the environment ...

OPTIONAL

We will also need the following rule, which will apply at the end of the rules of coreference:

(4.26) (Noncoreferentiality rule)

If for any NP^1 and NP^2 in a sentence, there is no entry in the table $NP^1 \pm$ coref NP^2, enter in the table $NP^1 -$ coref NP^2.

OBLIGATORY

This rule says that any noun phrases that have not yet been related by a rule of coreference are noncoreferential. The application of (4.26) ensures that every pair of NPs appears in the table.

To illustrate how these rules interact with the reflexive rule and with each other, return to (4.21)–(4.24). In (4.21), reflexivization obligatorily applies, entering *John* − coref *him* in the table. If pronominalization were then to apply, it would enter *John* coref *him* in the table. But then the reading of the sentence would be anomalous, since the table would assert that *John* and *him* both do and do not refer to the same individual. The Consistency Condition rejects this interpretation. Therefore, the only consistent reading is produced by refraining from applying pronominalization. In (4.22), reflexivization does not apply, but pronominalization may apply, entering *John* coref *him* in the table. If pronominalization does not apply, the table is empty when the noncoreferentiality rule is applicable, so the rule enters *John* − coref *him* in the table, producing the other possible reading of the sentence. In (4.23) and (4.24), only the noncoreferentiality rule is applicable, so the two NPs are marked distinct.

Next let us consider a slightly more complicated example.

(4.27) John said that Bill had shot him.

Reflexivization applies to *Bill* and *him*, entering *Bill* − coref *him* in the table. As in (4.21), if pronominalization applies between *Bill* and *him*, an inconsistent reading will result. But a good reading can be produced by applying pronominalization between *John* and *him*. The noncoreferentiality rule will apply between *John* and *Bill*. Thus for this reading the table of coreference will be

(4.28) *Bill* − coref *him*
     John   coref *him*
     John − coref *Bill*

Alternatively, we can choose not to apply pronominalization at all, in which case the noncoreferentiality rule also applies between *John* and *him*, yielding the table

(4.29) *Bill* − coref *him*
     John − coref *him*
     John − coref *Bill*

Incidentally, it should be noticed that no ordering has been established between reflexivization and pronominalization. Each makes independent entries in the table, then the table is inspected for consistency. The non-coreferentiality rule must, however, follow both of these rules.

4.4 The Environment for Pronominalization

In the transformational account of pronominalization, the transformation can be stated roughly as (4.30), following Langacker (1969).

(4.30) $NP^2 \Rightarrow +pro$ if NP^1 is identical with NP^2 and if NP^2 does not both precede and command NP^1.
     OBLIGATORY

The relation *command* is defined as follows (Langacker 1969): "We will say that a node *A* 'commands' another node *B* if (1) neither *A* nor *B* dominates the other; and (2) the *S*-node that most immediately dominates *A* also dominates *B*." The typical paradigm produced by (4.30) is illustrated in (4.31)–(4.34) (*Jake* and *he* to be understood as coreferential in each case).

(4.31)   Jake left town after he robbed the bank.

(4.32) *He left town after Jake robbed the bank.

(4.33)   After Jake robbed the bank, he left town.

(4.34)   After he robbed the bank, Jake left town.

With the antecedent to the left ("forward pronominalization"), pro-nominalization is generally possible. With the antecedent to the right ("backward pronominalization"), the pronoun must not command the antecedent.

Since the environment for the transformational rule seems to be essentially correct, it would be nice to preserve it as the environment in an interpretive theory. However, it is easy to see that the pronominalization transformation is ordered after many other transformations, for example adverbial preposing, which relates (4.32) and (4.33). To maintain this environment, therefore, we will have to give up any hope of having the interpretive rule for pronominalization apply to deep structure.

We can preserve the environment of (4.30) if we place the interpretive rule for pronominalization at exactly the point in the grammar where (4.30) takes place in the transformational theory. The complete form of the pronominalization rule will then look like (4.35).

(4.35) (Pronominalization)

Enter in the table: NP^1 coref $\begin{bmatrix} NP^2 \\ +pro \end{bmatrix}$ unless NP^2 both precedes and

commands NP^1

OPTIONAL

Each time (4.35) is reached after a series of transformations, pairs of noun phrases will be available for interpretation, and (4.35) will read off co-reference relations and insert them in the table.

To illustrate the operation of pronominalization beyond the examples of the last section, we consider (4.36)–(4.37), which are related to the examples discussed in Ross (1967b). (We cannot deal with Ross's actual examples until section 5.3, when we have developed an interpretive equivalent of the complement subject deletion transformation). Recall that in the interpretive theory, *him* is generated by the base.

(4.36) The fact that Mary realized John was sick bothered him.

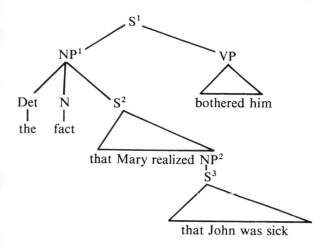

(4.37) The fact that he realized John was sick bothered him.

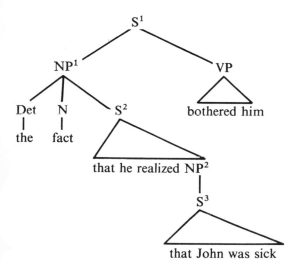

In (4.36), *John* and *him* may be coreferential, as expected from the environment of the pronominalization rule. But in (4.37), surprisingly, forward pronominalization fails between *John* and *him*. However, we will show this fact to be a natural consequence of the way the coreference rules have been stated.

In (4.36), there are two possible environments for pronominalization, using either *Mary* or *John* as NP^1, and *him* as NP^2. Of course, if *Mary* is used, a bad reading will result. If *John* is used, the noncoreferentiality rule will fill out the rest of the NP pairs, producing the table (4.38), the correct reading.

(4.38) *John*   coref *him*
          Mary − coref *John*
          Mary − coref *him*

Consider now (4.37). The possible environments for pronominalization are between *he* and *him* and between *John* and *him*, but not between *he* and *John*, since *he* precedes and commands *John*. Suppose that pronominalization applies in both environments. Then the noncoreferentiality rule will apply to the remaining pair *he* and *John*, yielding the complete table

(4.39) *he*   coref *him*
          John   coref *him*
          he   − coref *John*

But this table is inconsistent: it asserts that *him* is the same individual as two distinct individuals. Therefore the reading must be rejected. This leaves open only the possibility of marking *him* coreferential with one or the other of the other two NPs, letting the noncoreferentiality rule to mark it noncoreferential from the other.

In fact, the predominant reading of (4.37) is the one in which *him* is coreferential with *he* and distinct from *John*. The other reading is difficult to get unless contrastive stress is placed on *he*. This suggests that stress plays a part in making one reading predominate over the other. That this is the case elsewhere is pointed out dramatically by the following pair:

(4.40) John hit Bill and then MAX hit him. (him = Bill)
(4.41) John hit Bill and then Max hit HIM. (him = John)

I have no account at present of how stress interacts with anaphora. For more examples see Akmajian and Jackendoff (1970). However, it should be noted that the range of acceptable readings predicted by the interpretive rule in (4.37) is exactly the same as that predicted by the transformational rule.

The analysis of (4.37) illustrates the importance of letting the rules of coreference operate pairwise without use of the logical notion of transitivity of coreference. The noncoreferentiality rule must apply to pairs of NPs literally unmentioned in the table, without inferring any further coreference relations.

For a case where there are three NPs, all of which are marked pairwise coreferential, interchange *John* and *he* in (4.37) to form (4.42).

(4.42) The fact that John realized he was sick bothered him.

In (4.42), pronominalization may apply between all three pairs to produce the table (4.43), a correct interpretation.

(4.43) *John* coref *he*
    John coref *him*
    he   coref *him*

4.5 The Ordering of Pronominalization

Ross (1967b) gives a very elegant argument to show that certain apparently abnormal examples of pronominalization, related to (4.36) and (4.37), can be explained by simply assuming that the pronominalization transformation is a cyclic rule. On the other hand, G. Lakoff (1968b) and Postal (1970b) argue that pronominalization is last-cyclic, so that some ad hoc adjustment must be made to the environment of the rule to account for Ross's examples. In this section we will review Lakoff's and Postal's arguments, then show that the interpretive theory can resolve the conflict.

4.5.1 Arguments that Pronominalization Is at the End of the Cycle

Lakoff's ordering arguments fall into two parts. First, he shows that pronominalization must follow all reordering transformations in a particular cycle, making it the last rule in the cycle. Second, he purports to show that pronominalization is last-cyclic. Only the second argument raises a conflict with Ross's results. However, we will briefly give a version of his first argument, as it pertains to the interpretive theory as well.

Most reordering rules change pronominalization possibilities. (4.31)–(4.34) show that adverbial clause preposing does, and similar results obtain for *Wh*-preposing, which relates (4.46)–(4.47) to (4.44)–(4.45), and for extraposition, which derives (4.50)–(4.51) from (4.48)–(4.49) (*she* and *Mary* to be understood as coreferential).

(4.44)   Mary visited someone she knows.
(4.45) *She visited someone Mary knows.
(4.46)   Who that she knows did Mary visit?
(4.47)   Who that Mary knows did she visit?

(4.48)   That Mary is pregnant disturbs her.
(4.49)   That she is pregnant disturbs Mary.
(4.50) *It disturbs her that Mary is pregnant.
(4.51)   It disturbs Mary that she is pregnant.

Note that *Wh*-preposing increases pronominalization possibilities, but extraposition decreases them. This is a natural consequence of the pronominalization environment if pronominalization is ordered after these rules.

Certain cases of preposing rules do not increase pronominalization possibilities in the expected way. We illustrate for adverb preposing. Lakoff gives similar illustrations for topicalization and cleft-sentence formation (assuming that it is a transformation).

(4.52)   Mary smokes pot in her apartment.
(4.53) *She smokes pot in Mary's apartment.
(4.54)   In her apartment, Mary smokes pot.
(4.55) *In Mary's apartment, she smokes pot.

The unexpected result here is (4.55), where forward pronominalization fails. This could be explained by ordering the preposing rule after pronominalization. Then at the time of pronominalization, (4.55) would have the form (4.53) and so pronominalization could not take place. If this is the proper analysis, pronominalization could not be the last rule in the cycle.

However, Lakoff points out that ordering arguments do not suffice to account for the total range of facts. Consider (4.56)–(4.59), also related by adverb preposing.

(4.56)   Mary smokes pot in the apartment she rents.
(4.57) *She smokes pot in the apartment Mary rents.
(4.58)   In the apartment she rents, Mary smokes pot.
(4.59)   In the apartment Mary rents, she smokes pot.

If ordering of rules accounted for the unacceptability of (4.55), we would expect (4.59) to be bad also. To allow (4.59), we will have to order the rules *adverb preposing-pronominalization*, and account for (4.55) some other way, perhaps by altering the environment for pronominalization. In section 4.14 we will see some more cases like (4.55) and show that there is a systematic phenomenon, of somewhat wider range than Lakoff suggests, into which (4.55) fits. We will unfortunately not be able to propose a general solution.

So far, then, we have established that pronominalization is at the end of the cycle and that we have not stated the environment completely. These arguments apply equally to the pronominalization transformation and the interpretive rule, as they depend only on the environment and ordering of the rules, which are identical.

4.5.2 A Nonargument Based on Extraposition Rules
One set of arguments that pronominalization is last-cyclic involves the rules *extraposition* and *extraposition from NP* (cited by Lakoff 1968b). Lakoff argues in three steps: (1) the extraposition rules must be last-cyclic, (2) pronominalization must follow the extraposition rules; (3) hence pronominalization must be last-cyclic too.

Extraposition is the rule that produces, for example, (4.61) from (4.60) (this rule was proposed originally in Rosenbaum 1967).

(4.60) That Bill is sick bothers John.
(4.61) It bothers John that Bill is sick.

Ross (1967a, Chapter 5) gives two arguments to show that extraposition is last-cyclic. The first argument (pp. 271–276) is based on the necessity of producing correct derived constituent structure and hence correct intonation breaks in sentences such as (4.62), where extraposition takes place out of deep-structure subordinate clauses.

(4.62) It appears to be true that Harry likes girls.

For reasons that we will not go into here, only a last-cyclic rule of extraposition will derive the correct major constituent break after *true*. Ross's second argument (pp. 276–281) is based on the fact that extraposition must follow *particle movement*. Particle movement, he argues, must in turn be last-cyclic in order for the derivation of action nominalizations, such as *her rapid looking up of the information*, to come out right, under the assumption that action nominalizations are derived by a transformation from related sentences such as *she rapidly looked up the information*.

Since extraposition can change pronominalization possibilities, it must precede pronominalization:

(4.63) That John is sick bothers him.   coreferential or noncoreferential
(4.64) It bothers him that John is sick. noncoreferential only

Under the assumption that extraposition is last-cyclic, Lakoff argues that pronominalization must be also, on the basis of examples like (4.65).

(4.65) $[_{S_1}$Frank thinks $[_{S_2}$that it bothers him that John is sick.$]]$

The argument goes as follows. If pronominalization is cyclic, it can apply on the S^2 cycle, at which stage S^2 has the form (4.63). Thus we would expect it to be possible for *him* and *John* to be coreferential in (4.65). Since they are not, we must conclude that pronominalization may take place only after extraposition, that is, on the last cycle only.

Lakoff's argument based on extraposition from NP is similar. Extraposition from NP is the rule that produces, for example, (4.67) from (4.66).

(4.66) A man who was ten feet tall lumbered into the room.
(4.67) A man lumbered into the room who was ten feet tall.

Ross argues (pp. 281–285) that extraposition from NP is last-cyclic, again on the ground that it must follow the last-cyclic rule particle movement. Like extraposition, this rule decreases pronominalization possibilities, as seen from (4.68)–(4.69).

(4.68) A woman who hated John spoke to him.   coreferential or
                                               noncoreferential

(4.69) A woman spoke to him who hated John.   noncoreferential only

Hence pronominalization must follow extraposition from NP. Furthermore, if extraposition from NP is last-cyclic, pronominalization must be
also, as (4.70) shows, by an argument parallel to that for (4.65).

(4.70) $[_{S^1}$ Mary said $[_{S^2}$ that a woman spoke to him who hated John$]]$

To answer Lakoff's arguments, we first notice that if extraposition and
extraposition from NP are cyclic, pronominalization can be cyclic as well.
A cyclic extraposition rule will apply on the S^2 cycle in (4.65), before pronominalization, so that pronominalization can apply correctly on the S^2
cycle. Likewise in (4.70), if extraposition from NP is applied on the S^2
cycle instead of the S^1 cycle, pronominalization can apply correctly on the
S^2 cycle. Therefore, to retain a cyclic pronominalization rule, we must
refute Ross's arguments for the last-cyclic nature of the extraposition rules.
    Ross's first argument uses intonation contours as evidence for derived
structure. But, as Ross admits, the intonation contours may be produced
by late readjustment rules of the sort that give derived structure the correct
form in sentences such as (4.71), whose periodic intonation pattern cannot
be the result of the usual derived structure for relative clauses.

(4.71) This is the dog that chased the cat that caught the rat that ate the
       cheese.

Hence this argument is not especially compelling.
    The second argument, used as evidence for both rules, is that particle
movement is last-cyclic. But this argument is based on the assumption that
action nominals are derived transformationally, which cannot be the case
in the version of transformational grammar we are adopting here. A nominalization transformation would involve changing adverbs into adjectives,
as shown by the example above; such a derivation violates the Extended
Lexical Hypothesis. If action nominals are generated as NPs in the base
(perhaps as VP dominated by $\overline{N}$), Ross's argument does not go through.
Particle movement can then be put back in the cycle, and therefore the
extraposition rules and pronominalization can be cyclic as well. In Chapter

9, we will present some rather disastrous consequences of the assumption that extraposition and particle movement are last-cyclic, further undermining Ross's argument.

4.5.3 An Argument Based on *Wh*-Preposing

Postal (1970b) gives an independent argument that pronominalization is last-cyclic. This argument is specific to the transformational version of the rule, since it depends crucially on the fact that the rule is obligatory. (Recall that the interpretive rule (4.35) is optional.)

The form of Postal's argument is as follows (I have changed a few details for the purposes of exposition, without, I hope, affecting the validity of the argument): (1) *Wh*-preposing must be able to prepose material over a number of clauses; (2) doing pronominalization obligatorily in the cycle entails that it take place before certain applications of *Wh*-preposing; (3) pronominalization must take place after all occurrences of *Wh*-preposing in order to generate the full range of sentences; (4) therefore pronominalization must be last-cyclic.

Step (1) in the argument follows from the existence of sentences like (4.72).

(4.72) To whom did you expect Max to say Fred gave the donuts?

To whom has been moved out of the lowest clause (*Fred gave the donuts to Wh-someone*) in this sentence, and Postal gives evidence to show that the movement must be in one step, rather than one clause at a time. Hence the preposing only takes place on the cycle of the clause in which *Wh* eventually appears.

Step (2) in the argument follows from examples like (4.73).

(4.73) To whom did you expect Max to say he gave the donuts?

If pronominalization is obligatory and cyclic, the reading of (4.73) in which *he* is *Max* must result from pronominalization on the cycle *for Max to say he gave the donuts to Wh-someone*. But *to whom* is not fronted until the final cycle. Hence pronominalization can precede *Wh*-preposing, if they take place on different cycles.

Step (3), that pronominalization cannot take place until after *Wh*-preposing, is shown by (4.74).

(4.74) Who that Mary knew do you think she visited?

(4.75) is the underlying structure of this in the transformational theory, and (4.76) the surface structure.

(4.75)

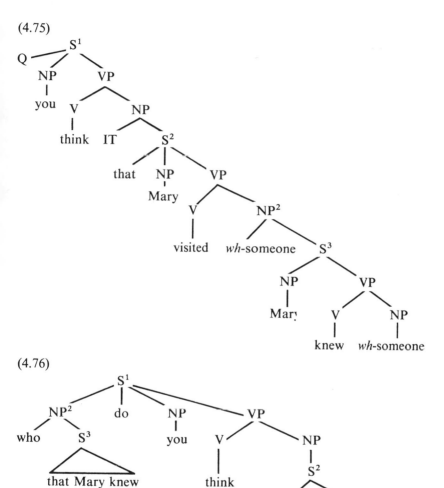

(4.76)

Under a cyclic pronominalization rule like Ross's, *Mary* in S^3 must oblig-atorily become *she* on the S^2 cycle; pronominalization may not proceed in the other direction. Thus when NP^2 is fronted on the S^1 cycle by the *Wh*-preposing rule, we can get only (4.77).

(4.77) Who that she knew do you think Mary visited?

Since the pronominalization transformation is obligatory, there is no way to hold it off until the S^1 cycle to produce (4.74). On the other hand, if we make pronominalization last-cyclic, it will not take place until after the fronting of NP^2. By this time an environment is created in which pronominalization can go either backwards or forwards, so we can get either (4.74) or (4.77), the correct result.

This argument that pronominalization is last-cyclic of course raises a serious conflict with Ross's argument that it is cyclic. Lakoff proposes to resolve the conflict by adding what he admits to be an ad hoc modification to the environment of pronominalization, just to handle Ross's crucial example. He then tries to show that his modification is needed anyway to handle some examples that should be handled by Ross's rule but that are not. These examples, to be discussed in section 5.3, will be shown to be less than convincing.

4.5.4 An Argument Based on Other Preposing Rules
There are several other rules which move phrases forward over a variable, as *Wh*-preposing does. Three constructions produced by such rules are (4.78)–(4.80).

(4.78) How brave Bill is! (*How* exclamation fronting)
(4.79) Beans I'll never eat. (Topicalization)
(4.80) Handsome though Melvin is, Dolores will never marry him. (*Though*-movement)

As Ross shows (1967a, Chapter 6), these rules all involve crucial use of a variable; the phrases can be moved up from indefinitely deep embeddings, subject to Ross's constraints. For example:

(4.81) How brave John thinks Mary said Bill was!
(4.82) Beans you'll never persuade me to force my kids to eat.

(4.83) Handsome though it is said by many people that Melvin is, Dolores will never marry him.

Like *Wh*-preposing, each of these rules must take place in a single step, on the cycle governed by the clause in which the preposed constituent appears in surface structure. If this were not the case, we might expect intermediate steps of preposing such as (4.84)–(4.86) to appear:

(4.84) *John thinks how brave Mary said Bill was.
(4.85) *You'll never persuade me beans to force my kids to eat.
(4.86) *Though it is said by many people that handsome Melvin is, ...

These rules all increase pronominalization possibilities. In the untransformed sentences below, *he* and *John* are noncoreferential, but in the transformed version, *he* and *John* may be the same.

(4.87) Mary thinks he is SO fond of the girl John kicked yesterday.
(4.88) How fond of the girl John kicked yesterday Mary thinks he is!

(4.89) Mary thinks he secretly loves the girl who kicked John.
(4.90) The girl who kicked John Mary thinks he secretly loves.

(4.91) Though Mary thinks he is fond of the girl John kicked yesterday, ...
(4.92) Fond of the girl John kicked yesterday though Mary thinks he is, ...

For each of these three rules, then, we can construct an argument that the pronominalization transformation must be last-cyclic. The arguments are exactly parallel to Postal's argument involving *Wh*-preposing, with (4.88), (4.90), and (4.92) functioning as the crucial examples in place of (4.74). Thus the ordering paradox for the transformational theory of pronominalization looms larger.

4.5.5 Avoiding the Paradox
Let us turn now to the interpretive pronominalization rule. So far it does not matter whether or not this rule is cyclic: we did not make use of the cyclic property of pronominalization in any of the examples in sections 4.3 and 4.4. However, it will prove important presently that the rule be cyclic, since it will be shown that it should partially generalize with the cyclic rules reflexivization and complement subject interpretation. We must show, then,

that a cyclic interpretive rule avoids Postal's argument concerning *Wh*-preposing and the parallel arguments for *How* exclamation fronting, Topicalization, and *Though*–movement.

The crucial step in Postal's argument is that the pronominalization transformation is obligatory, and it irretrievably turns an NP into a pronoun too soon for the full pronominalization possibilities to be realized. With the interpretive rule (4.35) no such problem arises. Consider again (4.74) and (4.77), assuming a last-cyclic *Wh*-preposing.

(4.74) Who that Mary knew do you think she visited?
(4.77) Who that she knew do you think Mary visited?

In the interpretive theory these have the respective underlying structures (4.93)–(4.94), with *she* generated in the base.

(4.93) $[_{S^1}$You think $[_{S^2}$she visited who $[_{S^3}$that Mary knew$]]]$
(4.94) $[_{S^1}$You think $[_{S^2}$Mary visited who $[_{S^3}$that she knew$]]]$

In (4.93), the environment for pronominalization does not appear on the S^2 cycle. However, after fronting on the S^1 cycle to form (4.74), the pronoun and NP can be marked coreferential. In (4.94), pronominalization can take place either on the S^2 cycle or after fronting on the S^1 cycle.

Notice, however, that we have not yet mentioned the noncoreferentiality rule (4.26). If it were in the cycle, too, it would apply obligatorily on the S^2 cycle of (4.93), to mark *she* and *Mary* distinct, since that pair is not yet entered in the table of coreference. This would prevent the correct reading from being derived by pronominalization on the S^1 cycle. But if we make the noncoreferentiality rule last-cyclic, pronominalization will have a second chance to apply to *she* and *Mary*, on the S^1 cycle, giving the correct reading. Only if pronominalization does not apply at any point in the derivation, then, do we want the conditions for the noncoreferentiality rule to be met.

Thus a cyclic rule of pronominalization combined with a last-cyclic noncoreferentiality rule can cope with the examples that are problematic to the cyclic theory of pronominalization. Both rules, furthermore, occur at the end of the transformations. This ordering of the rules makes an interesting prediction which unfortunately does not seem to have any application in English. All the rules which are relevant to the last-cyclic argument (*Wh*-preposing, *How* exclamation preposing, Topicalization, *Though–* movement) are preposing rules which move phrases over a variable. All of them cause increases in pronominalization possibilities, since they can move an antecedent in a subordinate clause from the right of a pronoun to the left. Conversely, a last-cyclic postposing rule involving a variable would move antecedents from the left of pronouns to the right, destroying pronominalization environments. However, the interpretive rule we have stated would predict that pronominalization can operate on a lower cycle, before the postposing rule can destroy the environment, so that pronominalization possibilities will not decrease under the postposing. Unfortunately, I know of no such rule in English with which to test the theory. The two extraposition rules mentioned above appear at first to be counterexamples, but we have shown that it is possible to put them back in the cycle, so they pose no problem.[2]

4.6 Some Problems of Reflexivization

The standard transformational account of reflexives is given by Lees and Klima in "Rules for English Pronominalization" (1963). This analysis gives the following rule:

(4.95) (Lees and Klima reflexive rule)

$$X \quad NP^1 \quad Y \quad NP^2 \quad Z$$
$$1 \quad 2 \quad 3 \quad 4 \quad 5 \Rightarrow 1 \quad 2 \quad 3 \quad \begin{bmatrix} 4 \\ +\text{refl} \end{bmatrix} \quad 5$$

Conditions:

1. NP^1 and NP^2 are (referentially and morphologically) identical
2. NP^1 and NP^2 are in the same simplex S

OBLIGATORY

This rule accounts for the simple reflexive sentences such as (4.96).

(4.96) John shaved himself.

In addition, with the mechanisms of the complement system and the transformational cycle discussed in great detail in Rosenbaum (1967), this rule can also account nicely for the reflexives in (4.97) and (4.98).

[2]Ross (1967a, p. 307) says that he knows of no rules of movement to the right that are not upward bounded. The rules that are upward bounded, but which Ross treats as last-cyclic, may in general be cyclic under the lexicalist treatment. Thus they will not test the present claim.

(4.97) Mary forced Bill to shoot himself.
(4.98) John expected himself to be able to abstain from eating.

In (4.97), reflexivization takes place in the first cycle (*for Bill to shoot himself*); then, on the second cycle, *Bill* is deleted from the complement by complement subject deletion, leaving *himself* still standing. In (4.98), reflexivization takes place in the second cycle, after *John* has been moved up into the main clause by complement subject raising. The restriction to simplex S prevents sentences like (4.99) and (4.100): there is never a point in the derivation in which *John* and *himself* are in the same simplex S (see, however, section 5.6).

(4.99)   *John forced Mary to shoot himself.
(4.100) *John saw the girl who hated himself.

The first doubts about rule (4.95) began to arise upon investigation of the so-called picture-nouns, first discussed in a transformational framework in Warshawsky (1965). Sentences like (4.101) and (4.102) are handled by rule (4.95) without difficulty; two different NPs can fulfill the structural condition for NP^1, and so there are two possible reflexivizations.

(4.101) I told Bill a story about myself.
(4.102) I told Bill a story about himself.

Thus we correctly predict the ambiguity of (4.103).

(4.103) John told Bill a story about himself.

Following this line of analysis, we would expect three readings for (4.104), but unfortunately there is only one, with *himself* referring to *Harry*.[3]

(4.104) Tom told Dick Harry's story about himself.

This fact becomes clearer when we substitute for *Harry* a noun that cannot be coreferential with *himself*.

[3]There are some speakers who claim that (4.104) has three readings, and that (4.105) has acceptable readings. See p. 138, footnote 5.

(4.105) *Tom told Dick $\left\{\begin{matrix} \text{Mary's} \\ \text{the newspaper's} \end{matrix}\right\}$ story about himself.

In (4.104) and (4.105) the appropriate way to refer to Tom or Dick is to use a pronoun instead of a reflexive.

(4.106) Tom told Dick $\left\{\begin{matrix} \text{Harry's} \\ \text{Mary's} \\ \text{the newspaper's} \end{matrix}\right\}$ story about him.

These examples show that even within the same simplex sentence there are times when reflexivization cannot take place.

A common suggestion for accounting for (4.104)–(4.106) is to introduce another S node into the underlying form, deriving *story* from an "abstract" underlying verb "to story." This extra S, it is alleged, would prevent reflexivization because of the simplex S condition. Then some further argument must be made to show why reflexivization does in fact take place in (4.103).

The immediate trouble with this approach is that it requires all kinds of abstract verbs for which there is no other justification. To be sure, *description* and *picture* and *photograph* have corresponding verbs, but what about *story, poem, novel, biography, portrait, watercolor,* and many others which take part in the same construction? These represent precisely the kinds of derivation we wish to disallow in adopting the Extended Lexical Hypothesis.

As it turns out, this attempt to save the simplex sentence condition on reflexivization would still not work. In addition to the cases where reflexivization cannot occur in the same simplex S, there are sentences which contain perfectly respectable reflexives in a different simplex S from their antecedents.

(4.107) Tom believes that there is a picture of himself hanging in the post office.

(4.108) Tom made the claim that the picture of himself hanging in the post office is a fraud.

(4.109) That the picture of himself in the newspaper is ugly enrages Charlie.

(4.110) The fact that there is a picture of himself hanging in the post office frightens Tom.

(4.111) The picture of himself that John saw hanging in the post office was ugly.
(4.112) The description of himself that John gave the police was a pack of lies.

All of these sentences exhibit reflexives in a different simplex sentence from their antecedents. In (4.107) and (4.108), the reflexive is to the right, as in normal simplex S cases. However, in (4.109) and (4.110) the reflexive is to the left, violating even the basic structural description of the reflexivization rule (4.95). In the first four examples the reflexive is in a lower S than the antecedent. However, in (4.111) and (4.112), the reflexive is not only to the left of the antecedent, but also in a higher simplex sentence.

A curious fact about reflexives noticed by Lees and Klima is that they cannot occur in passive sentences, either as surface subject or *by*-phrase:

(4.113) *Himself was shaved by John.
(4.114) *John was shaved by himself. (ok only with stress on *himself*)

A principled account of this fact will be deferred to section 4.11. However, there are passive sentences with picture-nouns where this constraint does not apply. Furthermore, in such cases the reflexive may occur to the left of its antecedent even in the same simplex S, a further violation of the rule (4.95).

(4.115) The king was hit over the head by a massive portrait of himself which had fallen off the wall.
(4.116) Unflattering descriptions of himself have been banned by our beloved president.

One could try to account for the behavior of picture-noun phrases by retaining Lees and Klima's rule and claiming that an extra, mysterious rule handles (4.101)–(4.116). This is the approach of Postal (1971, Chapter 17), who alludes to, but does not state, a rule of "late reflexivization." It would be more interesting, though, if all cases could be handled under a single rule. Such an account will be attempted here. Although it will not be able to handle all the phenomena of reflexivization that I am aware of, it will be considerably more comprehensive than earlier analyses. I will not be able to account here for the use of emphatic reflexives (*John himself did it*), or the lack of reflexives in locatives such as *John saw a snake beside him(*self)*. See also section 4.12 for reflexivization phenomena which I leave unaccounted for.

4.7 The Environment for Reflexivization

First a position must be taken on the structure of picture-noun constructions. I will assume the type of structure given in Chomsky (1970a), with the possessive in the determiner, and the head noun and *of*-phrase under a node $\overline{N}$. Thus *Mary's picture of Bill* will have the underlying structure (4.117).

(4.117)

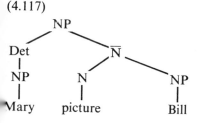

The possessive ending is put on *Mary* by a late transformation which applies to any NP in the determiner; another late transformation inserts *of* between N and NP.

This structure is very close to the structure of a simple sentence such as *Mary saw Bill*, with the highest NP in (4.117) corresponding to the S node of the sentence, the $\overline{N}$ corresponding to the VP, and the N corresponding to the V. Chomsky shows that this analysis leads to various desirable conclusions, in particular the generalization of various rules such as the passive to NP constructions as well as Ss. (For other work on generalizations of this sort, see Bowers 1968, 1969a and Jackendoff 1968c, 1971a as well as Chapter 3.)

Given the fact that constructions like (4.117) behave like sentences with respect to certain transformations, it is not unreasonable to suppose that the transformational cycle takes as its domain not only Ss, but sufficiently complex NPs, that is, NPs containing some complement structure. Under this assumption, the rule (4.118) will account for most of the hitherto unexplained examples of the last section.

(4.118) (Reflexivization)

Enter in the table:

$NP^1 \; \alpha \; coref \begin{bmatrix} NP^2 \\ \alpha reflexive \end{bmatrix}$ if each of the following conditions holds:

(a) NP^2 has not yet appeared on the right-hand (i.e.,) anaphoric expression) side of the table;

(b) NP^2 is immediately dominated (except for a possible preposition) by VP or $\overline{N}$;

(c) NP^1 is in the main clause of the present cycle;

(d) NP^2 does not both precede and command NP^1.

If NP^1 precedes NP^2 (forward reflexivization), rule is OBLIGATORY. (Backward reflexivization is OPTIONAL.)

We will now show the relevance of each of the conditions in the rule.

Condition (a) combined with the obligatoriness of forward reflexivization ensures that the rule will mark an NP for coreference with respect to the first and only the first NP encountered that stands in the proper structural relation. We will use this condition crucially at several points, both when NP^2 is reflexive and when it is not.

Condition (b) prevents the rule from applying in sentences with a reflexive in the subject such as (4.119).

(4.119) *John thinks that himself is sick.

This condition is now necessary since we have given up the simplex sentence condition, which prevented (4.119) in Lees and Klima's rule.[4] In section 5.4, the complementarity of this condition to one in the complement subject rule will be pointed out, further motivating it.

Condition (c) prevents reflexivization from applying in sentences such a (4.120)–(4.122).

(4.120) *The book which I gave John impressed himself.

(4.121) *I gave a book about John to himself.

(4.122) *The fact that there is a picture of himself in the post office proves that Tom is guilty.

---

[4]In a formalization of the rule along the lines of Chomsky (1970a), node labels will be represented as feature complexes, and the nodes $\overline{N}$ and VP will form a natural class.

We will show presently that apparent counterexamples like (4.123) can be derived.

(4.123) The fact that there is a picture of himself hanging in the post office is believed (by Mary) to be disturbing Tom.

Condition (d) allows both backward and forward reflexivization. It is identical to the structural relation for pronominalization. If this environment is correct, it is a significant generalization heretofore unnoticed. In section 4.8 it will be shown that this generalization can be captured by ordering the reflexivization and pronominalization rules at the same point in the grammar. They will be collapsed in section 4.14. Condition (d) prevents such sentences as *I talked about himself to John.

Finally, the distinction between obligatory forward reflexivization and optional backward reflexivization is necessary because of the contrast of the paradigm (4.124)–(4.125) to (4.126)–(4.128). (*Him* is to denote *John*.)

(4.124)   John saw a picture of himself in the post office.
(4.125) *John saw a picture of him in the post office.
(4.126)   The picture of himself in the post office enraged John.
(4.127)   The picture of him in the post office enraged John.
(4.128)   The picture of John in the post office enraged him.

Example (4.125) does not have the coreferential reading because reflexivization must apply, marking *him* and *John* noncoreferential. But in (4.127)–(4.128) we can choose not to apply reflexivization, which would mark noncoreference; then normal pronominalization can apply, forwards or backwards, giving the desired reading.

All the standard cases of simple reflexives not involving picture-noun constructions (e.g., *Max shot himself*) will undergo the reflexive rule obligatorily on the first cycle they are encountered, in the manner demonstrated in section 4.3: the subject of a sentence will always fulfill the conditions for interpretation as antecedent of a reflexive in the object. In sentences containing more than one cycle, condition (a) comes into play. Compare (4.129), the example discussed in section 4.3, with (4.130).

(4.129) John said that Bill had shot him. (= (4.27))
(4.130) John said that Bill had shot himself.

On the first cycle (*that Bill had shot him(self)*), reflexivization produces the partial tables (4.131) and (4.132), respectively (remember that the rule is an α rule, obligatory in this environment):

(4.131) *Bill* — coref *him*
(4.132) *Bill*   coref *himself*

On the second cycle, including the whole sentence, *him* and *himself* already appear in the right-hand side of the table. Therefore, because of condition (a), reflexivization cannot apply to them again to mark them with respect to *John*. Thus pronominalization can apply in (4.129) as discussed in section 4.3 to produce the correct range of readings.

Since the cycle may take NP as its domain as well as S, it comes into play in interpreting picture-noun constructions.

(4.133)   John showed Bill a picture of himself.
(4.134) *John showed Bill Mary's picture of himself.

In (4.133), the first cycle deals with the NP *a picture of himself. Himself* obeys conditions (a) and (b) of the reflexivization rule, but there is no NP^1 in the domain of this cycle, so nothing happens. The second cycle includes the whole sentence. On this cycle, *John* and *Bill* are eligible to be NP^1 in the reflexivization rule, and so one or the other of them must be assigned as the antecedent of *himself*, producing the two possible readings.

On the other hand, the first cycle in (4.134) deals with *Mary's picture of himself. Mary* is eligible to be NP^1 in the reflexivization rule, and since the rule is obligatory in this environment, *Mary* coref *himself* is entered in the table. Of course, the reading is then anomalous because of gender disagreement, and so the sentence is rejected. Because of the presence of *Mary* on the first cycle, the reflexive rule does not get a chance to pair *himself* with *John* or *Bill* on the second cycle. Similarly, in *John showed Bill Harry's picture of himself, Harry* is marked coreferential with *himself* on the first cycle, and so the reflexivization rule never has a chance to refer to *John* and *Bill* as possible antecedents.[5]

It is important to note that there is no natural way to state a transformation which is cognate to this cyclic reflexive rule. To see this, assume a

---

[5] For the dialect mentioned in footnote 3, we must relax condition (a) somewhat.

transformational theory of reflexives, and consider the underlying structure (4.135). (Subscripts are indices of coreference.)

(4.135) John$_i$ showed Bill$_j$ Mary$_k$'s picture of John$_i$.

On the first cycle, *Mary's picture of John*, nothing can happen since there are no two identical noun phrases. On the second cycle, the whole sentence, we face the old problem of how to prohibit reflexivization. The only way to do it is to mark on the first cycle that *John* cannot be subject to reflexivization because it and *Mary* fulfill all of the conditions for reflexivization except identity. The reflexive transformation will thus have to look like (4.136).

(4.136) $NP^2 \Rightarrow \begin{cases} [+\text{reflexive}] \text{ if } NP^2 \text{ is identical with } NP^1 \\ [-\text{reflexivization rule}] \text{ if } NP^2 \text{ is not identical with } NP^1 \end{cases}$
$$\text{in the environment} \ldots$$

The second part of this rule, which introduces a rule feature under conditions of nonidentity, is very strange: nothing like it occurs anywhere in the literature. It thus constitutes strong evidence against a transformational theory of reflexives. This and the ability to order pronominalization consistently are two important substantive differences between the interpretive and transformational theories.

An apparent counterexample to the analysis presented so far is (4.137).

(4.137) John showed Mary his picture of himself.

On the first cycle, the reflexivization rule will enter *his* coref *himself* in the table. On the second cycle, pronominalization may apply between *John* and *his*, but condition (a) will prevent reflexivization from applying between *John* and *himself*. How, then, can we prevent the noncoreferentiality rule from applying between these two, producing the anomalous table (4.138)?

(4.138) *his*   coref *himself*
　　　　 John   coref *his*
　　　　 John −coref *himself*

The solution lies in the fact that reflexives are marked not just [+refl], but

$\begin{bmatrix} + \text{pro} \\ + \text{refl} \end{bmatrix}$. Reflexivization indeed may not apply between *John* and *himself* on the second cycle, but pronominalization, which does not contain condition (a), is still applicable. Thus it is possible to mark all three NPs pairwise coreferential by making use of the fact that reflexives are pronouns as well. (This suggestion, however, is not quite right: it predicts that pronominalization should produce a reading for *John thinks that himself is sick*. See section 4.14 for one way to remedy this.)

Using the cyclic reflexivization rule, we can derive more of the examples mentioned in section 4.6 as well. Consider first the passives (4.115) and (4.116).

(4.115) The king was hit over the head by a massive portrait of himself which had fallen off the wall.

(4.116) Unflattering descriptions of himself have been banned by our beloved president.

(4.115) will be handled in the same fashion as the examples just discussed. (4.116) presents the problem of backwards reflexivization. Under the standard definition of "command," the first S node above *himself* also dominates *our beloved president*, so *himself* both precedes and commands *our beloved president*, violating condition (d). However, a simple change will make reflexivization applicable: we will replace the term "S" in the definition of command with "node that defines a cycle." In the theory assumed by Langacker in which he defines command, the two terms are interchangeable, since only Ss define cycles. In the theory we have adopted here, however, NPs may also define cycles; thus the two terms will differ in their consequences. Since the NP node dominating *unflattering descriptions of himself* defines a cycle under this revised definition of command, *himself* does not command *our beloved president*. Thus condition (d) is satisfied, permitting reflexivization.

Next let us discuss some cases involving three cycles.

(4.107) Tom believes that there is a picture of himself hanging in the post office.

(4.110) The fact that there is a picture of himself hanging in the post office
frightens Tom.

On the first cycle, only *a picture of himself* is involved, and there is no way
for the reflexive rule to apply. The second cycle involves *there is a picture of
himself hanging in the post office*. *There* is a dummy noun phrase, totally
nonreferential; this seems sufficient reason not to consider it as a possible
antecedent of *himself*. *Post office* could in principle serve as an (anomalous)
antecedent for *himself*, cutting off any further acceptable readings. But
since it is to the right of *himself*, reflexivization is optional. We can therefore bypass *post office*, having chosen no antecedent for *himself* on either
the first or the second cycle. Going on to the third cycle, the entire sentence, we encounter *Tom*, which meets all the structural conditions and
therefore can serve as NP^1 in reflexivization, providing the correct reading.

Finally, consider (4.139), which apparently violates condition (c) of
reflexivization (NP^1 must be in the main clause of the present cycle), and
compare it with some similar sentences.

(4.139) The fact that there is a picture of himself hanging in the post office
is believed (by Mary) to be disturbing Tom. (= (4.123))
(4.140) The fact that there is a picture of her(?self) hanging in the post
office is believed by Mary to be disturbing Tom.
(4.141) The fact that there is a picture of himself hanging in the post office
is believed by Max to be disturbing Tom.
(4.142) The fact that there is a picture of himself hanging in the post office
is deplored by Max.

My (admittedly not solid) judgments in (4.139), (4.140), and (4.142) are
self-evident. In (4.141), I understand *himself* to refer preferably to *Tom*,
not to *Max*. If the reflexivization rule operated only on the final cycle, these
judgments could not be explained, since we would expect *herself* to be
appropriate in (4.140) and *himself* to be able to refer to *Max* in (4.141), as
it does in the similar (4.142). Furthermore, there is no structural way to
distinguish (4.139) from (4.143) on the basis of surface structure.

(4.143) *The fact that there was a picture of himself hanging in the post
office induced the police to arrest Tom.

Sentences like (4.143), it will be recalled, were the motivation for condition (c) of the reflexive rule; the antecedent cannot generally be in a lower clause.

Cyclic application of reflexivization turns out to make the correct predictions. In (4.139), (4.140), and (4.141), the deep structure is of the form (4.144).

$$(4.144) \quad \left\{ \begin{matrix} \text{Mary} \\ \text{Max} \end{matrix} \right\} \text{ believes } [_s \text{the fact } [_s \text{that there is a picture of} \left\{ \begin{matrix} \text{her(self)} \\ \text{himself} \end{matrix} \right\}$$
$$\text{hanging in the post office}]_s \text{ disturbs Tom}]_s$$

Thus part of the derivation involves a subordinate cycle of the form (4.110), whose interpretation we have just explained. On the final cycle, complement subject raising will take place, breaking up the lower clause. The reflexivization rule will then be encountered, with the following effects. In (4.139), *Tom* violates condition (c) as a possible antecedent and *Mary* does not. But the reflexive already appears in the table, violating condition (a), having been marked coreferential with *Tom* on the lower cycle, so reflexivization does not apply anyway. In (4.141), the same thing happens: reflexivization on the lower cycle precludes the interpretation of *Max* as antecedent on the upper cycle. In (4.140), *herself* will have been marked (anomalously) coreferential with *Tom*, on the earlier cycle, precluding reflexivization on the final cycle. *Her* is marked noncoreferential with *Tom* on the lower cycle, so pronominalization can take place on the final cycle, creating the correct reading.

By contrast, in (4.142) there is no lower cycle on which *himself* can be entered in the table, so on the final cycle reflexivization can apply. In (4.143), the lower cycle is *the police arrested Tom*, not *the fact that there was a picture of himself hanging in the post office arrested Tom*. Thus *himself* is not subject to the reflexivization rule until the final cycle, when *Tom* violates condition (c) but *the police* does not. Thus the usual anomaly results. Substitution of *Harry* for *the police* provides the expected acceptable, nonambiguous reading.

While these sentences do not induce tremendously clear-cut judgments, because of their complexity, they provide further evidence for two important points. First, the difference between (4.139) and (4.143) cannot be accounted for unless reflexivization is cyclic. Second, the interpretive account of these sentences cannot be directly translated into a transformational account. As in the simple two-cycle picture-noun cases such as *John showed Bill Mary's picture of himself*, the interpretive solution hinges on the assumption that a reflexive is obligatorily marked with respect to the first possible antecedent on the left it encounters. As we have seen, this procedure cannot be mirrored in any simple way in a transformational theory. In a transformational theory, the reflexives in (4.140)–(4.141) are assumed to result from deletion from fully specified NPs. Suppose then that *Max* is the underlying form of *himself* in (4.141). The lower cycle will somehow have to use the nonidentity of *Tom* and *Max* to mark reflexivization inapplicable on the main cycle, where the appropriate context (identical to that in (4.142)) arises. Thus the transformational theory is again compelled to state reflexivization in the totally unnatural form (4.136).[6]

4.8 The Ordering of Reflexivization

Remembering that the environments of pronominalization and reflexivization are very similar, it would be an important result if they could be ordered together and hence partially collapsed. However, Postal claims (1971, section 10.B) that reflexivization and pronominalization must be ordered quite differently. There are two reasons why Postal cannot collapse the rules in his framework: first, reflexivization is cyclic, whereas pronominalization is last-cyclic; second, *Wh*-preposing intervenes between the two rules. The first argument we have already disposed of: in section 4.5 we justified putting pronominalization back in the cycle.

Postal's argument that the reflexivization transformation precedes *Wh*-preposing depends on the operation of the process *node-pruning*, discussed by Ross (1967a, Chapter 3). Ross argues that there is a general convention that deletes an S node in the course of a derivation if it comes to dominate only NP or VP. In (4.145), the deep structure of *Who did you see stab you*,

---

[6]Since the derivation of these sentences depends crucially on the use of the cycle, they provide further evidence that the theory of coreference rules in Postal (1970b, 1971) is incorrect. Postal attributes the reflexives in these examples to a rule of late reflexivization. But since he claims pronominalization is last-cyclic, and we have shown that the putative rule late reflexivization must be cyclic, the theory is inconsistent. Presumably Postal would advocate a solution similar to his "doom marker" for complement subject deletion, about which we will have more to say in Chapter 5.

the application of *Wh*-preposing on the S^1 cycle causes the node S^2 to prune, since it dominates only a VP.

(4.145)

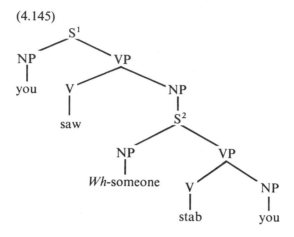

The result is the derived structure (4.146).

(4.146)

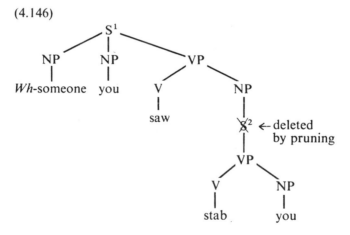

If the reflexivization transformation took place after the formation of (4.146), the surface structure would be (4.147) rather than the correct (4.148) since the two *you*s would now be in the same simplex S.

(4.147) *Who did you see stab yourself?
(4.148) Who did you see stab you?

Therefore, Postal concludes, reflexivization must take place before S^2 is pruned by the application of *Wh*-preposing. Since pronominalization follows *Wh*-preposing (see section 4.5.3), pronominalization and reflexivization cannot collapse.

In the interpretive theory, however, this problem does not arise. On the S^2 cycle, reflexivization will apply, making the entry *Wh-someone* — coref *you*. Then, in the S^1 cycle, even if the node S^2 has been pruned, the *you* from S^2 violates condition (a) of reflexivization, since it already appears in the table. Thus it can undergo normal pronominalization and be marked coreferential with the other *you*, even though they are now in the same simplex sentence. On the other hand, if *yourself* is substituted for *you* in S^2, it is (anomalously) marked coreferential with *Wh-someone* on the S^2 cycle, so (4.147) is predicted to be unacceptable.

Thus, even with the pruning of the S^2 node, the interpretive theory of reflexives permits reflexivization to be ordered after *Wh*-preposing and hence to be collapsed with pronominalization, a significant generalization. On the other hand, the transformational theory, in order to collapse reflexivization and pronominalization, must either give up the generality of the pruning convention or again put the very strange condition (4.136) on the reflexivization transformation. (See (4.248)–(4.249) for further evidence that reflexivization must follow *Wh*-preposing).

We now have used condition (a) of the rule crucially in explaining three disparate phenomena: the basic two-cycle picture noun cases (4.125)–(4.126), the four-cycle cases (4.140)–(4.141), and the *Wh*-preposing cases (4.147)–(4.148). We will see yet one more application in Chapter 5, in connection with the rule that raises complement subjects. With so much motivation, it has less of the character of an ad hoc trick than it might have seemed to at first.

4.9 Some Unexpectedly Bad Cases of Reflexivization—The So-Called Crossover Principle

We still have not accounted for the fact that reflexives are not allowed as the NP in the *by*-phrase of passives:

(4.149) *John was shaved by himself. (= 4.114)

This cannot be accounted for by ordering reflexive before passive, since (4.150), the then predicted result, is much, much worse.

(4.150) *Himself was shaved by John. (= 4.113)

Postal (1971) cites four more sets of cases of unexpectedly bad reflexivization like (4.149).

Tough Movement (Postal, 1971, Chapter 3)

(4.151) It is $\left\{ \begin{array}{l} \text{easy} \\ \text{tough} \\ \text{a breeze} \end{array} \right\}$ for Jack to hit Tony.

(4.152) Tony is tough for Jack to hit.
(4.153) It is tough for Tony to shave himself.
(4.154) *Tony is tough for himself to shave.
(4.155) *Himself is tough for Tony to shave.

It-Replacement (Postal 1971, Chapter 4)
(4.156) It seems to me that Schwarz is clever.
(4.157) Schwarz seems to me to be clever.
(4.158) It seems to me that I am clever.
(4.159) ?I seem to myself to be clever.
(4.160) *Myself seems to me to be clever.

About Movement (Postal 1971, Chapter 5)
(4.161) I talked to Mary about Louise.
(4.162) I talked about Louise to Mary.
(4.163) I talked to Thmug about himself.
(4.164) *I talked about Thmug to himself.
(4.165) *I talked about himself to Thmug.

Psychological Predicates (Postal 1971, Chapter 6)
(4.166) I regard myself as pompous.
(4.167) ?I strike myself as pompous.

(4.168) I like myself.
(4.169) ?I please myself.

(4.170) I smelled myself.
(4.171) ?I smelled funny to myself.

(4.172) I am amused with myself.
(4.173) ?I am amusing to myself.

...and a host of similar contrasts: look at/?look funny to, disgusted with/?disgusting to, horrified at/?horrifying to, irritated at/?irritating to, loathe/?be loathsome to, accept/?be acceptable to, familiar with/?familiar to, be impressed with/?impress, annoy/?be annoying to, frighten/?be frightening to, be pleasèd with/?be pleasing to

Postal proposes accounting for these facts by means of a constraint on movement transformations, called the Crossover Principle, which says roughly that a transformation may not move an NP over another NP with which it is coreferential. Example (4.149) is then ruled out because the passive moves the deep subject over the object into the *by*-phrase; since the two NPs are coreferential, the Crossover Principle rules out the result. Likewise, (4.154) and (4.155) are ruled out by the movement of the object of the subordinate clause over the subject of the subordinate clause; (4.159) and (4.160) are out because of the movement of the complement subject over the *to*-phrase (assuming the account of *It*-replacement in Rosenbaum 1967); (4.164) and (4.165) are out because of the movement of the *about*-phrase over the *to*-phrase; and (4.167), (4.169), (4.171), and (4.173) are out because of an alleged rule of *psych movement* which derives them from underlying forms in which the positions of the subject and object are the opposite of their surface forms.

In an interpretive theory of coreference, the Crossover Principle cannot be stated, since coreferentiality, a purely semantic concept, cannot be referred to in transformations, and since conversely, semantic rules cannot depend on what transformations have taken place, but only on the resulting structural configurations. Furthermore, if we want to maintain the Extended Lexical Hypothesis, we cannot simultaneously maintain the Crossover Principle: the transformation psych movement is just the kind of rule the Extended Lexical Hypothesis seeks to exclude. But if (4.167), (4.169), (4.171), and (4.173) are not the output of a movement rule, then they cannot be ruled out by a constraint on movement.

Therefore these cases of bad reflexivization must be taken care of in some way other than a constraint on movement of coreferential NPs. As there does seem to be a generalization lurking somewhere in the data, Postal is right in claiming that merely naming the particular cases is not enough. Accordingly, I will propose a constraint, involving the thematic relations of reflexives and their antecedents with respect to the verb of their clause. This constraint will account for not only the cases cited above, but additional cases that Postal cannot account for conveniently.

4.10 A Second Thematic Hierarchy Condition

Section 2.5 introduced the Thematic Hierarchy (4.174) and stated the Thematic Hierarchy Condition on the passive transformation.

(4.174) (The Thematic Hierarchy)
    1. Agent
    2. Location, Source, Goal
    3. Theme

We will now show how a second Thematic Hierarchy Condition does away with the need for the Crossover Principle.

(4.175) (Thematic Hierarchy Condition on Reflexives)
    A reflexive may not be higher on the Thematic Hierarchy than its antecedent.

(4.175) is a well-formedness condition on semantic interpretations, relating a complete table of coreference to the thematic relations expressed in functional structure. Violation of the condition will result in sentences that are not fully grammatical, yet that are not nearly so bad as sentences which violate the structural conditions of the reflexive rule.

4.10.1 Passive

First look at (4.149) and (4.150), the passive reflexives.

(4.149) *John was shaved by himself.
(4.150) *Himself was shaved by John.

In (4.149), *John* is the deep structure object and the Theme of the sentence. *Himself* is the deep structure subject and the Agent. Therefore *himself* is higher on the Thematic Hierarchy than *John*, so the THC is violated. (4.150) obeys the THC but violates the structural condition for reflexivization, so it is much more crashingly ungrammatical. In the corresponding active *John shaved himself*, the Agent is to the left of the Theme, so both the structural condition of reflexivization and the THC can be met, permitting a good sentence.

What about the actives and passives of sentences that do not necessarily have an Agent subject? Take for example sentences with *touch* or *hit*, which have Theme in the subject and Location or Goal in the object, but only optionally Agent in the subject.

(4.176) The tree was touching the wire.
(4.177) The falling rock hit the car with a crash.
(4.178) John was touching the bookcase.
(4.179) John hit the car with a crash.

(4.178) and (4.179) are ambiguous between an Agent and non-Agent reading of *John*. However, the parallel reflexive sentences have only the Agent reading.

(4.180) John was touching himself.
(4.181) John hit himself (?with a crash).

This is predicted by the THC, for if *John* were only the Theme, the Thematic Hierarchy would be violated. Therefore the only acceptable reading has *John* as Agent as well.

We would expect then that the passives of (4.180) and (4.181) would be acceptable, in the interpretation that the deep subject is only the Theme. Unfortunately this is not the case, for such passives are independently blocked by the Thematic Hierarchy Condition on the Passive (section 2.5), which requires the *by*-phrase to be higher on the Thematic Hierarchy than the derived subject.

(4.182) *John was being touched by himself.
(4.183) *John was hit by himself.

What would disprove this alleged explanation of the reflexive passive? If there were an acceptable sentence with an inanimate (and therefore non-Agent) subject, but with a semantically plausible reflexive object, and with a verb like *touch*, which marks the subject as Theme, such a sentence would violate the THC, since the reflexive would have to be higher on the Thematic Hierarchy than its antecedent. Such a sentence is *The tree was touching itself*, which sounds to me somewhat less acceptable than (4.180). According to the analysis so far, this feeling should be due either to a violation of the THC or to a dubious attribution of volition to trees.

4.10.2 Psychological Predicates

There are some verbs whose active forms potentially yield violations of the THC, for example, *impress NP as* and *strike*. In section 2.5 we established that the subject of these verbs is the Theme and the object is Goal, while *regard* reverses these relations.

(4.184) Bill $\left\{ \begin{array}{l} \text{strikes} \\ \text{impresses} \end{array} \right\}$ Harry as pompous. (= 2.74)

(4.185) Harry regards Bill as pompous. (= 2.75)

We used this difference in thematic relations to explain why *strike* and *impress* do not undergo the passive but *regard* does.

Now notice what the THC predicts about reflexives with these verbs. Since with *strike* and *impress* the Theme is on the left, but the reflexivization rule permits reflexives only on the right, the THC should be violated and we predict (correctly) the unacceptability of *?I* $\left\{ \begin{array}{l} \text{strike} \\ \text{impress} \end{array} \right\}$ *myself as pompous*. *Regard*, with Theme on the right, should function normally with respect to reflexivization, and as expected, *I regard myself as pompous* is acceptable. The passive **I am regarded by myself as pompous* then violates the THC. The passives of *strike* and *impress*, of course, are independently eliminated by the Passive THC of section 2.5.

Please, like *strike* and *impress*, has the Theme in the subject and a Goal in the direct object, as pointed out by the variant *is pleasing to*. Thus it also cannot have reflexive objects without violating the THC. Note, too, that its passive sounds a bit strange unless the *by*-phrase is construed as an Agent or Instrument (a surrogate or intermediate Agent):

(4.186) Bill was pleased by $\left\{ \begin{array}{l} \text{?Harry. (Agent)} \\ \text{Harry's performance. (Instrument)} \end{array} \right.$

To fill the semantic gap, there is the adjective form *pleased with*.

(4.187) Bill was pleased with Harry.

The thematic relations of *pleased with* are not immediately clear. By the usual arguments from parallelism, the subject should be Goal and the *with*-phrase Theme. This analysis and the THC correctly predict the acceptable reflexives with *pleased with, amused with, disgusted with,* and *impressed with*. Though Gruber (1965) does not discuss thematic relations involving this *with*-phrase, the following examples suggest that there are more concrete cases where a *with*-phrase is Theme.

(4.188) The spy $\begin{Bmatrix} \text{supplied} \\ \text{provided} \end{Bmatrix}$ information to the enemy.

(4.189) The spy $\begin{Bmatrix} \text{supplied} \\ \text{provided} \end{Bmatrix}$ the enemy with information.

In (4.188) the thematic relations are identical to those with *give*: the subject is Source and Agent, the direct object is Theme, and the indirect object is Goal. In the semantically parallel forms (4.189) then, we expect the *with*-phrase to be Theme and the direct object Goal (note that this *with*-phrase is semantically distinct from the instrumental).

Turning to the adjectives with *to*-phrases (e.g., *striking, impressive, pleasing, amusing, disgusting, irritating, horrifying, familiar, annoying,* and *frightening*),[7] we remember that the *to*-phrase marks an expression of Goal. This means that the Theme is in the subject, which is what we predict if the adjective attributes an abstract Location to the Theme. If the subject is purely Theme, then a reflexive in the *to*-phrase will violate the THC.

Can the subject of these adjectives be Agent as well? If so, reflexives in the *to*-phrase should be permissible. The use of progressive aspect with these adjectives, where at all felicitous, does give a reading of volition to the subject:

(4.190) John is (deliberately) being $\begin{cases} \text{disgusting.} \\ \text{amusing.} \\ \text{frightening.} \\ \text{impressive.} \end{cases}$

But in this usage the expression of Goal seems to be ruled out: adding *to Bill* in (4.190) makes the sentence sound odd. We predict from the THC that the addition of *to himself* in (4.190) should not make it any worse than *to Bill* does. But my judgments fail me at this point.

---

[7]There is an interesting correlation here: the adjectives ending in *-ed* take *with*, and those ending in *-ing* take *to*, with concomitant correlation in induced thematic relations. I have no explanation to offer for this fact.

The last of the psychological predicates are those that occur in patterns like (4.171) (*NP V Adj to NP*): *look*, *sound*, *taste*, and *smell*. But these fall into a by now familiar pattern: the *to*-phrase is a mark of the expression of Goal, the adjective is an abstract Location attributed to the subject, and so the subject is the Theme. The subject is *not* an Agent: **I smelled funny to Bill in order to get rid of him.*[8] Therefore these verbs cannot take part in reflexive sentences either, without violating the THC. On the other hand, the use of *smell* in *I smelled myself* allows an Agent subject (*I smelled myself in order to see if I needed a shower*) so the THC can be met, permitting reflexivization.

4.10.3 *About* Movement

(4.161)   I talked to Mary about Louise.
(4.162)   I talked about Louise to Mary.
(4.163)   I talked to Thmug about himself.
(4.164) *I talked about Thmug to himself.
(4.165) *I talked about himself to Thmug.

Talk, *tell*, *speak*, etc. can be analyzed as verbs of motion, where the thing undergoing the motion is the information being conveyed by the speech-act (see Gruber 1965, section 7.2). This means that the subject is Agent and Source, and the *to*-phrase is the Goal. Then the *about*-phrase must be the Theme. Gruber does not mention any instances of Themes in PPs, but an extension of his arguments about the Themes of *look* and *see* (in Gruber 1967a) might lead one to conclude that, for example, in (4.161), the Theme is some abstract instantiation of *Louise*. If the *about*-phrase is Theme, then we can explain (4.164) as follows. In (4.163) the Goal is to the left of the Theme, so the THC and the structural description of the reflexive rule can be met simultaneously. But in (4.164), the Theme is to the left of the Goal, so the THC must be violated. (4.165) of course violates the reflexivization rule.

Consider also the following sentences.

(4.191) I talked to Thmug about myself.

[8]For the sense of volition in sentences like *John tried to look sick*, see section 5.12. Note also the strangeness of *John tried to seem sick to Bill*. As with the adjective constructions just discussed, the Agent subject and the expression of Goal seem to be mutually exclusive.

(4.192) I talked about myself to Thmug.
(4.193) I talked to myself about myself.
(4.194) I talked about myself to myself.

(4.191) and (4.192) are both all right, since *I*, the Agent and Source, is to the left of the Theme whether or not *about*-movement takes place. (4.193), which has the *to*-phrase and the *about*-phrase in underlying order, has reflexives in both Goal and Theme, with the Agent as antecedent.

(4.194), which for Postal should be a violation of the Crossover Principle, is unexpectedly good, and he goes to a great deal of trouble to explain it away. The interpretive theory takes care of it without inordinate difficulty. The table of coreference generated for (4.194) by the reflexivization rule for (4.194) is (4.195), where $myself_1$ is the reflexive after *about* and $myself_2$ is the reflexive after *to*.

(4.195) I coref $myself_1$
$\qquad$ I coref $myself_2$
$\qquad$ $myself_1$ coref $myself_2$

The third entry in the table will violate the THC, since $myself_1$ is Theme and $myself_2$ is Goal. However, if we alter the THC to read "A reflexive must be lower on the Thematic Hierarchy than at least one of its antecedents," table (4.195) will meet the condition.

4.10.4 *It*-Replacement

(4.156)   It seems to me that Schwarz is clever.
(4.157)   Schwarz seems to me to be clever.
(4.158)   It seems to me that I am clever.
(4.159)   ?I seem to myself to be clever.
(4.160)   *Myself seems to me to be clever.

Example (4.160) is of course out because it violates the reflexivization rule. But (4.159) is more difficult. Let us make the usual assumption that *Schwarz* in (4.157) and *I* in (4.159) arise from a rule moving them from the complement subject into the position of the *it* in (4.156) and (4.158), respectively. The Thematic Hierarchy Condition as stated will not account for all cases of this sort, since it is easy to find a sentence in which the subject is an Agent, yet the reflexive *to*-phrase (a Goal) is still bad.

(4.196) ?John appears to himself to have hit Bill.

Since there is nothing we can do about the thematic relations in (4.196), we will have to modify the Thematic Hierarchy Condition. One possibility that suggests itself is to say that the condition applies only to thematic relations *induced by the verb of the lowest cycle* in which the reflexive has antecedents. It is reasonable that a raised NP such as the derived subject of *seem* has no thematic relation at all with respect to its new clause, since thematic relations are related to deep structure grammatical relations; *John* in (4.196) is an Agent only with respect to the complement. Then, to prevent (4.159) and (4.196), we need assume only that lack of thematic relation counts as the lowest position on the Thematic Hierarchy. Under this assumption, the derived subject, having no thematic relation, is lower on the hierarchy than the reflexive, which is an expression of Goal.

4.10.5 *Tough* Movement
(4.151)   It is tough for Jack to hit Tony.
(4.152)   Tony is tough for Jack to hit.
(4.153)   It is tough for Tony to shave himself.
(4.154) *Tony is tough for himself to shave.
(4.155) *Himself is tough for Tony to shave.

Postal claims in his monograph that there is a rule *Tough* movement that takes the object out of the complement sentence in (4.151) and puts it in the subject of the main clause to produce (4.152). This, he says, causes a crossover violation in cases like (4.154). For an account of these sentences involving the THC, the crucial factor, I claim, is that the *for*-phrase is a deep structure constituent of the main clause, but the subject is a deep structure constituent of the complement. If this is the case, the subject has no thematic relation in the main clause, whereas the *for*-phrase does. The modification of the Thematic Hierarchy Condition we have just proposed to handle *It*-replacement guarantees that whatever the thematic relation of the *for*-phrase, it will be higher on the hierarchy than the subject. Hence a reflexive in the *for*-phrase will violate the THC and the sentence will be unacceptable.

To establish the claim that the *for*-phrase in (4.154) is a constituent of the main clause, consider the following sentences.

(4.198) The problem is easy (for John).
(4.199) Shaving Bill is easy (for John).
(4.200) For John, shaving Bill is easy.

(4.198)–(4.200) show that there is an independently motivated *for*-phrase in the complement of *easy*. Now we must show that when *Tough* movement takes place, the *for*-phrase that appears is this main clause *for*-phrase and not the *for*-phrase of the *for-to* complement.

(4.201) *John's shaving Bill is easy.
(4.202) ?To shave Bill is easy (for John).
(4.203) It is easy (for John) to shave Bill.
(4.204) *For John to shave Bill is easy.

These examples show that the *for*-phrase originating as complement subject with *easy* must usually be deleted. (4.201) shows that a gerund subject cannot itself have a subject. With an infinitive subject (4.202), extraposition is preferred, as in (4.203), but an infinitive in subject position is much worse if it has an overt subject, as in (4.204).

There are a few cases where both *for*-phrases show up on the surface.

(4.205) It would be easier for me for John to do the job than for me to do it
        myself.
(4.206) It is a waste of time for me for John to try to help with this job.

However, these sentences do not have the corresponding form with the object fronted from the subordinate clause.

(4.207) *This job would be easier for me for John to do (than for me to do
        myself).
(4.208) *This job is a waste of time for me for John to try to help with.

Thus, when both *for*-phrases are present, *Tough* movement cannot take place.

For further evidence that the *for*-phrase is part of the main clause, notice that in the cases where the complement object is fronted, the *for*-phrase can still prepose, as in (4.209).

(4.209) For John, Bill is easy to shave.

These examples argue that *Tough* movement can take place only if the complement subject has been deleted, since every time there is an acceptable *for*-phrase in such sentences, it turns out to be the main clause *for*-phrase. If the *for*-phrase is in the main clause, the Thematic Hierarchy Condition can account for the violation (4.154) in the manner shown above.

4.10.6 Dative Shifts
In addition to the cases given so far, there are two cases which Postal cites (1971, Chapter 15) as "non-counterevidence" to the Crossover Principle. These actually turn out to be evidence against the Crossover Principle and for the Thematic Hierarchy Condition. The rules are *To*-dative shift and *For*-dative shift, the effects of which we now illustrate.

(4.210) Dave sold a book to Pete. ⎫
(4.211) Dave sold Pete a book.   ⎬ (*To*-dative)
(4.212) Dave bought a book for Pete. ⎫
(4.213) Dave bought Pete a book   ⎬ (*For*-dative)

Each of these rules permutes the two objects and deletes or inserts a preposition, depending on one's assumptions about the underlying order.

Which member of the pairs above has the underlying order of objects? I maintain that the upper member is more primitive since the order of complements NP-PP is widespread in English and hence a plausible base rule, whereas the order PP-NP is unknown except in these two constructions and the order NP-NP is rare. Hence for economy in the base it seems wiser to assume that the dative rules produce (4.211) from (4.210) and (4.213) from (4.212).

Furthermore, in the nominalized form, the direct object always directly follows the head and is followed by the *to*-object or *for*-object.

(4.214) Dave's sale of a book to Pete
(4.215) ?Dave's sale to Pete of a book
(4.216) *Dave's sale Pete of a book

(4.217) Dave's painting of a picture for Mary
(4.218) *Dave's painting for Mary of a picture
(4.219) *Dave's painting Mary of a picture

Under our usual assumptions about the base rule schema, as in Chomsky (1970a), these facts can best be captured by supposing (4.210) and (4.212) to have the underlying order of objects in sentences, corresponding to (4.214) and (4.217). The two dative rules, however, do not generalize to NP constructions, but occur only in sentences; thus they produce only (4.211) and (4.212), not (4.215), (4.216), (4.218), or (4.219).

Postal points out that the direct and indirect objects cannot be coreferential, no matter what their order.

(4.220) ?*I sold the slave to himself.
(4.221)　*I sold the slave himself.
(4.222) ?*I bought the slave for himself.
(4.223)　*I bought the slave himself.

Since only (4.221) and (4.223) can be instances of crossover violations, Postal alludes to "some mysterious, independent constraint which prevents the direct and indirect objects from being coreferential in such cases" (p. 126).

Actually, these examples are a great deal more transparent in light of the present treatment of reflexivization. Consider the thematic relations of these sentences. With *sell*, the subject is Agent and Source, the direct object is Theme, and the indirect object is Goal. With *buy*, the subject is Agent, the direct object is Theme, and the *for*-phrase is Goal. The *from*-phrase, if it occurs, is Source. In (4.220), then, the reflexive is the Goal, but its antecedent is Theme, so the THC is violated. Likewise, in (4.222), the reflexive is the Goal, but its antecedent is Theme, so the THC rules the sentence out.

What then of (4.221) and (4.223), where the reflexive is Theme and its antecedent Goal, so that the THC is met? We can account for these by appeal to the well-known constraint that dative shifts may not move definite pronouns out of postverbal position:

(4.224)　I gave it to John.
(4.225) *I gave John it.
(4.226)　I bought it for John.
(4.227) *I bought John it.

Since reflexives are definite pronouns, they fall under this restriction as well. As further evidence, observe that the violation in (4.221) has nothing to do with coreference with the object, only with the presence of a reflexive pronoun:

(4.228) *I sold the slave myself. (= I sold myself to the slave.)

(This example was suggested to me by George Bedell.)

Thus we see that the combination of the THC and this condition on dative shift rules out both possible orders, accounting nicely for (4.220)–(4.223). Notice also that the relative force of the two conditions we have invoked accounts for the difference in acceptability, correctly predicting (4.221) and (4.223) to be worse than (4.220) and (4.222).

The Crossover Principle, on the other hand, can rule out only (4.221) and (4.223), since no movement takes place in (4.220) and (4.222). (4.220) and (4.222) cannot be ruled out by a condition on pronouns like that which rules out (4.225) and (4.227), since pronouns are acceptable in *to*-phrases and *for*-phrases:

(4.229) I gave the book to him.
(4.230) I bought the book for him.

4.10.7 Emphasis

The only remaining reflexive cases that Postal discusses are emphatic reflexives, which are often acceptable even when they violate the Crossover Principle:

(4.231) John was shaved by HIMSELF.

Postal explains these by getting them from pseudocleft sentences by a derivation that somehow manages not to violate the Crossover Principle. However, notice that (4.231) can be used only as an answer to some question like (4.232).

(4.232) Who was John shaved by?

Thus in this particular case there is no more appropriate way to answer than (4.231). Notice also that (4.233), a nonreflexive answer to (4.232), is more acceptable than (4.231).

(4.233) John was shaved by BILL.

This suggests that (4.231) in fact is a violation of the Crossover Principle or the Thematic Hierarchy Condition, but that the exigencies of the discourse permit one to override the relatively weak force of the violation.

What evidence is there to decide whether the Crossover Principle or the Thematic Hierarchy Condition is the better way of accounting for all these facts of reflexivization? It is of course impossible to compare them in relative complexity. But we can compare them with respect to the number of phenomena they can explain, and the Thematic Hierarchy Condition seems to explain more. It explains the dative shift case, which the Crossover Principle cannot. It also explains the double reflexive case of *About* movement, which the Crossover Principle cannot explain without resort to a more complex deep structure. The Crossover Principle purports to explain some aberrant cases of pronominalization that could not be explained by the THC, but the next section will show that Postal's account cannot be correct. Thus the Thematic Hierarchy Condition must be chosen as the analysis of greater generality.

The existence of the Reflexive and Passive Thematic Hierarchy Conditions is in addition a striking corroboration of Gruber's system of thematic relations, with which we have chosen to represent the functional structure. By strictly following Gruber's principles for determining thematic relations of verbs, we have been able to account for a wide variety of apparent exceptions by a very simple principle. Since it is not clear that any other proposed description of functional structure can capture the same generalization, we have strong reason to prefer Gruber's system. More evidence for this system, from an entirely unrelated set of phenomena, will appear in the next chapter.

The other cases Postal discusses in connection with the Crossover Principle have to do with pronouns. We will turn to these cases now.

4.11 Some Unexpectedly Bad Cases of Pronominalization—The Failure of the Crossover Principle

Postal (1971, Chapter 10) brings up a class of sentences in which understood coreference apparently should be possible, but is not. Contrast the following pairs of questions, in which *he* or *himself* and *who* are to be understood as coreferential.

(4.234) Who shaved himself?

(4.235) *Who did $\begin{Bmatrix} \text{he} \\ \text{himself} \end{Bmatrix}$ shave?

(4.236) Who does Mary think hurt himself?
(4.237) *Who does Mary think he hurt?

(4.238) Who did the police accuse of trying to enrich himself?
(4.239) *Who did the police accuse him of trying to enrich?

(4.240) *Who did the girl $\begin{Bmatrix} \text{he hated} \\ \text{who hates him} \end{Bmatrix}$ describe?

(4.241) *Who did you talk to the girl $\begin{Bmatrix} \text{he likes} \\ \text{who likes him} \end{Bmatrix}$ about?

Exactly the same judgments obtain for parallel relative clause constructions. Postal suggests that the Crossover Principle can take care of these bad sentences, since in each case, *Wh*-preposing has moved *who* over the pronoun. Then, to account for the fact that (4.242) is good with *he* and *Charley* coreferential,

(4.242) Who that Charley knows did he criticize?

Postal incorporates Ross's suggestion that the Crossover Principle is operative only when that one of the coreferent NPs that moves is the NP "mentioned" in the structural description of the rule that moves it. Then, to account for the fact that (4.243) is bad, even though the *wh*-word is only a subpart of the NP being moved,

(4.243) *Evidence for whose claim did he deduce?
        (contrast with: Who deduced evidence for his claim?)

Postal goes through a long discussion of the Pied Piping Convention, first proposed in Ross (1967a), which enables the *wh*-fronting rule to "mention" only the *wh*-word but still carry along larger NPs.

   I will not discuss Postal's analysis in detail because it seems to me to be unable to handle the whole range of relevant facts. Consider the following sentences. (*Whose* and *him* to be coreferential, as usual.)

(4.244) *Whose mother did you talk to the girl who likes him about?

(4.245) *Whose mother did you talk about to the girl who likes him?
(4.246) *Whose mother did you talk about the girl who likes him to?
(4.247) *Whose mother did you talk to about the girl who likes him?

The Crossover Principle can handle (4.244) and (4.246), since *whose* is "mentioned" by the fronting rule and it crosses over *him*. But (4.245) and (4.247) cannot be covered, since *whose mother* has been moved away from the left of *him*. It might be argued that the violation in these sentences is produced by the crossing in *About* movement, but this proposal can handle only one of the two: whichever one has the underlying order of *to*-phrase and *about*-phrase still has no crossover violation. Furthermore, an appeal to *About* movement would be specious anyway, since *About* movement would have to "mention" the whole NP *whose mother* in moving the PP.

Another counterexample concerning *About* movement is the fact that (4.248) seems good, in fact better than the nonquestion version (4.249).

(4.248)   ?Whom did you talk about himself to?
(4.249)   *I talked about himself to John.

It is only by virtue of the fact that *whom* has crossed over that (4.248) is good. These examples also argue for ordering reflexivization after *Wh*-preposing, as we claimed in section 4.8, since only if this is the case can the two sentences be distinguished in acceptability.

In search for another way to deal with these examples, we separate these anomalies into two cases: (a) no coreference between *wh*- and the subject of the clause it came from, as in (4.235), (4.237), (4.239), and (4.243); and (b) no coreference between *who* and pronouns that are in certain relative clauses, as in (4.240), (4.241), and (4.244)–(4.247).

Going to a wider range of data, we find some other constructions which have paradigms at least partially like questions.

(4.250)   In Mary's apartment, a thief assaulted her.
(4.251)   ?In Mary's apartment, she was assaulted by a thief.

(4.252)   It was John's dog that bit him.
(4.253)   *It was John's dog that he bit.

Note that in none of these examples has a movement rule "mentioned" one of these coreferential NPs. In (4.250)–(4.251) this is obvious, since the adverb preposing rule moves adverbials. In the cleft sentences (4.252)–(4.253), there is a relative clause movement involved, but the NP "mentioned" by the relative clause rule is *John's dog*, not *John*. But notice that if the Crossover Principle were altered to cover (4.251), it would also cover (4.250), since the adverbial moves from the extreme right-hand end of the sentence. Furthermore, G. Lakoff shows (1968b) that neither the adverbial cases nor the cleft cases can be handled by ordering a rule of adverbial fronting or cleft formation *after* pronominalization, since pronouns within relative clauses contained in the adverbial or clefted NP exhibit the possibilities one would expect if the rule were ordered *before* pronominalization (recall the discussion of section 4.5). Since neither the Crossover Principle nor ordering of rules can explain these examples, we conclude that there must be some additional specifications in the environment for pronominalization, or else some other principle not yet discovered. I will not try to discuss here what modifications must be made. But whatever the principle is, it can be seen to easily generalize to cover case (a) of the *wh*-anomalies, since the relevant distinction is subject versus nonsubject.

Thus we have found an independently needed constraint that handles case (a) of pronominalization violations allegedly due to the Crossover Principle. What about case (b)? There seems to be a variety of factors interacting in these sentences. For one thing, some sentences of this form sound bad even without an anaphoric pronoun: (4.254) does not seem appreciably worse than (4.255).

(4.254) Who did the man who hated him see?
(4.255) Who did the man who hated John see?

This seems to be only a stylistic violation of some sort, but it does serve to confuse the issue of coreferentiality in (4.254).

Second, there seems to be a great deal less freedom in the way pronouns can relate to *whose* than there is in their use with definite or even some indefinite (generic) NPs.

(4.256) John's mother hit him in the nose.
(4.257) ?Whose mother hit him in the nose?
(4.258) In $\begin{Bmatrix} \text{a pedant's} \\ \text{John's} \end{Bmatrix}$ mind, no possible argument against him can ever be justified.

(4.259) ?In whose mind can no possible argument against him ever be justified?

The difference is not just a result of the "mention" clause in the Crossover Principle, since there is not even any movement taking place in (4.257). This factor plays a part in the anomalies of (4.244)–(4.247).

A third factor is that which distinguishes (4.260) from (4.261), and (4.262) from (4.263).

(4.260) ?During what movie do you cry every time you see it?
(4.261) During what movie do you cry every time you get drunk?
(4.262) ?Who do you talk about to people that respect his work?
(4.263) Who do you talk about to people that respect Bill's work?

(4.260) and (4.262) seem to me to be good only as echo questions. This corresponds precisely to my feelings about the anomalies of (4.239), (4.241), (4.243), and perhaps (4.244)–(4.247), (4.254), (4.257), and (4.259). Yet again there is no possibility for the questioned phrase to cross over the anaphoric pronoun. In section 7.6 we will show that these differences are consequences of the modal structure associated with *wh-*.

Thus virtually all the pronominalization cases adduced as evidence for the Crossover Principle should actually be handled by other processes that capture a wider range of phenomena. Since these other processes are not known to conflict with the interpretive theory of pronouns, whereas the Crossover Principle does, the discussion in this section can be taken as a vindication of the interpretive theory even if not all the problems have been solved.

4.12 Some Further Cases of Reflexivization

This section will tend to throw a certain amount of doubt on the analysis given so far. However, the evidence will show that, if anything, reflexivization is *more* dependent on semantics than has been claimed. Thus the transformational theory of reflexives will be made to seem even less plausible.

One pair of sentences mentioned in section 4.6 is still not accounted for by the reflexivization rule of section 4.8.

(4.264) The picture of himself that John saw hanging in the post office was ugly. (= 4.111)

(4.265) The description of himself that John gave the police was a pack of lies. (= 4.112)

The structure of these sentences looks like (4.266) at the time reflexivization applies. (I assume, with Chomsky, that restrictive relative clauses are daughter-adjuncts to the NP at this stage of derivation, not Chomsky-adjuncts.)

(4.266)

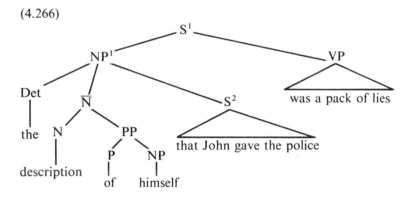

The difficulty is that on the NP^1 cycle, when *himself* is first encountered, *himself* both precedes and commands *John*, violating condition (d) of reflexivization, which rules out exactly this case. Furthermore, *John* is in the subordinate clause S^2, violating condition (c), which requires the antecedent to be in the main clause. We thus predict that (4.264)–(4.265) should be unacceptable.

To see that conditions (c) and (d) are well motivated here, compare (4.265) and its structure (4.266) to (4.267) and its structure (4.268).

(4.267) *It bothered himself that John was sick.

(4.268)

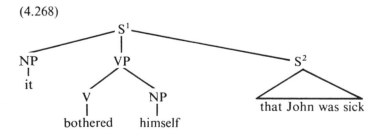

Comparing the whole of (4.268) to NP^1 in (4.266), we observe a total parallelism of structure. Any change in conditions (c) and (d) that allows (4.265), then, will also allow (4.267), which must be excluded.

One difference between (4.265) and (4.267) is that a possessive NP may be added in the determiner of (4.265), but the subject of (4.267) admits of no such addition. In other words, (4.269) is possible, but (4.270) is not.

(4.269)   John's picture of himself, which he gave the police, was ugly.
(4.270)   *John bothered himself that he was sick.

John in the determiner of (4.266) would be sufficient to produce the reflexive by the regular rule. Therefore one's immediate reaction is to claim that all relative clause reflexivizations like (4.264)–(4.265) start out like (4.269), with an NP in the determiner which gets deleted later. Unfortunately, this will not work, since there are sentences where putting the necessary NP in the determiner destroys the correct interpretation:

(4.271) The unflattering descriptions of himself which our beloved president has banned from the public press still circulate underground.
(4.272) Our beloved president's unflattering descriptions of himself, which he has banned from the public press, still circulate underground.

So in general a possessive NP cannot be added to the underlying form without producing disastrous results in other aspects of the interpretation.

Another possible suggestion is that the relative clause transformation actually moves the relativized noun and its complements from the relative clause into the head position in the NP. Thus (4.265) would be derived from an underlying structure of the form $[_{NP_1}$*the one* $[_{S_2}$*that John gave the police a description of himself*$]]$ *was a pack of lies.* The reflexive could be interpreted on the S^2 cycle, then *description of himself* could replace *one* later by relative clause formation. This explanation fails too, because reflexivization does not invariably take place in these clauses, particularly with an indefinite determiner:

(4.273) *I painted a picture of himself that John saw yesterday.

Since we probably do not want to have two separate relative clause transformations, one moving the noun up from the relative clause and one not doing so, we have to reject this solution too.

Exploring more data, we notice the startling fact that the choice of verbs in the main clause and the relative clause affects the acceptability of reflexives in the relativized noun phrase. We get paradigms like these:

(4.274) I hate the story about $\left\{ \begin{array}{l} \text{*him} \\ \text{himself} \\ \text{me} \\ \text{*myself} \end{array} \right\}$ that John always tells.

(4.275) I told the story about $\left\{ \begin{array}{l} \text{*him} \\ \text{*himself} \\ \text{*me} \\ \text{myself} \end{array} \right\}$ that John likes to hear.

(4.274) and (4.275) are structurally identical with respect to the relevant NP relationships:

(4.276)

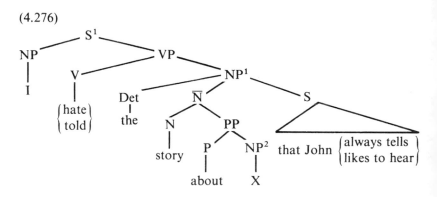

Assume that there is a semantic rule that can duplicate the subject of a sentence in the determiner of an object, and that this rule is ordered before reflexivization. If this rule puts *John* in the determiner of NP¹ in (4.276), we will get the paradigm (4.274): *himself* will be coreferential with *John*, *me* will be noncoreferential, *him* will be noncoreferential, and *myself* will be (anomalously) coreferential. If the rule puts *I* in the determiner of NP¹, we will get the paradigm (4.275): *him* is marked noncoreferential with *I*, but it both precedes and commands *John*, so they cannot be marked coreferential

Himself is anomalously marked coreferential with *I*, *me* is anomalously marked noncoreferential with *I*, and *myself* is correctly marked coreferential with *I*. Thus the postulation of this duplication rule gives exactly the right results, though its status as a possible semantic rule is still very much open to question.

The conditioning of the duplication rule, as we have noticed, seems to depend on some semantic property of the verb. I suggest that the property in question may have something to do with the subject's being marked with the thematic relation Agent by the verb: *tell* certainly has an Agent subject, whereas *hate* and *like to hear* do not. Perhaps some extension of the Thematic Hierarchy Condition (section 4.10) comes into play.

Semantic properties of verbs seem to play a part in reflexivization in a much more familiar construction, too. The rule proposed in section 4.7 correctly predicts the ambiguity of the reflexive in (4.277).

(4.277) John told Bill a story about himself. (= 4.103)

In the structurally very similar (4.278) and (4.279), the rule predicts the same ambiguity. But, unaccountably, *himself* is read only as *John* here.

(4.278) John criticized Bill in a story about himself.
(4.279) John learned about Bill from a story about himself.

The way to refer to *Bill* in this construction is to use *him*.

(4.280) John criticized Bill in a story about him.
(4.281) John learned about Bill from a story about him.

One might suppose from these examples that the difference has to do with a condition on reflexivization which keeps it from applying when the picture-noun construction is in a prepositional phrase. But the problem is not that easy. Changing the verb again changes the paradigm, although the structure remains the same. (The following examples were pointed out to me by Gary Martins.)

(4.282) John collaborated with Bill on a story about himself.
(4.283) John agreed with Bill on an alibi for himself.

As in (4.278)–(4.279), *himself* can only be *John*. However, in this case there seems to be no way at all to refer to *Bill*: *him* must be someone else in (4.284)–(4.285).

(4.284) John collaborated with Bill on a story about him.
(4.285) John agreed with Bill on an alibi for him.

Admittedly, these judgments are not very secure, but comparison of the acceptability of (4.286)–(4.289) is a further test: the latter two feel somewhat worse, with *her* understood as *Mary*.

(4.286)   John learned about Mary from a story about her(*self).
(4.287)   John criticized Mary in a story about her(*self).
(4.288) ?John collaborated with Mary on a story about her(*self).
(4.289) ?John agreed with Mary on an alibi for her(*self).

The difference seems to be due to the fact that the *with*-phrases in (4.288)–(4.289) are semantically co-Agents along with the subject, whereas the objects in (4.286)–(4.287) are not. What the connection is between this difference and the coreference phenomena is extremely unclear to me, however.

   Note, by the way, that a transformational explanation appealing to Lakoff and Peters's (1969) rule of conjunct movement is not as easy as it might first appear. The argument might be that (4.288) is derived from *John and Mary collaborated on a story about her(self)*, and that the coreference rules take place before *Mary* is moved to the right of the verb. However, then it would be impossible to explain why *John and Mary collaborated on a story about himself* is rendered acceptable by doing conjunct movement. In any event, Dougherty (1971) casts a great deal of doubt on the plausibility of this transformation.

4.13 *Each Other*
Dougherty (1970) points out that the distribution of the expression *each other* is governed by a simplex sentence condition like that for reflexivization.

(4.290)   John and Bill like each other.
(4.291) *John and Bill thought that Mary liked each other.

An alternative construction with similar meaning uses the discontinuous formatives *each . . . the other*. This construction is not subject to a simplex sentence condition.

(4.292) John and Bill each like the other.
(4.293) John and Bill each thought that Mary liked the other.

Dougherty maintains that (4.290) is derived from (4.292) by an *each*-movement transformation. The restriction of this transformation to simplex sentences will explain the unacceptability of (4.291). Call this the transformational theory of *each other*.

A possible alternative proposal for the syntax of *each other*, the phrase-structure theory, is that it is generated in something relatively close to its surface form, as part of the regular paradigm exemplified in (4.294).

$$(4.294) \quad \begin{Bmatrix} \text{one} \\ \text{each} \end{Bmatrix} \text{ of the } \begin{Bmatrix} \text{houses} \\ \text{men} \\ \text{others} \end{Bmatrix}$$

$$\begin{Bmatrix} *\text{one} \\ *\text{each} \end{Bmatrix} \text{ of } \begin{Bmatrix} \text{houses} \\ \text{men} \\ \text{others} \end{Bmatrix}$$

$$\begin{Bmatrix} \text{one} \\ \text{each} \end{Bmatrix} \begin{Bmatrix} \text{house} \\ \text{man} \\ \text{other} \end{Bmatrix}$$

According to this paradigm, it is a syntactic fact about *each* that it can be followed by *of the* $\begin{bmatrix} N \\ \text{plur} \end{bmatrix}$ or by $\begin{bmatrix} N \\ \text{sing} \end{bmatrix}$. Similar paradigms exist for many quantifiers; rules which express these generalizations have been discussed in Jackendoff (1968a). Since *each other* can be generated as a regular member of this paradigm, it is a loss of generality to derive it by an *each*-movement transformation, as Dougherty proposes.

Dougherty does provide evidence against the phrase-structure theory. He points out that his proposal, but not one which generates *each other* as a single constituent in the base, can explain the ungrammaticality of (4.295) with no further effort.

(4.295) *John and Bill each like each other.

Under his analysis, the two positions of *each* have the same underlying source, so they cannot co-occur, as in (4.295). If there are two independent sources in the base, extra constraints will be needed to rule out (4.295). Thus the two theories are apparently at a standoff with respect to the data given so far: each appears to miss an important generalization.

The following sentence seems to argue against Dougherty's analysis, however, in that it contains both a preverbal quantifier and *each other*.

(4.296) John and Bill and Harry all like each other.

If the *each* of *each other* comes from the preverbal position, Dougherty's argument predicts that (4.296) should be bad also. Dougherty permits, for various reasons, the quantifier combination *each of all* to be generated in the base, providing a possible source for (4.296). But since in general such combinations are not permitted, this solitary example looks suspicious, particularly since it never appears at the surface.

It appears, then, that the transformational approach to *each other* cannot generate (4.296) without ad hoc restrictions on permitted quantifier combinations. Hence the apparent advantage it had in rejecting (4.295) is offset by further complication. It seems reasonable, then, to adopt the phrase-structure theory and find some other restriction to eliminate (4.295). Informally, the appropriate restriction seems to be that a sentence may not contain markers that designate a multiplicity of events (Dougherty's feature [− totality]) unless these markers can be semantically realized nonredundantly.

Under the phrase-structure theory we will have to somehow incorporate the observation that *each other* does not generally occur in clauses subordinate to its antecedent. I suggest that the appropriate account is to treat *each other* as a specialized plural pronoun, indicating coreference of the sets designated by plural NPs, but noncoreference with respect to individual actions within that set. Like all other pronouns, its antecedent will be designated by the rules of coreference. We can capture the simplex sentence condition by treating *each other* as a *reflexive* pronoun.

If *each other* is a reflexive pronoun, it should be subject to all the other conditions which reflexives obey. This prediction seems to be largely borne out. First of all, it is self-evident that *each other* cannot occur without an antecedent. Second, the conditions on its occurrence are not strictly limited to simplex sentences, but rather to the enlarged set of environments found for reflexives in section 4.6.

(4.297)   John and Bill told me stories about $\begin{Bmatrix} \text{themselves} \\ \text{each other} \end{Bmatrix}$.

(4.298)   I told John and Bill stories about $\begin{Bmatrix} \text{themselves} \\ \text{each other} \end{Bmatrix}$.

(4.299)   *John and Bill told me Mary's stories about $\begin{Bmatrix} \text{themselves} \\ \text{each other} \end{Bmatrix}$.

(4.300)   ?John and Bill are disturbed that there are pictures of $\begin{Bmatrix} \text{themselves} \\ \text{each other} \end{Bmatrix}$ hanging in the post office.

(4.301)   *John and Bill are disturbed that I found pictures of $\begin{Bmatrix} \text{themselves} \\ \text{each other} \end{Bmatrix}$ hanging in the post office.

(4.302)   The stories about $\begin{Bmatrix} \text{themselves} \\ \text{each other} \end{Bmatrix}$ that John and Bill tell are fascinating.

The facts of section 4.12 involving agency hold here too.

(4.303)   I like the stories about $\begin{Bmatrix} \text{themselves} \\ \text{each other} \end{Bmatrix}$ than John and Bill tell.

(4.304)   *I told the stories about $\begin{Bmatrix} \text{themselves} \\ \text{each other} \end{Bmatrix}$ that John and Bill like.

(4.305)   John and Bill told the stories about $\begin{Bmatrix} \text{themselves} \\ \text{each other} \end{Bmatrix}$ that I like.

(4.306)   John and Bill like the stories about $\begin{Bmatrix} \text{?themselves} \\ \text{*each other} \end{Bmatrix}$ that I tell.

(4.307)   John and Bill criticized Mary in stories about $\begin{Bmatrix} \text{themselves} \\ \text{each other} \end{Bmatrix}$.

(4.308)   ?*Mary criticized John and Bill in stories about $\begin{Bmatrix} \text{themselves} \\ \text{each other} \end{Bmatrix}$.

(4.309)   John and Bill collaborated with Mary on stories about $\left\{\begin{array}{l}\text{themselves}\\\text{each other}\end{array}\right\}$.

(4.310) ?*Mary collaborated with John and Bill on stories about $\left\{\begin{array}{l}\text{themselves}\\\text{each other}\end{array}\right\}$.

The Thematic Hierarchy Condition holds, for a wide range of examples. Compare the following examples to those in section 4.9.

Passive

(4.311)   John and Bill arrested $\left\{\begin{array}{l}\text{themselves}\\\text{each other}\end{array}\right\}$.

(4.312) ??John and Bill were arrested by $\left\{\begin{array}{l}\text{themselves}\\\text{each other}\end{array}\right\}$.[9]

Tough Movement

(4.313)   It is tough for John and Bill to shave $\left\{\begin{array}{l}\text{themselves}\\\text{each other}\end{array}\right\}$.

*John and Bill are tough for $\left\{\begin{array}{l}\text{themselves}\\\text{each other}\end{array}\right\}$ to shave.

It-Replacement

(4.314) ?John and Bill seem to $\left\{\begin{array}{l}\text{themselves}\\\text{each other}\end{array}\right\}$ to be clever.

About Movement

(4.315) ?I talked to John and Bill about $\left\{\begin{array}{l}\text{themselves}\\\text{each other}\end{array}\right\}$.

*I talked about John and Bill to $\left\{\begin{array}{l}\text{themselves}\\\text{each other}\end{array}\right\}$.

Psychological Predicates

(4.316)   John and Bill regard $\left\{\begin{array}{l}\text{themselves}\\\text{each other}\end{array}\right\}$ as pompous.

?John and Bill strike $\left\{\begin{array}{l}\text{themselves}\\\text{each other}\end{array}\right\}$ as pompous.

---

[9](4.312) is good if *each other* is stressed, exactly as with reflexives, further extending the generalization.

John and Bill like $\begin{Bmatrix}\text{themselves}\\ \text{each other}\end{Bmatrix}$.

?John and Bill please $\begin{Bmatrix}\text{themselves}\\ \text{each other}\end{Bmatrix}$. (in nonagentive sense)

John and Bill smelled $\begin{Bmatrix}\text{themselves}\\ \text{each other}\end{Bmatrix}$.

?John and Bill smell funny to $\begin{Bmatrix}\text{themselves}\\ \text{each other}\end{Bmatrix}$.

Thus the environments of *each other* seem to be virtually identical to those of reflexives, and any analysis which does not capture this fact is missing an important generalization. As we have seen, a phrase-structure theory of *each other* combined with an interpretive theory of pronominalization can capture this generalization. A transformational theory of *each other* combined with an interpretive theory of coreference can probably capture it, but with somewhat more effort. In the phrase-structure theory, *each other* is generated within a single constituent. Thus the lexicon can list it as an idiom, with special semantic interpretation, including the feature [+refl], which is not shared by *the others* (as can be seen from (4.293)). The reflexivization rule will then have to make no special mention of *each other*. In the transformational theory, the surface form *each other* is taken to have no lexical significance; hence *each other* and its special interpretation will have to be specified within the reflexivization rule itself, certainly a less pleasing place in the grammar to have to state the facts. Furthermore, the *each*-movement transformation will have to be considerably complicated to derive the "backwards" cases like (4.302).

Under a transformational theory of *coreference*, the situation seems hopeless. In this theory, the interpretation of *each other* requires a conjoined source for (4.290) something like (4.317), with an intermediate step (4.318) (see Gleitman (1965) and Lakoff and Peters (1969) for this approach, and Dougherty (1970) for arguments against it).

(4.317) John likes Bill and Bill likes John.

(4.318) John and Bill like Bill and John, respectively.

I can see no way in which reflexivization can be tied into this sort of derivation in order to capture the generalization. We must conclude again in favor of the interpretive theory.

4.14 Generalizing Pronominalization and Reflexivization

We have established that pronominalization and reflexivization are both cyclic rules of interpretation ordered at the end of the transformational cycle. Furthermore, we have noticed an important similarity in the environments of the two rules. The basic pronominalization environment (NP^2 must not both precede and command NP^1) appears as condition (d) of the reflexivization rule.

In addition, there are two rather interesting restrictions which apply to both rules equally, giving us more reason to want to collapse them. The first concerns animacy: apparently backward reflexivization does not apply if the antecedent is inanimate. Observe the following contrasts:

(4.319)   The newspaper printed a story about itself.

(4.320) *A story about itself appeared in the newspaper.

(4.321) ?A strange story about himself intrigued Frank.

(4.322) *A model of itself was put in the auditorium.

(4.323)   A picture of himself was given to Bill.

In similar contexts the same constraints hold for pronominalization.

(4.324)   The newspaper printed Harry's story about it.

(4.325) *Harry's story about it appeared in the newspaper.

(4.326)   Harry's story about him intrigued Frank.

(4.327) *Mary's model of it was put in the auditorium.

(4.328) ?Mary's picture of him was given to Bill.

The second restriction has been alluded to with respect to pronominalization in sections 4.5.1 and 4.11. It concerns an asymmetry between subject and object position for pronouns whose antecedent is in a preposed constituent:

(4.329)   It was John who bit his dog.⎫
(4.330) *It was John who his dog bit.⎭ (*John = him*)
(4.331)   Who talked about his mother?⎫
(4.332) *Who did his mother talk about?⎭ (*Who = him*)

By an argument similar to that given for adverb preposing in section 4.5.1, it can be shown that these asymmetries are not due to the ordering of rules: if the antecedent is embedded under an S, the asymmetry disappears and forward pronominalization is always possible (see the examples in section 4.5.1). In section 4.11 we showed that a solution involving the Crossover Principle cannot successfully account for these violations either. We must conclude that the asymmetry is stated somewhere in the environment of pronominalization.

The same asymmetry is present in parallel examples with reflexives:

(4.333)   It was John who saw a picture of himself.
(4.334) *It was John who a picture of himself startled.

(4.335)   Who saw a picture of himself?
(4.336) *Who did a picture of himself fall on?

This further strengthens the generalization of the two rules.

In collapsing the rules, I will take into account one thing that has been left hanging. In section 4.7 we pointed out the necessity of having pronominalization apply to reflexive forms in sentences like *John saw his picture of himself*. However, as pointed out on page 140, simply letting pronominalization apply freely to reflexives would have the disastrous consequence of producing a reading for *John thinks that himself is sick*. What seems to be the case is that pronominalization can apply only to reflexives which already appear in the table, i.e., do not satisfy condition (a) of the reflexive rule.

The collapsed form of the two rules can be represented schematically as (4.337).

(4.337) Enter in the table:

$$NP^1 \; \alpha \; coref \begin{bmatrix} NP^2 \\ +pro \end{bmatrix} if$$

(A) general conditions on the two rules
and either
(B) special conditions for reflexivization
or
(C) special conditions for pronominalization.

One collapsing that works is (4.338); there may be other, better ones.

(4.338) Enter in the table:

$$NP^1 \; \alpha \; coref \begin{bmatrix} NP^2 \\ +pro \end{bmatrix} if$$

(A) a. NP^2 does not both precede and command NP^1;
     b. if NP^1 is inanimate, NP^2 follows NP^1;
     c. restrictions to account for (4.319)–(4.336)

and either

(B) a. NP^2 does not appear in the right-hand side of the table;
     b. NP^2 is dominated by $\overline{N}$ or VP;
     c. NP^1 is in the main clause relative to this cycle;
     d. NP^2 is $[\alpha \; refl]$;
     e. if NP^1 precedes NP^2, rule is OBLIGATORY

or

(C) either
     a. NP^2 is $[-refl]$
     or
     b. NP^2 appears in the right-hand side of the table

The conditions (A) have just been discussed. Conditions (B. a, b, c, e) are the conditions from the reflexivization rule, discussed in section 4.7. Condition (B.d) makes the rule mark reflexive pronouns coreferential with NP^1 and nonreflexive pronouns noncoreferential with NP^1, as did the reflexivization rule of section 4.7. Condition (C.a) makes pronominalization apply to nonreflexive pronouns; (C.b) makes it apply to reflexives that have already undergone reflexivization, as just mentioned.

Two slight changes from the original rules should be mentioned. If case (C) is chosen, the α in the first line of the rule has no counterpart in the conditions on the rule, as it does in case (B). In the original statement of pronominalization in section 4.4, this sign was always +. However, it causes no difficulty to let α be chosen freely as + or − : if − is chosen, a pair will simply be marked noncoreferential that would be marked later anyway by the noncoreferentiality rule.

In the statement of reflexivization in section 4.7, NP^2 in the first line of the rule carried $[\alpha \; refl]$ rather than $[+pro]$. $[\alpha \; refl]$ has now been placed in condition (B.d). The specification $[+pro]$ simply means that reflexivization will no longer mark noncoreference in nonpronominal environments such as *John saw Bill*. However, the noncoreferentiality rule will take care of these cases, so the change is irrelevant.

The final form (4.338) leaves me somewhat dissatisfied, in that one would hope to be able to eliminate condition (C.b) in some way. It remains for further research to determine whether this can be done, and if so, whether only minor adjustments to the system are needed or whether some drastic reorganization is called for. I conjecture that the correct modification will involve a much more essential use of the Thematic Hierarchy Condition and Modal Structure.

The completed system works as follows: (4.338) will apply at the end of each transformational cycle, entering relations between pairs of noun phrases in the table of coreference. After the application of (4.338) on the final cycle, the noncoreferentiality rule (4.26) marks any pair of NPs not yet related in the table as noncoreferential. The completed table is subject to well-formedness conditions, three of which have been mentioned so far: the Consistency Condition, the condition that reflexives must have antecedents, and the Thematic Hierarchy Condition.[10]

[10] I would like to mention three pieces of work that have appeared since this book first went to press. A case where the cyclic rule of reflexivization proposed here predicts an incorrect result has been pointed out in S. I. Harada and Sakio Saito, "A Non-Source for Reflexives," *Linguistic Inquiry* 2(4): 546–557. However, their alternative theory of reflexivation, a mixed transformational and interpretive approach, completely ignores the difficulties of the picture-noun constructions we have discussed here in detail. I do not know if there is a simple solution to this apparent counterexample.

Further examples of coreference violating condition (A.a) of (3.338), parallel to those discussed in section 4.12, have been pointed out in Edward Witten, "Pronominalization and Sloppy Identity," unpublished, and in Adrian Akmajian, "Getting Tough," *Linguistic Inquiry*, 3(3): 373–377. These examples show that the solution proposed in section 4.12 is not general enough; however, I do not care to speculate here what the correct solution might be. Witten's paper, incidentally, contains much else of importance to the theory of coreference.

CHAPTER FIVE

Coreference and the Complement System

5.1 The Problem

One of the more thoroughly explored problems in English syntax is the system of sentential complements to verbs. Rosenbaum (1967) gives an extensive range of data and proposes rules to account for most of it. The rules have subsequently been refined by, among others, G. Lakoff (1966), Ross (1967a), Kiparsky and Kiparsky (1968), and Perlmutter (1971).

There has been general agreement that there are three basic transformational processes in the complement system: (1) extraposition of the complement, relating sentences such as (5.1) and (5.2):

(5.1) That Irving is indisposed doesn't bother anyone.
(5.2) It doesn't bother anyone that Irving is indisposed.

(2) raising of the complement subject (also called *It*-replacement or pronoun replacement), relating derived forms like (5.4) to underlying structures like (5.3):

(5.3) Bill believes [$_s$for the doctor to have examined Max]$_s$
(5.4) Bill believes the doctor to have examined Max.

and (3) complement subject deletion (also called equi-NP deletion), relating derived forms like (5.6) to underlying forms like (5.5):

(5.5) Fred attempted [$_s$for Fred to escape the snark]$_s$
(5.6) Fred attempted to escape the snark.

These accounts of the complement system are all incompatible with the interpretive theory of coreference presented in the last chapter. The fundamental problem is that the rule of complement subject deletion requires identity of referential indices in its structural description. The interpretive theory, however, claims that coreference is a semantic property and hence that no syntactic rule can be contingent on it. In order to maintain the interpretive theory it will therefore be necessary to treat complement subject deletion so that the referential identity is handled within the semantic component.

This chapter will explore the consequences of an interpretive theory of the complement subject. In section 5.2 we will state the rule, illustrating it with a number of examples in section 5.3. Section 5.4 will demonstrate that the complement subject rule generalizes nearly completely with the interpretive rules for pronominalization and reflexivization developed in Chapter 4. The following three sections show how the interpretive rule deals with various well-known derivations involving deleted complement subjects. The rest of the chapter is devoted to the *control problem*, the problem of determining which NP in the main clause is the antecedent of the complement subject on the basis of information in the main verb. It will be shown that the choice of antecedent is determined from the interaction of two independent factors in the lexical entry of the verb, networks of coreference and assignment of responsibility.

5.2 An Interpretive Rule

Let us try to state an interpretive rule for the complement subject. To avoid complications due to complement subject raising, we will first use verbs whose complements do not undergo subject raising, for example, *wait*, *hope*, and *pray*.[1]

(5.7)   Bill hoped to be able to leave soon.

(5.8)   Bill hoped for Sam to be able to leave soon.

(5.9)   Bill hoped for Bill to be able to leave soon.

(5.10) Bill hoped for him to be able to leave soon.

We observe that only when the complement subject is absent on the surface (5.7) is it interpreted as coreferential with the subject of the main clause. In particular, if the complement subject is morphologically identical to the main clause subject (5.9), or if the complement subject is an appropriate pronoun (5.10), it is still distinct from the main clause subject.

The rule apparently looks rather like reflexivization. In reflexivization, we recall, there is given a particular structural relation between two NPs,

---

[1] We see that they do not undergo subject raising because of bad passives like **Bill was prayed for by Max to go*; contrast this with *Bill was believed by Max to have gone*. The simplest explanation of this difference seems to be that the passive can move only noun phrases dominated by the VP of the main clause (with a possible intervening PP), and that *Bill* is still dominated by the complement S node in the *pray* sentence, but has been raised in the *believe* sentence. Note that an NP object of *pray* does passivize: *Bill's recovery was prayed for by everyone.*

NP^1 and NP^2. Assuming that the structural relations hold, the NPs are marked in the table as coreferential if and only if NP^2 is reflexive. In the case of complement subjects the structural relation is that obtaining between the complement subject and some NP in the clause above it; the effect of the rule is then similar. The problem of deciding which NPs in the upper clause are permissible as coreferents of the complement subject is called the *control problem*; the NP selected as coreferent is called the *controller* (these terms are introduced in Postal 1970b). We will discuss the control problem in sections 5.8–5.12; for the moment, we will merely say that the complement subject is coreferential with some NP in the upper clause.

What is the nature of the NP in the complement subject when it is interpreted as coreferential with the controller NP? It clearly cannot be any normal pronoun or NP, as we can see from (5.7)–(5.10). One solution might involve a special pro-NP (call it DEL) which has no phonological interpretation and serves the sole semantic function of acting as a coreferential subject complement. Then the interpretive rule for complement subjects would be something like (5.11).

(5.11) (Complement Subject Rule, first approximation)
      Enter in the table:
      NP^1 α coref NP^2 if NP^2 is the subject of a *for-to* or *poss-ing* complement, NP^1 is in the main clause of the present cycle, and NP^2 is α equal to DEL.
      OBLIGATORY

In addition to this rule, we will need a well-formedness condition, rejecting any reading in which there remains an uninterpreted DEL. This pair of rules is formally similar to the pair of rules needed for reflexivization.

To see how (5.11) works, let us apply it to (5.7)–(5.10). In (5.7), the deep structure is *Bill hoped for DEL to be able to leave soon*. On the first cycle, nothing happens; on the second cycle, *Bill* is eligible to be NP^1 and DEL to be NP^2. Since NP^2 is equal to DEL, (5.11) enters *Bill* coref *DEL* in the table of coreference. In (5.8)–(5.10), *Bill* is again NP^1, but NP^2 is *Sam, Bill* or *him*. Since NP^2 is unequal to DEL, (5.11) enters $Bill - \text{coref} \begin{Bmatrix} Sam \\ Bill \\ him \end{Bmatrix}$ in the table of coreference.

(5.11) is problematic in that it requires a special pro-NP which is required nowhere else in the grammar, and which never appears on the surface. This pro-form violates the Extended Lexical Hypothesis. One might raise a further objection to DEL: suppose that it were desirable to extend the interpretive theory to other systems of rules presently handled with deletion transformations having identity conditions. For a consistent approach, one would want to use the same formalism for all of the interpretive rules. The use of a special pro-form such as DEL presupposes that the missing elements in the surface form a constituent. This is not always the case; for example, a comparative construction such as (5.12) has a missing subject and verb after *than*.

(5.12) Stanley smokes more pot than tobacco.

I do not intend to propose an interpretive analysis of comparatives at this point, but it would be nice to have an interpretive theory of complement subjects that leaves open the possibility of doing comparatives with similar mechanisms.

One general mechanism that will *not* work is to simply have the syntax generate only the nodes that appear in the surface, and to have the semantic rules conjure up the missing nodes. Ross (1969b) shows convincingly that such an approach inevitably leads to a totally unconstrained base component that can generate arbitrary phrase-markers. This is clearly an undesirable result.

Chomsky has suggested (personal communication) a more satisfactory approach. Suppose that the phrase structure rules and lexical insertion are optional, so that potential deep structures can be generated containing nonterminal nodes at the end of one or more branches (empty nodes, symbolized by Δ). It was assumed in *Aspects of the Theory of Syntax* that such structures would block at the end of the transformations. Observe, however, that these structures would be semantically ill-formed, since no semantic information would be available for empty nodes. I propose that the semantic blocking rather than surface structure blocking be taken as the criterion for rejecting empty nodes. Suppose then that some rules of semantic interpretation give readings to empty nodes (or combinations of them) under certain conditions. Then the semantic blocking of an empty node can be prevented, just in case it is interpreted by one of these rules.

An empty node can undergo transformations like any other node. If such a node is either deleted or else interpreted by convention as phonologically null, without blocking, a legal surface structure will result. If, however, an empty node is not given a semantic interpretation, the sentence it is in will be semantically ill-formed.

The reader may wonder whether the introduction of empty nodes makes the concept of grammaticality totally different than previously, since strings such as *John* $[_V\Delta]$ *of the* $[_N\Delta]$ can be generated as syntactically well-formed by the base rules, and interpreted phonologically as **John of the*. However, this seems to me only a problem with the use of the term "grammaticality." By introducing empty nodes, we have not changed the considerations excluding any sentences previously generated by the grammar; we have only added a new set of phrase-markers, whose unacceptability in most cases is accounted for by an obvious semantic well-formedness condition. It is only if we insist that every crashingly unacceptable sentence is an instance of a syntactic violation that the empty node convention is counterintuitive. But there is no basis for such insistence; native speakers have no intuitions of what kind of rule a bad sentence violates.

In the interpretive theory, the semantic rules which interpret empty nodes will correspond to the transformations of the standard theory which delete items under identity. Possible examples of this kind of rule are the complement subject rule, the comparative rules, the gapping rule (cf. Ross 1967c, Jackendoff 1971a), the rule for deletion of a noun phrase in the complements of *too* and *enough*, the rule of Sluicing (Ross 1969b), and VP-deletion (cf. section 6.8).

The second approximation to the complement subject rule, then, will simply substitute Δ for DEL. All interpretive rules of this type likewise mention Δ rather than some specialized pro-form.

There is another rule besides the complement subject rule that can provide an interpretation for a Δ in a complement subject: This rule assigns to Δ the generic indefinite subject *one* just in case a generic reading is possible. This interpretation can be detected by the use of the reflexive *oneself*, as in *Scratching oneself can be painful*.

5.3 Examples
In this section we explore the interpretation possibilities of several examples.

(5.13) Mary told Bill that helping herself could be difficult.

In the deep structure, the subject of *helping* is Δ. Assume for the present (we will show it shortly) that the complement subject rule is cyclic. On the first cycle, Δ *helping herself*, we get the table of coreference Δ *coref herself* by the application of the reflexivization rule (p. 176). On the next cycle, Δ *helping herself could be difficult*, no coreference rules apply, since no new NPs have come into play. On the third cycle, including the entire sentence, the complement subject rule applies to establish the antecedent of Δ, and pronominalization applies to establish the antecedent of *herself*. Finally, the noncoreferentiality rule marks all remaining pairs of NPs noncoreferential. (5.13) thus yields the following possible tables.

(5.14) Δ   coref *herself*   Reflexivization
  Mary   coref Δ   Complement subject
  Mary   coref *herself*   Pronominalization, case (C.b) p. 176
  Bill   − coref Δ   ⎫
  Bill   − coref *herself*   ⎬ Noncoreferentiality rule
  Bill   − coref *Mary*   ⎭

(5.15) Δ   coref *herself*   Reflexivization
  Bill   coref Δ   Complement subject
  Mary   coref *herself*   Pronominalization
  Mary − coref Δ   ⎫
  Bill − coref *herself*   ⎬ Noncoreferentiality rule
  Bill − coref *Mary*   ⎭

(5.16) Δ   coref *herself*   Similar derivation
  Mary   coref Δ
  Bill   coref *herself*
  Mary − coref *herself*
  Bill − coref Δ
  Bill − coref *Mary*

(5.17) Δ   coref *herself*   Similar derivation
  Bill   coref Δ
  Bill   coref *herself*
  Mary − coref *herself*
  Mary − coref Δ
  Bill − coref *Mary*

Of these four tables, we can readily verify by inspection that only (5.14) is internally consistent. So the only correct interpretation of (5.13) is that in which *Mary* is understood as the subject of *help*. Similarly, in *Mary told Bill that helping himself could be difficult*, the subject of *help* must be understood as *Bill*.

In *Mary told Bill that helping oneself could be difficult*, suppose that the complement subject rule marks Δ coreferential with either *Mary* or *Bill*. An internally consistent table would require *oneself* to be coreferential with *Mary* or *Bill* too. But *oneself* may have only a generic indefinite antecedent. Thus the only acceptable reading comes from not interpreting Δ by the complement subject rule at all, but by assigning it the reading *one*.

In (5.18) there are five possible consistent readings.

(5.18) Mary told Bill that helping him could be difficult.

First assume that the pronoun is not marked coreferential with any NP in the sentence, so that it denotes someone mentioned earlier in the discourse. Then Δ can be interpreted as *Mary*, *Bill*, or *one*: the possibilities in (5.19) are all consistent for (5.18).

(5.19) a. Δ   − coref *him*   Reflexivization
        Bill   coref Δ   Complement subject
        Mary − coref Δ   ⎫
        Bill   − coref *him*   ⎬   Noncoreferentiality rule
        Mary − coref *him* ⎬
        Bill   − coref *Mary* ⎭

     b. Δ   − coref *him*   Similar derivation
        Mary   coref Δ
        Bill   − coref Δ
        Bill   − coref *him*
        Mary − coref *him*
        Bill   − coref *Mary*

     c. Δ   − coref *him*   Reflexivization
        Bill   − coref Δ   ⎫
        Mary − coref Δ   ⎪
        Bill   − coref *him*   ⎬   Noncoreferentiality rule
        Mary − coref *him* ⎪
        Bill   − coref *Mary* ⎭

In (5.19a), Bill is helping someone else; in (5.19b) Mary is helping someone else; and in (5.19c), *one* is helping someone else.

Alternatively, suppose that pronominalization marks *him* and *Bill* coreferential. Of the three possibilities (5.20) for the complement subject rule, only two are consistent:

(5.20) a. Δ $-$ coref *him*   Reflexivization
      Bill   coref *him*   Pronominalization
      Bill   coref Δ Complement subject
      Mary $-$ coref Δ ⎫
      Mary $-$ coref *him* ⎬ Noncoreferentiality rule
      Bill $-$ coref *Mary* ⎭

   b. Δ $-$ coref *him*   Similar derivation
      Bill   coref *him*
      Mary   coref Δ
      Bill $-$ coref Δ
      Mary $-$ coref *him*
      Bill $-$ coref *Mary*

   c. Δ $-$ coref *him*   Reflexivization
      Bill   coref *him*   Pronominalization
      Mary $-$ coref Δ ⎫
      Bill $-$ coref Δ ⎬ Noncoreferentiality rule
      Mary $-$ coref *him* ⎬
      Bill $-$ coref *Mary* ⎭

(5.20a) is an inconsistent interpretation because it asserts that *Bill* and *him* are the same person, yet Δ and *him* are distinct and Δ and *Bill* are the same. Thus the only possible readings are with *Mary* or *one* helping Bill.

One further sentence of this type is of interest.

(5.21) Mary told Bill that helping themselves could be difficult.

Presumably this possibility arises by marking Δ and *themselves* coreferential with both *Mary* and *Bill*, an option which has so far been overlooked, and which is impossible in a transformational theory of coreference.[2] A proper account of this sentence would involve the analysis of set and individual coreference to which I have alluded several times earlier. Since that issue is being left aside here, we will not go any further into this example.

Given an account of the complement subject rule even in the rather rudimentary stage we have arrived at, we can also do Ross's crucial example in "On the Cyclic Nature of English Pronominalization" (Ross 1967b), in which *John* and *him* cannot be the same person.

(5.22) Realizing that John was sick bothered him.

This has the following structure, in the present theory.

(5.23)

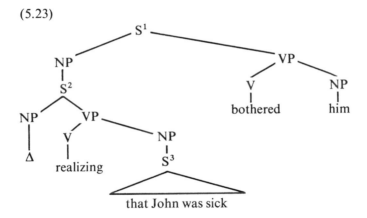

[2]Dougherty (1969) gives many examples of pronominal forms referring simultaneously to two NPs which together do not form a conjoined NP. He shows the myriad difficulties encountered in accounting for these sentences in a transformational theory of pronominalization. Cases like (5.21) have been cited (e.g. in McCawley (1968a)) as evidence that plurals like *themselves* must sometimes be derived transformationally from conjoined NPs, in this case *herself and himself*. As Anderson (1970) has pointed out, this approach has its dubious points. Both (i) and (ii) could undergo conversion to (iii).

I saw John and Mary. $\begin{cases} \text{(i) He and she} \\ \text{(ii) She and he} \\ \text{(iii) They} \end{cases}$ were eating an apple and an orange, respectively.

Thus if the reduction transformation exists, we would incorrectly predict (iii) to be ambiguous between (i) and (ii). The phrase structure-interpretive approach to *respectively* constructions proposed in Dougherty (1970) seems to hold more promise.

On the S^3 cycle, nothing of interest happens. On the S^2 cycle, pronominalization cannot apply between Δ and *John*, so they are eventually marked distinct by the noncoreferentiality rule (on the final cycle). On the S^1 cycle, the complement subject rule applies, marking Δ coreferential with *him*. Now if pronominalization also applies, between *John* and *him*, a paradoxical reading will result, since we will have formed a table of coreference:

(5.24) *John* coref *him*

    him coref Δ

    Δ $-$coref *John*

Thus the only alternative is not to apply pronominalization between *John* and *him*, so that they will be marked distinct by the noncoreferentiality rule. This gives the correct reading for (5.22).

On the other hand, *John* and *him* can be the same person in (5.25).

(5.25) Bill's realizing that John was sick bothered him.

In this sentence, application of the complement subject rule on the S^1 cycle results in *him* and *Bill* being marked noncoreferential, because the rule is an α rule. Therefore *him* and *John* can be marked coreferential by pronominalization without producing a strange reading like (5.24).[3]

[3]Lakoff (1968b) gives examples that purport to show that the principle of the cycle cannot handle all cases like (5.22) and that it therefore must be replaced by an ad hoc constraint on a last-cyclic pronominalization rule. The first two examples are based on the last-cyclic nature of the rules of extraposition from NP and *wh*-preposing; we disposed of these in sections 4.5.2 and 4.5.5. Lakoff's third argument is based on the assumption that in (i), *Mary* is understood as the subject of *realizing*; he is trying to construct an example which behaves like Ross's but for which Ross's argument will not work.

(i) *Realizing that John had cancer seemed to him to have been bothering Mary.

But Lakoff's assumption about the subject of *realizing* seems false to me; I can't find any subject for *realizing*, whether or not *John* and *him* are coreferential. This can be more readily seen from the simpler example (ii), which involves no pronouns at all.

(ii) *Realizing that John had cancer was bothering Mary.

Note that if *the realization* is substituted for *realizing* in these sentences, they are acceptable, and in (i) *John* and *him* can be coreferential. The sentences can also be fixed up by substituting *bother* for *have been bothering*. Thus the violation in (i) has to do with something like sequence of tenses, and not at all with pronominalization. This redeems Ross's argument, at least for the interpretive theory.

5.4 The Generality of the Complement Subject Rule, Reflexivization, and Pronominalization

This section will show that the complement subject rule shares most aspects of its structural description and application conventions with reflexivization, and therefore that it is of utmost importance that the grammar collapse the rules together and with pronominalization. There are of course two things that will not generalize: the complement subject rule concerns NP^2 in subject position that is α equal to Δ, but reflexivization concerns NP^2 in object position that is α reflexive. However, we have already seen one generalization: both rules are α rules, obligatory when NP^2 is on the right.

Two other generalizations are only slightly less obvious. First, in the complement subject rule, the position of NP^1 has been specified as *in the main clause of the present cycle*, which is also one of the conditions on reflexivization. Second, the general pronominalization condition NP^2 *does not both precede and command* NP^1 can easily be seen to hold for the complement subject rule. If NP^2 does not command NP^1, but is in a lower clause, the complement subject rule can take place in either direction.

(5.26) Max tried to sock Harry.
(5.27) Socking Harry disturbs Max.

Under the conditions of the Complement Subject Rule, NP^2 must be the subject of a *for-to* or *poss-ing* complement, and NP^1 must be in the main clause of the present cycle. Thus if NP^2 commands NP^1, there is only one possible position for NP^1 in which the rule could apply: the object of the complement. Unless the condition NP^2 *does not both precede and command* NP^1 is added, we might expect the complement subject rule to take place on the first cycle of (5.28), marking Δ coreferential with *Bill*.

(5.28) $[_s$for Δ to love Bill$]_s$ would be hard for me.

Since this reading obviously does not exist, the pronominalization condition can be added to the complement subject rule. In fact, this reading of (5.28) can be eliminated by the normal obligatory application of reflexivization, which would mark Δ and *Bill* distinct. However, the fact that the complement subject rule is consistent with the pronominalization condition (i.e. yields no counterexamples to it) is still an important generalization.

Like reflexivization, the complement subject rule is obligatory when NP^2 is on the right but optional when NP^2 is on the left. (*John* and *him* to be coreferential in the following examples.)

(5.29) John prayed to win the prize. ⎫
(5.30) *John prayed for him to win the prize. ⎬ forwards

(5.31) To lose the game would disturb John. ⎫
(5.32) ?For him to lose the game would disturb John. ⎬ backwards
(5.33) For John to lose the game would disturb him. ⎭

This paradigm is exactly parallel to that for reflexivization; compare to these examples from section 4.7.

(5.34) John saw a picture of himself in the post office. ⎫
(5.35) *John saw a picture of him in the post office. ⎬ forwards

(5.36) The picture of himself in the post office enraged John. ⎫
(5.37) The picture of him in the post office enraged John. ⎬ backwards
(5.38) The picture of John in the post office enraged him. ⎭

The crucial cases in the cyclic analysis of reflexivization were the picture-noun examples. These examples showed that reflexivization always chooses as antecedent an NP on the lowest possible cycle. Thus we distinguished *John saw a picture of himself* and *John saw Mary's picture of himself* by the fact that *Mary* on the lower NP cycle has to serve as antecedent for the reflexive. On the other hand, the assignment of an antecedent can be put off for several cycles, if no available NPs are forthcoming: in *John believes that there is a picture of himself in the post office* reflexivization cannot take place until the third cycle.

Although most discussion of the complement subject rule in the literature deals only with NP^1 in the clause immediately above the deleted complement subject, NP^1 may be higher, a possibility that was pointed out to me by John Grinder. In (5.39) there are three cycles.

(5.39) $[_{S_1}$Max finds $[_{S_2}$it to be difficult $[_{S_3}$to shave himself.$]]]$

On the second cycle, the domain is *for it to be difficult* $[_{S_3} \Delta$ to shave himself$]$ which presents no possible antecedent for Δ. Only in the third cycle does the antecedent *Max* appear. Our earlier example (5.13) is similar.

(5.13) Mary told Bill that helping herself could be difficult.

Cases with more intervening cycles can be constructed: (5.40) has (at least) four cycles.

(5.40) $[_{S^1}$ The fact $[_{S^2}$ that it tends $[_{S^3}$ to seem difficult $[_{S^4}$ to shave himself $]]]$ annoys Max.$]$

If two possible antecedents appear on different cycles, the one in the lower cycle is always chosen.

$$(5.41) \quad \left[_{S^1} \text{Max believes} \left[_{S^2} \text{that Mary finds it} \left[_{S^3} \text{to be difficult} \right.\right.\right.$$

$$\left.\left.\left[_{S^4} \text{to shave} \begin{Bmatrix} \text{herself} \\ \text{*himself} \\ \text{Bill} \end{Bmatrix} \right]\right]\right]\right]$$

The reflexive clearly indicates the identity of Δ, but with *Bill* in the same position, Δ still designates *Mary*.

Thus we see that the complement subject rule is of the same cyclic character as reflexivization. The conditions can be captured by adding the condition to the complement subject rule NP^2 *does not appear in the right-hand side of the table.*

Recall the consequences of the cyclic solution for reflexivization. It was shown in section 4.7 that although the interpretive theory of coreference can express this solution with the usual kind of α-rule, a transformational theory will need a rule that introduced the rule feature $[-$reflexivization rule$]$ in case of nonidentity. Thus if the cyclic solution is correct, the interpretive solution must be preferred, since it avoids the need for introducing rule features by means of transformations. Now we have seen the identical solution arise for the complement subject rule; an identical argument must hold.[4]

[4] One might imagine handling these cases by the use of something like Rosenbaum's "minimal distance principle." The distance principle does not work within simple clauses, as will be shown in section 5.10. Thus its use will have to be restricted to NPs in different clauses. Since the complement subject rule is cyclic, the distance principle will have to be applied in the following way. If, say on the second cycle, an NP is encountered that is not identical to the complement subject, nothing happens. Then, if on the third cycle, a possible antecedent is discovered, the distance principle will throw out the derivation because of the intervening nonidentical NP. Instead of a transformation introducing a rule feature, we will have a transformational filter with a rather strange condition.

This way of stating the complement subject rule explains very simply an otherwise ad hoc condition noticed in Postal (1970a). Postal is dealing with sentences like (5.42), with missing complement subjects in both subordinate clauses.

(5.42) Shaving oneself is like torturing oneself.

He observes that the complement subjects can be coreferential with an NP in the next higher clause.[5]

(5.43) Walt believes that shaving himself is like torturing himself.
(5.44) It strikes Harry that shaving himself is like torturing himself.

Then he observes that in (5.45) the missing subjects must be identical to the object of *remind*, not to the NP (*Fred*) in the higher clause.

(5.45) Fred thinks that shaving himself reminds Bill of torturing himself.

Postal attempts to explain these facts by stating a new constraint, that the missing subject must be coreferential with an NP two sentences up; then he disposes of (5.45) by supposing an internal structure for *remind* involving an embedded clause (the existence of this structure being what Postal is trying to prove).

However, the facts are explained with no special apparatus in the present system. In (5.43) and (5.44) there is no NP on the second cycle that can serve as an antecedent for Δ. Hence an antecedent is not chosen until the final cycle. In (5.45), however, *remind* allows an NP object in addition to the two clauses; this NP, encountered on the second cycle, obligatorily becomes the antecedent of Δ. The contrast of (5.43) and (5.45) is thus exactly parallel to the picture-noun pair *John saw a picture of himself* and *John saw Bill's picture of himself*. Postal's conclusion is reached only because he has stated the conditions on complement subject interpretation incorrectly.

Once Δ appears on the right-hand side of the table, we must allow it to undergo normal pronominalization, so that we can produce the complete table (5.46) for (5.47).

---

[5]Postal claims only that coreferentiality is possible under a verb of saying or thinking: *Max says that shaving himself is like torturing himself*. But in fact any verb taking an appropriate information clause as complement will do, for example *Max makes shaving himself like torturing himself by using a penknife*.

(5.46) [Ted thinks [that he should try [Δ to win the race.]]]

(5.47) *he*   coref Δ   Complement subject rule, 2nd cycle

   Ted coref *he*   Pronominalization, 3rd cycle

   Ted coref Δ   Pronominalization, 3rd cycle

This is exactly parallel to the cases where reflexives have to undergo pronominalization after they have been assigned antecedents, for example (5.48), with table (5.49).

(5.48) Max lost his picture of himself.

(5.49) *his*   coref *himself*   Reflexivization, 1st cycle

   Max coref *his*   Pronominalization, 2nd cycle

   Max coref *himself*   Pronominalization, 2nd cycle

Consider next the (unstated) restriction having to do with clefts and *wh*-questions mentioned in section 4.14. Here are the relevant examples from Chapter 4.

(5.50) It was John who bit his dog.

(5.51) *It was John who his dog bit.

(5.52) Who talked about his mother?

(5.53) *Who did his mother talk about?

(5.54) It was John who saw a picture of himself.

(5.55) *It was John who a picture of himself startled.

(5.56) Who saw a picture of himself?

(5.57) *Who did a picture of himself fall on?

The pronouns and reflexives are good only if their antecedent has been preposed from subject position, not from object position. Exactly the same restriction holds for complement subjects.

(5.58) It was John who liked socking Harry.

(5.59) *It was John who socking Harry amused.

(5.60) Who likes socking Harry?

(5.61) *Who does socking Harry amuse?

Finally, there is the condition which prohibits backwards pronominalization and reflexivization to inanimate antecedents. It is hard to find a relevant example for the complement subject rule, since most verbs taking complement clauses have animate subjects. I will assume the condition to hold vacuously. This exhausts the set of conditions we have stated on the reflexivization rule; all of them generalize to complement subjects as well.

Postal (1970b) gives some further arguments showing the similarity of the complement subject rule and pronominalization. The most interesting examples are cases in which an indefinite NP and a complement subject on its left cannot be coreferents. (All following examples from Postal 1970b, section V.B).

(5.62) *Finding out Greta was a vampire worried somebody.
(5.63) *Discovering that their daughters were pregnant worried some old ladies.
(5.64) *Kissing was fun for some kids.
(Unstressed *some* in all these sentences.)

Contrast these with the acceptable sentences below, where the complement subject is distinct from the object of the main clause.

(5.65) Bill's finding out that Greta was a vampire worried somebody.
(5.66) My discovery that their daughters were pregnant worried some old ladies.
(5.67) Tony and Betty's kissing was fun for some kids.

The same paradigms seem to hold for backwards pronominalization to indefinites: contrast (5.68)–(5.69), with anaphoric pronouns, to (5.70)–(5.71), without them.

(5.68) *The man who lost it$_i$ needs to find something$_i$.
(5.69) *It was their$_i$ strength that made some gorillas$_i$ famous. (unstressed *some* again)
(5.70) The man who lost the camel needs to find something.
(5.71) It was my strength that made some gorillas famous.

That the conditions are the same is further borne out by derived nominal constructions, in which complement subject deletion is optional (at least in Postal's dialect—I'm not sure about mine).

(5.72) His$_i$ realization that you knew Greta disturbed Tony$_i$.

(5.73) The realization that you knew Greta disturbed Tony.

In neither case can the object of the main clause be indefinite. (Capitals denote stress.)

(5.74) *His$_i$ realization that the Earth was exploding WORRIED some-body$_i$.

(5.75) *The realization that the Earth was exploding WORRIED some-body.

Some more similar examples:

(5.76) My discovery that Johnson was a puppet scared some congressmen.

(5.77) Schwarz's realization that God was dead didn't WORRY anybody.

(5.78) $\left\{ \begin{array}{l} \text{*Their} \\ \text{*The} \end{array} \right\}$ discovery that Johnson was a puppet SCARED some

congressmen. (where the congressmen discovered it)

(5.79) $\left\{ \begin{array}{l} \text{*His}_i \\ \text{* The} \end{array} \right\}$ realization that God was dead didn't WORRY anybody$_i$.

Although I don't agree entirely with Postal's data, of which (5.62)–(5.79) constitute only a small sample, it is evident that there is a correlation be-tween complement subject deletion and pronominalization constraints on indefinite NPs. In fact, the same constraint holds for reflexives in similar constructions.

(5.80) *A picture of himself fell on somebody.

There is not space here to go into the rest of Postal's examples. Suffice it to say that he has given more evidence that a theory which combines the complement subject rule and pronominalization in some interesting way is to be preferred to a theory which does not do so.

In Postal's theory, since the pronominalization transformation is non-cyclic but complement subject deletion is cyclic, it is necessary to introduce a special device called the Doom Marker, which is placed as a feature on a complement subject by a cyclic rule. Then if, in the last cycle, Doom is also marked [+Pro] by pronominalization, it can delete, producing a correct surface form. Otherwise, the derivation blocks.

There is, I believe, a fundamental metatheoretical flaw in Postal's solution. In effect, what his solution does is to circumvent the ordering of rules by use of an arbitrary, otherwise unmotivated diacritic feature: an NP is allowed to delete at the time of pronominalization just in case at some stage earlier in the derivation it satisfies a certain structural relation. Since one of the primary insights of transformational grammar is that rules are ordered, a trick to get around ordering can be seen only as a breach of the ground rules of the investigation. Even if we have no clearly articulated principle in the theory to prevent such a proposal (such a principle as is discussed for phonology in, for example, Kiparsky 1968), one would hope that there is a more interesting way of capturing the facts than Postal points out.

The interpretive theory of coreference appears potentially to have more promise. First of all, pronominalization is a cyclic rule, as is the complement subject rule, so the immediate conflict presented by Postal's theory does not arise. It remains to be shown that the complement subject rule can take place at the end of the cycle, so that whatever it shares with pronominalization and reflexivization can be collapsed into a single statement.

Assuming that the complement subject rule can be ordered at the end of the cycle (which sections 5.8–5.12 will demonstrate), we can collapse the complement subject rule with the pronominalization-reflexivization rule of Chapter 4 into the rule (5.81). I will assume, for convenience, that the relevant occurrences of Δ are designated by the features $[+\text{pro}, -\text{lexical}]$ (see Example (5.81) on the following page).

(5.81) (Pronominalization-reflexivization-complement subject)
Enter in the table:

$$\text{NP}^1 \; \alpha \; \text{coref} \begin{bmatrix} \text{NP}^2 \\ +\text{pro} \end{bmatrix} \text{if}$$

(A) a. NP² does not both precede and command NP¹;
   b. if NP¹ is inanimate, NP² follows NP¹;
   c. restrictions to account for preposed NPs;
   d. if NP¹ is indefinite, NP² follows NP¹
      (Postal's constraint)

and either

(B) a. NP² does not appear in the right-hand side of the table;
   b. either

      (1) NP² is [α refl] and is dominated by $\overline{\text{N}}$ or VP

      or

      (2) NP² is [−α lexical] and the subject of a *for-to* or *poss-ing*
          complement;
   c. NP¹ is in the main clause relative to the present cycle;
   d. if NP¹ precedes NP², rule is OBLIGATORY

or

(C) either

   a. NP² is $\begin{bmatrix} -\text{refl} \\ +\text{lexical} \end{bmatrix}$
   or

   b. NP² appears in the right-hand side of the table

The general form of the structural description can be seen more clearly in
the outline form (5.82).

(5.82) Enter in the table:

$$NP^1 \; \alpha \; coref \begin{bmatrix} NP^2 \\ +pro \end{bmatrix} if$$

(A) Conditions common to pronominalization, reflexivization, and complement subject

and either

(B) Conditions common to reflexivization and complement subject
   (b) (1) Condition specific to reflexivization
      (2) Condition specific to complement subject,

or

(C) Conditions for pronominalization

All of the conditions have been illustrated in the course of this section.

An interesting observation emerges from this rule. The complement subject rule and reflexivization are identical except for the nature of NP^2 and its position in the clause. The two rules are in some sense complementary, since the complement subject rule applies to subjects and reflexivization to objects. We will see the effects of this complementarity in the next section.

5.5 Interaction of the Complement Subject Rule with Movement Transformations

We want to show that the complement subject rule can take place at the end of the cycle. Its transformational equivalent, equi-NP deletion, in fact, is usually assumed to be ordered at the beginning of the cycle. The reason for this ordering has to do with selection of the controller. In the accounts of Rosenbaum (1967) and Perlmutter (1971) it is assumed that the selection of the controller NP in the higher clause is based on structural principles— either the grammatical relations of subject and object, or something equally dependent on the structure, like Rosenbaum's distance principle (see section 5.10 for more discussion of this). It is important that these structural relations be captured before transformations start distorting the main clause, because of pairs like (5.83)–(5.84).

(5.83) Bill forced John to wash the dishes.
(5.84) John was forced by Bill to wash the dishes.

If the controller is selected on the basis of grammatical relations, i.e., *objec*
in this case, it must be the *deep* object in (5.84), since there is no surface
object, and the controller is the surface subject. If the controller is selected
on the basis of a distance principle, then it must be the underlying structure
distance, since in (5.84) *Bill* is in the VP and hence nearer to the complement than *John*.

We will show, however, in section 5.11 that probably a better principle
for selecting the controller NP can be based on the thematic relations intro
duced in Chapter 2. Thematic relations are not altered by transformations
since they are properties of the semantic reading which correlate to the
deep structure grammatical relations. Hence the selection of controller
does not depend on whether or not transformations have distorted the
main clause, and examples like (5.83)–(5.84) do not argue against ordering
the complement subject rule at the end of the cycle along with pronominalization.

The one distortion we will still have to worry about is the one that move
the complement subject itself, the complement subject raising transformation (often called *It*–replacement). This transformation breaks up a *for-to*
complement, moving the VP of the complement to the end of the VP of the
main clause, and raising the complement subject to the position originally
occupied by the complement. Thus, for example, (5.85) becomes (5.86) by
subject raising.

(5.85)

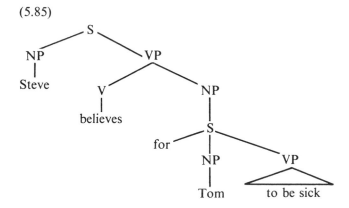

(5.86)

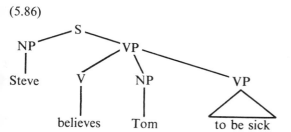

Various ways of accomplishing this change have been proposed (Rosenbaum, Kiparsky and Kiparsky, Lakoff), but for this discussion all that is relevant is the difference in structure due to the disappearance of the S node.

How will raising affect the interpretation of Δ? The complement subject rule applies to Δ only if it is in complement subject position. But inadvertently, raising may be applied to a complement containing Δ. Contrast the two derived structures (5.87) and (5.88).

(5.87) $[_{S^1}$John expects $[_{S^2}\Delta$ to go$]_{S^2}]_{S^1}$
(5.88) $[_{S^1}$John expects Δ $[_{VP}$to go$]]_{S^1}$

In (5.87) raising has not applied, and the complement subject rule can operate properly on the S^1 cycle. In (5.88) raising has applied, and now the complement subject rule is not applicable on the S^1 cycle. Therefore, if this is the end of the derivation, the sentence must be rejected as semantically ill-formed since there is an uninterpreted empty node present.

However, if (5.88) is embedded in another clause, as in (5.89), the derivation can be saved.

(5.89) $[_{S^1}$Sam hoped $[_{S^2}$for John to expect Δ $[_{VP}$to go.$]]]$

Assume that (5.89) is a stage in the S^2 cycle, after subject raising. Then the passive can take place in S^2 to form (5.90).

(5.90) $[_{S^1}$Sam hoped $[_{S^2}$for Δ to be expected by John $[_{VP}$to go.$]]]$

Now on the S^1 cycle, the complement subject rule can mark Δ coreferential with *Sam*, giving the correct reading of (5.91).

(5.91) Sam hoped to be expected by John to go.

Although Δ has moved around in the tree quite a bit by the time its antecedent is established, it can still be identified in the semantic reading as the subject of *go*, since this is a property of the reading which is identified in the deep structure.

To point out the independence of coreference relations from grammatical relations, let us see what happens if (5.87), which has not undergone raising, is embedded.

(5.92) $[_{S^1}$Sam hoped $[_{S^2}$for John to expect $[_{S^3}\Delta$ to go.$]]]$

This time, the complement subject rule applies in the S^2 cycle, making *John* the antecedent of Δ. Then in S^1 the rule marks *Sam* and *John* distinct. Thus we get the correct reading for (5.93).

(5.93) Sam hoped for John to expect to go.

The difference in meaning between (5.91) and (5.93) is purely one of coreference, and hence not represented in the deep structure, which says only that Δ is the subject of *go*. The difference in coreference is produced by the application of the optional rules raising and passive; if only raising applies (if, for example (5.89) is the final derived structure), then still another variant is produced, this one without a well-formed semantic reading.

How does the reflexivization rule interact with the rules we have just discussed? First of all, there is the fairly trivial observation that a reflexive can be marked coreferential with Δ. We have used this fact several times already in this chapter.

(5.94) Frank tried $[\Delta$ to scratch himself$]$

More interesting things happen if we put a reflexive in place of Δ in examples like (5.87)–(5.93). Take the analogues of (5.87)–(5.88), which differ by the application of raising.

(5.95) John expects $[_S$himself to like Bill$]$
(5.96) John expects himself $[_{VP}$to like Bill$]$

What happens to these on the lower cycle? The reflexivization rule does apply in this cycle, with *himself* as NP^1 (the antecedent) and *Bill* as NP^2, making the table entry *himself* — coref *Bill*. However, *himself* does not yet appear on the right-hand side of the table, so it is still without an antecedent: recall the exact statement of condition (B.a) of the rule (5.81), which we use here crucially.

On the upper cycle, if *himself* is not raised (5.95), the complement subject rule applies, marking it noncoreferential with *John*. But this leaves *himself* without an antecedent, and so the reading is ill-formed. On the other hand, if *himself* is raised (5.96), the reflexive rule applies, marking *himself* coreferential with *John* to give a good reading.

If, however, the passive takes place on the second cycle of (5.96), *himself* will be moved into subject position, forming (5.97), and the reflexivization rule again cannot find it an antecedent.

(5.97) Himself is expected by John [to like Bill]

But if (5.96) is embedded,

(5.98) [$_{S^1}$Sam believed [$_{S^2}$for John to expect himself [$_{VP}$to like Bill]]]

then passive is applied in S^2,

(5.99) [$_{S^1}$Sam believed [$_{S^2}$for himself to be expected by John [$_{VP}$to like Bill]]]

we can save the day by raising *himself* on the S^1 cycle.

(5.100) [$_{S^1}$Sam believed himself [$_{VP}$to be expected by John [$_{VP}$to like Bill]]]

Now reflexivization can apply on the S^1 cycle, marking *Sam* as the antedent of *himself*, giving the correct interpretation of (5.100).

Again in the case of reflexivization, we see the independence of coreference relations from deep structure grammatical relations. For if (5.98) does not undergo any further transformations, *himself*, the deep subject of *like*, will be coreferential with *John*. But by application of passive and raising, *himself* comes to be coreferential with *Sam*, though it is still understood as the subject of *like*.

The discussion of examples illustrates clearly the complementarity of the complement subject rule and reflexivization. We have followed Δ and *himself* through derivations involving cyclic iterations of raising and passive, sometimes getting good sentences, sometimes bad ones. Those acceptable sentences containing *himself* are bad if Δ is substituted, and vice versa. This is because a reflexive can get a good interpretation only in *object* position, and Δ only in *subject* position.

Note also that in this discussion we make crucial use of the asymmetry of condition (B.a) of the coreference rule, (5.81) i.e. that a reflexive or Δ counts as having been marked only if it has served as NP^2 in the rule. This is important just for the case where a reflexive is generated as a deep subject, as in (5.95), where we want it to be interpreted on the following cycle, by which time it has become an object, as in (5.96).

We have also made crucial use of this condition in finding coreferents of complement subjects, in similar situations. In sentences like (5.94), the first cycle makes an entry Δ coref *himself*. Since Δ is not yet on the right-hand side of the table, the complement subject rule can still apply on the second cycle. But once the complement subject rule has applied once, it cannot apply to the same occurrence of Δ on a subsequent cycle.

To further see the force of this condition, recall that the complement subject rule can apply to two NPs simultaneously on one cycle, receiving a plural interpretation:

(5.101) Mary told Bill that helping themselves could be difficult. (= 5.21)

But if the two NPs are on different cycles, such an interpretation is impossible, as predicted by this condition.

(5.102) *Max says that shaving themselves reminds Bill of torturing themselves.

Only *himself* is appropriate here, referring to *Bill*, the lower NP.

Incidentally, it should be noticed that the Thematic Hierarchy Condition (section 4.10) causes no difficulties with these raised reflexives. Recall that in the final form of the condition (section 4.10.5), it applies to the thematic relations defined by the verb of the clause in which reflexivization takes place. A raised reflexive, having no thematic status in its new clause, is considered lowest on the hierarchy. Hence whatever the thematic relation of the subject, reflexivization will be permitted. Furthermore, passives such as (5.103) are prohibited by the condition,

(5.103) *Tom is believed by himself to have hit Norman.

since *Tom* comes from the lower clause and therefore is lower on the hierarchy than *himself*.

5.6 Reflexives, Raising, and Pruning—More Evidence for Condition (B.a)

In the transformational account of reflexivization, the derived structure after complement subject raising poses an interesting problem. Because raising leaves only the VP dominated by the subordinate S node, the pruning convention proposed in Ross (1967a) dictates that the derived structure contain only the VP of the complement sentence attached at the right-hand end of the matrix VP, the S node having been pruned.

(5.104)

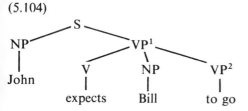

Since now VP^2 is in the same simplex sentence as the subject, we would expect the reflexivization transformation to take place, producing, for example (5.106) from (5.105).

(5.105) I expect [for Bill to examine me].
(5.106) *I expect Bill to examine myself.

The only way to stop this in the transformational theory is to somehow retain the S node above VP^2, by restricting pruning in some way that will throw the generality of pruning into doubt.

However, in the interpretive theory of reflexives, this problem does not arise. We can deal with this example much as we dealt with sentences like (5.107) and (5.108).

(5.107) *John showed Bill Mary's picture of himself. (section 4.7)
(5.108) *Who did you think stabbed yourself? (section 4.8)

(5.106) will have the underlying structure (5.109).

(5.109) I expect [for Bill to examine myself].

On the inner cycle, before the complement is broken up, *myself* and *Bill* are marked coreferential by the reflexive rule; since the reflexive rule is obligatory, the sentence is anomalous.

The problem really arises for the interpretive theory in handling the interpretation of what starts as (5.105) and ends up as (5.110).

(5.110) I expect Bill to examine me.

Why, once the complement S node has pruned, cannot the reflexive rule apply to mark *I* and *me* as noncoreferential, ruining the interpretation? The key lies in the first cycle, in which reflexivization enters *Bill* − coref *me* in the table. This marking on the first cycle prevents the structural description of reflexivization from being met on the second cycle, after the S node has pruned: condition (B.a) of rule (5.81) is not met since *me* appears on the right-hand side of the table already. Therefore the reflexive rule cannot apply in the second cycle between *I* and *me*, leaving pronominalization free to mark them coreferential, even though at this point they are in the same simplex sentence.

The interdependence of proposals on reflexivization and proposals on complement subject raising is thus as follows: the interpretive theory of reflexives is consistent with the standard complement subject-raising transformation whether or not pruning takes place. The transformational theory of reflexives, on the other hand, is consistent only with a derived structure for subject raising that retains an S node above the postposed complement VP. Such a derived structure is possible only if the pruning convention is modified in some ad hoc fashion so as to prevent the S from disappearing; the interpretive theory requires no such modification.

Note also the complete parallelism of this argument and that presented for the interaction of reflexivization with *wh*-preposing in section 4.8. There also, the pruning convention caused difficulty for the transformational theory. In that case, it could be circumvented by ordering reflexivization before *wh*-preposing, but this of course made it impossible to capture in a natural way any generalizations between pronominalization and reflexivization. In the present case, a reordering of the two is impossible, since reflexivization must follow raising to get *John believes himself to be beautiful*. Thus here the plight of the transformational theory is more acute.

It is because of condition (B.a) of the interpretive reflexivization rule combined with the fact that it is an α rule that these cases are both handled nicely. These conditions, it will be recalled, cannot be stated naturally in a transformational framework. It is cases like these that decide between the theories.

5.7 The Behavior of Plurals in Coreference Rules

Another difficulty with the standard transformational account of complement subject deletion is that the behavior of quantified phrases under the identity requirement is not exactly as expected. (5.111) and (5.112), though they apparently have the same deep structure (5.113) in the transformational analysis, have rather different meanings.

(5.111) Some of the men expected to be drafted.
(5.112) Some of the men expected some of the men to be drafted.
(5.113) Some of the men expected [$_s$for some of the men to be drafted]$_s$

A widely accepted solution, proposed by Carden (1967, 1968), claims that it is not the identity requirement at fault here, but the analysis of quantifiers. He shows that (5.111)–(5.113) can be accounted for by treating quantifiers as main verbs of higher clauses in deep structure. The surface main clause is embedded as a sort of relative clause into the higher clause; the surface structure is reached by a transformation called quantifier lowering, which deletes the higher clause and inserts the quantifier into its surface position.

The transformation quantifier lowering, it should be noted, differs substantially from the traditional battery of syntactic transformations. None of the well-known transformations result in the deletion of a main clause, and it is not clear that any of them insert lexical material from a main clause into a subordinate clause. In addition, most quantifiers will have to be listed as positive absolute exceptions to quantifier lowering, since sentences of the form (5.114), the proposed deep structure, are usually out.

(5.114) The men who came were $\begin{cases} \text{?many.} \\ \text{*all.} \\ \text{*some.} \\ \text{*each.} \\ \text{?three.} \end{cases}$

Thus adopting Carden's proposal commits us to a sizable expansion of the power of the transformational component.

Since there is other evidence that this solution is inadequate (cf. Jackendoff 1968a, 1969b, 1971b, and Chapters 7 and 8), and since it requires otherwise unwarranted power, we will consider another approach. One could claim that the difficulty in (5.111)–(5.112) has nothing to do with the syntax of quantifiers, but that the problem lies in the formulation of coreferentiality of plural and quantified noun phrases. As suggestive evidence for this, note first that (5.111)–(5.112) have exact parallels with pronominalization and reflexivization.

(5.115) Some of the men think they are sick.
(5.116) Some of the men think some of the men are sick.

(5.117) Some of the men believe themselves to be sick.
(5.118) Some of the men believe some of the men to be sick.

Second, notice that plurals can exhibit the same differences.
(5.119) Senators from New England expect to be treated with respect.
(5.120) Senators from New England expect Senators from New England to be treated with respect.

These examples show that the problem is much more general than merely the correct interaction of complement subject deletion and quantifiers.

To see that the proper place to expand the theory is in the meaning of the identity condition for plurals, observe that a simple index of coreference is insufficient to characterize the difference between (5.121) and (5.122).

$$(5.121) \begin{cases} \text{John and Bill and Max} \\ \text{Some of the boys} \\ \text{The boys} \end{cases} \text{ were kicking themselves.}$$

$$(5.122) \begin{cases} \text{John and Bill and Max} \\ \text{Some of the boys} \\ \text{The boys} \end{cases} \text{ were kicking each other.}$$

In both of these examples, the set of individuals denoted by the object is coextensive with the set denoted by the subject. But the individual actions of each member of the set are different in the two examples: in (5.121) each individual is inflicting kicks on himself; in (5.122), on someone else. Thus given set coreference, we see that ordinary pronouns, reflexives and deleted complement subjects denote individual-by-individual coreference, while *each other* indicates individual-by-individual noncoreference.

Again, I will refrain from making any proposals about the formalization of coreference for plural, conjoined, and quantified noun phrases. Dougherty (1970) has a rather comprehensive discussion of this aspect of the grammar, in a framework largely compatible with the assumptions here. However, it seems fair to assume that the explanation of (5.111)–(5.112) and (5.115)–(5.122) lies in the interpretation of the relations *coreferential* and *noncoreferential* marked in the table of coreference, as applied to plural NPs, and not in any peculiarities of deep structure.

The rest of this chapter will discuss the control problem.

5.8 Three Aspects of the Control Problem

There are two aspects of the selection of the antecedent for the complement subject (the *controller*) that immediately strike the eye: finding which NP in the main clause Δ is coreferential with, and deciding whether coreference is obligatory or optional. These two factors interweave in interesting ways, varying more or less independently from one class of verbs to another. Here are some examples of different combinations.

A. VP dominates only complement; subject controller; optional control:
   wait, pray, hope, decide
   John prayed to leave.
   John prayed for Bill to leave.
B. VP dominates only complement; subject controller; obligatory control:
   try, learn, condescend, be lucky, be wise
   John tried to leave.
   *John tried (for) Bill to leave.
C. VP dominates only complement; raising obligatory, so no control:
   believe, imagine
   *John believed to be going.
   John believed himself to be going.
   John believed Bill to be going.

D. VP dominates only complement, raising optional; if no raising, subject
controller, obligatory: *expect, want* (in some dialects)
John expects to leave.
*John expects for Bill to leave.
John expects himself to leave.
John expects Bill to leave.

E. VP dominates NP and complement; object controller; obligatory control: *permit, persuade, force*
*John permitted to leave.
John permitted Bill to leave.
*John permitted Bill (for) Harry to leave.

F. VP dominates complement and optional NP or PP; subject controller;
obligatory control: *promise, vow (to NP), agree (with NP), learn
(from NP)*
John agreed to leave.
John agreed with Bill to leave.

G. VP dominates complement and optional NP; object controller obligatory if present, otherwise subject controller obligatory: *get, keep*
John got Bill to leave.
John got to leave.
*John got there to be an explosion.

H. VP dominates complement and optional NP; object controller optional
if present: *shout, scream* (but see section 5.10)
John shouted for Bill to leave.
John shouted to Bill to leave.
John shouted to Bill for Harry to leave.
*John shouted to leave.

I. Subject complement, VP dominates NP; object controller; optional
control: *bother, benefit*
(For John) to leave so early would bother Bill.

G. Lakoff (1971) and Perlmutter (1971) attempt to account for the op-
tional-obligatory distinction in different ways. Lakoff uses the device of
positive absolute exceptions: verbs can be marked as positive absolute exceptions to equi-NP deletion, which means that the structural description
of equi-NP deletion must be met and the transformation must take place.
This kind of exception is illustrated in Lakoff (1971) with three other kinds
of examples. The first involves verbs that must have reflexive objects, such
as *behave* and *perjure*. The second is the adjective *gala*, which must undergo

wh-be deletion to derive *gala affair*, but not **affair that was gala*. This may be a true exception (but see section 3.5.1). The third example involves "verbs" which must nominalize (in his theory of nominalizations), such as *aggress* and *king*; this kind of case will not arise under the Extended Lexical Hypothesis, in which nominalizations are independent lexical items and not transformationally derived. Thus the need for a device as powerful as the positive absolute exception rests on only three cases. It would be nice to find a more constrained way to talk about them, particularly in view of the fact that the verbs with obligatory control hardly seem "exceptional" among the types listed above. We will deal here only with those examples of Lakoff's that involve coreference.

Perlmutter tries to do away with the need for positive absolute exceptions for equi-NP deletion by showing that obligatoriness of complement subject deletion can be expressed as a constraint on coreference of deep structure matrix and complement subjects. To maintain this, he must show that all cases of deleted derived structure subjects of complements are deep structure subjects as well. An apparent counterexample that comes immediately to mind is a sentence with a passive complement like (5.123), in whose deep structure *the doctor*, not *John*, is complement subject.

(5.123) John tried to be examined by the doctor.

Perlmutter claims that (5.123) is not a counterexample, because its deep structure contains an additional clause which satisfies the deep structure constraint, as in (5.124).

(5.124) John tried $\left[_s \text{John} \left\{ {\text{get} \atop \text{let}} \right\} \left[_s \text{the doctor examine John}\right]\right]$.

To derive (5.123), a transformation deletes *get* or *let*. Perlmutter's argument is based on the claim that the extra clause in (5.124) reflects the actual meaning of (5.123), and that all the constraints on these passive complements follow from the constraints on passive complements of *get* and *let*.

But even if this somewhat counterintuitive analysis of the deep structure of (5.123) can be worked out, it is not general enough to cover all verbs which require the complement subject to be missing at the surface. There are many verbs and adjectives, including *get* itself, which, like *try*, have obligatory control, but unlike *try*, have passive complements not paraphraseable with an extra clause involving *get* or *let*.

(5.125) John was lucky to be examined by the doctor.

John got to be examined by the doctor.

Bill permitted John to be examined by the doctor.

(5.126) John was lucky to $\begin{Bmatrix} \text{get} \\ \text{let} \end{Bmatrix}$ the doctor (to) examine him.

John got to $\begin{Bmatrix} \text{get} \\ \text{let} \end{Bmatrix}$ the doctor (to) examine him.

Bill permitted John to $\begin{Bmatrix} \text{get} \\ \text{let} \end{Bmatrix}$ the doctor (to) examine him.

(5.125) and (5.126) are not paraphrases: (5.126) expresses a sense of volition on John's part which is absent in (5.125). Hence (5.126) cannot be the source for (5.125), as required for Perlmutter's analysis to be correct. Verbs such as *try*, *condescend*, and *intend* express this sense of volition anyway, so a paraphrase with *get* or *let* is generally possible. In section 5.12 we will return to the problem of expressing the difference between these verbs and the verbs in (5.125), and show that the lexical property of expressing volition cross-classifies with the aspects of the control problem previously mentioned.

Since Lakoff's account of obligatory control is too powerful, and Perlmutter's is too restricted, we will develop a fresh approach in the next two sections.

5.9 Networks of Obligatory Coreference

Among Lakoff's four examples of absolute exceptions, two have to do with coreference. This suggests the use of a much less powerful device than absolute exceptions, one dealing only with properties of coreference. It appears that verbs can require certain of the NPs around them to be co-referential. Besides the case of obligatory complement subject deletion, we have the reflexive cases (5.127) mentioned by Lakoff,

(5.127) Harry behaved $\begin{Bmatrix} \text{himself} \\ \text{*Bill} \end{Bmatrix}$.

Teddy perjured $\begin{Bmatrix} \text{himself} \\ \text{*Mack} \end{Bmatrix}$.

a case (5.128) where both object and complement subject are required to be coreferential to the subject,

(5.128) Frank prides $\left\{\begin{array}{l} \text{himself} \\ *\text{Jack} \end{array}\right\}$ on (*Bob's) being intelligent.

and many expressions with obligatory pronouns or possessive pronouns:

(5.129) Bill took Mary at $\left\{\begin{array}{l} \text{her} \\ *\text{his} \\ *\text{Walt's} \end{array}\right\}$ word.

Gerald blew $\left\{\begin{array}{l} \text{his} \\ *\text{Tom's} \end{array}\right\}$ stack.

Ron knows Sue for what $\left\{\begin{array}{l} \text{she} \\ *\text{he} \\ *\text{Dave} \end{array}\right\}$ is: a liar.

Millie has a wart on $\left\{\begin{array}{l} \text{her.} \\ \text{her nose.} \\ *\text{Bill's nose.} \end{array}\right.$

In these expressions the meaning of the verb or idiom requires that the two NPs be coreferential. In a sense the second NP is redundant semantically, but it is present because of the syntactic vagaries of the expressions. If the two NPs are referentially distinct, the semantic reading comes out wrong, in that there are two individuals in evidence where the verb presupposes only one.

To capture this intuition, we can allow a verb to introduce a well-formedness condition on the semantic representation of sentences in which it occurs. The well-formedness condition requires certain NPs to be coreferential; it is violated if two NPs, independently determined noncoreferential by the rules of coreference, fill semantic places which are required by the condition to be coreferential. We will call such a condition a *network of coreference*. A network of coreference will appear in the lexical entry of any verb that requires coreference restrictions. (Postal 1970b hints at the need for this kind of restriction toward the end of the Appendix.)

This proposal obviously can account for cases like (5.127)–(5.129). Its extension to obligatory complement subject identity depends on the assumption that "surface complement subject" is an identifiable position in the semantic representation. If this were not so, there would be no way for a verb like *try* to specify that the surface complement subject is identical to the matrix subject. This does not seem too extravagant an assumption, since we showed in section 3.9 that the derived subject is semantically a privileged position in another respect: it serves as an argument of the projection rule for subject-oriented sentence adverbs (see Appendix to this chapter for more discussion).

We conclude, then, that an appropriate and sufficiently restricted device for expressing the obligatory absence of a complement subject for verbs like *try*, *get*, *persuade*, and so forth, is a network of coreference given within the verb's lexical entry, requiring the coreference of two NPs in the sentence.

5.10 When There Is a Unique Controller

So far we have specified how a controller is imposed on the complement subject. Now we must ask how the controller is to be selected. Rosenbaum (1967) proposes a general principle for the selection of the controller. He says that the choice of controller can be made purely on the basis of structural considerations, by means of a "minimal distance principle." According to this principle, the controller is always the noun phrase "nearest" to the complement subject, where distance is measured by counting nodes along the path in the tree joining the complement subject to the noun phrase. This principle successfully predicts the controller in all cases listed in section 5.8 except the *promise* class, and furthermore, it correctly predicts that the controller of sentence adverbial clauses (*in order to* and *by -ing* clauses) is always the subject.

This principle, if correct, would be a very surprising result. Nothing like it has been found elsewhere in the grammar; the device of node-counting somehow seems foreign to our formalisms. Furthermore, the glaring exception *promise* throws doubt on its correctness; it seems no accident that the meaning of *promise* correlates with its formal behavior under complement subject deletion.

An underlying assumption of Rosenbaum's principle is that there is never more than one NP in a sentence that can serve as antecedent of the complement subject. Yet, as Postal points out (1970b, section V.D), this assumption is invalid, since the following sentences are ambiguous as to the reference of the deleted complement subject (see also example (5.21), p. 185).

(5.130) Harry talked to Bill about kissing Greta.
Harry wrote to Bill about not voting for Humphrey.
Harriet argued with Betty about visiting you.

There are in fact three branches of the ambiguity: the complement subject can be coreferential with either upper NP or with both jointly. As Postal points out, this is exactly parallel to the ambiguity of the pronoun in (5.131).

(5.131) Mary argued with John about their getting married in a church.

Their can denote *Mary* and someone else, *John* and someone else, or *Mary* and *John*. (The first two readings are more apparent if *Bill* is substituted for *Mary*.) In general, the environments for joint interpretations of Δ are just like those for joint interpretation of pronouns (see Postal 1970b, section V.E, for the evidence).

The ambiguities of (5.130) show that it is not always possible to pick a unique NP which will serve as controller. The proposal made in the last section suggests the condition for choosing a unique NP: just when the matrix verb establishes a network of coreference involving the complement subject, i.e. when the verb requires the complement subject to be missing. If there is no network of coreference imposed by the verb, selection of a controller should be free within the constraints imposed by pronominalization.

To test this claim, let us look through the classes of verbs listed at the beginning of section 5.8. Only three classes there have optional control. Two of these—*wait, hope, pray, decide*, and *bother, benefit*—only have one possible NP in the clause other than the complement, so they do not test the present claim. The other class includes *shout* and *scream*. In the examples given, only object controller was illustrated. But in fact subject controller is also possible, as Perlmutter (1971) points out.

(5.132) I screamed (to Bill) to be allowed to go.[6]

[6]This class of verbs is G. Lakoff's (1971) only example of *negative absolute exceptions*, lexical items which must not meet the structural description of a transformation. Lakoff bases his argument on examples like *I shouted for John to go* but **I shouted (for me) to go*, where the main subject cannot be coreferential with the complement subject. But Perlmutter's examples such as (5.132) show that Lakoff's proposal is incorrect. Hence there is no evidence that negative absolute exceptions are ever needed in grammar. As we have argued against Lakoff's positive absolute exceptions in the last section and elsewhere, there seems to be no evidence for any kind of absolute exceptions within the interpretive theory.

In this case and in the examples given in section 5.8, there is no ambiguity in the complement subject. What we have established, however, is that the controller is not always the same NP in the matrix, and that the variation depends on the content of the complement clause. We will show in section 5.12 why these sentences are unambiguous; the extra readings of coreference will be blocked by an independent constraint having to do with volition, the third factor in the control problem mentioned in section 5.8.

In addition to the examples in section 5.8, there are the constructions (5.130) we originally cited as ambiguous. But these, too, have merely optional coreference between the complement subject and something in the main clause.

(5.133) Harry talked to Bill about Sam's kissing Greta.

Harry wrote to Bill about Walt's not voting for Humphrey.

Harriet argued with Betty about Jerry's visiting you.

Thus, assuming that we can account for the lack of ambiguity in sentences with *scream* and *shout*, the generalization is that there is a unique identifiable controller position if and only if control is obligatory.

5.11 The Position of the Obligatory Controller

Having decided when we must specify a controller, we must now decide how to specify where it is. Compare *get* and *promise*.

$$(5.134)\ \text{John} \begin{Bmatrix} \text{got} \\ \text{promised} \end{Bmatrix} \text{to leave.}$$

$$(5.135)\ \text{John} \begin{Bmatrix} \text{got} \\ \text{promised} \end{Bmatrix} \text{Bill to leave.}$$

The controller for a particular verb cannot always be identified with its subject or with its object, because *get* switches controller position when an object is added. Nor can we use Rosenbaum's distance principle, which predicts this switching will always take place, because *promise* does not switch.

Nor would it be especially general to state that for *promise*, whether or not there is a direct object, the subject is controller; but with *get*, the object is controller if present and otherwise the subject is controller. A more interesting theory would predict this difference on the basis of independently motivated differences between *promise* and *get*.

Toward such a theory, notice the similarity in the following sets of examples.

(5.136)   Joe got to Philadelphia.
            Frank got Joe to Philadelphia.
(5.137)   Joe got furious at Henry.
            Frank got Joe furious at Henry.
(5.138)   Joe got to wash the dishes.
            Frank got Joe to wash the dishes.
(5.139)   ?Joe kept $\left\{ \begin{array}{c} \text{to} \\ \text{in} \end{array} \right\}$ his room.
            Frank kept Joe in his room.
(5.140)   Joe kept at the job.
            Frank kept Joe at the job.
(5.141)   Joe kept working on the problem.
            Frank kept Joe working on the problem.

The interesting thing about these examples is that the switching of understood complement subjects in (5.138) and (5.141) is exactly parallel to the switching of attribution of the adjectives and locatives in the rest of the examples. And this switching in turn is exactly parallel to the switching of attribution of motion in (5.142).

(5.142) The rock rolled away.
       Bill rolled the rock away.

In other words, we appear to be dealing with a manifestation of the system of thematic relations introduced in Chapter 2.

    The thematic relations in (5.136) and (5.139) are transparent. In each case, *Joe* is the Theme; with *get* he is asserted to have undergone a motion resulting in achievement of the Goal *Philadelphia*; with *keep* his Location over a certain period of time is asserted to be *his room*. In the transitive members of the pairs, *Frank* is acting as an Agent to bring about this state of affairs. By the usual analogies, we can consider the adjectives and complements in the other examples to be abstract Goals and Locations.

    We could explain the variable controller position for *get* by claiming that networks of coreference are defined on *thematic relations* rather than *grammatical relations*. Then the controller of *get* could always be the *Theme*, no matter what its position. Since the fact that the Theme of *get* occurs in various positions must be expressed in the grammar anyway, there will be nothing special about the way *get* behaves under the complement subject rule.

It still must be shown, however, that thematic relations can distinguish *get* from *promise*. *Promise* unfortunately cannot describe concrete events, so we have no direct analogy as we do with *get*. However, compare *promise* with *sell*.

(5.143) John sold a bathtub.

John sold Bill a bathtub.

(5.144) John promised to go straight.

John promised Bill to go straight.

In both pairs, a transfer is effected away from John—in (5.143), a bathtub is transferred; in (5.144), information (that John will go straight) is transferred. The thing transferred is obviously Theme in both pairs. *John* is in all four sentences the Source (and Agent). With both verbs, the inclusion of a Goal, in these examples *Bill*, is optional. The fact that *Bill* is the Goal is made clearer by the variant with *to*, just in case the theme is placed next to the verb (this is of course impossible if the Theme is a clause).

(5.145) John sold a bathtub to Bill.

John would promise nothing to a scoundrel like Bill.

If this analysis of *promise* is correct, we see that the controller can always be the Source, whether or not the Goal is present. Thus the difference between *get* and *promise* is that *promise* does not switch position of Source when a Goal is added, but *get* switches position of Theme when an Agent is added.

Next compare *give* and *permit*.

(5.146) Sylvia gave Joe a tricycle.

(5.147) Sylvia permitted Joe to cross the street.

In (5.146) *a tricycle* is being transferred; in (5.147) the information that Joe may cross the street is being transferred. These are the Themes of their respective sentences. In both cases, *Sylvia* is the Source and Agent, and *Joe* is the Goal. As with *sell* and *promise*, the Goal can be marked in certain constructions with *to*, identifying it more clearly.

(5.148) Sylvia gave a tricycle to Joe.
        Sylvia's permission to Joe to cross the street

The interpretation of the complement subject in (5.147) indicates that the controller must be the Goal of the matrix sentence. Thus *permit* differs from *promise* only in that Goal rather than Source is controller; the correspondence of thematic relations to grammatical relations is identical.

Another example: the positional and abstract forms of *force* have the same syntax, and by the usual assumptions, the same thematic relations.

(5.149) George forced the ball into the hole.
(5.150) George forced Bob into selling his car.
(5.151) George forced Bob to sell his car.

Here *George* is Agent, *the ball* and *Bob* are Themes, and *the hole* and *sell his car* are Goals, as shown by the directional preposition *into*, which deletes in (5.151) by the well-known rule deleting prepositions before *that* and *for-to* complements. The controller of *force* can be identified with the Theme.

Examples could be multiplied, but the point is clear. It is possible, using thematic relations, to explain the position of controller NP by means of a single marking, and to differentiate the various classes of verbs without any special exception apparatus. The crucial cases showing that thematic relations are the correct device are *get* and *promise*, which have an optional element in the VP. If all verbs with an optional NP behaved like *promise*, maintaining a fixed control position when the optional object is added, this would argue that grammatical relations determine control. If all such verbs behaved like *get*, switching the control position when the object is added, this would argue that some restricted variant of the distance principle determines control. But the fact that both types occur, correlated exactly with differences in thematic relations, argues that thematic relations are the factor determining control.

The linking of controller position to thematic relations offers some insight into a long-standing puzzle connected with the control problem. (5.152) and (5.153) differ in interpretation of complement subject, but there is no difference either in distance or in grammatical relations.

(5.152) Mary gave Alex permission to go.
(5.153) Mary received permission to go from Alex.

As we showed earlier, the Goal of *permit* controls complement subject co-reference. However, in the nominal form *permission* the Goal is optional, and not present in these examples.

However, examine the thematic relations in the main sentences. In (5.152), *Mary* is Source and *Alex* Goal; in (5.153) it is the other way around. In each sentence, it turns out that the *Goal of the main clause* is interpreted as complement subject. If some semantic rule could establish an understood identity between the Source-Goal patterns in the sentence and the NP, it could be inferred that in (5.152) *Alex* is the Goal of *permission* and in (5.153), *Mary*. Then the network of coreference associated with *permission* would give the correct result. This rule may be related to the rule proposed in section 4.12, which creates a surrogate Agent for *picture* in *The picture of himself that John saw is ugly.*

Such an analysis would also predict correctly the complement subject in (5.154) and (5.155), since control with *promise* goes with the Source instead of the Goal. Note that the complement subjects in these examples are the reverse of those in (5.152)–(5.153).

(5.154) Mary gave Alex a promise to go.
(5.155) Mary received from Alex a promise to go.

I don't know the conditions under which this rule requiring identity of Source-Goal patterns is enforced, but the assumption of such a rule gives beautiful predictions in these heretofore refractory examples.

Thus, if control is established by networks of coreference which refer to thematic relations, we have solved the ordering problem brought up in section 5.4. The complement subject rule can now be ordered at the end of the cycle, since it is free to assign coreference between the complement subject and any NP at all in the main clause, subject to pronominalization constraints. When there is a restricted choice of coreferents for the complement subject, the restriction is imposed independently by a network of coreference. Like the Thematic Hierarchy Condition, a network of coreference is a well-formedness condition on semantic readings, having nothing to do with the derivation of the semantic reading.

The appearance of thematic relations in the solution to the control problem is a third independent justification of thematic relations as the correct device for expressing the functional structure. The fact that networks of coreference and the Thematic Hierarchy Conditions for reflexives and passive make use of thematic relations for unexpected generalizations indicates that the relations defined by Gruber and the principles for finding them are more than simply an arbitrary descriptive system. These independent applications should convince us rather that thematic relations must play an important part in linguistic theory.

5.12 Agents Not Conditioned by the Verb of Their Clause

English has various ways of expressing a person's being responsible for bringing an event about. First, a subject of a sentence can be marked Agent by the verb. Second, there are sentences in which the deliberate influence of some individual other than the Agent defined by the verb is expressed by an adverb or adverbial clause:

(5.156) Tom intentionally struck Bill as rude.
(5.157) Willy was examined by the doctor in order to prove to his uncle
        that he didn't have rickets.

Strike (*as Adj*) does not normally mark its subject as Agent, yet in (5.156) the adverb *intentionally* implies that Tom went out of his way to cause Bill to consider him rude. Likewise, since Agents are generally marked by the verb in (deep) subject position, the surface subject of a passive such as (5.157) cannot have been marked Agent by the verb. Yet the *in order to* clause implies that Willy deliberately made sure he underwent examination. Third, some interpretations of modals mark their subjects as Agents:

(5.158) Billy will not (i.e. refuses to) be examined by Dr. Gronk.

$$\text{You} \begin{Bmatrix} \text{must} \\ \text{should} \end{Bmatrix} \text{ (i.e. are obliged to) be examined by Dr. Schlepp.}$$

Fourth, as remarked in Chapter 2, the imperative expresses volition on the part of the surface subject, suggesting that it too introduces the reading Agent on its subject. Note, by the way, that the last three of these devices that mark Agents mark the *surface subject*. This is further evidence that the surface subject plays some special role in semantic interpretation, as was suggested in section 5.9. It is unclear to me, however, what this special role is.

A fifth way of expressing volition was discovered in section 5.8. There we saw that *try*, *condescend*, and *intend* express volition over the event described in the complement, but *lucky*, *get*, and *permit* do not. In this section we will discuss the nature of this expression of volition and its interaction with the complement subject rule and networks of coreference.

First of all, we observe that there are many cases where the introduction of an Agent marking by something other than the verb renders a sentence unacceptable:

(5.159) ?*John intentionally knew the answer.

(5.160) ?*Harold tried to be small.

(5.161) ?*You must be judged inadequate.

Thus we must ask what sentences permit Agents and which NPs in those sentences can be Agents.

Fischer and Marshall (1969), in discussing Perlmutter's (1970c) theory of *begin*, deal with this question. They show that the ability of an NP to be an Agent is a complex and subtle property, tied very closely to the meaning of the sentence. Of course, if the verb marks the subject as an Agent, there can be no conflict if something else marks the subject as Agent, too. So the interesting cases are sentences in which the verb does not mark the NP in question as an Agent, such as passives with Agentive surface subjects.[7]

Fischer and Marshall show that the ability of a sentence to take an Agent (surface) subject cannot be identified with the feature [−stative] on the verb (recognizable by the ability to take present progressive aspect), as Perlmutter claims. For example, *know*, a stative verb, may occur under *try* if accompanied by an appropriate adverb, but *sweat*, a nonstative verb, seems strange.

[7]There appears to be a rough criterion for distinguishing Agents marked by the verb from Agents marked by other than the verb. If the subject is an Agent not marked by the verb, there will be a plausible paraphrase with *NP brought it about that . . .*, whereas with Agents marked by the verb such a paraphrase seems odd or redundant. Compare (i), which have Agents marked by the verb, with (ii), where the subject is marked Agent by something else. Their paraphrases are (iii) and (iv), respectively.

   (i)   John (intentionally) moved away from the wall.
         The doctor tried to examine John.
  (ii)   John intentionally struck Bill as pompous.
         John tried to be examined by the doctor.
 (iii)   ?John (intentionally) brought it about that he moved away from the wall.
         ?The doctor tried to bring it about that he would examine John.
  (iv)   John intentionally brought it about that he struck Bill as pompous.
         John tried to bring it about that he would be examined by the doctor.

(5.162)   John tried to know the answer by the next morning.
(5.163)   ?John tried to sweat.

In fact, the ability to take a plausible Agent subject is often a matter of factual knowledge about the world, as illustrated by Fischer and Marshall's discussion of an extreme case (section 4):

As one might expect from the idiosyncratically oriented lexicon, there are wide differences among speakers as to what is self-controllable [i.e. can take an Agent subject (R. J.)] and what is not, and even in the same speaker, one verb may be self-controllable, while its semantic opposite or a close synonym may not. For example, one of the authors (S. D. F.) can say
(109) a.   Be taller by next year.
        b.   I let myself be rumored to enjoy surfing.
but not
(110) a.   *Be shorter by Friday.
        b.   *I let myself be said to enjoy surfing.
The reason for this is that she knows of hormones that can produce growth, but none (discounting hookah-smoking caterpillars and mushrooms) that produce shrinkage, and that one can start or quash rumors about oneself, but one cannot stop people from saying things. . . .

If the ability of a sentence to take an Agent subject is this intimately bound up with the meaning of the sentence and with the real-world consequences of the sentence, a formal criterion for appropriateness of Agent subject is obviously unstable within the scope of discussion to which we are limited here. This does not, however, prevent us as linguists from using our knowledge of the language to tell us when something is intended to be the Agent of a sentence. If we can describe the behavior of Agents informally, we can discover interesting things about sentences containing Agents even if we do not know formal criteria for agenthood.

Besides the class containing *try* and *condescend*, we know of several classes of verbs that mark Agents. *Persuade* and *force* take direct objects as well as the complement; the object and complement subject are coreferential, and the complement subject must be an Agent. *Promise* and *vow* take optional indirect objects; the subject and complement subject are coreferential, and the complement subject must be an Agent.

In all the cases mentioned so far, since the complement subject is always coreferential with some NP in the main clause, we could have the verb mark either the complement subject or its controller as the NP that is the Agent of the complement. However, consideration of another class of verbs shows that it is the NP in the *main clause* which should be marked, not the complement subject. Recall the discussion in section 5.10, in which we concluded that there is no network of coreference invoked by verbs like *scream* and *shout*. For these verbs, we get the following paradigms:

(5.164) *I screamed to go.
(5.165) I screamed to Bill to go.
(5.166) I screamed to Bill for Harry to go.
(5.167) I screamed to be allowed to go.
(5.168) I screamed to Bill to be allowed to go.
(5.169) I screamed to Bill for Harry to be allowed to go.

Note first of all that in (5.166) and (5.169) I am asking Bill to bring it about that Harry go or be allowed to go; it is only by virtue of action on Bill's part that anything will happen to Harry. *Bill* thus meets our intuitive criteria for being an Agent of the complement clause, suggesting that it is indeed the NP in the main clause that is marked as Agent, not the complement subject.

   Consideration of the meaning of (5.166) reveals an interesting thing about sentences with two Agents. Notice that *Harry* is the Agent marked by the verb in the complement clause. The relation of Bill's action to Harry's action indicates that the Agent defined in the higher clause has some kind of causal or temporal priority over the Agent defined by the verb: the former must exert volition first. This is in fact also true in sentences like (5.170), in which *Bill*, the Agent marked by the adverb, must act before *the doctor*, the Agent marked by the verb, can do so.

(5.170) Bill was intentionally examined by the doctor.

   Sentences like (5.166) also show the dependence of the ability to take an Agent on the meaning of the sentence. Compare the following:

(5.171) *I shouted to Bill to be tall.
(5.172) *I shouted to Bill for Harry to be tall.
(5.173) I shouted to Bill for the next recruit to be tall.

Be tall does not normally allow an Agent in the subject. In fact, because it is impossible for someone to make someone else tall, (5.172) is out: Bill cannot be an Agent of the complement. Why is (5.173) good? The meaning of (5.173) is that Bill should exercise choice in selecting the next recruit, and that the one he selects should be tall. The supposition that Bill is responsible for the choice of the next recruit is the only plausible way in which *Bill* can be understood as an Agent over the sentence. I take it that this supposition is inferred from Bill's agenthood and not the other way around: what would be a syntactically motivated deep structure that explicitly represented Bill's making a choice?

Let us return to (5.164)–(5.169). In (5.168), since there is no network of coreference with *scream*, we would anticipate that the complement subject could be coreferential with either *I* or *Bill*. But assume that *Bill* is chosen as antecedent of the complement subject. Then *Bill* ($= \Delta$) would be Agent of the complement. But since *be allowed to go* does not permit its subject to be an Agent (as shown by, for example, **I intended to be allowed to go*), this reading would not be acceptable. Therefore *I* must be the antecedent of the complement subject for a consistent reading. Similarly, in (5.167), *I*, not being an Agent of the complement, may serve as antecedent of Δ.

For (5.164) and (5.165), these considerations are unfortunately not enough. In (5.165), what is to prevent *I* from being the antecedent of Δ, even if *Bill* is the Agent? If this reading were possible, we would get a reading of (5.165) rather like (5.166). A possible addition to the grammar to account for this situation might be a rule that, whenever possible, the Agent marked by the verb over a particular clause must be the same as the Agent marked by other factors (such as the dominating verb). This rule bears some similarity to the rules of sections 5.11 and 4.12 in requiring parallelism of thematic relations in two structurally related Ss or NPs. Then, for example, Δ, the Agent of the complement marked by the verb *go* in (5.165), would preferably be identified with *Bill*, the Agent marked by the upper verb *scream*; the complement subject in (5.164) could not refer to *I* because of the implicit Agent. Admittedly, there is so far no other evidence for such a rule, but it seems to me to point toward the correct sort of account.

Some support for this analysis comes from a slightly different class of verbs, including *beg* and *ask*. These have the same paradigm as *scream* except that the counterpart of (5.164) is acceptable.

(5.174) I begged to go.
(5.175) I begged Bill to go.
(5.176) I begged Bill for Harry to go.

(5.177) I begged to be allowed to go.
(5.178) I begged Bill to be allowed to go.
(5.179) I begged Bill for Harry to be allowed to go.

Note that (5.174) is synonymous with (5.177). They both paraphrase the direct question *May I go?* whereas (5.175) paraphrases the direct question *Will you go?* In a theory accepting the strong Katz-Postal Hypothesis, we would thus be compelled to posit two complementary verbs *beg*, or two drastically dissimilar deep structures for (5.174) and (5.175).

In the present theory these interpretations make more sense: we need posit no lexical or deep structure differences. The similarity between the two sentences lies in the fact that I am requesting someone to act as Agent over the event of the complement clause. In (5.175), he can do so directly by being the Agent marked by the verb; in (5.174), the implicit recipient of the plea can act only indirectly, by granting permission or otherwise making my going possible. But how the agency of the indirect object is carried out is perhaps not specified in the meaning of *beg*, but is rather a consequence of the meaning of the sentence. Again, I cannot be more specific about this analysis, or how to differentiate these verbs from those like *scream*. However, the fact that this kind of account appears to lead potentially toward a more sophisticated semantic analysis and away from systems of arbitrary exception features seems to me a strong incentive to continue work along these lines.

Perhaps a few words should be said here about the so-called Modal Constraints discussed in Postal (1970b). Postal observes that with verbs of linguistic performance such as *beg*, *scream*, *shout*, *ask*, and so forth, the subjects of certain *that*-complements obey the same coreference conditions as the deleted subject of *for-to* complements. For example, in the following sentences, under the interpretation of the modal in which Bill is requesting action, not just communicating information, Postal says that *he* can only be *Harry*.

(5.180) Bill told Harry that he ought to leave.
       Bill shouted to Harry that he should stop.

These parallel the coreference in

(5.181) Bill told Harry to leave.
       Bill shouted to Harry to stop.

Postal tracks down the exact senses of the *that*-complements for which this correspondence holds; he discovers that they are the ones that paraphrase direct discourse in which the speaker requests some action on the part of the hearer. When all that is happening is that information is being transmitted, the correspondence does not hold.

In the analysis given here, this fact is meaningful: if only information is being transmitted, the hearer is obviously not being asked to act. If the hearer is being asked to act (i.e. asked to be an Agent) the additional coreference constraints follow from the semantic principles governing Agents. Since *for-to* complements with these verbs always request action, the coreference constraints always hold.

Note, by the way, that in (5.182) the Agent restriction operates in the usual fashion to make *Bill* the antecedent of *he* in the "action" reading.

(5.182)   Bill told Harry that he ought to be allowed to leave.
(5.183) *Bill told Harry to be allowed to leave.

The same thing should happen in (5.183), but the network of coreference established by *tell* (over its *for-to* complements only) says that only *Harry* is allowed to be the antecedent. Since neither condition can be satisfied without violating the other, the sentence is ruled out. This is a further illustration of the interdependence of the network of coreference and Agent constraints.

5.13 Summary

In adopting an interpretive theory of coreference, we must state the complement subject rule as an interpretive rule. It is best stated as a rule marking coreference between an empty node (Δ) complement subject and an NP in the main clause. Aside from the subject-object distinction, all aspects of the environment for the complement subject rule generalize with reflexivization. This generalization can be expressed in the rule (5.81), if the complement subject rule can be ordered at the end of the cycle, like reflexivization and pronominalization. To make this ordering possible, it is necessary to show that the selection of obligatory controller NP does not depend on where the rule is ordered.

The problem of selecting an obligatory controller can be broken into three parts: how a verb governs an obligatory controller, how the controller position is located, and how an Agent reading is superimposed on the complement. Networks of coreference are proposed as a highly restricted device to replace positive absolute exceptions in expressing obligatoriness of a controller. It turns out that there is a unique controller position designated exactly when there is a network of coreference. The position of the obligatory controller is determined by thematic relations, not by structural relations. This verifies the semantic character of the network of coreference, and permits the required ordering of the complement subject rule. Finally, a verb can mark an NP in its clause as Agent over the complement clause, and restrictions on coreference independent of the network of coreference result.

5.14 Appendix

We should show that networks of coreference are limited in power and cannot refer to arbitrary surface positions. To do so, let us briefly examine two other rules which involve NPs in complement clauses and which might be thought to require networks of coreference.

Tough movement (which produces *John is tough to please*), discussed briefly in section 4.10.5, can be stated in two possible ways. It can apply to a phrase marker like (i), moving the object of the complement clause into the position of the main subject *it*.

(i)   It is tough $[_{VP}$to please John$]$.

Alternatively, the underlying phrase marker might be (ii).

(ii)   John is tough $\left[\begin{array}{l} \text{to please} \left\{ \begin{array}{l} \text{John} \\ \Delta \end{array} \right\} \\ {}_{VP} \end{array} \right]$ (transformational theory)
(interpretive theory)

Tough movement will then be an object deletion in the transformational theory and a semantic coreference rule in the interpretive theory. If the latter solution is chosen, a network of coreference must be imposed by *tough* between the main clause subject and the complement object, in order to prevent *John is tough to please Bill*. Since complement objects, as far as I know, have no particularly privileged semantic status, it would be preferable to avoid this extension of the power of networks of coreference by adopting the movement rule version of *Tough* movement.

The only objection to this solution is that the movement does not preserve meaning, since (iii) can be transformed either into (iv) or into (v) by *Tough* movement (as pointed out by Edward Klima).

(iii) It is easy to play sonatas on this violin.
(iv) Sonatas are easy to play on this violin.
(v) This violin is easy to play sonatas on.

But only in the context of the Katz-Postal Hypothesis is this argument valid. The functional structure of (iii) is preserved in (iv)–(v); only the presuppositions differ. Similar differences in meaning appear when emphatic stress is added to (iii).

(vi) It is easy to play sonatas on this VIOLIN.
(vii) It is easy to play SONATAS on this violin.

Chapter 6 will show such differences to follow from rules of interpretation which apply to surface structure, so the interpretive theory can account for the differences without a difference in deep structure. Hence *Tough* movement can be stated as a topicalization-like movement rule, eliminating the need for an extension of networks of coreference on its account.

Another rule that affects NPs in complements is the rule for the complements of degree modifiers like *too* and *enough*.

(viii) This pig is $\begin{Bmatrix} \text{old enough} \\ \text{too young} \end{Bmatrix}$ for Harry to kill. (object missing)

(ix) This pig is $\begin{Bmatrix} \text{old enough} \\ \text{too young} \end{Bmatrix}$ to climb the fence. (subject missing)

(x) This pig is $\begin{Bmatrix} \text{fat enough} \\ \text{too fat} \end{Bmatrix}$ to eat. (ambiguous)

For this rule, a coreference assignment is obviously necessary, since there is no possible source sentence like *It is too fat to eat the pig* which could undergo something like *Tough* movement. Sometimes pronouns are needed instead of Δ in the position of coreference:

(xi) The pig is fat enough that we can eat it.
  Saskatchewan is too far away for you even to start to conceive of
  getting there in one day by unicycle.

If there are networks of coreference in the representations of *too* and
enough, they will have to refer to an NP in the complement which need not
be the subject, again an undesirable extension of the notion. But in fact, the
restriction on the complement is weaker than coreference, for there are
sentences like (xii) with no coreference at all.

(xii) This room is too chilly to turn on the air-conditioning.
  The weather is warm enough for us to go swimming.

From these sentences we see that the restriction is something more like
"the complement sentence must be directly relevant to the matrix," where
"directly relevant" is a euphemism for a semantic relation I don't understand. The same sort of relation, however, must hold between *of*-objects
and *that*-complements of *believe*, as pointed out by J. R. Ross (personal
communication):

(xiii) I believe of Holland that $\begin{cases} \text{the tulips are beautiful.} \\ \text{Amsterdam is a swinging place.} \\ \text{*New York is a drag.} \end{cases}$

Thus no network of coreference need be established for *too* and *enough*,
and we can still maintain that the subject is the only position within the
complement to which a network of coreference ever needs to refer.

Focus and Presupposition

Stress and intonation in English have been commonly regarded as "mere stylistic factors" which do not contribute to the essential meaning of sentences. In this chapter we will begin to construct an account of the semantic effects of these phonological phenomena and show how they fit into the general theory proposed here and into a possible theory of discourse. It is hoped that this will provide a framework in which more detailed studies of intonation such as Kingdon (1958) and Bolinger (1965b) can be brought to bear on generative grammar.

The first three sections of the chapter introduce the notion of focus and presupposition and sketch an approach to the rule *focus assignment*. Section 6.4 proposes a formalism for the semantic representation of focus and presupposition. Sections 6.5 and 6.6 discuss *association with focus*, a rule that plays an important part in the interpretation of such words as *even*, *only*, and *not*. Section 6.7 shows how two intonation contours affect the interpretation, and in particular how they interact with negation. Sections 6.8–6.9 concern a number of rules of anaphora which crucially use focus and presupposition. Section 6.10 briefly discusses lexical items which introduce presuppositions other than those marked by stress.

6.1 Focus and Presupposition in Yes-No Questions

Chomsky (1970b) discusses the relation between yes-no questions and their "natural" responses. Following his discussion, consider a question like (6.1), in which the capitalized word represents the main stress and highest pitch of the sentence, using a normal stress and intonation contour for this sentence.

(6.1) Is it JOHN who writes poetry?

There is a sense in which (6.2) is a "natural" response to this, but (6.3) is not.

(6.2) No, it is BILL who writes poetry.
(6.3) No, it is JOHN who writes short stories.

To give some structure to this intuition, we introduce the notions of *focus* and *presupposition*. As working definitions, we will use "focus of a sentence" to denote the information in the sentence that is assumed by the speaker not to be shared by him and the hearer, and "presupposition of a sentence" to denote the information in the sentence that is assumed by the speaker to be shared by him and the hearer. Intuitively, it makes sense to speak of a discourse as "natural" if successive sentences share presuppositions, that is, if the two speakers implicitly agree on what information they have in common.

In (6.1) the presupposition is that someone writes poetry. *John* is the focus: in the case of a question, the status of the constituent being questioned is assumed by the speaker to be known by the hearer, but it is obviously not known to the speaker. In (6.2) the presupposition is also that someone writes poetry, and *Bill* is the focus, the new information being conveyed. In (6.3), however, the presupposition is that someone writes short stories; we can attribute the unnaturalness of (6.3) as a response to (6.1) to the disparity in presuppositions.

To account for these intuitions about (6.1)–(6.3), we must suppose that one aspect of the semantic representation of a sentence is a division of the reading into presupposition and focus, and that this division is reflected somehow in the syntactic structure of the sentence. Within the linguistic theory being pursued here, this claim will be embodied in a rule which we can call *focus assignment*, which will divide the reading into focus and presupposition on the basis of some aspect of the syntactic representation.

What aspect of the syntactic representation correlates with choice of focus? Assuming a deep structure for (6.1) on the order of (6.4), as given by the analysis of Akmajian (1970a), one might suppose that the focus is the predicate of the higher clause in deep structure (the deep structure theory).

(6.4) the one [*wh*-someone writes poetry] is John

Alternatively, Chomsky suggests that the focus is determined by the surface structure, as a phrase containing the main stress of the sentence. This notion will be made more explicit in section 6.2; for the present, we will leave it in this rough form. In the case of (6.1)–(6.3) the two theories make the same predictions.

Next consider (6.5)–(6.6).

(6.5) Did Maxwell kill the judge with a HAMMER?
(6.6) Was it with a HAMMER that Maxwell killed the judge?

Both of these have as a "natural" response (6.7) but not (6.8), for example.

(6.7) No, he killed him with a ZAPGUN.
(6.8) No, it was SAM who killed the judge.

(6.5)–(6.7) share the presupposition that Maxwell killed the judge; they differ only in the focus. (6.8), on the other hand, denies the presupposition of (6.5)–(6.6), agreeing only that someone killed the judge, but asserting that it was Sam rather than Maxwell. The difference between (6.7) and (6.8) as natural responses to (6.5)–(6.6) can thus be interpreted as a difference in presuppositions.

Now notice that the two theories of focus assignment put different requirements on the deep structure of (6.5). In the deep structure theory, it will be necessary to claim that the deep structure of (6.5) resembles the deep structure of (6.6), that is, that it has a form roughly like (6.9).

(6.9) the thing [Maxwell killed the judge with *wh*-something] was a hammer

The deep structure theory must thus claim that the single surface clause of (6.5) is derived from a deep structure source with two clauses. The surface structure theory, on the other hand, can retain the traditional single-clause analysis of (6.5), simplifying the syntax. The same difference in the two theories arises with a wide range of adverbials:

(6.10) Does John read poetry in the GARDEN?
(6.11) Did John leave at six o'CLOCK?
(6.12) Did Fred slice the bread CAREFULLY?

In each case the deep structure theory will claim that the adverbial is the predicate of a higher clause, and the surface structure theory will be able to retain the traditional single-clause source for these sentences.[1]

Chomsky's next examples amplify the difference in the two theories.

[1]The deep structure theory is argued for in G. Lakoff (1971). Note incidentally that the surface structure theory is consistent with the source for manner adverbs argued for in Chapter 3, and that the deep structure theory is probably consistent with the source for manner adverbs that we argued against, on independent grounds.

(6.13) Was it an ex-convict with a red SHIRT that he was warned to look out for?

(6.14) Was it a red-shirted ex-CONVICT that he was warned to look out for?

(6.15) Was it an ex-convict with a shirt that is RED that he was warned to look out for?

The deep structures of these are all of the form (6.16).

(6.16) the one [he was warned to look out for *wh*-someone] was X

Thus the deep structure theory predicts, correctly, that (6.17) is an appropriate response to (6.13)–(6.15), since the presupposition is that he was warned to look out for someone.

(6.17) No, it was an AUTOMOBILE salesman he was warned to look out for.

But notice that (6.18)–(6.20) are also appropriate responses to (6.13)–(6.15), respectively, but they are not interchangeable.

(6.18) No, it was an ex-convict with a red TIE that he was warned to look out for.

(6.19) No, it was a red-shirted AUTOMOBILE salesman that he was warned to look out for.

(6.20) No, it was an ex-convict with a shirt that is GREEN that he was warned to look out for.

The presuppositions shared by the question-response pairs (6.13/6.18), (6.14/6.19), and (6.15/6.20) appear to be (6.21), (6.22), and (6.23), respectively.

(6.21) He was warned to look out for an ex-convict with $\begin{cases} \text{something red.} \\ \text{a red piece of clothing.} \end{cases}$

(6.22) He was warned to look out for $\begin{cases} \text{someone with a red shirt.} \\ \text{a red-shirted person.} \end{cases}$

(6.23) He was warned to look out for an ex-convict with a shirt of some particular color.

These examples show that the clefted phrase (the predicate of the higher clause) in surface structure is not necessarily identical with the focus, and that the lower clause is not necessarily identical with the presupposition, as the deep structure theory claims they are in deep structure. The strongest statement we can make is that in cleft sentences, the focus must be *included* in the clefted phrase, and that the presupposition *includes* the lowest clause. Furthermore, it seems quixotic to try to save the deep structure theory by claiming that there is an additional clefting in the deep structure of (6.13)–(6.15) which disappears in the surface:

(6.24) *Was it (a) shirt that it was an ex-convict in a red (one) that he was
       warned to look out for?
(6.25) *Was it (an) ex-convict that it was a red-shirted (one) that he was
       warned to look out for?
(6.26) *Was it red that it was an ex-convict with a shirt that is that he was
       warned to look out for?

One might try to argue that (6.24)–(6.26) are bad solely because they violate Ross's Complex NP Constraint (Ross 1967a), which prohibits relativization from inside a relative clause. But this argument will not account for examples to be discussed shortly, in which uncleftable morphemes such as verbs, prefixes, and tense function as focus because of emphatic stress. Furthermore, the deep structure theory must violate the constraint if it produces emphatic stress from cleft constructions, since emphatic stress may be marked within a relative clause.

In the surface structure theory, we can accept the weaker account of the meaning of cleft sentences that is suggested above and still deal with the differences in (6.13)–(6.15). If focus assignment refers to "a phrase containing the main stress," focus can be chosen in (6.13), for example, as any of the following phrases:

(6.27) (an) ex-convict with a red shirt
(6.28) with a red shirt
(6.29) a red shirt
(6.30) shirt

Corresponding to these choices of focus are the following "natural" responses:

(6.17) No, it was an AUTOMOBILE salesman . . .
(6.31) No, it was an ex-convict wearing DUNGAREES . . .
(6.32) No, it was an ex-convict with a CARNATION . . .
(6.18) No, it was an ex-convict with a red TIE . . .

Example (6.14) has (6.33)–(6.35) as possible choices of foci; (6.15) has (6.36)–(6.39).

(6.33) a red-shirted ex-convict
(6.34) ex-convict
(6.35) convict

(6.36) an ex-convict with a shirt that is red
(6.37) with a shirt that is red
(6.38) that is red
(6.39) red

Of all the possible foci in (6.13)–(6.15), only the choices (6.27), (6.33), and (6.36) are semantically equivalent; these correspond to the common "natural" response (6.17). Other choices of focus lead to responses not compatible with all three questions.

To further show that stress and not clefting is the criterion for focus assignment, we observe that emphatic stress occurring anywhere in a sentence attracts the focus. (I use # to mark an inappropriate response.)

(6.40) Did Fred HIT Bill?
   $\Big\{$ No, he KISSED him.
     # No, he hit TOM.
(6.41) Does Walt UNDERrate the opposition?
   $\Big\{$ No, he OVERrates it.
     # No, CHARLEY underrates the opposition.
(6.42) Can Willy do SIXTY pushups?
   $\Big\{$ No, he can only do forty-FIVE.
     # No, he can do sixty SITUPS.

Since clefts involving verbs, prefixes, and quantifiers are impossible,

(6.43) *Was it HIT that Fred (did to) Bill?
(6.44) *Is it UNDER that Walt rates the opposition?
(6.45) *Is it SIXTY that Willy can do (of) pushups?

the cleft theory of focus assignment can be maintained only with a great deal of artifice; the surface structure theory requires no modification.

One might abandon the cleft theory yet maintain that focus is marked in deep structure, by claiming that some deep structure node is marked with the semantic feature FOCUS, which has a phonological realization as high stress. However, Chomsky shows that choices of focus correspond to constituency in surface structure, not deep structure; hence this alternative deep structure theory also loses plausibility. For example, (6.46) has (6.47)–(6.49) as possible responses.

(6.46) Is John certain to WIN?

(6.47) No, he is certain to LOSE.
(6.48) No, he is likely not even to be NOMINATED.
(6.49) No, the election may not even take PLACE.

These responses correspond to the foci *win*, *certain to win*, and *is John certain to win*, respectively. But the second of these is not a deep structure constituent, since the deep structure of (6.46) is usually taken to be of the form (6.50).

(6.50) $[_S$ for John to win$]_S$ is certain

The choice of focus and presupposition giving (6.48) as a response is therefore not available until after the transformation of complement subject raising has taken place.

Similarly, the passive construction (6.51) has (6.52)–(6.53) as possible responses.

(6.51) Was *The Sound Pattern of English* reviewed by the New York TIMES?
(6.52) No, it was reviewed by the Reader's DIGEST.
(6.53) No, it was made into a MOVIE.

These answers correspond to the foci *New York Times* and (*was*) *reviewed by the New York Times*, respectively. Again, the second of these is not a deep structure constituent, but rather a derived structure constituent created by the passive transformation.

A third example involves *Tough* movement. Among the possible responses to (6.54) is (6.55), and among the responses to (6.56) is (6.57); the responses are not interchangeable.

(6.54) Is a krummhorn easy to play twelve-tone MUSIC on?

(6.55) No, a krummhorn isn't even easy to BLOW into.

(6.56) Is twelve-tone music easy to play on a KRUMMHORN?

(6.57) No, twelve-tone music isn't even easy to SING.

In (6.54) the focus is apparently (*easy*) *to play twelve-tone music on,* and in (6.56), (*easy*) *to play on a krummhorn.* But neither of these is a deep structure constituent; in deep structure, the complement of *easy* must be (*for someone*) *to play twelve-tone music on a krummhorn* in order to capture the understood grammatical relations (see however section 5.14). The focus constituents exist only by the grace of the *Tough* movement transformation.

Chomsky establishes, therefore, that the evidence leads one to prefer the surface structure theory of focus assignment. As he points out, if one is determined to maintain the Katz-Postal Hypothesis and represent focus in deep structure, one can do so. It is simple to allow an initial expansion of the sentence S → S' − Focus, then to expand S' in the usual way. A late filtering transformation can reject a derivation if focus does not correspond to a surface structure constituent containing the main stress. Unfortunately, the examples given here show that the expansion of focus must permit the generation of rather arbitrary pieces of structure, including the entire range of surface structures (or pieces of underlying structure corresponding to surface structure constituents, which is probably worse) and even certain ranges of prefixes. The Katz-Postal Hypothesis has been preserved, but at the expense of a host of very strange phrase-structure rules which have no motivation other than the preservation of the Katz-Postal Hypothesis.[2]

[2]G. Lakoff (1970b) seems to advocate a position of this sort. As he is very vague about the contents of the presupposition and focus constituents in his semantic representation, it is difficult to tell whether his account successfully avoids the difficulties Chomsky points out. The problems that Lakoff claims to find in Chomsky's approach seem to me to be due to errors of his own. The first case, involving stressed prenominal adjectives, is perfectly straightforward; Lakoff's argument is based on the unsupported (and in this case incorrect) claim that restrictive relative clauses are presupposed. The second case involves the following two sentences, in which I have indicated the surface structure bracketing:

(i) John [$_{VP}$looked up [$_{NP}$a girl [$_S$whom he had once met in Chicago]$_S$]$_{NP}$]$_{VP}$
(ii) John [$_{VP}$looked [$_{NP}$a girl]$_{NP}$ up [$_S$whom he had once met in Chicago]$_S$]$_{VP}$

Lakoff asserts that these sentences have identical ranges of foci, and therefore that a theory that bases focus on surface structure constituency is disconfirmed. However, a cursory look at the predictions made by the surface structure theory shows Lakoff's assertion to be incorrect. Assuming that main stress is on *Chicago*, (i) has as one possible focus the constituent *a girl whom he had once met in Chicago.* Since (ii) has under-

6.2 Stress Assignment and Focus

It is not quite correct to characterize the focus assignment rule as establishing the focus on "a phrase containing the main stress." Containing the main stress is a necessary but not sufficient condition for a phrase to be focus. To see this, observe that in (6.40)–(6.42), the VP is a constituent containing the main stress, yet it certainly cannot be focus.

A more precise condition can be stated more conveniently as a dependence of stress position on choice of focus:

(6.58) If a phrase P is chosen as the focus of a sentence S, the highest stress in S will be on the syllable of P that is assigned highest stress by the regular stress rules.

According to this principle, the possible foci of a sentence are the domains of phonological cycles in which the syllable with main stress is assigned [1 stress]. Hence a sentence will be ambiguous as to focus just in case the highest stressed syllable has received [1 stress] on more than one phonological cycle.

Let us see how principle (6.58) applies to some examples. Start with an example from section 6.1, which is reproduced below with its surface structure.

(6.5) Did Maxwell kill the judge with a hammer?

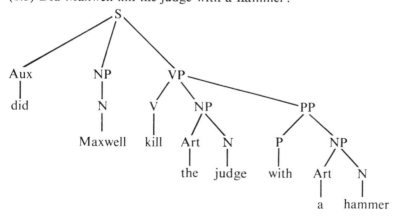

If the focus is *Maxwell*, emphatic stress will be placed on the first vowel,

gone relative clause extraposition, this phrase is no longer a constituent. Thus the theory predicts that (i) should be a more natural answer than (ii) to *Whom did John look up?* Insofar as my intuitions are applicable to this example, this prediction seems correct.

since the Main Stress Rule of Chomsky and Halle (1968) assigns it the
stress *Máxwell*. Likewise, if the focus is any of the other single words, emphatic stress will be placed on the main stress of that word (we discuss the
semantic infelicity of certain choices of focus in section 6.3). Suppose that
the focus is one of the NPs or PPs. In the case of (6.5), the articles and the
preposition are treated as proclitics by the stress rules, so emphatic stress
will fall on the main stress of the noun. Suppose that the focus is the entire
VP (asking "What did Maxwell do?"). Since the Nuclear Stress Rule will
assign the stress *kíll the júdge with a hámmer*, emphatic stress will again be
placed on the first syllable of *hammer*. If the focus is the entire sentence
(asking "What happened?"), *hammer* will again receive the main stress,
since the Nuclear Stress Rule puts [1 stress] on the final constituent. Hence
unless the main stress falls on *hammer*, (6.5) is unambiguous as to focus
(except for the trivial *judge/the judge* distinction). If the main stress falls on
hammer, though, the sentence can be read with any of the five nodes dominating it as focus. It is likely that at least some of these readings can be
sorted out by further subtleties of stress and intonation; some suggestions
will be made later in this section.

Next, consider (6.13), reproduced here with its surface structure.

(6.13) Was it an ex-convict with a red shirt that he was warned to look
out for?

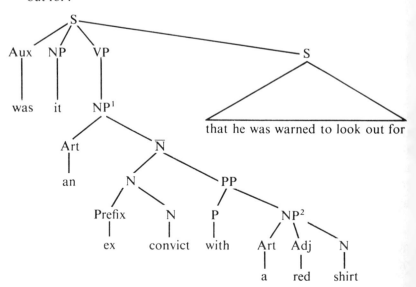

First, recall that it is inherent in the meaning of the cleft construction that the focus must be included in the copula of the main clause. Thus a choice of focus outside of NP^1 would be semantically inconsistent; this is reflected in the unacceptability of main stress anywhere in the complement S (except as an echo question, when the meaning of the sentence is not at issue, only its phonology; see p. 242). However, the cleft construction allows focus to be chosen on any node within NP^1. Of these nodes, the articles and the preposition can be excluded for semantic reasons. Any other lexical material can be focused, receiving main stress. Note in particular that the prefix *ex-* can be focused and that it will then receive main stress. Also, if *convict* is focused, main stress will fall on the first syllable, where [1 stress] is placed by the Main Stress Rule. If the larger noun *ex-convict* is focused, main stress will again go on the first syllable of *convict*, as predicted by the stress rules and principle (6.58). Hence this surface form will be ambiguous between focus on *ex-convict* (contrasting with *automobile salesman*) and *convict* (contrasting with *ex-boxer*). The surface form with main stress on *shirt* will have as possible foci the noun *shirt*, NP^2, PP, $\bar{N}$, and NP^1, since in each of these cycles *shirt* is assigned [1 stress] by the stress rules. These are exactly the foci observed in (6.17)–(6.18) and (6.31)–(6.32) (where the difference between $\bar{N}$ and NP^1 is probably indistinguishable with the fineness of judgments we are applying here).

Finally, consider the following example, in which the choice of focus and the syntactic ambiguity interact in an interesting way. (This example was pointed out to me by Vicki Fromkin.)

(6.59) Was it $\begin{cases} \text{(a) } [_{NP}\text{a } [\text{black}]_{Adj} [\text{bird}]_N]_{NP} \\ \text{(b) } [_{NP}\text{a } [_N[\text{black}]_{Adj} [\text{bird}]_N]_N]_{NP} \end{cases}$ that you saw?

Case (a) is the normal adjective-noun construction *black bird*; case (b) is the compound *blackbird*. In either case, there are three possible choices of focus: *black*, *bird*, and *black bird*. Assume first that only *black* is focused and hence that main stress falls there. Natural responses will then be like (6.60) for (6.59a) and like (6.61) for (6.59b); note that the stress patterns are identical in the replies as well as in the questions.

(6.60) No, I saw a PURPLE bird.
(6.61) No, I saw a BLUEbird.

If *bird* is focus and stress falls there, natural responses are (6.62) and (6.63), respectively.

(6.62) No, I saw a black CAR.
(6.63) No, I saw a blackBOARD.

If the entire phrase is focused, however, the two cases differ in surface form, because the stress rules apply differently. In (6.59a), the Nuclear Stress Rule applies, placing [1 stress] on *bird*. Hence principle (6.58) dictates that the surface form be *black BIRD*. But in (6.59b), the Compound Rule applies, stressing *black*, so (6.58) requires the surface form to be *BLACKbird*. Both of these have (6.64) as a natural response.

(6.64) No, I saw a GHOST.

The surface form (6.59) with main stress on *black* is therefore three ways ambiguous: case (a) with focus on *black*, or case (b) with focus on *black* or *blackbird*. Similarly, main stress on *bird* is ambiguous between case (a) with focus on *black* or *black bird*, or case (b) with focus on *bird*.

How can principle (6.58) be incorporated into the grammar? I suggest the following way, which does minimal violence to the theory as a whole. One artificial construct is required: a syntactic marker F which can be associated with any node in the surface structure. Since F is of relevance only in the surface structure and phonology, it can be introduced in either of two ways, either by an attachment transformation like the *Syntactic Structures* rule for introducing negation and the rules discussed in Kuroda (1969), or by an extension of the phrase structure rules (assuming that no new nodes are introduced by the transformations, which is an open question). The choice between these two methods is immaterial to present concerns, so I will simply assume that F is present in surface structure.

Two systems of rules will make use of the marker F, one in the semantics and one in the phonology. The former system contains at least the rule of focus assignment, which we present here in preliminary form.

(6.65) (Focus assignment, first approximation)
    The semantic material associated with surface structure nodes dominated by F is the Focus of the sentence. To derive the Presupposition, substitute appropriate semantic variables for the focused material.

Since a well-formed semantic interpretation of a sentence must be divided into Focus and Presupposition, well-formedness conditions will indirectly ensure that F occurs somewhere in the surface structure.

There are perhaps two phrases in (6.65) that deserve further comment. One, "appropriate semantic variables," will be discussed in section 6.3. The other, "the semantic material associated with surface structure nodes," has been subject to some misinterpretation (for example in Ross 1969b, section 1.1, in a somewhat different, but relevant context). To see the apparent difficulty, consider the reading of (6.66) in which the VP *arrested by the police* is focus.

(6.66) Was Ted arrested by the POLICE?

To identify the semantic material associated with the focus, one might think that it is necessary to perform a semantic rule "Anti-Passive" to undo the effects of the transformation. This of course would result in needless duplication in the grammar as a whole.

What is really needed is a way of tracing material throughout the course of a derivation despite any changes it may undergo, for example by associating with each node a unique identification index. These indices will of course be of considerably different theoretical import than the referential indices of Chomsky (1965), as they have no purpose other than identification. They may be compared to memory locations in a computer program, which serve to identify information but which do not contribute to its content. Their use is already implied in the common notation for transformations which uses numerals to identify various parts of the structural description in the structural change.

Under this proposal, focus assignment has merely to use the identification indices to locate the portions of the semantic representation derived by various rules at various levels that correspond to the surface structure nodes dominated by F. Hence there is no need for "anti-transformations."

Turning to the phonological realization of the marker F, we can get a first approximation to the correct stress patterns with the following rule.

(6.67) (Emphatic Stress Rule)
$$V \rightarrow [\text{emph stress}] \, / \, [X \, [\overline{1 \text{ stress}}] \, Y]_F$$

(6.67) will be in the phonological cycle, following all the other stress rules. We will establish the convention that [emph stress] does not weaken on successive cycles, as do other stresses. Thus in the assignment of stress contour, the main stress of the constituent marked F will receive emphatic stress and all other stresses will have the values assigned by Chomsky and Halle's rules.

One might want to refine (6.67) to account for Chomsky's observation that for narrower choices of focus, the emphatic stress seems more prominent relative to its surroundings. For example, it is possible to disambiguate (6.5)

(6.5) Did Maxwell kill the judge with a HAMMER?

with a certain degree of reliability by changing the prominence of the emphatic stress on *hammer*. This suggests that perhaps *all* stresses dominated by F are exempted from weakening on successive cycles, preserving their strength relative to F, but ending up with higher stress relative to the rest of the sentence than would otherwise be the case. However, as judgments on stress become unreliable beyond a certain point, and as they are intimately tied up with intonation (see section 6.7) as well as intensity, I would hesitate to propose much beyond this point without thorough experimental work.

This proposal will not account for examples like Chomsky's *I'm talking about AFfirmation, not CONfirmation*, since *af-* and *con-* never receive [1 stress]. In most examples of this type the contrast being made is phonological rather than semantic, in that the speaker is trying to correct the hearer's mistaken impression of what words were just said. There seem to be three alternatives: first, accounting for these cases with an entirely different rule; second, extending the Emphatic Stress Rule to these cases; third, calling these cases ungrammatical but necessary to say sometimes, and hence derivatively generated by a temporary weakening of the conditions on the Emphatic Stress Rule. The first alternative probably misses the generality of the phenomenon. Of the other two, I lean toward the third, though without much argument.

6.3 The Nonsyntactic Basis of Contrast
Some remarks are called for on the notion of "appropriate semantic variables" to be substituted for the focus in forming the presupposition. The problem of defining appropriateness is amenable to linguistic analysis only to a limited extent. Beyond a rather quickly attained point, however, it becomes clear that the solution deeply involves conceptual structure and

knowledge of the world, which we are (arbitrarily) not investigating here. Hence we will be relying heavily on unanalyzed intuition in certain aspects of the discussion.

In accordance with the definition of the presupposition given in section 6.1, the variable must be chosen in such a way that it defines a coherent class of possible contrasts with the focus, pieces of semantic information that could equally well have taken the place of the focus in the sentence, within bounds established by the language, the discourse, and the external situation. The class of possible contrasts represents the range of information over which either the speaker or the hearer is uncertain (depending on whether the sentence is interrogative or declarative). Each possible contrast will share with the focus the semantic content of the variable in the presupposition, but will differ in other semantic content.[3]

An obvious condition on choice of variable, then, is that the variable have the same functional semantic form as the focus. As a crude example, a variable with the functional form of predicate cannot be substituted for a focus denoting an individual: the presupposition would be grossly ill-formed semantically. Similarly, a variable with the form of a one-place predicate cannot substitute for a focused two-place predicate; a variable manner adverb cannot be substituted for a focused locative.

It is important to observe that this condition does not imply anything about the syntax of the variable or of the possible contrasts. Within certain limits, the syntax is open to variation. For example, (6.68) seems a natural question-response pair.

(6.68) Did the cop ARREST Bill?
    No, he only LEERED at him.

The foci of the two sentences are both two-place predicates, but *arrest* is a transitive verb and *leer* takes a PP object. The presupposition is not clearly expressible in English, but an approximation might be a sentence of still another syntactic form:

(6.69) The cop did something nasty to Bill.

[3]We can actually think of the focus as consisting of only those semantic markers which are not contained in the variable; in fact this is the proper way to satisfy the definition of focus in section 6.1. However, for convenience we will continue to refer to the focus in terms of full lexical items or phrases.

Thus there appears to be no syntactic motivation for placing requirements on the form of the presupposition beyond those imposed by the form of semantic representations and the rules deriving them. (6.68) forms a natural pair because the projection rules sketched in Chapter 3 assign both sentences a semantic structure of the form (6.70),

(6.70) f(the cop, Bill)

in which *the cop* is marked as the Agent, and the function f specifies a point-action in which the individual denoted by the first variable does something having unpleasant consequences for the individual marked by the second variable. The presupposition goes no further than this, but each sentence in the actual discourse mentions a particular f having these properties. Since there is no verb in English having the necessary semantic properties for the presupposition, we must build up f as a composite of the items *do something nasty to* in order to express the presupposition in English. Thus a syntactic nonconstituent can be interpreted by the projection rules as having the semantic structure of f in (6.70). This point will be of great important in subsequent discussion.

We have seen then that syntactic similarity is not a necessary condition for possible contrast. Neither is it a sufficient condition. Consider some discourses involving verb-particle constructions.

(6.71)   Did Fred turn the lights ON?
          No, he turned them OFF.
(6.72)   Did Fred turn the proposal IN?
      #(*)No, he turned it OUT.

Both discourses involve a contrast only on closely related particles. But the items *turn on/turn off* happen to form a semantic contrast that can be concentrated solely in the particle, and *turn in/turn out* do not. In (6.71), then, there exists an appropriate semantic variable that can be substituted for the particle, having just the range *on/off* (and perhaps *up/down*). In (6.72) there is no such variable, so a well-formed presupposition cannot be derived if the particle is focused. Syntactically, however, there is no difference between (6.71) and (6.72).

It appears, then, that the semantic variable in the focus assignment rule must be assigned with respect to the semantic interpretation of the sentence, disregarding the syntax, in particular the deep structure. The rule refers to two levels of derivation, the surface structure and the semantic representation, in forming focus and presupposition.

6.4 A More Precise Hypothesis of Presupposition and Assertion

Having presented a range of material concerning presuppositions, we will now propose a formalism for the semantic reading resulting from the application of focus assignment. The reasons for choosing this particular formalism will not be immediately evident; however, subsequent sections will show how this analysis leads to interesting accounts of the relation of negation to focus and presupposition and of the effect of certain aspects of intonation on meaning.

The derivation of the semantic representation proceeds in three steps. First, as in section 6.2, focus assignment derives two formal objects from the otherwise determined semantic representation SR of a sentence S. The first, the Focus, consists of that semantic material associated with surface structure nodes dominated by the marker F. The second is a one-place predicate $Presupp_s(x)$, formed by replacing the Focus by an appropriate semantic variable x in SR. As section 6.3 showed, the variable x is limited by the semantic notion "possible contrast," and the function $Presupp_s(x)$ is independent of the functional structure based on deep structure grammatical relations. For example, if the focus is the verb *like* in (6.73), the functional structure is (6.74), but the function $Presupp_s(x)$ is something like (6.75).

(6.73) John LIKES Bill.

(6.74) LIKE (JOHN, BILL)

(6.75) the $\begin{Bmatrix} \text{relation between John and Bill} \\ \text{attitude of John toward Bill} \end{Bmatrix}$ is x

The second step in the derivation constructs another formal object, the presuppositional set, defined as the set of values which, when substituted for x in $Presupp_s(x)$, yield a true proposition. We will symbolize the presuppositional set with the expression $\lambda x Presupp_s(x)$. (The lambda notation $\lambda x P(x)$ is originally due to Church. This particular interpretation of it discussed in Carnap 1956.)

The third step in the derivation constructs the presupposition and assertion from the presuppositional set. The presupposition takes a form roughly expressed by (6.76).

$$(6.76)\ \lambda x\mathrm{Presupp}_s\,(x) \begin{cases} \text{is a coherent set} \\ \text{is well-defined} \end{cases}\text{in the present discourse} \\ \text{is amenable to discussion} \\ \text{is under discussion}$$

The form (6.76) must be chosen in preference to an existential presupposition "there exists something satisfying $\mathrm{Presupp}_s\,(x)$" because $\lambda x\mathrm{Presupp}_s\,(x)$ can be the empty set, as in *NOBODY likes Bill*.

The assertion of a declarative sentence S claims that the focus is a member of the presuppositional set (i.e. satisfies the presuppositional function):

$$(6.77)\ \mathrm{Focus} \in \lambda x\mathrm{Presupp}_s\,(x)$$

For other sentence types, such as questions and imperatives, the assertion will obviously take a different form.

Because of the way the assertion is defined, its truth conditions will be the same as the original representation SR, with the exception that the presupposition (6.76) must be true before the assertion is meaningful. Formally, this is so because of the definition of the lambda function; intuitively, because we have extracted the focus from SR in the first step of the derivation, then reintroduced it in an equivalent position in the third step.

We have already pointed out two cases in which (6.76) can be violated. The first case, illustrated in the "unnatural" dialogues of section 6.1,

(6.78)   Is it JOHN who writes poetry?   (= 6.1)
      # No, it is JOHN who writes short stories.   (= 6.3)

occurs when the two speakers do not agree on what is under discussion. The second case, discussed in section 6.3, occurs when no appropriate variable x is available, so the presuppositional set cannot be formed or is not well defined.

The rule of focus assignment can now be restated as (6.79).

(6.79) (Focus assignment)

In a sentence S, with otherwise determined semantic representation SR, the semantic material associated with surface structure nodes dominated by F is the Focus of S. Substitute an appropriate semantic variable x for Focus in SR to form the function $\text{Presupp}_s(x)$. The presupposition of S is then formed as (6.76), and the assertion is (6.77).

To return to example (6.73), focus assignment derives the function $\text{Presupp}_s(x)$ as (6.75). Hence the presupposition is (6.80) and the assertion is (6.81).

$$(6.80)\ \lambda x \left[\text{the} \begin{Bmatrix} \text{relation between John and Bill} \\ \text{attitude of John toward Bill} \end{Bmatrix} \text{is } x \right] \text{is} \begin{Bmatrix} \text{well-defined} \\ \text{under discussion} \end{Bmatrix}$$

$$(6.81)\ like \in \lambda x \left[\text{the} \begin{Bmatrix} \text{relation between John and Bill} \\ \text{attitude of John toward Bill} \end{Bmatrix} \text{is } x \right]$$

These interpretations can be represented intuitively as (6.82) and (6.83), respectively.

$$(6.82)\ \text{We're talking about possible} \begin{Bmatrix} \text{relations between John and Bill.} \\ \text{attitudes of John toward Bill.} \end{Bmatrix}$$

$$(6.83)\ like \text{ is one of} \begin{Bmatrix} \text{the relations between John and Bill.} \\ \text{John's attitudes toward Bill.} \end{Bmatrix}$$

Our account of the assertion, however, is not quite accurate. An additional element due to the intonation contour will be introduced in section 6.7.

6.5 Association with Focus

The interpretation of words such as *even*, *only*, and *just* is intimately tied up with focus and presupposition, as pointed out by Fischer (1968). These words can occur before NPs and in the auxiliary. Before a simple NP, no ambiguity results. But if *even* is in the auxiliary, a number of possible readings present themselves. (Subsequent remarks referring to *even* apply, with one exception, identically to *only* and *just*, though the examples have to be changed for appropriateness.)

(6.84) Even John gave his daughter a new bicycle.
(6.85) John gave even his daughter a new bicycle.
(6.86) John gave his daughter even a new bicycle.
(6.87) John even gave his daughter a new bicycle.

In (6.87) the readings are associated with different choices of focus: *even* can go with *a new bicycle*, the VP, and perhaps the entire S. In (6.87) S focus is not so clear, but in (6.88) (due to Steve Anderson) it is.

(6.88) The results of today's games will be remarkable: Harvard will even defeat Loyola.

Note however that emphatic stress in (6.87) results in lack of ambiguity. *Even* must go with the stressed constituent.

(6.89) JOHN even gave his daughter a new bicycle.
John even gave his DAUGHTER a new bicycle.
John even gave HIS daughter a new bicycle.
John even gave his daughter a NEW bicycle.
John even gave his daughter a new BICYCLE.
John even GAVE his daughter a new bicycle.

Furthermore, stresses in (6.84), (6.85), and (6.86) render the sentences unacceptable unless the stress is in the NP preceded by *even*.

(6.90)	Even JOHN gave his daughter a new bicycle.				
	*Even John	GAVE			
	*		HIS		
	*			DAUGHTER	
	*				NEW
	*					BICYCLE.

(6.91)	*JOHN gave even his daughter a new bicycle.				
	*	GAVE			
	ok	HIS			
	ok	DAUGHTER			
	*		NEW		
	*			BICYCLE.	

(6.92)   *JOHN gave his daughter even a new bicycle.
      *   GAVE
      *   HIS
      *   DAUGHTER
    ok   NEW
    ok   BICYCLE.

To account for these facts, let us consider the meaning of *even* (cf. Anderson 1969). The association of *even* with a constituent implies that there is something special, unusual, or unexpected about the connection of that constituent with the event. If there is something unexpected about the constituent, it must be new to the hearer, and hence by definition part of the focus.

We will propose a rule *association with focus*, which applies to *even* to associate its reading with the focus. Unfortunately, at the present stage of research the formal nature of this rule cannot be specified. The reason there must be a rule accomplishing this association, and not just a general semantic convention, is that there are particular structural conditions under which the association takes place. To specify these conditions, we need to define the notion of *range*. (I avoid the usual term *scope* here because it will be introduced for a different purpose in Chapter 7.) Certain lexical items, among them *even*, will define a range, that is, a set of nodes in the surface structure bearing a particular structural relation to the lexical item, where the relation is defined by the lexical item itself. Assuming that *even* in (6.89) is dominated by S, and in (6.90)–(6.92) by the following NP, the range of *even* can be defined as (6.93).

(6.93) (Range of *even*)
    If *even* is directly dominated by a node X, X and all nodes dominated by X are in the range of *even*.

Association with focus will be able to take place only if the focus is within the range of *even*. If the focus is not within the range of *even*, association with focus will not apply and hence an unacceptable reading will be generated.

To illustrate this analysis, return to (6.89)–(6.92). In (6.90)–(6.92), the range of *even* is only the NP it precedes, so focus can be only within that NP, although it may be any element within the NP. In (6.89), where *even* is attached to S, the entire VP is within the range of *even*, as is the subject, so any constituent can be chosen as focus.

As Anderson points out, this analysis of the grammar of *even* eliminates the need to syntactically restrict the occurrences of *even* to one per sentence. Such a need prompted Kuroda's proposal (1969) for handling *even* by means of an attachment transformation that changed meaning. Since there is only one focus per sentence, and since one can (presumably) mention only once that the focus is remarkable, this leaves semantic room for only one *even* per sentence. In the syntax, then, we can generate *even* freely in all constituents it occurs with. There is no need for transformations to move *even* around, and no need to make any syntactic restrictions on its occurrence.[4]

The single difference between *even* on one hand, and *only* and *just* on the other, is that *only* and *just* cannot substitute for *even* in the first sentence of (6.89).

(6.94) *JOHN $\begin{Bmatrix} only \\ just \end{Bmatrix}$ gave his daughter a new bicycle.

We can account for this difference by defining the range of *only* and *just* as follows:

(6.95) (Range of *only* and *just*)
   If *only* or *just* is dominated by a node X, X and all nodes dominated by X and to the right of *only* or *just* are in the range of *only* or *just*.

The specification "to the right of" will make no difference except in this one case, where the focus is to the left of *even*, *only*, and *just*. Here *even* will be able to undergo association with focus, and *only* and *just* will not.

This analysis provides confirmation of the theory of the auxiliary presented in section 3.8, in which it was argued that, in the surface structure,

---

[4]One particular theory of *even* that is inadequate on other grounds is one in which *even* is syntactically associated with the focus in deep structure, then moved transformationally to its surface position in the auxiliary. Such a movement transformation would violate Ross's (1967a) Complex NP Constraint, which prohibits moving material out of relative clauses, as shown by the following example:

Sam even saw the man who was wearing a RED hat.

the first auxiliary is dominated by S and the other auxiliaries are dominated by VP. This analysis predicts that the subject is within the range of *even* only if *even* comes before the second auxiliary, since otherwise *even* would be dominated by VP, not S. The following examples bear this out: *even* after the second auxiliary is unacceptable with subject focus, although other foci are possible.

(6.96) JOHN (even) will (even) have (*even) given his daughter a new bicycle.

JOHN (even) has (even) been (*even) giving his daughter French lessons.

(6.97) John will have even given his DAUGHTER a new bicycle.

etc.

As further data bearing on the definition of range, we notice that preposed constituents are not within the range of an *even* or *only* in the aux, except in "Yiddish" dialects: compare (6.98) with (6.99).

(6.98) *In the GARDEN Max $\begin{Bmatrix} \text{even} \\ \text{only} \end{Bmatrix}$ reads comic books.

*MAX I $\begin{Bmatrix} \text{even} \\ \text{only} \end{Bmatrix}$ hate to bother.

(6.99)   Even in the GARDEN Max reads comic books.

Only in the GARDEN does Max read comic books.

Even MAX I hate to bother.

Only MAX do I hate to bother.

Only automatically excludes constituents to the left from its range, so its behavior in (6.98)–(6.99) is already accounted for. The range of *even*, however, so far should include topicalized phrases, so there is not yet a way to explain why it is bad in (6.98). Two alternatives suggest themselves. First, we can adopt the more complex definition (6.100) for the range of *even*.

(6.100) (Range of *even*)

If *even* is dominated by a node X, the range of *even* includes X and all nodes dominated by X to the right of *even*, plus the subject if X is an S.

Alternatively, we could claim that preposed constituents are adjoined to a new S node introduced above the original S (so-called Chomsky-adjunction), giving the derived structure (6.101) for (6.98).

(6.101) [$_s$in the garden [$_s$Max even reads comic books]$_s$]$_s$
[$_s$Max [$_s$I even hate to bother]$_s$]$_s$

Then the range of *even* as originally defined includes only the lower S, so association with focus cannot be applied correctly. I have no evidence in favor of either of these approaches; note, however, that the need for Chomsky-adjunction in linguistic theory is very much open to question.[5]

Also in the class of words that undergo association with focus are the *-ly* adverbs *merely, truly, simply,* and *hardly.* (6.102) is ambiguous in the usual way for such words, depending on choice of focus; stress automatically attracts the adverb.

$$(6.102) \text{ Tom } \begin{Bmatrix} \text{merely} \\ \text{simply} \\ \text{truly} \\ \text{hardly} \end{Bmatrix} \text{ put the book on the table.}$$

$$(6.103) \text{ Tom } \begin{Bmatrix} \text{merely} \\ \text{simply} \\ \text{truly} \\ \text{hardly} \end{Bmatrix} \text{ put } \begin{cases} \text{the BOOK on the table.} \\ \text{the book on the TABLE.} \end{cases}$$

These adverbs seem to be more restricted in use than the *even* group. Like *only* and *just,* their range only goes to the right. Their occurrence in front of NPs seems to be restricted largely to indefinite NPs.

[5]These solutions make different claims about the "Yiddish" dialect which accepts *even* in (6.98). I assume the difference between the "Yiddish" and the standard dialects is not a matter of daughter-adjunction versus Chomsky-adjunction in the preposing rules, since this would be a drastic change in linguistic theory. In the Chomsky-adjunction solution, the "Yiddish" dialect can be accommodated by allowing the scope of *even* to include higher nodes than that immediately dominating *even,* probably a complication of the definition. On the other hand, the daughter-adjunction solution can describe the "Yiddish" dialect simply by reverting to definition (6.93) for the range of *even,* a simplification. In a similar way, the two solutions make different claims about the relative complexity of *even* and *only*: *even* is simpler than *only* in the Chomsky-adjunction solution and more complex than *only* in the daughter-adjunction solution.

6.104) Donald brought along $\begin{Bmatrix} \text{simply} \\ \text{merely} \end{Bmatrix}$ $\begin{Bmatrix} \text{a piece of cheese} \\ \text{*the first thing he found} \end{Bmatrix}$ for lunch.

6.105) This is truly $\begin{cases} \text{a fantastic result.} \\ \text{*the fantastic result you've been expecting.} \end{cases}$

6.106) Hardly $\begin{Bmatrix} \text{a mouse was} \\ \text{*the mice were} \end{Bmatrix}$ stirring.

(note however: *Hardly even the mice were stirring.*)

Syntactically, these constructions seem to be related to *many a, such a,* and *not a*, which are also only indefinite. In particular, the appearance of the quantifiers *many* and *hardly* seems no coincidence. There is undoubtedly also a relation between these constructions and things like *a mere boy, a true believer*, and *a simple contradiction*. Under our assumptions this cannot be a transformational relationship. Rather these are the syntactic analogues of (6.102) generated by the base rule schema of Chapter 3 when the head is a noun instead of a verb.

At least two of the adverbs that occur in the auxiliary position only, *utterly* and *virtually*, are still more restricted than the ones we have discussed so far. These probably also attract to focus, but they only allow the focus to be the verb. Contrastive stress is bad elsewhere in examples like 6.107).

6.107) The enemy $\begin{Bmatrix} \text{utterly} \\ \text{virtually} \end{Bmatrix}$ destroyed the city.

*	ENEMY	
ok	DESTROYED	
*		CITY

Also, they do not occur in front of indefinite NPs.

6.108) *This is virtually a fantastic result.
　　　*Utterly a mouse was stirring.

The same is probably true of one sense of *really*, at least when it occurs in auxiliary position.

There is at least one other semantic rule that is similar to association with focus. Bowers (1969b) points out that in the preposed *of*-phrase connected with superlatives, the reference shifts with contrastive stress.

(6.109) Of the three men,
$$\begin{cases} \text{John hates BILL the most.} \\ \text{*John hates MARY the most.} \\ \text{JOHN hates Bill the most.} \\ \text{*MARY hates Bill the most.} \end{cases}$$

This cannot be a syntactic linkage originating in deep structure: **John of the three men* is impossible, and the *of*-phrase really goes syntactically with the superlative.

(6.110) John hates Bill the most of the three men.

With the *of*-phrase here, however, stress sounds good only on *Bill*. In the passive, stress sounds good only on *John*.

(6.111) Bill is hated by JOHN the most of the three.

This may be another range phenomenon. Note that when the *of*-phrase is in the VP, only the noun phrase within the VP can be stressed. But when the *of*-phrase is attached to S, as in (6.109), either NP can be stressed. However, I would prefer not to speculate further on this construction.

6.6 Negation: Preliminary Account

It has frequently been noted that there is a connection between focus and the interpretation of negation. Often negation does not seem to apply to an entire sentence, but only to part of it. For example, (6.112) is multiply ambiguous, having (6.113)–(6.115) among its paraphrases (possibly differentiated by degree of emphasis on *hammer*).

(6.112)   Maxwell didn't kill the judge with a silver HAMMER.

(6.113)   It wasn't with a silver hammer that Maxwell killed the judge.
(6.114) (*)Kill the judge with a silver hammer isn't what Maxwell did.
(6.115)   It's not the case that Maxwell killed the judge with a silver hammer.

This ambiguity is similar to the ambiguities with *even* and *only* in section 6.5, related to the possible choices of foci. (6.113)–(6.115) correspond to focused final PP, VP, and the entire S, respectively. It appears then that negation can undergo the rule association with focus. This is confirmed when we shift the stress in (6.112). For example, if *judge* receives emphatic stress, (6.116) is a paraphrase.

(6.116) It's not the judge that Maxwell killed with a silver hammer.

For the reasons already discussed in section 6.1, it would be difficult to maintain instead that these semantic differences are the result of different deep structures of some cleft-like form, as claimed by G. Lakoff (1971). There are too many forms that would have no motivation other than to provide interpretations, for example (6.114), or (6.117) for still another reading of (6.112).

(6.117) *It wasn't (a) hammer that Maxwell killed the judge with a silver (one (of)).

Furthermore, if the phenomenon that we have called association with focus is general enough to include *even*, *only*, and *merely* as well as negation, a derivation from some cleft form looks still less plausible, since (6.118)–(6.119), for example, seem unlikely sources for (6.120)–(6.121).

(6.118) ?*It was even Bill that I saw.
(6.119) ?*It was merely *War and Peace* that I read last night.
(6.120)   I even saw BILL.
(6.121)   I merely read *War and PEACE* last night.

Hence we will continue to suppose that the ambiguity of (6.112) results from the interaction of the placement of the marker F with focus assignment and association with focus.

Most negated sentences have a set of paraphrases like (6.113)–(6.115), in which we have supposed that the negation has undergone association with focus. In many cases there is another set of paraphrases as well. For example, (6.122) has readings falling into the groups (6.123) and (6.124).

(6.122) Karl doesn't write radical pamphlets in the BATHROOM.

(6.123)a. It isn't in the bathroom that Karl writes radical pamphlets.

   b. (*)Write radical pamphlets in the bathroom isn't what Karl does.

(6.124)a. It is in the bathroom that Karl doesn't write radical pamphlets.

   b. What Karl doesn't do is write radical pamphlets in the bathroom.

The readings paraphrased in (6.123) are (perhaps uninformative) answers to the questions (6.125); the readings (6.124) are answers to (6.126).

(6.125)a. Where does Karl write radical pamphlets?

   b. What does Karl do?

(6.126)a. In which room doesn't Karl write radical pamphlets?

   b. Which of those perverted things doesn't Karl do?

The ambiguity between the two sets of readings is in fact present only on paper; there is a phonetic difference marked in the intonation contour, to be discussed more fully in section 6.7.

The difference between the (a) readings and the (b) readings of (6.122) is clearly due to choice of focus: the (a) readings have PP focus and the (b) readings have VP focus. What, however, is the difference between the (6.123) and (6.124) readings? In the (6.124) readings the negation is clearly part of the presupposition, as can be seen from the related questions. In the formalism of the previous section, then, we can express the (6.124a) reading of (6.122) as (6.127).

(6.127) Presupposition:

λx [Karl doesn't write radical pamphlets at x] is $\begin{cases} \text{well-defined} \\ \text{under discussion} \end{cases}$

Assertion:

(in) the bathroom $\in \lambda x$ [Karl doesn't write radical pamphlets at x]

In the (6.123) readings, on the other hand, the negation does not form part of the presupposition, as can be seen from the corresponding questions. (6.128) seems to be an appropriate expression of the (6.123a) reading.

(6.128) Presupposition:

λx [Karl writes radical pamphlets at x] is $\begin{cases} \text{well-defined} \\ \text{under discussion} \end{cases}$

Assertion:
(in) the bathroom $\notin \lambda x$ [Karl writes radical pamphlets at x]
     or
not [in the bathroom $\in \lambda x$ [Karl writes radical pamphlets at x]]

We would like to attribute the difference between (6.127) and (6.128) to the process of association with focus (which in fact might be better named disassociation from presupposition). *Even* and *only*, because of the nature of their interpretations, must undergo association with focus; they make no sense as part of the presupposition. Negation, however, undergoes association with focus optionally.

Apparently if an element undergoes association with focus, it makes no contribution to the presupposition, but instead alters the form of the assertion. In the case of negation the assertion is negated. Another semantic element that associates with the focus is the Yes-No question, as we saw in section 6.1; this element obviously changes the form of the assertion. Horn's (1969) semantic analysis of *only* shows that it too changes the form of the assertion.

We saw in section 6.5 that association with focus can take place only under certain structural conditions, namely, when the focus is within the range of the associating word. To demonstrate that negation is similar to *even* and *only* in this respect, we will show that there is at least one structural configuration in which negation cannot associate with the focus.

Observe first that sentences with focused instrumentals such as (6.112) cannot have the reading in which negation does not associate with the focus, as shown by the corresponding clefts and questions.

(6.112) Maxwell didn't kill the judge with a silver HAMMER.
(6.129) ??It was with a HAMMER that Maxwell didn't kill the judge.
(6.130) ??What didn't Maxwell kill the judge with?

For this reading of (6.112), we would derive the presupposition (6.131).

(6.131) λx [Maxwell didn't kill the judge with x] is $\begin{cases} \text{well-defined} \\ \text{under discussion} \end{cases}$

The oddness of (6.129)–(6.130), then, is due to the unusual presupposition that it makes sense to speak of using some instrument not to do something.

This reading is plausible just in case one is given a choice of weapons and is asked "Which of these didn't Maxwell use to kill the judge?" This sentence has the required negative presupposition. However, the normal reading of (6.112), which we claim has undergone association with focus, is acceptable, because the presupposition is positive.

Second, we note that instrumental phrases normally can be preposed:

(6.132) With a hammer (,) Maxwell killed the judge.

However, this is not the case in negative sentences:

(6.133) ?*With a hammer (,) Maxwell didn't kill the judge.

One explanation of this is that preposing the instrumental removes it from the range of the negation, so that association with focus cannot take place. Hence (6.133) receives the unacceptable interpretation (6.129). This explanation is enhanced by the fact that preposed constituents cannot associate with an *even* in the auxiliary either, as noted in section 6.5. Also, notice that (6.134), though unacceptable for independent syntactic reasons (the *not* cannot be preposed here), seems to have the correct interpretation, just as with *even* and *only* (compare with (6.98)–(6.99)).

(6.134) *Not with a hammer did Maxwell kill the judge.

We can conclude then that *not* in the auxiliary undergoes optional association with focus, and that its range is identical with *even* in the same position. If it undergoes association with focus, it modifies the normal assertion form from (6.135) to (6.136).

(6.135) Focus $\in \lambda x \text{Presupp}_s(x)$ ($= 6.77$)
(6.136) Focus $\notin \lambda x \text{Presupp}_s(x)$

6.7 Two Intonation Contours
We noted in the previous section that intonation contour disambiguates certain uses of negation. The intonation contours we are interested in are part of a more general phenomenon called by Bolinger (1965b) *pitch accent*. A pitch accent consists of the intonation on an emphatically stressed syllable plus the intonation following until the next emphatically stressed syllable or the end of the sentence, whichever comes first.

In the theory we have been discussing, emphatic stress is assigned according to placement of the focus marker F. So far we have presented only examples with a single focus marker. We will first describe the pitch accents for this case, then go on to examples of multiple foci. Finally, we will give an account of the semantics of pitch accents that makes their interaction with negation part of a more general process.

The two pitch accents we are interested in are called A and B accents by Bolinger. In both accents, the focus syllable has a high pitch. By the onset of the next vowel there is an abrupt drop to low pitch. The two accents differ in that the A accent concludes with a fall in pitch, and the B accent concludes with a rise in pitch. In the cases seen so far, the fall or rise occurs at the end of the sentence, since there is only one focus syllable.

In the example previously cited, (6.112),

(6.112) Maxwell didn't kill the judge with a silver HAMMER.

the focus syllable is at the very end of the sentence, so the intonation contour is difficult to analyze. It becomes clearer in an example like (6.137).

(6.137) FRED doesn't write poetry in the garden.

This has two possible readings, paraphrased by the clefts (6.138). (6.138b), it will be recalled, is the reading in which negation has undergone association with focus.

(6.138)a. It is Fred who doesn't write poetry in the garden.
     b. It isn't Fred who writes poetry in the garden.

In both readings, *Fred*, the focus syllable, has high pitch. After the focus syllable there is an abrupt drop to low pitch, which is maintained until almost the end. The ends, however, are different: the (a) reading has the falling coda of an A accent and the (b) reading has the rising coda of a B accent. (6.139) represents the intonation contours.

(6.139)a. FRED doesn't write poetry in the garden.

     b. FRED doesn't write poetry in the garden.

As the focus is shifted, the same patterns appear in the intonation contour to the right of the focus. (We will not concern ourselves here with the prefocal contour.)

(6.140)a. ?Fred doesn't <u>WRITE</u> poetry in the garden.

　　b.　Fred doesn't <u>WRITE</u> poetry in the garden.

(6.141)a.　Fred doesn't write <u>POETRY</u> in the garden.

　　b.　Fred doesn't write <u>POETRY</u> in the garden.

In case the focus is in the final word, the pitch contour is compressed, but still recognizable.

(6.142)a. Fred doesn't write poetry in the <u>GARDEN</u>.

　　b. Fred doesn't write poetry in the <u>GARDEN</u>.

So far we have no evidence that these pitch contours are syntactically associated with the focus rather than with the entire sentence, since the difference between them always appears at the end of the sentence. To show that the pitch contours are a part of the focus constituent, we must turn to sentences with multiple foci.

We have not yet dealt with sentences with multiple foci, but their interpretation is a straightforward extension of the single-focus case. For example, (6.143) has two foci, on *Fred* and *beans*.

(6.143) FRED ate the BEANS.

(6.143) can be derived phonetically by generating the marker F in two positions in the sentence. To form the presupposition, we remove both foci and substitute variables, getting x *ate* y. Since there are two variables, the lambda-operator is applied to ordered pairs, forming the function $\lambda(x, y) [x$ ate $y]$. The assertion of (6.143) is therefore (6.144).

(6.144) (Fred, the beans) $\in \lambda(x, y) [x$ ate $y]$

In general, then, for sentences with n foci, the interpretation contains a lambda-operator over ordered $n$tuples.

There are two possible intonation contours for (6.143). To make it easier for the reader to generate these contours himself, I will provide discourse settings. We presuppose, as indicated by (6.144), that there were a number of people and a number of different things to eat, and that various people ate various things. Speaker A in the discourse is asking questions of the form *Who ate what?* and Speaker B is answering. For the first intonation pattern, A is asking person by person:

(6.145) A: Well, what about FRED? What did HE eat?
    B: FRED ate the BEANS.

For the second pattern, A is asking by foods:

(6.146) A: Well, what about the BEANS? Who ate THEM?
    B: FRED ate the BEANS.

In each example we find the typical fall-rise of the B pitch accent and the fall of the A accent, but in different positions: (6.145) has B on *Fred* and A on *beans*, and (6.146) is the other way around. If the focus positions are moved, the same two patterns appear:

(6.147) A: Well, what about FRED? What did HE do to the beans?
    B: FRED ATE the beans.
                                    (B–A)
(6.148) A: I know who COOKED the beans. But then, who ATE them?
    B: FRED ATE the beans.
                                    (A–B)

(6.149) A: I know what Fred COOKED. But then, what did he EAT?
    B: Fred ATE the BEANS.
                                    (B–A)

(6.150) A: Well, what about the BEANS? What did Fred do with THEM?
    B: Fred ATE the BEANS.
                                    (A–B)

We conclude that one pitch contour must be assigned for each focus in the sentence.

For a minimal formalization of the pitch accents, we will assume that each focus marker F contains a feature marking the pitch contour to be applied. This feature will be realized phonetically by rules whose nature need not concern us here. Henceforth, for convenience, we will simply indicate pitch contour by an A or B under the associated focus. For example, (6.145) will be represented as (6.151).

(6.151) FRED ate the BEANS.
       B   A

So far we have identified the phonetic shape of the two pitch contours and shown that they are syntactically associated with focus constituents. It remains to characterize their contribution to the reading of the sentence. We begin with the two-focus case, as it is more transparent. In the pairs of examples above, the presupposition contains two variables; the difference in intonation is due to the order in which values for the variables are chosen. The B accent occurs on the variable whose value is chosen first, the one which speaker A above is asking about. The A accent occurs on the variable whose value is chosen second, so as to make the sentence true for the value of the other variable. In formal terms, the presupposition is a mapping from a set of values defined by the variable x, marked with a B accent, into a set of values defined by the variable y, marked with an A accent, such that given any value of x there is a corresponding value of y. Thus the B accent defines an *independent variable* and the A accent a *dependent variable*.

This interpretation of the pitch accents bears on the traditional notions of *topic* and *comment*. In many simple sentences, the stress and intonation contours divide the sentence exhaustively into two foci, the subject and the predicate, with a B pitch accent on the former and an A accent on the latter.

(6.152) The man in the purple VEST has delivered the stolen
                                        B

RHINOCEROS tusks.
    A

Under our analysis of the pitch accents, we can take the subject to be the traditional "topic," chosen freely, and the predicate to be the "comment," that is, what there is to be said about the topic. In this particular example, nothing is presupposed, so the comment will be the entire second focus. If there is a presupposition, the comment will include the presupposition as well as the second variable: this accords with the structure of the discourses in (6.145)–(6.150).

Notice further that the idea of the B-accented focus as topic accords with the intonation on preposed (or "topicalized") phrases, which almost always receive a B accent.

(6.153) BAGELS I don't like to EAT.
     B   A

At six o'CLOCK, FRED walked in.
        B   A

Of all the people I've ever MET, you are undoubtedly
                B

the UGLIEST.
   A

As for FRED, I don't think HE can MAKE it.
    B   B   A

The major exceptions to this generalization are precisely the phrases which produce subject-auxiliary inversion when preposed, e.g. negative constituents, *wh*-constituents, and *only*-phrases. They will be discussed in section 8.8.

For full generality, we must now show how these interpretations can be extended to the case of sentences with only a single focus. First consider a sentence with a single A accent. We have conjectured that the A accent marks its focus as a dependent variable, a value chosen not freely, but rather in such a way as to make the sentence true. For a value to be chosen under these conditions, there is no need for a second variable; the presupposition alone suffices to determine the correct value of the focus. Hence our interpretation of the A accent can be extended with no effort to the single focus case.

On the other hand, the interpretation of the B accent as an independent variable requires that it be freely chosen. Under this assumption, it would seem impossible ever to have a B accent associated with a single focus, since the presupposition uniquely determines the appropriate values, violating freedom of choice. One way to circumvent this problem is to use the affirmation-negation distinction as a dependent variable just in case there is a single B accented focus. In this way, the focus can be chosen freely; the choice of affirmation or negation will then be determined uniquely.

If the affirmation-negation distinction is to be chosen as the dependent variable, it obviously cannot form part of the presupposition. But we have already seen a way in which a negation can be removed from the presupposition, namely by applying the rule association with focus. And in fact it is exactly those cases in which negation has been removed from the presupposition that have a B accent on the focus, as noted at the beginning of this section. Affirmation too is possible with a B accent: the first clause of (6.154) is a case where the value of the dependent variable is affirmation.

(6.154) (Did John and Bill leave yet?)
　　　　Well, JOHN has left, but BILL hasn't.
　　　　　　　　B　　　　　　　　B

For a further confirmation of this hypothesis, we note that affirmation and negation can themselves be focused by stressing the first auxiliary (or *not*). The associated intonation, however, must be an A accent.

$$(6.155) \text{ Max} \begin{Bmatrix} \text{WILL} \\ \text{DOESN'T} \\ \text{does NOT} \end{Bmatrix} \text{ like Myra's cooking.}$$

$$\begin{Bmatrix} \text{A} \\ \text{*B} \end{Bmatrix}$$

This can be explained easily in terms of our assumptions. The use of a B accent on a single focus requires that affirmation-negation be chosen as the dependent variable, in order to preserve freedom of choice. But if it has already been chosen as the independent variable, the difficulty is obvious. Hence it can only be chosen as the dependent variable, if it is the only focus. On the other hand, if there is a second focus, either can be chosen as the independent variable, given the proper discourse.

(6.156) Max WILL like MYRA'S cooking; he WON'T like REX'S.
$$\begin{Bmatrix} \text{A} & \text{B} & \text{A} & \text{B} \\ \text{B} & \text{A} & \text{B} & \text{A} \end{Bmatrix}$$

We have shown it to be plausible, then, that the intonation curve associated with a focus indicates whether it is a dependent or independent variable, and that association with focus allows affirmation-negation to be used as a dependent variable when there is a single focus used as an independent variable. We will use this analysis further in section 8.6, showing its application to the interpretation of several examples. There are of course many other interesting questions raised by this hypothesis for which there is no space in this study.

We now turn to another group of processes in English that are intimately related to focus and presupposition, those rules which interpret anaphoric expressions which are more complex than the definite pronouns we studied in Chapters 4 and 5.

6.8 VP-Anaphora

There are a number of constructions in English in which all or part of a sentence, including the verb, is replaced by a pro-form or deleted. Here are examples of some of them.

(6.157) Max has often thought of emigrating to Albania, and Janice has too. (VP deletion)

(6.158) Kurt plays krummhorn, Ivan alphorn, Frank fluegelhorn, and Boris bassethorn. (gapping)

(6.159) I'll leave the room if you consent to do so. (*Do So*)

(6.160) Johnny threw stones at the cops, and now his brother wants

to do $\begin{cases} \text{it.} \\ \text{likewise. } (Do\ It) \\ \text{the same.} \end{cases}$

(6.161) Though we never believed it could happen, Charlie seduced Ermintrude.

Harry believes that Sally is innocent, although no one else believes it. (prosententialization)

Each of these rules has its own peculiar restrictions, and their behavior has received wide attention in the literature (cf. G. Lakoff 1971, 1970a; Ross 1967a; Anderson 1968a; Lakoff and Ross 1966; Akmajian 1970b; and Jackendoff 1971a for some discussion of these rules. In this section and the next, I draw heavily on Akmajian's work, which discusses the interpretive approach in more detail.)

It is assumed in most of the literature on these rules that they resemble the pronominalization transformation, i.e. that they are transformations which delete a constituent or replace it by a pro-form just in case it is morphologically and semantically identical with a constituent in some other position in the sentence. Under this assumption, G. Lakoff (1970a) concludes that various adverbial phrases are predicates of higher sentences. His argument is based on examples like (6.162).

(6.162) Goldwater won in the West, but it could never happen here.

The antecedent of *it* is *Goldwater won*. If we assume that pronouns always stand for constituents, we must conclude that *Goldwater won* is a constituent of the first clause, so the structure must be something like (6.163) at the time prosententialization takes place, rather than the more traditional (6.164).

(6.163) $[_s[_s$Goldwater won$]$ in the West$]$
(6.164) $[_s$Goldwater $[_{vp}$won in the West$]]$

However, Chomsky (1970b) shows that there is something seriously wrong with this argument: (6.165) and (6.166) are acceptable, at least for many speakers. (I indicate emphatic stress with capitals again.)

(6.165) Fred turned the HOTDOG down flat, but that wouldn't have happened with FILET MIGNON.
(6.166) FRED turned the hotdog down flat, but that wouldn't have happened with SALLY.

Lakoff's assumptions lead to the conclusion that in (6.165) *Fred turned down flat* is a constituent and *hotdog* a predicate of a higher sentence, and in (6.166), *turned the hotdog down flat* is a constituent and *Fred* a predicate of a higher sentence. These conclusions violate our most fundamental intuitions about constituent structure; we can only conclude that there is something wrong in the initial assumption about the source of *it*.[6]

---

[6]G. Lakoff's defense of the assumption (1970a) is dependent on the use of the transformation *Not*-transportation, whose existence is called into question in Jackendoff (1971b). There it is shown that the formulation of such a transformation would lead to loss of generality on several important points, but that a semantic account of the same data can be formulated quite satisfactorily. The main syntactic argument for the rule is based on the distribution of *until*; Lindholm (1969) shows this argument to be based on faulty data. The only other defense of the rule that I know of is R. Lakoff (1969a). In that paper she mentions a suggestion by Bolinger that the rule changes meaning, undermining the primary reason for its existence; then she proceeds to give an argument based on a very poorly understood group of tag questions. This argument too turns out to be based on insufficient data, as shown in Jackendoff (1971b). Thus the thread of argument supporting G. Lakoff's widely accepted conclusion is sufficiently slender to justify attempting another approach. Furthermore, as we have just seen, his argument leads to clearly unsatisfying results.

The approach to the constructions (6.157)–(6.161) to be sketched here will start from rather different assumptions. In line with the interpretive theory of pronominalization developed in Chapters 4 and 5, we will assume that the pro-forms *it, do it, do so*, etc. are inserted in the base as lexical items and that their antecedents are determined by interpretive rules; we will also assume the apparent deletions in (6.157)–(6.158) are represented syntactically as empty nodes (cf. section 5.2) which receive interpretation by semantic rules. Furthermore, to avoid Chomsky's argument, we will assume that at least sometimes a pro-form need not have a complete syntactic constituent as its antecedent. (Ross 1969b shows that even in a strongly transformational theory, it will be necessary to delete nonconstituents.)

As with definite pronominalization, there is a small amount of semantic and lexical evidence that an interpretive theory has advantages. There is a sizable range of expressions that can be used as pro-forms in (6.160), for example *do it, do likewise, do the same (thing)*, and more distant, *do something like that*. Furthermore, there is the form *do something else*, which indicates nonidentity (but within the range of possible contrasts), and the rather precise form *do (just) the opposite*, which can be used as a pro-form for verb phrases with a well-defined two-way semantic opposition. This variety of expressions is similar to that found with pronouns, where we had forms like *someone else* and *the other* to contend with. Another relevant piece of evidence is pointed out by Bolinger (1970), who shows that *do so* is not semantically neutral, but often carries implications of adversity. This is similar to the cases of pronominal epithets like *the bum* and *the bastard*; there is no way for a transformation introducing the pro-form to check for this information. Under the interpretive hypothesis, however, all of the pro-forms will appear in the lexicon, and their differing meanings can be marked there, the natural place for such information.

It is easy to show, furthermore, that an interpretive theory of pronominalization forces us to adopt an interpretive theory of these other constructions. For suppose that (6.167) is derived from (6.168) by a transformation deleting the VP *kiss him*.

(6.167) Fred got SALLY to kiss him, but SUE refused to.
(6.168) Fred got SALLY to kiss him, but SUE refused to kiss him.

The interpretation of (6.167) will not be complete unless it includes the fact that Fred is the one Sue wouldn't kiss. According to the interpretive theory developed in Chapter 4, the antecedent of the second *him* in (6.168) is determined on the final cycle, after all the transformations. But if the deletion of the VP in (6.167) is accomplished by a transformation, *him* will have been deleted before pronominalization can apply to it, so there will be no way for the grammar to derive the coreference of *Fred* and *him*. Hence a VP -deletion transformation is inconsistent with the interpretive theory. Similar arguments obtain for all the constructions in (6.157)–(6.161). An interpretive theory of these constructions is therefore necessary.

Let us first try to state the interpretive equivalent of VP-deletion, perhaps the simplest case. As an interpretive rule we will call it VP-anaphora. Assume that in the second clause of (6.157), the missing VP is represented syntactically as an empty VP node, or a VP node dominating no lexical items, represented in the rule by Δ. The conventions of section 5.2 on empty nodes will apply: an empty node is treated syntactically like any other node and phonologically unrealized. Unless it receives semantic interpretation by some rule, the sentence containing it will be semantically ill formed since it contains uninterpreted nodes.

(6.169) (VP-anaphora)

Associate with VP^2 the semantic representation of VP^1 if

(a) VP^2 is Δ; and

(b) VP^2 does not both precede and command VP^1.

The environment (b) is approximate; it is intended to account for the range of facts in (6.170)–(6.173). Obviously, refinements will be necessary.

(6.170)   Charlie will leave town if his mother-in-law doesn't.
          (VP^1 precedes and commands VP^2)
(6.171)   Whenever Russia has made a major political blunder, the U.S. has too.
          (VP^1 precedes VP^2, VP^2 commands VP^1)
(6.172)   If he hasn't yet, John should try to climb the Eiffel Tower.
          (VP^2 precedes VP^1, VP^1 commands VP^2)
(6.173) *Charlie will, if his mother-in-law doesn't leave town.
          (VP^2 precedes and commands VP^1)

(6.169) must be a derived structure rule of interpretation, since it depends on the position of subordinate clauses and on derived, not deep constituency of VPs. (6.174) and (6.175) show that it must take place after passive and *Tough* movement, respectively.

(6.174) Tom was arrested by the pigs, but Fred wasn't.
(6.175) Walt is tough to get along with, but Vera isn't.

The deep structures of these will be (6.176) and (6.177), respectively.

(6.176) The pigs arrested Tom, but $[_{NP}\Delta]$ past not $[_{V}\Delta]$ Fred
(6.177) $[_{S}$(for) Δ to get along with Walt$]$ is tough, but $[_{S}$(for) $[_{NP}\Delta]$ $[_{V}\Delta]$ Vera$]_{S}$ isn't $[_{Adj}\Delta]$

(6.176) undergoes the passive to form (6.178).

(6.178) Tom was arrested by the pigs, but Fred wasn't $[_{VP}[_{V}\Delta]$ (by) $[_{NP}\Delta]]_{VP}$

By is deleted in (6.178) by the general rule that deletes *by* in agentless passives (*by someone* in Chomsky 1965), leaving the entire VP free of lexical items and thus eligible to be interpreted by (6.169). Likewise, (6.177) undergoes extraposition and *Tough* movement in both clauses to become (6.179).

(6.179) Walt is tough to get along with, but Vera isn't $[_{VP}[_{Adj}\Delta]$ (to) $[_{V}\Delta]]$

A rule deleting *to* in these circumstances will not be difficult to state (if *to* is even present in the base structure of this clause), leaving the entire second VP empty and thus subject to interpretation by (6.169). (Akmajian 1970b points out a number of problems in applying transformations correctly to phrase-markers containing empty nodes; their solutions must be left to future research.) We see from these examples, then, that VP-anaphora must make reference to two levels of derivation: the surface structure (or perhaps end-of-cycle structure, because of the similarity to pronominalization), and the semantic interpretation.

Let us be more explicit about the meaning of the phrase in (6.169) "Associate with VP^2 the semantic representation of VP^1." Call the clauses containing VP^1 and VP^2, respectively, S^1 and S^2. The semantic association can be done, informally, by inserting all semantic material mentioning parts of

VP^1 into structurally parallel places in the reading of S^2; when an element of S^1 outside of VP^1 is involved in a binary relation with an element of VP^1, the corresponding element of S^2 is substituted for it.

For an example, we will derive the reading of (6.167). The first clause has the derived structure (6.180) (according to the discussion of Chapter 5), and a semantic representation of approximately the form (6.181).

(6.180) $[_S$Fred got Sally $[_S\Delta^1$ to $[_{VP}$kiss him$]]]$.
(6.181) Functional structure:

GET (FRED, SALLY, (KISS (Δ^1, HIM)))

Table of coreference:

Δ^1	$-$coref *him*	(reflexivization, 1st cycle)
Sally	coref Δ^1	(complement subject, 2nd cycle)
Fred	coref *him*	(pronominalization, 2nd cycle)

(The entries in the table of coreference made by the noncoreferentiality rule have not been made at the time of VP-anaphora, so they are left out here.) The second clause has the derived structure (6.182) and a partial reading (6.183), before the application of VP-anaphora; the unspecified function f indicates that Δ^2 has grammatical relations with respect to some as yet unknown verb.

(6.182) Sue refused $[_S[_{NP}\Delta^2]$ to $[_{VP}\Delta^3]]$
(6.183) Functional structure:

REFUSE (SUE, $f(\Delta^2)$)

Table of coreference:

Sue coref Δ^2 (complement subject, 2nd cycle)

If VP-anaphora were not applicable, (6.183) would not meet the well-formedness conditions on semantic representations, since it is incompletely filled out. However, we can take the VP *kiss him* as VP^1 and Δ^3 as VP^2 in the structural description of VP-anaphora. To apply the rule, we must substitute $KISS(\ldots, HIM)$ for f in (6.183), and in addition, copy over those parts of the table of coreference in (6.181) that refer to *him*, making appropriate substitutions, in this case Δ^2 for Δ^1. We thus get the reading (6.184).

(6.184) Functional structure:
    REFUSE (SUE, (KISS (Δ^2, HIM)))
    Table of coreference:
    Δ^2 $-$coref *him*
    Sue   coref Δ^2
    Fred   coref *him*

Finally, the noncoreferentiality rule will apply in both clauses, filling out the table of coreference. Note that since the noncoreferentiality rule makes no reference to syntactic structure, it can be stated as a rule applying solely to semantic representation, obviating the need to duplicate a syntactic structure for S^2.

Hence we have succeeded in creating the correct reading for (6.167), including its pronoun, by referring only to surface structure and semantic representation. There is no need to use an intermediate structure or deep structure to understand the pronoun, since we duplicate the semantic interpretation of the VP *including* the interpretation of the pronoun, rather than copying over the VP in some form, then interpreting it.

Ross (1967a, section 5.2; 1969) mentions an interesting phenomenon which occurs in these constructions. (6.185) is for many speakers ambiguous as to whose arm Bill scratched.

(6.185) John scratched his arm and Bill did, too.

Because of Ross's assumption of a transformational theory of pronouns and VP-deletion, he must explain the ambiguity of (6.185) in terms of a relaxation of the identity conditions in VP-deletion, in order to permit deletion in (6.185) even though *Bill* and *John* are not identical (hence his term "sloppy identity"). In the interpretive theory, the ambiguity can be accounted for with a rather simple mechanism. The table of coreference in the first clause of (6.185) will be *John* coref *his*. In substituting the reading of the VP for the VP in the second clause, the rule apparently has the option of carrying over the table of coreference intact or substituting *Bill*, the NP in corresponding position, for *John*, to form the table *Bill* coref *his*.

The problem still remains of specifying what semantic features can be ignored in substituting corresponding constituents. For example, many speakers get the same ambiguity in (6.186) as in (6.185).

(6.186) John scratched his arm and Mary did, too.

For the reading in which Mary scratched her own arm, the VP-anaphora rule will derive a table of coreference *Mary* coref *his*, which under normal conditions would be ill–formed. Evidently the rule can leave out certain conflicting semantic markers in duplicating the reading of the first VP. I will not attempt to make the necessary modifications here.

6.9 Anaphoric Expressions for Presuppositions

In the case of VP-anaphora, we can identify the missing part of the second sentence with the derived VP of the first sentence. Similarly, in the case of gapping (6.158),

(6.158) Kurt plays krummhorn, Ivan alphorn, Frank fluegelhorn, and Boris bassethorn.

the missing verb of the second clause can be filled with the reading of the verb in the first clause. However, in the other constructions the relevant semantic information to substitute into the second clause cannot be identified with any single constituent: in (6.162), (6.165), and (6.166) the same anaphoric expression *it happened* is apparently used for widely divergent sets of constituents.

(6.162) Goldwater won in the West, but it could never happen here.

(6.165) Fred turned the HOTDOG down flat, but that wouldn't have happened with FILET MIGNON.

(6.166) FRED turned the hotdog down flat, but that wouldn't have happened with SALLY.

Akmajian (1970b) suggests that a rather simple principle is operating here: the anaphoric expression receives the semantic interpretation of the *presupposition* of the first clause, rather than the semantic interpretation of some particular constituent. This seems particularly plausible in light of the importance in (6.165)–(6.166) of stress, the phonetic marker of focus.

To see how Akmajian's semantic rule would operate, let us illustrate with the derivation of (6.162), which has the surface structure (6.187). Note that the locative phrases in the two classes are marked F, resulting in main stress being assigned to *West* and *here*.

(6.187) $\begin{bmatrix} \text{Goldwater} \begin{bmatrix} \text{won} \begin{bmatrix} \text{in the West} \end{bmatrix} \end{bmatrix} \end{bmatrix}$ but $\begin{bmatrix} \text{it could never} \end{bmatrix}$

$\begin{bmatrix} \text{happen} \begin{bmatrix} \text{here} \end{bmatrix} \end{bmatrix}$

The presupposition of the first clause is formed by substituting a variable for the focus; it can be represented roughly as "Goldwater won somewhere." The partial reading of the second clause, before the interpretive rule of prosententialization, has roughly the form (6.188), ignoring the auxiliary for the moment.

$(6.188) f(\text{HERE})$
  Presupposition: $f(\text{SOMEWHERE})$
  Focus: HERE

(6.188) is of course an ill-formed reading if no further semantic rules apply. But if prosententialization can apply, as it does in this case, the presupposition of the first clause is substituted for the empty presupposition of the second clause. The functional structure of the second clause is constructed by substituting the focus back for the variables in the presupposition. Hence (6.188) will become (6.189).

(6.189) WIN (GOLDWATER, HERE)
  Presupposition: WIN (GOLDWATER, SOMEWHERE)
  Focus: HERE

Returning to the auxiliary, we notice that the reading of the second clause is "Goldwater could never win here." Apparently prosententialization also substitutes the new tense, modal, and sentence adverbs. The rule treats (6.165) and (6.166) the same way. (6.165) has the presupposition "Fred turned something down flat"; (6.166) has "someone turned the hotdog down flat." But since the rule refers to presupposition and focus, which are independent of grammatical relations, it is perfectly possible to substitute the *with*-phrase in the first case for the object, and in the second case for the subject.

We cannot, however, assume that the assertion of the second clause is formed simply by substituting the new focus and new modality into the presupposition of the first clause. The antecedent of *it happen* must be an event, not a simple statement of fact:

(6.190) *4 is a perfect square, but it doesn't happen with 6.

If we assume instead that *it happen* has some minimal semantic markers over which the presupposition is superimposed, we can account for the anomaly of (6.190) with no special mechanism. The well-formedness conditions will simply note that *6 is a perfect square* is not an event but is marked as one. Similarly, the preposition following *happen* has semantic effects that must be recognized in the reading: *to* indicates a benefactive function, often an adverse one; *with* is more neutral.

(6.191) They tore down PENN STATION; I hope that doesn't happen
$\begin{Bmatrix} \text{with} \\ \text{to} \end{Bmatrix}$ CARNEGIE HALL.

(6.192) FRED turned the hotdog down flat, but that would never happen
$\begin{Bmatrix} \text{with} \\ ?*\text{to} \end{Bmatrix}$ BILL.

Again, if the presupposition of the first sentence is superimposed on the minimal reading of the second sentence, rather than substituted for it, the difference between *with* and *to* will appear in the reading. *To* will be unacceptable in (6.192), then, because of well-formedness conditions concerning what NPs in a sentence can be possible benefactors of an action.

The rule can be stated roughly as follows, then:

(6.193) (*Happen* prosententialization)

Let S^2 be an anaphoric sentence of the form $\begin{Bmatrix} that \\ it \end{Bmatrix}$ *aux happen PP*, in which the PP is the focus, and let S^1 be its antecedent. To form the reading of S^2, (a) substitute the reading of the aux and sentence adverbs in S^2 for those in the presupposition of S^1; (b) superimpose the resulting reading on the (minimally specified) presupposition of S^2; (c) substitute the focus of S^2 for the variables in the presupposition to form the assertion.

Similar rules can be stated for the constructions with *do* $\begin{Bmatrix} so \\ it \\ the\ same \end{Bmatrix}$. The situation is slightly more complicated, since the status of the derived subject comes into play. As usual, call S^2 the sentence containing the proform, and

S^1 its antecedent. Besides the conditions of *Happen* prosententialization, the rules for *do* will have at least the following additions:

(6.194)a. In creating the reading of S^2, substitute the reading of the derived subject of S^2 for all occurrences of the reading of the derived subject of S^1.
   b. The derived subject of S^2 is an *Agent*.

The reason for (6.194a) is clear: the *do* constructions only substitute for a VP, not an entire sentence. (6.194b) is to prevent non-Agent constructions like (6.195).

(6.195) *Richie inherited a million dollars, and I'd like to do so too.

Anderson (1968a) points out further semantic differences between *do it* and *do so*, which we will not discuss here.

Akmajian (1970b) observes that there are some rather complex *do the same* constructions with multiple foci.

(6.196) Maxwell killed the JUDGE with a silver HAMMER, and I'd like to do the same thing to that COP, $\begin{Bmatrix} \text{with} \\ \text{using} \end{Bmatrix}$ a CUDGEL.
(6.197) Fred hung TESSIE up in a tree and poured PAINT on her, but I bet he wouldn't do it to SUE with GLUE.

Note that in the second clause, the linear order of the corresponding foci in the first sentence must be preserved, although the syntactic constructions involved may be entirely different.

The derivation of the reading for (6.197) will proceed along the following lines. The presupposition of the first clause is "Fred hung someone up in a tree and poured something on her." To form the reading of the *do it* clause, we must first establish the proper pairing of foci, on the basis of surface structure order: *Tessie* pairs with *Sue*, and *paint* pairs with *glue*. Then to form the reading of the second clause, we substitute the readings of the new subject, *he*, the new auxiliary, *wouldn't*, and the new foci, to get "He wouldn't hang Sue up in a tree and pour glue on her."

Note in particular the treatment of the pronoun *her* in this example, parallel to the example discussed before. The table of coreference for the first clause will have an entry *Tessie* coref *her*. When the presupposition is formed, a variable will be substituted for *Tessie* in this entry as well as in the functional structure. The substitution of the new focus for the variable will give the correct new entry *Sue* coref *her* for the second clause.

There are of course many problems with these constructions that have not been touched upon here. A full discussion would be beyond the scope of the present study. I hope to have shown at least that an interpretive approach to this type of anaphora is feasible and insightful.

6.10 Inherent Presuppositions

In addition to the presupposition derived by focus assignment, the reading of a sentence may contain presuppositions introduced by other elements of the sentence. A well-known example is the presupposition introduced by "factive" verbs such as *know* and *realize*. As pointed out by Kiparsky and Kiparsky (1968), the complements of these verbs are understood as true whether or not the main clause is negated. (Karttunen 1970, discusses a related class, the "implicative" verbs, which are also of interest here.) This is not in general true of complements; contrast the factives in (6.198) with the nonfactives in (6.199).

$$(6.198) \text{ Bill} \begin{cases} \text{knows} \\ \text{doesn't know} \\ \text{realizes} \\ \text{doesn't realize} \end{cases} \text{that eating tennis balls makes you sick.}$$

$$(6.199) \text{ Bill} \begin{cases} \text{thinks} \\ \text{doesn't think} \\ \text{concluded} \\ \text{didn't conclude} \end{cases} \text{that eating tennis balls makes you sick.}$$

Let us refer to the presupposition derived by focus assignment as the *focal presupposition*, and to presuppositions such as those introduced by factive verbs *inherent presuppositions*. Inherent presuppositions satisfy the general definition "Information assumed by the speaker to be shared by him and the hearer": if the information turns out not to be shared, "unnatural" or "surprising" discourses such as (6.200) can result.

(6.200) A :   I didn't realize that Bill ate a tennis ball.
   B :   # But Bill didn't eat a tennis ball.

In (6.198) the focal and inherent presuppositions are (6.201), assuming normal stress and the subordinate clause as focus.

(6.201) Focal presupposition: Bill knows something
Inherent presupposition: Eating tennis balls makes you sick

Note that if the focus is shifted by stressing *TENNIS balls*, the presuppositions are (6.202); the inherent presupposition is unchanged.

(6.202) Focal presupposition: Bill knows that eating a certain thing makes you sick.
Inherent presupposition: Eating tennis balls makes you sick.

Another example of an inherent presupposition is that induced by the definite article. Definite noun phrases presuppose that they describe an entity uniquely identifiable within the bounds of the discourse. In the case of NPs like *the sun* and *the moon*, common knowledge provides the unique identification requisite to interpretation of *the*. Likewise, common knowledge among, say, members of a family explains the uniqueness in examples like *Have you fed the dog?* Anaphoric *the* is a similar case, but the knowledge shared by speaker and hearer has been introduced earlier in the discourse. If a definite NP used anaphorically does not sufficiently identify its antecedent, it has a feeling of inappropriateness.

(6.203) A: I saw a tall boy and a short boy.
B: # Was the boy eating a candy bar?

If *girl* is substituted for one occurrence of *boy* in the first sentence, the question is appropriate.

Alternatively, the noun phrase itself can provide the information necessary for unique identification. Certain kinds of noun phrase adjuncts allow nothing but a unique interpretation, and so the definite article is obligatory, for example *the fact that Bill came*, *the probability that he will win*. In other cases, the adjunct may, but need not, designate uniqueness. For example, restrictive relative clauses can occur with either definite or indefinite articles: $\begin{Bmatrix} a \\ the \end{Bmatrix}$ *man I met yesterday*. In case the definite article is used, the focal and inherent presuppositions can overlap as they did in (6.201)–

(6.202). For example, (6.204), with focus on *ex-convict*, has presuppositions (6.205).

(6.204) He was looking for the EX-CONVICT who was wearing a red shirt.
(6.205) Focal presupposition: He was looking for a certain person who
was wearing a red shirt.
Inherent presupposition: There is only one ex-convict who was
wearing a red shirt.

The insertion of inherent presuppositions into a semantic interpretation must obviously depend on lexical information. We will not discuss a specific mechanism here. However, it seems likely that inherent presuppositions can be formalized like selectional restrictions: just as a verb can presuppose that its object is human or animate or mass, it can presuppose that its complement is true. Another possibility is that presuppositions are incorporated somehow into the modal structure to be proposed in Chapter 7, as there are certain parallels in their effects on interpretation.

6.11 Summary
We have shown that focus and presupposition of a sentence are determined on the basis of surface structure constituency, supplemented by inherent presuppositions introduced by lexical items. We have proposed that focus and focal presupposition be related to a syntactic marker F, which directly affects the assignment of stress contours; and to features A and B on the focus marker, which result in the assignment of A and B pitch accents. The choice of focus is constrained by the notion of "possible contrast," which we have shown is a semantic notion, not a syntactic one. By means of the semantic rule association with focus, various items other than the focus, such as *even*, *only*, and negation, can be disassociated from the presupposition so that they affect only the form of the assertion. The form of the assertion is also affected by the choice of pitch accents: a B accent on a focus denotes an independent variable, and an A accent denotes a dependent variable. In case there is only one focus, bearing a B accent, the affirmation-negation distinction functions as the dependent variable. Finally, we have shown that focus and presupposition play an important part in the interpretation of anaphoric expressions such as *do it*; we have stated the interpretive rules in preliminary form.

CHAPTER SEVEN

Modal Structure

In this chapter I will propose a simple rule of semantic interpretation and a formalism for semantic representation to account for the ambiguity of *a fish* in *John wants to catch a fish*. I will then show how this rule and this formalism can be applied with a minimum of extension to describe a wide range of linguistic phenomena that have never before been considered to be intimately related.

7.1 *Want* Contexts

The well-known ambiguity of (7.1)

(7.1) John wants to catch a fish.

has been discussed in, among others, Baker (1966), Dean (1968), and Heringer (1969). On one reading, there is a particular fish that John wants to catch (the specific reading). On the other reading, the predominant one, this claim is not made (the nonspecific reading): rather there will be a fish to point to just in case John succeeds in catching one. The ambiguity is possible with indefinites anywhere within the object or the object complement of the verb *want*:

(7.2) a. John wants $\left\{ \begin{array}{l} \text{a new bicycle} \\ \text{to see a friend of his catch a fish} \end{array} \right\}$.
      b.

In fact (7.2b) is four ways ambiguous, since *a friend of his* and *a fish* are independently subject to the ambiguity. The ambiguity is not present in the subject of *want*; for example, only the specific interpretation of *a man* is possible in (7.3):

(7.3) A man wants to see you.

The class of verbs inducing this particular ambiguity includes the following:

(7.4) want, look for, hope for, wish for, hunt for, ask for, try for, plan (for), expect, attempt, intend

Ask is an interesting example, in that it shows that the ambiguity is not induced everywhere to the right of the verb. For example, *a cigar* in (7.5) has both specific and nonspecific readings, but *a man* must be specific.

(7.5) Bill asked a man for a cigar.

Suppose we embed a sentence containing a verb of the class (7.4) as the complement of another verb of class (7.4), as in (7.6).

(7.6) Fred wants a man to ask him for a cigar.

We notice first that although *a man* is the subject of *ask*, it may be non-specific, apparently due to the influence of *want*. Second, and more subtle, we observe that *a cigar* is now three ways ambiguous. In the first interpretation, there is a particular cigar that Fred wants someone (specific or nonspecific) to ask for; in the second Fred wants someone to ask "Will you give me that cigar?" where the person asking has a particular cigar in mind but Fred does not know which one it will be; in the third interpretation, Fred wants someone to ask, "Will you give me a cigar?" having no particular cigar in mind. Thus there are in all six interpretations for (7.6).

These facts suggest the following preliminary description. It is normally the case that noun phrases are interpreted as specific. For example, in *a man ran into a tree* both noun phrases are specific. However, under the influence of the verbs in class (7.4), noun phrases within a certain portion of the sentence are optionally open to a nonspecific interpretation. The portion of the sentence in which the ambiguity is possible is determined by the verb; we will call this portion of the sentence the *scope* of the verb *with respect to specificity*. The scope of *want*, for example, is its direct object: *a fish*, *a new bicycle*, and *a friend of his* are subject to the ambiguity in (7.1) and (7.2), but *a man*, in subject position in (7.3), is not. The scope of *ask* consists of the object of *for* but not the direct object, as shown by the range of ambiguity in (7.5). I will discuss the interpretation of (7.6) in a moment.

We must immediately clarify the terminology. The use of the term *scope* in the preceding paragraph is somewhat different from the usual use of the term. In the more common usage, one would say that a noun phrase is within the scope of the verb only if it is interpreted as nonspecific; the scope of the verb in this sense depends on the interpretation chosen for the sentence. In our usage, the scope is the area in which nonspecificity is *possible*; the scope is thus invariant throughout all interpretations. To describe the two interpretations of (7.1), then, we will not say that *a fish* may be inside or outside of the scope of *want*. Rather we will say that because *a fish* is within the scope of *want*, it is subject to ambiguity. I will describe the nonspecific interpretation by saying that *a fish* is *dependent* on *want*; in the specific interpretation, I will say that *a fish* is not dependent on *want*.

Returning to (7.6), we see that the threefold ambiguity of *a cigar* militates against a semantic description in which noun phrases are simply marked [±specific]. Such a description cannot distinguish the two interpretations in which Fred has no particular cigar in mind, since in both readings *a cigar* is nonspecific. These two interpretations, we observe, correspond precisely to the two interpretations of the subordinate clause *a man asks him for a cigar*; that is, they differ in whether or not *a cigar* is dependent on *ask*. In (7.6), however, *a cigar* is within the scope of *want* as well as the scope of *ask*. *Want* as usual can produce ambiguity within its scope, as can be seen from the ambiguity of *a man* in (7.6). Therefore it is plausible to assume that the ambiguity of *a cigar* is due to the influence of both *want* and *ask*. In the specific reading, *a cigar* is dependent on neither verb. In the second reading, it is dependent on *want*, accounting for its nonspecificity, but it is not dependent on *ask*, parallel to the specific reading of *a man asks him for a cigar*. In the third reading, it is dependent on both verbs, as in the nonspecific reading of *a man asks him for a cigar*. A fourth conceivable reading, in which *a cigar* is dependent on *ask* but not on *want*, seems not to exist; an adequate theory of the semantics of specificity will have to account for the lack of such a reading.

How should the difference between these various interpretations be reflected in semantic representation? One solution, variants of which are proposed by Baker (1966) and Bach (1968), is to represent the specific interpretation of (7.1) by some form of an existential quantifier whose scope includes *want*, as in (7.7a), and the nonspecific interpretation by an existential quantifier whose scope does not include *want*, as in (7.7b).

(7.7)a. $\exists x$ (x is a fish and John wants to catch x)

b. John wants ($\exists x$ (x is a fish and John catches x))

These can be paraphrased by (7.8a) and (7.8b), respectively.

(7.8)a. There is a fish such that John wants to catch it.
   b. John wants there to be a fish such that he catches it.

In this approach, dependence of *a fish* on *want* is represented by putting the existential quantifier for *a fish* within the scope of *want*.

There are several difficulties with this solution. First, if the rule relating (7.7) or (7.8) to the surface form (7.1) is a transformation, that is, if (7.7) or (7.8) is taken to be an underlying structure (as in fact it is by Bach and Baker), the transformation performs a suspiciously complex set of operations in producing the surface form.

We notice in particular that the transformations deriving (7.1) from (7.7) or (7.8) must delete the main clause and insert lexical material into the subordinate clause, which now becomes the main clause of the sentence. Such transformational operations are not attested among the standard repertoire of transformations; they occur only in those transformations associated with the term "abstract syntax," in which many semantic properties are accounted for by "higher abstract verbs" that must be deleted by transformations. As a theory of grammar which permits transformations to perform such operations is far more powerful than a theory which does not permit them, it would be preferable to do without them if at all possible. Aside from this rather general remark, it is difficult to comment on the transformations relating (7.7) or (7.8) to (7.1), because they have never been stated with sufficient precision to allow one to work out their interaction with the rest of the grammar.

Alternatively, one could propose that (7.7) is the semantic representation of (7.1), related to it by a nontransformational projection rule. Still, by whatever means (7.7) is related to (7.1), one can raise objections to (7.7) purely on the grounds of its adequacy as a semantic representation of (7.1). Consider the sentence (7.9), in which *a pretty girl* is ambiguous in specificity. (7.10a) and (7.10b) would be the semantic representations of the two readings.

(7.9) Bill is trying to find a pretty girl.
(7.10)a. $\exists x$ (x is a pretty girl and Bill is trying to find x)
     b. Bill is trying ($\exists x$ (x is a pretty girl and Bill finds x))

(7.10b), the putative nonspecific reading, does not convincingly represent this reading: its most direct paraphrase is the nonsensical sentence *Bill is trying for there to be an* x *such that* x *is a pretty girl and Bill finds her.* Even the more natural realization *Bill is trying to cause there to be an* x *such that* . . . is not an accurate paraphrase of (7.9), since in (7.9) Bill is not trying to make someone exist. Hence it is not clear that (7.10b) can function as a semantic representation of (7.9).

A second respect in which a representation of the form (7.7) or (7.10) fails is in the description of discourse. Suppose that the person to whom (7.9) is addressed replies with (7.11).

(7.11) Have you met her yet?

(Notice that (7.11) is an appropriate reply to (7.9) only under the specific reading of (7.9).) What is the semantic representation of (7.11), in particular the representation of the pronoun *her*? *Her* cannot be represented as x, the variable bound by the existential quantifier in (7.10a), since it is outside the scope of the quantifier, and bound variables are meaningless outside the scope of the quantifier that binds them. One might suggest that the scope of the quantifier be extended to include the question as well. But the scope of a quantifier is (traditionally at least) a proposition; it is not immediately clear how one could extend the formalism to include a statement and a question, uttered by two different speakers.

Alternatively, one might suggest that the semantic representation of *her* is approximately of the form *the* x *such that* x *is a pretty girl and Bill is trying to find her*. However, this approach necessarily leads to an inconsistent treatment of pronominalization. Such a form for the pronoun is impossible within sentences such as (7.12a), since an infinite regress of the form (7.12b) would result.

(7.12)a. John wants to show a pretty girl that he likes her.
   b. $\exists x$ (x is a pretty girl and John wants to show x that he likes the x such that x is a pretty girl and John wants to show x that he likes the x such that . . .)

Rather, in this case, the bound variable x must be used to represent *her*, as in (7.13).

(7.13) $\exists x$ (x is a pretty girl and John wants to show x that he likes x)

Hence it must be concluded that pronominalization within sentences is not the same process as pronominalization across a discourse, and it is thus accidental that the same forms are used. But this conclusion flies in the face of the very strong intuition that pronominalization is a unified process.

The fundamental inadequacy in this approach to specificity, I claim, is the inability of the traditional quantificational formalism to cope with natural language semantics. The necessity for the scope of a quantifier to be as large as an entire proposition in (7.9) makes a convincing interpretation difficult to construct. On the other hand, the necessity for the scope of a quantifier to be as small as a single proposition makes it impossible to describe the discourse (7.9)–(7.11) without seriously disrupting the generality of pronominalization. Section 7.4.4 will show that the quantificational formalism fails in another respect: when dealing with quantifiers other than the universal and existential quantifiers, it cannot describe the complete range of readings. We will see that in sentences containing two quantifiers, three readings are possible, rather than the two predicted by the traditional mechanism of quantifier ordering.

In view of these difficulties with the traditional logical notation, it does not seem overly brash to consider other possible formalisms for representing the semantic properties of *Want* contexts. After all, the hypothesis that logical notation is appropriate for semantic description of natural language has priority only for historical reasons. Accordingly, we will now introduce an alternative theory of the semantics of *Want* contexts.

7.2 A Solution for *Want* Contexts

We want to choose a semantic description for *Want* contexts that reflects the properties observed in section 7.1. In this description, the normal interpretation of noun phrases is the specific interpretation; but if a noun phrase has the syntactic property of being within the scope of a verb of class (7.4), it is possible for it to acquire the semantic property of dependence on the verb, one of whose consequences is a nonspecific interpretation.

The projection rule (7.14) accurately expresses this description.

(7.14)a. If an NP is within the scope of a verb V of the class (7.4) in the syntactic structure, it is optionally, but preferably, dependent on V in the semantic interpretation.
   b. If an NP is not within the scope of V, it is not dependent on V.

We will represent dependence by parentheses. For example, in (7.1) we will represent the specific reading of *a fish*, in which *a fish* is not dependent on *want*, by (7.15a); we will represent the nonspecific reading, in which *a fish* is dependent on *want*, by (7.15b). Notice that *John*, which is outside the scope of *want*, is not dependent on *want* in either case.

(7.15)a. John, a fish, want (   )
      b. John, want (a fish)

To derive these representations by means of (7.14), we observe that *John* is not within the scope of *want*, so rule (7.14b) applies, making *John* not dependent on *want*. *A fish* is within the scope of *want*; we get its preferred reading by applying (7.14a), making it dependent on *want*, yielding representation (7.15b). However, (7.14a) is an optional rule; if we choose not to apply it, we get the representation (7.15a), in which nothing is dependent on *want*.

    An important consequence of the optionality of rule (7.14) is that it permits us to describe an ambiguity without recourse to either syntactic or lexical ambiguity. Two distinct semantic interpretations are formed from the same syntactic structure by choosing to apply or not to apply (7.14a). The logical possibility of accounting for ambiguity in this fashion has generally been ignored by transformational grammarians; the usual assumption is that if there are two interpretations, there must be two deep structures or two homophonous lexical items involved. However, the optional semantic rule (7.14a) is a very simple way of accounting for the ambiguity of (7.1) that does away with the need for distinct deep structures, which in any event have never been justified on independent syntactic grounds.

    In the more complicated case *John wants to see a friend of his catch a fish*, there are four readings, which we can represent by using the optionality of (7.14a) independently with respect to *a friend* and *a fish*, thus:

(7.16)a. John, a friend, a fish, want (   )   (both specific)
      b. John, a friend, want (a fish)   (*a friend* specific)
      c. John, a fish, want (a friend)   (*a fish* specific)
      d. John, want (a friend, a fish)   (neither specific)

Notice that in the notation we have just introduced, the linear order of elements need bear no relation to their order in the sentence. The only relevant property of this notation is whether or not an NP is within the parentheses associated with *want*.

The notion of dependence, introduced by the projection rule (7.14), gives us a way of differentiating between the various readings of sentences containing *Want* contexts. However, if the representation in (7.15)–(7.16) is to be part of semantic description and not a mere classification of readings, we must ascribe a semantic significance to dependence. To do this, we first observe that all of the verbs in the class (7.4) denote a state of affairs in which the subject is contemplating some yet unrealized situation and has some particular attitude or is taking some particular action toward the realization of this situation. For example, in *John wants to catch a fish* the unrealized situation is John's catching a fish, and John's attitude toward the realization of this situation is positive. In *John is afraid to catch a fish* the unrealized situation is again John's catching a fish, but John's attitude toward the realization of this situation is negative. *John is trying to catch a fish* and *John is avoiding catching a fish* have the same unrealized situation, but in these sentences John is exerting effort respectively toward and against the realization of this situation. *Bill asked John to catch a fish* expresses the same unrealized situation; Bill is exerting effort toward the realization of this situation by talking to John about it. Thus in general we can say that these verbs contain a semantic marker *unrealized* which is applied to some part of the semantic interpretation of the sentence.

Now consider the correspondence between a noun phrase in a sentence and actual things (e.g. individuals, objects, ideas, etc.), that is, the *extension* of the noun phrase. If the sentence claims such-and-such a state of affairs or event to have been realized in the real world, it follows that the participants in this state of affairs or event can be identified. But if the situation is as yet unrealized, there are two possibilities: either the participants can be identified already, and only their participation is unrealized; or the identity of the participants depends on possibilities inherent in the realization of the state of affairs. These two possibilities correspond precisely to the two possible readings of noun phrases in *Want* contexts. In the specific reading of *John wants to catch a fish*, the fish is identifiable even if John never succeeds in catching it; in the nonspecific reading, there is an identifiable fish only in the event that John actually catches one. That is, just in case *a fish* is dependent on *want*, it is subject to the condition that it has an identifiable referent only in the further instance that the unrealized situation comes to fruition. We will use the term $C_{unrealized}$ to denote this condition.

Under this interpretation of the projection rule (7.14), it is easy to see why proper nouns in *Want* contexts, for example *Bill* in (7.17), exhibit no ambiguity.

(7.17) John wants to meet Bill.

Since the use of the name *Bill* already implies the existence of an identifiable individual, it would be inconsistent to apply $C_{\text{unrealized}}$, which would say that *Bill* does not have an identifiable referent now but might in the future. Hence the reading in which *Bill* is dependent on *want* is rejected, leaving only the possibility of the specific reading. Similarly, the use of *certain* and some kinds of relative clauses will force the specific reading on an indefinite NP, since they imply that the NP can already be identified:

(7.18)a. John wants to meet a certain girl.
    b. John wants to meet a girl you told him about.

Definite NPs may be either specific or nonspecific, depending on their content. (7.19a) is clearly specific, but (7.19b) can well be nonspecific. In general, the definite article produces only a presupposition of uniqueness, but not a presupposition of identifiability.

(7.19)a. John wants to meet the girl in your bedroom.
    b. John wants to meet the girl of his dreams.

However, anaphoric definite NPs will generally be specific, for reasons which we must now make clear.

Suppose two noun phrases in a discourse are intended to be coreferential and are so marked by the use of the anaphoric definite article or a definite pronoun. Since their coreferentiality by definition entails that they have the same intended referent, the conditions under which they are claimed to have an identifiable referent must be the same. We will call this requirement, which follows from the consistency condition on pronominalization (cf. section 4.3), the *coreference condition on modal dependence*.

For example, consider the following sentences:

(7.20)a. John wants to touch a fish. You can see it over there.
    b. John wants to touch a fish and I want to kiss it.
    c. John wants to touch a fish and kiss it too.
    d. John wants to touch a fish. He saw one over there.

In (7.20a), only the specific reading of *a fish* is possible, because *it* is not within the scope of *want* and hence cannot be dependent on it. If *a fish* were marked dependent on *want* by rule (7.14a), the first sentence of (7.20a) would claim that *a fish* will have an identifiable referent only if John actually succeeds in touching a fish. But this would be inconsistent with the fact that *it* is claimed to have an identifiable referent already, since *it* is not dependent on *want*. Thus the specific reading of *a fish* must be chosen for a consistent semantic interpretation.

In (7.20b), again only the specific reading of *a fish* is possible. Again, if the nonspecific reading were chosen, the sentence would claim that *a fish* has an identifiable referent only when John touches a fish. But consider the intended referent of *it*. The two possible readings are that *it* has an identifiable referent and that *it* will have an identifiable referent only when I succeed in kissing a fish. Since the unrealized situations in the two clauses are different (though both determined by the word *want*), the same individual cannot be chosen depending on the outcome of both situations. Hence the only consistent characterization of *a fish* and *it* is that in which both are claimed to have an identifiable referent.

In (7.20c), however, *a fish* and *it* are within the scope of the same *want* and hence are participants in the same unrealized situation. It follows that they can have a common intended referent which cannot be identified until the situation is realized; in other words, a nonspecific reading is possible.

(7.20d) is presented for contrast. *One*-pronominalization, as in (7.20d), does not imply intended coreference, so the coreference condition does not apply across *one*-pronominalization. Hence *a fish* may be dependent on *want* and be read as nonspecific even though *one* is specific. This striking difference between the two kinds of pronominalization is by no means determinable a priori; one can well imagine a language in which (7.20d) has only a specific interpretation, like (7.20a). The fact that the difference between (7.20a) and (7.20d) is an automatic prediction of our account of the semantics of *Want* contexts is thus evidence for the correctness of the analysis.

We are now in a position to analyze (7.6), which we repeat here for convenience.

(7.6) Fred wants a man to ask him for a cigar.

In section 7.1 we showed that *a man* may or may not be dependent on *want*, and that *a cigar* may be dependent either on *want*, on *want* and *ask*, or on neither, yielding a total of six readings. We must show how this set of readings follows from the analysis we have presented. First consider the relation between *ask* and the NPs in the sentence. The only NP within the scope of *ask* is *a cigar*, so the other NPs must not be dependent on *ask*; *a cigar* may or may not be dependent on *ask*. (7.21) represents these two possible partial readings.

(7.21)a. Fred, a man, him, a cigar, ask (   )
     b. Fred, a man, him, ask (a cigar)

Next consider the relation between *want* and the NPs. All the NPs but *Fred* are within the scope of *want*. *Fred* is of course not dependent on *want*. *A man* may or may not be dependent on *want*, yielding the two readings we we have observed. *Him*, as far as rule (7.14) is concerned, may be dependent on *want*. But if this reading is chosen, the coreference condition will be violated: *Fred*, the antecedent of *him*, is already claimed to have an identifiable referent, so it cannot be claimed that *him* does not yet have an identifiable referent. Hence *him* may take only the specific reading. Finally, *a cigar* again may or may not be dependent on *want*. Thus we get the four partial readings given in (7.22).

(7.22)a. Fred, a man, him, a cigar, want (   )
     b. Fred, a man, him, want (a cigar)
     c. Fred, him, a cigar, want (a man)
     d. Fred, him, want (a man, a cigar)

At first blush we would expect there to be eight possible readings for the sentence rather than the observed six, derived by combining either of the partial readings in (7.21) with any of those in (7.22). However, a more careful examination of the semantic significance of the readings shows this initial expectation to be incorrect. The unrealized situation associated with *ask* is Fred giving a man a cigar; the unrealized situation associated with *want* is a man asking Fred for a cigar. If *a cigar* is independent of both verbs, it is claimed to have an identifiable referent regardless of whether either unrealized situation comes about. If *a cigar* is dependent on both verbs, it is claimed to have an identifiable referent just in case both unrealized situations come about. If a cigar is dependent on *want* but not dependent on *ask*, it is claimed to have an identifiable referent as soon as a man asks Fred for a cigar, whether or not Fred gives him one. For this to be the case, the man must ask Fred for a particular cigar, but Fred cannot know in advance which cigar the man will ask for. These are the three readings of *a cigar* we observed in section 7.1.

What about the other possibility, in which *a cigar* is dependent on *ask* but not on *want*? This reading would claim that *a cigar* has an identifiable referent only if Fred gives a man a cigar, but whether or not the man asks Fred for a cigar. However, consider the case in which Fred gives a man a cigar but the man has not asked Fred for a cigar. Under these circumstances, Fred's giving a man a cigar cannot be considered a genuine realization of the unrealized situation in *the man asked Fred for a cigar*, since the man has not exerted effort to bring the situation about. That is, it is in principle impossible to bring about a genuine realization of the *ask* situation without first realizing the *want* situation. We conclude, then, that a reading in which the identity of *a cigar* is dependent on the outcome of the *ask* situation but not on the outcome of the *want* situation is anomalous or incoherent. We have thus accounted for the full range of interpretations of (7.6).

Before going on to a more general form of this theory of *Want* contexts, let us briefly observe how it avoids the difficulties we pointed out in the theory of indefinites as existential quantifiers. The first difficulty was that with agentive verbs such as *try* involving unrealized situations, the analysis with an existential quantifier did not correctly characterize the nonspecific reading: *Bill is trying to find a pretty girl* does not mean *Bill is trying for there to be a pretty girl such that he finds her*. In the present analysis, however, the semantic representation of claims about reference is independent of the semantic representation of grammatical relations. That is, whether *a pretty girl* is dependent on *try* has no bearing on the fact that what Bill is trying to do is find a pretty girl. Hence no problem arises.

The second problem with the use of existential quantifiers was that the interaction of anaphora with the logical notation could not be worked out consistently. In our analysis, however, the representation of anaphora is treated as entirely independent from the representation of claims about intended reference, and any otherwise workable device can be used to account for anaphora. The only interaction between these two parts of the grammar is the coreference condition, a well-formedness condition on semantic representation which requires that if two NPs are to be coreferential they must have the same conditions for identifiability of reference. Any readings which violate the coreference condition are anomalous.

If the analysis of *Want* contexts we have presented here were an isolated solution, it would of course not be terribly interesting. In particular, we have given no systematic significance to the kind of representation we have introduced in (7.15)–(7.16) and (7.20)–(7.21), nor have we shown that the projection rule (7.14) is of an independently useful type. In the next section we will present a more general theory of the semantic representation of intended reference, the theory of modal structure, showing how our solution to *Want* contexts is an instance of this theory. We will then present several other linguistic phenomena as further instances of the theory, in order to demonstrate the theory's generality.

7.3 The Theory of Modal Structure

We observed in the analysis of *Want* contexts that the semantic interpretation of a sentence must include the conditions under which the various NPs in the sentence are claimed to have identifiable referents. It has generally been assumed that this semantic information is integrated into the functional structure. For example, Bach's treatment of *Want* contexts in terms of quantifiers supposes that the representations of grammatical relations form propositions which are embedded as the scope of the quantifiers which express referential information, and that these quantified expressions may in turn be embedded into other expressions involving grammatical relations.

However, this treatment leads to an interesting difficulty. For example, in the sentence *John wants to catch a fish*, we know that *a fish* is the object of *catch* and thus subordinate to *want* in the representation of grammatical relations; this relationship must hold in either the specific or the nonspecific reading. However, in the representation of specificity, *a fish* is subordinate to *want* only in the nonspecific reading. Bach's solution takes care of this fact by introducing into the single hierarchical representation two reflexes of *a fish*: the variable x within the proposition that expresses grammatical relations, and the quantifier binding x outside that proposition.

In the treatment of *Want* contexts in section 7.2, we made a different assumption about the representation of specificity, namely, that the representation of referential conditions is independent of the functional structure. We will claim that there is a second hierarchical structure in the semantic representation, the *modal structure*, and that the lexical items of a sentence may have reflexes in both hierarchies simultaneously. For example, the two readings of *John wants to catch a fish* will have the same functional structure but will differ in modal structure. *A fish wants to catch John*, on the other hand, will have a different functional structure than *John wants to catch a fish*, but it will have the same modal structure as the specific reading of *John wants to catch a fish*, since in both cases *a fish* and *John* are claimed to have identifiable referents.

The conditions on identifiability of referents will be determined by a class of semantic markers called *modal operators*. *Unrealized* is one modal operator, occurring in the semantic representation of the verbs in (7.4). Other modal operators we will discuss here are *future, possible, negative, multiple, generic*, and *wh-*. The lexical items containing modal operators can be of virtually any syntactic category; we will observe modal operators associated with verbs such as *want, hope*, and *doubt*, modals such as *will* and *may*, determiners such as *which, no*, and *five*, adjectives such as *possible* and *certain*, and the word *not* (whatever its category may be).

Associated with each lexical item bearing a modal operator will be a structural relation called the *scope* of the modal operator. The scope of the modal operator is that portion of the sentence within which the modal operator may affect claims about the identifiability of referents. For example, the scope of *unrealized* is that portion of the sentence within which nonspecifics of the type we discussed in sections 7.1–7.2 may arise. The verb *want* contains as part of its semantic representation the information that the scope of *unrealized* is the direct object; *ask* specifies that the scope of *unrealized* is the object of *for*. In general, it appears that if a lexical item containing a modal operator belongs to a category that strictly subcategorizes NPs (e.g. adjectives in copula position and verbs, but not determiners, modals, or *not*), the scope consists of one of the NPs it strictly subcategorizes. We will call this *type I scope*.

Among the examples of modal operators to be presented here, two other types of scope appear. One type appears with modal verbs such as *will* and *may*; the scope in these examples consists of everything commanded by the lexical item containing the modal operator. We will call this *type II scope*. The last type appears with various determiners and with *not*; it consists of all material commanded by and to the right of the lexical item containing the operator. We will call this *type III scope*.

How do modal operators affect interpretation of noun phrases within their scope? Each modal operator M (which may appear as a semantic marker in a variety of lexical items) has an associated *modal condition* C_M which may be placed on the identifiability of noun phrase referents within the scope of M. For example, a noun phrase subject to $C_{unrealized}$ is claimed to have an identifiable referent only upon realization of the unrealized situation. The modal conditions associated with other operators will be shown to make different claims about the identifiability of referents. For example, a noun phrase subject to the modal condition associated with negation is claimed to have no identifiable referent; a noun phrase subject to the modal condition associated with a number n is claimed to have n identifiable referents.

There must be a rule of semantic interpretation which establishes the claims made about particular noun phrases in a particular sentence, that is, which relates the modal structure of the sentence to its syntactic structure. This rule turns out to be only a slightly more general form of the rule we developed for *Want* contexts:

(7.23) (Modal projection rule)

Given a lexical item A whose semantic representation contains a modal operator M. If an NP is within the scope of A, it is optionally (with degree of preference d_M) *dependent on M* in the modal structure, that is, subject to C_M. If an NP is outside the scope of M, it is not dependent on M.

The only part of (7.23) that has not yet been explained is the degree of preference d_M. In general we will observe ambiguities in referential claims for noun phrases within the scope of modal operators, resulting from the optional application of the condition C_M. However, which of the readings is preferred seems to vary somewhat unsystematically from one modal operator to another and in some cases from one speaker to another. As I have no explanation of this variation, I have chosen to account for it by incorporating the factor d_M into the operation of the modal projection rule. A more interesting account of the variation would of course be welcome.

In analysis of *Want* contexts we discussed the interaction of anaphoric processes with the application of $C_{unrealized}$. From the quite general assumption that for two noun phrases in a discourse to be intended coreferents, they must be subject to the same conditions for identifiability of referents (the coreference condition), we predicted the behavior of pronouns and their antecedents in *Want* contexts. The coreference condition turns out to apply to all the examples of modal operators we will discuss. It appears in two variants, a strong form and a weak form. Which form applies depends on which modal operator is involved and to some extent on certain circumstances of the discourse. The division of modal operators into those requiring the strong condition and those requiring the weak condition appears to follow a systematic pattern, but the exact criteria for the division are not easy to characterize. For present purposes it will be sufficient to observe the division without explaining it.

(7.24) (Coreference condition on modal dependence)
    If NP^1 and NP^2 are intended to be coreferential, they must be dependent on

$\begin{cases} \text{the same type modal operators} & \text{(weak form)} \\ \text{the same token modal operators} & \text{(strong form)} \end{cases}$

Unrealized is subject to the strong form of the coreference condition, as shown by (7.20), which we repeat here for convenience.

(7.20)a. John wants to touch a fish. You can see it over there.
    b. John wants to touch a fish and I want to kiss it.
    c. John wants to touch a fish and kiss it too.
    d. John wants to touch a fish. He saw one over there.

In (7.20a) *it* is not dependent on *unrealized*, so its antecedent *a fish* may not be either. In (7.20c) *a fish* and *it* are within the scope of the same instance of *want*, so both can be dependent on the same token of *unrealized*. In (7.20b), however, they may be dependent only on different tokens of *unrealized*, that is, on different, instances of this general type of modal operator; the fact that we observe only the specific reading, in which neither is dependent on *unrealized*, shows that the strong coreference condition must hold. In the parallel example with the modal operator *future* (see section 7.4.1), on the other hand, the dependent reading will be possible and we will conclude that the weak coreference condition holds. (The generality of the coreference condition was suggested to me by the discussion in Karttunen 1969.)

    Before turning to further examples, it is important to make clear the claims we are making in presenting the theory of modal structure as an account of these phenomena. The theory of modal structure predicts that whenever a formative can be shown to affect the claim on identifiability of referents for an NP, it will have discrete scope within which any suitable NP may be similarly affected, that ambiguities will appear depending on whether or not the modal condition has been applied, and that the co-reference condition will hold in one of its two forms. In section 7.5 I will justify the further claim that any formative placing a condition on the identifiability of referents for NPs puts a similar condition on the realization of situations described by sentences. This is a highly structured set of claims about language; the class of possible grammars it predicts is restricted in a significant and interesting way not captured by other extant theories of semantic interpretation. Should these claims prove viable, they are independent justification for abandoning the description of *Want* contexts in terms of traditional logical notation, for they provide a more unified view of language.

7.4 Some Other Modal Operators

We will now present a number of modal operators other than *unrealized*. For each one, we will give evidence that it has a scope within which it induces an optional condition C_M on the identifiability of referents for NPs. In addition, we will try to give some idea of the nature of C_M in each case, and we will show that the coreference condition obtains.

7.4.1 Future

Nonspecificity is induced optionally by the modal *will*, as can be seen by the ambiguity of *a girl* in (7.25).

(7.25) John will bring a girl to the party.

Will can induce the ambiguity anywhere in its clause or in clauses it commands, as can be seen from (7.26).

(7.26)a. A unicorn will appear on your doorstep tomorrow.
      b. Max will learn that a girl is in his bedroom.

It cannot induce the ambiguity in clauses it does not command, as can be seen from the lack of ambiguity of *a girl* in (7.27).

(7.27) A girl said that Bill will see a unicorn.

We can account for the ambiguity by claiming that *will* contains a modal operator *future* and that its scope is of type II, the entire clause it commands. The ambiguity is due to the fact that the modal projection rule optionally marks NPs within the scope of *will* dependent on *future*. The two readings of (7.25) will be identical in functional structure, but the nonspecific reading will have the modal structure (7.28a) and the specific reading will have the modal structure (7.28b).

(7.28)a. John, the party, will (a girl)
     b. John, the party, a girl, will ( )

If an NP is dependent on *will*, the modal condition C_{future} is placed on it. C_{future} claims that there is no identifiable referent at present, but there definitely will be at the time in the future when the situation described by the sentence comes about. C_{future} thus contrasts with $C_{unrealized}$, which claims only the *possibility* of a future identifiable referent.

One might ask why there are no ambiguities associated with *John* and *the party* in (7.25), since both of these NPs are also within the scope of *will*. However, the theory of modal structure claims that the ambiguity involves different claims about the identifiability of referents. Since the referents of *John* and *the party* are independently claimed to be identifiable, the dependent reading, in which they are claimed not yet to be identifiable, is anomalous.

The weak form of the coreference condition applies to *future*:

(7.29)a. John will bring a girl to the party, and she is beautiful.
     b. John will bring a girl to the party, and she will be beautiful.
     c. John will bring a girl to the party and introduce her to everyone.
     d. John said he will bring a girl to the party, and that's why I've
        brought one.

In (7.29a), where *she* is outside the scope of *will*, *a girl* must be read as specific. In (7.29b), *a girl* and *she* are within the scope of different occurrences of *will*, but nonspecificity is permitted anyway. We conclude that only the weak coreference condition applies. (7.29c) has both *a girl* and *she* within the scope of the same *will*, and the ambiguity is possible. (7.29d) shows that *one*-pronominalization is not subject to the coreference condition, as predicted by the theory.

7.4.2 Possible

Also within the province of nonspecifics are the noun phrases commanded by various expressions of possibility, including the modal *may*.

(7.30)a. It is $\begin{Bmatrix} \text{possible} \\ \text{likely} \end{Bmatrix}$ that John caught a fish.

     b. John may have caught a fish.

For the adjectives of possibility, the ambiguity may appear in any NP originating in the complement of the adjective. For example, in (7.31a), *a fish* is inside a clause embedded within the complement of *likely*; in (7.31b), *a unicorn* originates as the subject of the complement. Both display the ambiguity.

(7.31)a. It is likely that John saw Bill catch a fish.

     b. A unicorn is likely to appear on your doorstep.

In case there is no complement, the subject NP is subject to the ambiguity:

(7.32) A catastrophe is quite likely in California.

However, NPs originating outside the complement are not subject to the ambiguity, for example *a friend of mine* in (7.33).

(7.33) It seems likely to a friend of mine that deep structures exist.

We conclude that the scope of these adjectives consists of the subject, and therefore that it is of type I.

    With the modal *may*, the ambiguity appears anywhere in the clause commanded by *may*:

(7.34)a. John may have seen Bill catch a fish.

     b. A unicorn may appear on your doorstep.

But it does not occur in clauses not commanded by *may*:

(7.35) A friend of mine said that deep structures may exist.

The scope of *may*, then, consists of its entire clause, i.e. it is of type II.

We can suppose, then, that these adjectives and *may* contain a modal operator *possible* which induces the ambiguity: noun phrases within the scope of *possible* may be marked dependent on it by the modal projection rule. The modal condition $C_{possible}$ placed on NPs dependent on *possible* claims that the existence of an identifiable referent is possible; the degree of possibility will vary among the lexical items containing the operator *possible*.

Apparently the nonspecific reading is highly preferred where possible, for when we construct the frames to test for the coreference condition, we get unnatural sentences where the specific reading is required:

(7.36)a. ??It is $\begin{Bmatrix} \text{possible} \\ \text{likely} \end{Bmatrix}$ that John has caught a fish, because he ate it.

b. ??It is $\begin{Bmatrix} \text{possible} \\ \text{likely} \end{Bmatrix}$ that John caught a fish, and $\begin{Bmatrix} \text{possible} \\ \text{likely} \end{Bmatrix}$ that he ate it too.

c. It is $\begin{Bmatrix} \text{possible} \\ \text{likely} \end{Bmatrix}$ that John caught a fish and ate it.

d. It is $\begin{Bmatrix} \text{possible} \\ \text{likely} \end{Bmatrix}$ that John caught a fish, because I saw him eat one.

(7.37)a. ??A man may have entered Leonora's bedroom, because I saw him leave.

b. ??A man may have entered Leonora's bedroom, and he may have left.

c. A man may have entered Leonora's bedroom and left right away.

d. A man may have entered Leonora's bedroom, because I saw one leave.

These examples are parallel to (7.20) and (7.29). In the (a) examples, the pronoun is not within the scope of *possible*, so the coreference condition predicts that only the specific reading is possible for its antecedent. Since the nonspecific reading is highly preferred, the specific reading is unnatural, and the unnaturalness of the (a) examples follows. In the (b) examples, the pronoun and its antecedent are within the scope of different instances of the modal operator. Since the strong coreference condition therefore cannot tolerate anything but the specific reading, but the modal projection rule strongly favors the nonspecific reading, the result is not fully accept-able.[1] In the (c) examples, the pronoun and its antecedent are within the scope of the same instance of the modal operator, so the nonspecific read-ing is possible. In the (d) examples, as predicted by the theory, the non-specific reading is possible because *one*-pronominalization does not entail coreference.

Even the extreme on the scale of possibility, certainty, apparently has a modal operator, since the weak coreference condition obtains: compare (7.38) to (7.29).

(7.38)a. ?It is certain that John caught a fish, because he ate it.
   b. It is certain that John caught a fish, and it is certain that he ate it.
   c. It is certain that John caught a fish and ate it.
   d. It is certain that John caught a fish, because he ate one.

The appearance of the weak condition here suggests a hypothesis: when-ever a modal operator makes a definite claim about the existence of an identifiable referent, the weak condition holds; whenever a modal operator leaves uncertainty as to the existence of an identifiable referent, the strong condition holds. This seems to be the generalization implicit in the facts presented so far: *future* and *certainty* have the weak condition, and *un-realized* and *possible* have the strong condition.

One might ask why no specific-nonspecific ambiguity is apparent in examples with *certain*. The reason is simple: an NP dependent on *certain* is claimed to be certain of having an identifiable referent, which is in effect the same claim made if it is not dependent on *certain*. The indistinguish-ability of the two readings makes the ambiguity disappear. For some speakers, this will be sufficient to satisfy the coreference condition, and sentences like (7.38a) will be acceptable.

Certainty and the various expressions of possibility apparently can be analyzed as a single operator of possibility with an added indication of degree; we discover then that the coreference condition holds in such a

---

[1]Speakers disagree on the degree of unacceptability of (7.36a, b) and (7.37a, b). In particular, one reader of an earlier version of this chapter claimed they were totally unacceptable, and another claimed they were totally acceptable in the specific reading. These differences can be captured in the degree of preference $d_{possible}$ associated with the modal operator. The more highly preferred the nonspecific reading is, the less acceptable the examples are which need a specific reading to satisfy the coreference condition. Apparently d_M is subject to individual variation.

way as to require a pronoun to be not more certain than its antecedent
(these examples were pointed out to me by George Lakoff):

(7.39)a. It is certain that John caught a fish, and it is possible that he ate it
     too.
   b. It is possible that John caught a fish, and it is certain that he ate
$$\left\{\begin{array}{c} ?\text{it} \\ \text{one} \end{array}\right\}.$$

Many of the adjectives which carry the modal operator *possible* have
cognate speaker-oriented adverbs. It is only natural that the adverbs carry
modal operators as well. One might conjecture, then, that the projection
rules for sentence adverbs proposed in Chapter 3 actually contribute (at
least in part) to the modal structure rather than to the functional structure.
The close semantic relationship between speaker-oriented adverbs and
epistemic modals, pointed out in Chapter 3, reinforces this suspicion. We
will not attempt an integration of the two systems of rules here, however.

We see from the results of sections 7.1 and 7.2 and the last two sub-
sections that *nonspecific* is a collective term for an assortment of modal
conditions, all of which give some degree of uncertainty to the existence of
an identifiable referent at the time the sentence is spoken. It is beyond doubt
that the modal operators *unrealized, future,* and *possible* should be analyzed
further into structures of great similarity. It is an important problem to
determine the exact way to analyze these operators, since the results are
likely to be of great significance for a theory of universal semantic prim-
itives.

7.4.3 Negation
Indefinite noun phrases in negative sentences can be read as nonspecific:

(7.40)a. John didn't catch a fish.
   b. John didn't see a man catch a fish.

In fact, a specific reading in (7.40) is unnatural; it is difficult to conceive of
a situation in which one would say (7.40) with a particular fish in mind.
We can attribute the nonspecificity in (7.40) to the presence of a modal
operator *neg. Neg* will be contained in all the negative morphemes such as
not, no, nobody, never, neither, and *nothing,* as well as in the morphemes
with "implicit" negation such as *few, little, seldom, doubt,* and *dissuade.*

The condition C_{neg} applied to NPs dependent on *neg* is that there is no identifiable referent at all.

To see that the application of C_{neg} is optional, consider the contrast in (7.41), where intonation contour changes the meaning.

(7.41)a. Fred didn't buy many of the eggs. (normal intonation)
     b. Fred didn't BUY MANY of the eggs.
                     A   B
        (A and B contours as introduced in Chapter 6.)

(7.41b) has the specific reading of *many of the eggs*: the eggs Fred didn't buy can be pointed out. (7.41a), on the other hand, is nonspecific: it only makes a claim about the number of eggs Fred didn't buy, not about their identity.

Observe that the strong form of the coreference condition obtains for *neg*. The paradigm (7.42) is precisely parallel to the earlier paradigms (7.20), (7.36), and (7.37).

(7.42)a. ?I didn't catch a fish, and it was ugly.
     b. ?I didn't catch a fish, and I didn't bring it home.
     c. I didn't catch a fish and bring it home.
     d. I didn't catch a fish, but Bill caught one.

As usual, the specificity of *a fish* is problematic only when it is coreferential with a definite pronoun; *one*-pronominalization, because it does not imply coreference, has no effect on conditions on identifiability of referent.

A complication arises in the theory at this point. The verbs we have discussed all take type I scope, and it appears that the determination of which NPs are within the scope takes place at the level of deep structure. For example, an NP can be passivized out of the object of *expect* and still retain its nonspecificity, as in (7.43a); or an NP can be topicalized out of the object of *want*, as in (7.43b).[2]

[2]The only transformation that affects the specificity of NPs originating within the scope of type I verbs is *There*-insertion, which requires specifics: note the strangeness of examples like *There is an earthquake expected to take place next week*. To account for this one apparent exception without requiring *There*-insertion to mention specificity, we could claim that *there* contains a modal operator with type III scope, whose modal condition is a claim that there is an identifiable referent. As will be shown directly, type III scope is determined at surface structure, so the *There*-insertion rule, like other movement rules, would affect meaning.

(7.43)a. A unicorn is expected to appear pretty soon.
   b. A Rembrandt(,) Bill wants very much to see.

For the modal verbs, which take type II scope, there is no way to ascertain at what level of derivation the scope is determined. Since there are no transformations which move NPs in or out of clauses containing modal verbs, we cannot see whether such transformations leave the range of readings unaffected, as is the case above, or change it, as we will now show to be the case with type III scope.

Evidence is plentiful that modal dependency on negation is contingent on surface structure configurations. A great deal of this evidence will be presented in detail in section 8.2; for the present a few examples will suffice.

Consider (7.44), in which *many* has a nonspecific reading unless intonation as in (7.41b) is applied.

(7.44) The cops didn't arrest many of the innocent bystanders.

Corresponding to (7.44) are two passives:

(7.45)a. Not many of the innocent bystanders were arrested by the cops.
   b. Many of the innocent bystanders weren't arrested by the cops.

(7.45a) has the nonspecific reading of (7.44). But (7.45b) has only a specific reading for *many*; this indicates that *many* is outside the scope of negation in (7.45b), which can be the case only if the scope is determined at surface structure. The passive construction has an extra reading only marginally present in the active (7.44), because the syntax happens to allow negation either to precede or to follow *many* in the passive, but only to precede *many* in the active.

Note that this cannot be stated as a special condition on that passive; rather it has to do with the relative configuration of negation and *many*. Sets of sentences like (7.44)–(7.45) exist where it is the active that has the extra reading:

(7.46)a. Not many of the arrows hit the target.
   b. Many of the arrows didn't hit the target.
   c. The target wasn't hit by many of the arrows.

(7.46c) has the specific reading of (7.46b) only under the special intonation pattern of (7.41b). Hence the presence of an extra reading must not depend on what transformations have taken place or what the deep structure is, but only on what surface configurations are possible.

Similar paradigms exist for transformations other than the passive. For example, (7.47b) and (7.47c) both result from (7.47a) by an adverb fronting rule.

(7.47)a. Tom didn't go to town very often.
    b. Not very often did Tom go to town.
    c. Very often Tom didn't go to town.

Often is subject to specific and nonspecific readings. In (7.47c) one can in principle mention the times Tom didn't go to town, but this is not possible in (7.47a) and (7.47b). Hence as a result of performing the adverb-preposing rule, there is another reading possible, because *often* has been moved to a position where it may be to the left of (i.e. outside the scope of) negation. Further examples will be presented in the next chapter.

Consideration of these examples makes it clear that no constraint on the transformations themselves can account for the differences in meaning: the semantic generalization has to do with the surface structure configurations, regardless of the derivation by which they are produced. We conclude then that the scope of negation must be determined at surface structure (or perhaps at end-of-cycle structure, like the pronominalization rules).

The claim that type I scope is determined at deep structure but type III scope is determined at surface structure calls for some discussion. We have proposed that a single projection rule, the modal projection rule, maps information from two distinct (but predetermined) levels of syntactic structure into a unified aspect of semantic representation, the modal structure. The logical possibility of such a projection rule has been overlooked in the past, though this not surprising, considering the dearth of work on projection rules of any type. However, in this case, the generalization is clear: all the lexical items containing modal operators affect semantic interpretation in the same way, though the syntactic environments in which they affect it differ. In other words, the generality of the modal projection rule itself is not curtailed; once the scope is defined, the modal projection rule can go on as before.

One might still contend that allowing scope to be determined at either of two levels increases the power of the theory greatly. However, as remarked before, the level at which scope is determined seems to be correlated precisely with the type of scope, which in turn seems to be correlated with lexical category. Furthermore, all of these properties seem to be independent of the semantics of the modal operators involved. If this generalization is correct, the theory of modal structure is still highly constrained, even if it is not constrained along lines usually considered "natural."

To illustrate the interaction of the syntactic properties associated with the determination of scope, we will consider the two lexical items *forbid* and *no one*, both of which contain the modal operator *neg*. Since *forbid* is a verb, we expect its scope to be its object, determined at deep structure. And this seems to be the case: *many people* in (7.48a) originates in the complement, as it does in (7.48b), and both have a nonspecific reading. In (7.48c) *many people* occupies the same surface position as it does in (7.48c), but only a specific reading is possible.

(7.48)a. Many people are forbidden to leave (at once).[3]
     b. They forbid many people to leave (at once).
     c. Many people forbid them to leave.

On the other hand, with *no one*, where *neg* is in the determiner, we expect the scope to be everything commanded and to the right in surface structure. This seems to be borne out by the contrast of (7.48) with (7.49):

(7.49)a. Many people are allowed by no one to leave (*at once).
     b. No one allows many people to leave (at once).
     c. Many people allow no one to leave.

Unlike (7.48a), (7.49a) lacks a nonspecific reading for *many people*, as shown by the inappropriateness of the adverbial *at once*. (7.49a) is derived from (7.49b), which has the nonspecific interpretation. However, with respect to modal structure it patterns like (7.49c), which has a similar configuration in surface structure. Thus the scope appears to be correlated with

---

[3]In order to claim that *many people* in (7.47a) originates in the complement, we will have to derive this reading syntactically from *someone forbids* [$_S$*many people to leave at once*], rather than from *someone forbids many people* [$_S$*many people leave at once*]. This derivation is justified by the existence of sentences like *I forbid there to be any noise in here,* in which *there* cannot be the deep object of *forbid*.

lexical category, independent of the nature of C_M, which is the same in (7.48) and (7.49).[4]

7.4.4 Quantifiers

There is an ambiguity present in sentences with quantifiers, such as (7.50a), which is not present in sentences with ordinary plurals, such as (7.50b).

(7.50)a. $\left\{\begin{array}{l}\text{Some}\\\text{All}\\\text{Five}\end{array}\right\}$ of the boys told me a story.

    b. The boys told me a story.

In (7.50a) it is possible that I heard either a single story or several stories, one per boy.[5] In (7.50b) only the former possibility exists. The ambiguity can be produced anywhere to the right of the quantifier and commanded by it, as shown by (7.51a), but not to the left (7.51b) or not commanded by the quantifier (7.51c).

(7.51)a. $\left\{\begin{array}{l}\text{Some}\\\text{All}\\\text{Five}\end{array}\right\}$ of the boys made Bill promise to tell me a story.

    b. A boy told me $\left\{\begin{array}{l}\text{some}\\\text{all}\\\text{five}\end{array}\right\}$ of the stories.

    c. That $\left\{\begin{array}{l}\text{some}\\\text{all}\\\text{five}\end{array}\right\}$ of the boys came bothered a friend of mine.

We can account for this ambiguity by making quantifiers carry a modal operator *multiple*. A noun phrase interpreted as dependent on *multiple* by the modal projection rule, then, is subject to the claim that there is a distinct identifiable referent corresponding to each member of the set being

[4]The status of *not* is somewhat open to question. The fact that *any* does not occur independently to the left of *not* may be solely due to the scope of *any* (cf. section 7.4.4), as there is some indication that the scope of *not* may extend to the left or be determined at deep structure, or both, classing it with the modals as a type II scope. Much depends on judgments of acceptability which are sufficiently subtle as to make strong statements unjustified at present.

[5]There is an additional ambiguity in this reading: whether the boys told me together, or whether they told me the same story one by one. The difference between these readings will be discussed in section 7.5.

quantified. The ambiguity of (7.50a) is predictable from the optionality of the modal projection rule.

The distribution of the ambiguity demonstrated in (7.51) shows that the scope of quantifiers is of type III. In the last section we claimed that type III scope is determined at surface structure. This claim appears to be true of quantifiers, as can be seen by passivizing (7.50a) and (7.51b):

(7.52)a. A story was told to me by $\begin{Bmatrix} some \\ all \\ five \end{Bmatrix}$ of the boys.

    b. $\begin{Bmatrix} Some \\ All \\ Five \end{Bmatrix}$ of the stories were told to me by a boy.

In (7.52a) *a story* is unambiguous, unlike in the active (7.50a); in (7.52b) *a boy* is ambiguous, unlike in the active (7.51b). Thus the passive simultaneously adds and deletes readings. The true generalization concerns the surface structure configuration: with respect to modal structure, (7.50a) and (7.52b) pattern together, and (7.51b) and (7.52a) pattern together.

As predicted from the interpretation of modal structure, the coreference condition obtains, in its strong form:

(7.53)a. I told $\begin{Bmatrix} some \\ all \\ five \end{Bmatrix}$ of the boys a story, even though I didn't like it (the story).

    b. I told $\begin{Bmatrix} some \\ all \\ five \end{Bmatrix}$ of the boys a story, and $\begin{Bmatrix} some \\ all \\ four \end{Bmatrix}$ of them liked it.

    c. $\begin{Bmatrix} Some \\ All \\ Five \end{Bmatrix}$ of the boys met a friend of mine and liked her.

    d. $\begin{Bmatrix} Some \\ All \\ Five \end{Bmatrix}$ of the boys told me a story, and Sally told me one too.

The multiple interpretation is possible only in (7.53c), where the pronoun is within the scope of the same quantifier as its antecedent, and in (7.53d), where *one*-pronominalization does not interfere with modal dependence in the first clause.

An additional example might be added to the paradigm (7.53) for quantifiers. It is (at least in my dialect) semigrammatical.

(7.54) ?Five of the boys gave Bill a cookie, and he ate them up.

Clearly *them* is comprehensible in (7.54) by virtue of the condition $C_{multiple}$ on *a cookie*, giving it multiple referents. In light of the semigrammaticality of (7.54), however, I will leave open the question of whether *them* is interpreted by rules of the grammar or by purely pragmatic considerations.

Of course a quantifier may contain other quantifiers within its scope. Since quantified noun phrases are themselves subject to external modal conditions, the usual ambiguity results. Read (7.55) with as neutral an intonation pattern as possible:

(7.55) I told three of the stories to many of the men.

The readings differ in whether *many of the men* is multiple or not. If it is not, the same group of many men heard all three stories. If *many of the men* is multiple, each story may have been told to a different group of many men; there is no single group of many men that heard all three stories. In each reading, however, a single group of three stories is referred to.

If we perform dative shift on (7.55), we get (7.56), in which *three* is within the scope of *many*.

(7.56) I told many of the men three of the stories.

The nonmultiple reading of (7.56) says that there is a particular group of many men that heard a particular group of stories. In the multiple reading, each member of a particular group of many men heard three stories, but it is not claimed that all of them heard the same three stories. Hence (7.55) and (7.56) share the reading in which neither quantifier is multiple, but they each have a reading not present in the other.[6]

The ambiguities of (7.55)–(7.56) have traditionally been assumed to be

[6]With appropriate stress patterns, 7.55 and 7.56 can each receive all three readings. This does not change the force of the argument of the next two paragraphs, but it is an apparent counterexample to the claim that the scope of quantifiers goes only to the right.

captured by the logical formalism of quantifier order. For the simplest examples of quantifiers, the universal and existential quantifiers, the logical formalism is indeed adequate. For example, the possible meanings of (7.57) can be represented in logical notation as (7.58).

(7.57)a. I have told one friend of mine all those stories.
   b. I have told all of those stories to one friend of mine.
(7.58)a. $\exists x \, [\forall y \, [(x \in$ friends of mine $\land \; y \in$ those stories) $\rightarrow$ I have told y to $x]]$
   b. $\forall y \, [\exists x \, [(x \in$ friends of mine $\land \; y \in$ those stories) $\rightarrow$ I have told y to $x]]$

(7.57a) has only the reading (7.58a), but (7.57b) has both readings. There are no other possible readings. The trouble in extending the notation of (7.56) to (7.55)–(7.56) is that we have found three readings for these two sentences, and the logical notation can express only two. The reading it cannot represent is the one in which neither quantifier is dependent on the other. The reason there are only two distinct readings in the case of (7.57) is that *all* denotes the same group regardless of whether it is subject to C_{multiple} or not: every time a group consisting of *all of those stories* is chosen from those stories, it will be the same group. Furthermore, C_{multiple} stemming from the quantifier *one* has a vacuous effect, since no duplication of intended referent results. Hence the only possible difference in meaning is in the multiplicity of *one*, which can be dependent on *all* in (7.57b) but not in (7.57a).

   Since the traditional logical notation is insufficient to describe the possible readings of multiple quantifiers, it is clear that the syntactic theory of quantifiers as higher verbs in deep structure, which claims the semantic representation to be a form isomorphic to the logical notation of (7.58), is likewise deficient. It would of course be possible to make various alterations in the theory (such as allowing conjoined higher predicates above a single main clause for nonmultiple readings), but it is not clear that such solutions would be of any generality. On the other hand, in the conception of modal structure and modal operators we have developed here, the correct set of readings emerges immediately from general properties of the system which have been justified on independent grounds. Thus we have further evidence to prefer the theory of modal structure for *Want* contexts over a solution involving quantifiers and bound variables.

7.4.5 Generic

Generic sentences seem to be another case where a modal operator is in evidence, since noun phrases with *a* or *any* and plural NPs without an article do not have specific referents:

(7.59)a. A rhinoceros eats small snakes.

b. Any beaver can build a dam.

It is hard to determine what syntactic element of the sentence should be considered to contain the modal operator *generic*. One might suspect the auxiliary or aspect system, since generic sentences have simple present tense with verbs that otherwise require present progressive (such as *eat* in (7.59a)), and since the modal *can* yields generic interpretations (as in (7.59b)). But in the past tense the auxiliary is not distinctive: (7.60) can be either generic or specific:

(7.60) A dinosaur ate the leaves of the tall trees.

Semantically, generic sentences resemble sentences with a universal quantifier. For example, (7.59)–(7.60) can be paraphrased by (7.61).[7]

(7.61)a. Every rhinoceros eats small snakes.

b. All beavers can build a dam.

c. All dinosaurs ate the leaves of the tall trees.

However, there is another possible interpretation: a generic sentence states a property of the surface subject, regardless of its referent. In other words, given an arbitrary rhinoceros, (7.59a) is asserted to be true of it. C_{generic} therefore must say that there is no particular identifiable referent, but that the speaker will accept as appropriate any referent the hearer wishes. In section 8.3, this interpretation will be shown consistent with the meaning of *any*.

The weak form of the coreference condition obtains:

[7]See, however, Vendler's (1967) discussion of *Any doctor will tell you that Stopsneeze helps*, where he demonstrates a subtle difference from parallel sentences with *all* and *every*.

(7.62)a. A rhinoceros eats small snakes. I saw it yesterday. (specific)
   b. A rhinoceros eats small snakes. It also likes to eat old shoes and
      '54 Chevrolets. (generic)
   c. A rhinoceros eats small snakes and digests them in its four stom-
      achs. (generic)
   d. A rhinoceros eats small snakes. I saw one doing just that yesterday.
      (generic)

For evidence for surface structure interpretation of generics, we need
only form the passives of (7.59)–(7.60).

(7.63)a. Small snakes are eaten by a rhinoceros.
   b. A dam can be built by any beaver.
   c. The leaves of the tall trees were eaten by a dinosaur.

In these sentences the *by*-phrases are not generic in the same sense as their
counterparts in (7.59)–(7.60); the surface subject is the thing whose properties are being described. We conclude that genericity is determined at
surface structure.[8] We have not described precisely how the interpretation
of the surface subject differs from that of the other NPs in the sentence;
nevertheless the similarity of generic interpretation and its derivation to the
other modal conditions is clear.

7.5 The Effect of Modal Operators on Clauses
So far we have spoken only of how modal operators affect the interpretation of noun phrases, by making different claims about the identifiability of
referents. But it is easy to see that modal operators have a related effect on
clauses as well. Consider the following examples:

(7.64)a. John wants to catch a fish.
   b. John will catch a fish.
   c. It is possible that John has a bicycle.
   d. John doesn't have a bicycle.
   e. Some of the boys built a house.

Just as the nonspecific reading of *a fish* in (7.64a) claims that there will be
an identifiable referent just in case John's wish is fulfilled, the truth con-

[8]Is there any connection between the surface-subject orientation of generics and subject-
oriented sentence adverbs, which are also affected by passive (cf. section 3.9)?

ditions of the subordinate clause *for John to catch a fish* are claimed to be satisfied by a state of affairs in the real world just in case John's wish is fulfilled. Similarly, just as the nonspecific reading of *a fish* in (7.64b) claims that there is an identifiable referent sometime in the future, the truth conditions of *John catch a fish* are claimed to be met sometime in the future. (7.64c) claims only the possibility of a realization of *John has a bicycle*; *a bicycle* in the nonspecific reading is claimed only possibly to have an identifiable referent. In (7.64d) the truth conditions of *John has a bicycle* are claimed not to be met, and *a bicycle* is claimed (optionally) to have no identifiable referent. In (7.64e), corresponding to the multiple reading of *a house*, there is a multiplicity of events being referred to, one building of a house per boy.

This similarity must be expressed somehow in the grammar. As an obvious extension of the formalism we have developed, we could permit modal conditions to be applied to Ss as well as to NPs, with the C_M affecting the conditions under which the truth conditions of an S are claimed to be satisfied in the real world. We can represent the dependence of an S on a modal operator by placing the verb of the S in the parentheses following the modal operator. For example, the two readings of (7.64a) can be represented as (7.65).[9]

(7.65)a. John, want (catch, a fish)
     b. John, a fish, want (catch)

I will briefly discuss two details involved in this extension of the modal projection rule. First consider the scopes of the modal operators in (7.64). The scopes of *want* and *possible* include the entire complement, so the S node of the subordinate clauses can be subjected to the modal conditions in these examples with no difficulty. In the other three examples some modification is necessary: the scope of *will* consists of all commanded material, and the scopes of *not* and *some* consist of all commanded material

[9]To make the parallelism more precise along the lines of the Lexicalist Hypothesis, we might represent an NP's dependence on an operator by placing only the head N in parentheses, rather than the whole NP. There is some independent justification for his modification. In cases such as the nonspecific reading of *I want to buy a picture of Mao*, the NP *a picture of Mao* is dependent on *want*, but the NP *Mao* is not. This situation is expressed only awkwardly in the notation we have used so far. However, if we represent dependence by putting the head of the phrase in parentheses, there is no problem with this example.

to the right. Under the standard definition of "command," a node A commands a node B if the lowest S node dominating A also dominates B. This definition excludes the S node in (7.64b, d, e) from the scope of the modal operators. However, there seems to be nothing in the established uses of command that conflicts with an extension of the definition, allowing A also to command the lowest S dominating it. With this extension of command, the modal projection rule will automatically place the modal condition on the immediately dominating S, when establishing modal dependence on *will*, *not*, and *some*.[10]

To see that this is the correct extension to make (rather than, for instance, determining modal dependence on the basis of the verb's position), consider a sentence like (7.66).

(7.66) We saw nobody.

The interpretation of (7.66) is that no events of our seeing someone took place—that is, the S is dependent on negation. The verb of course is not within the scope of *nobody*, since it is to the left of *nobody*. However, the S node is commanded by *nobody*, and since it dominates *nobody*, no question can arise as to whether it is to the left or right. Hence we can consider the S to be within the scope of *nobody* and consequently subject to the modal condition.

The other detail that we must discuss in the extension of modal conditions to Ss concerns choice in the application of modal conditions. So far we have been able to maintain that modal conditions are always optional, or at most very highly preferred where semantically consistent. However, in (7.64a–d) it would be nonsensical to look for a reading in which the S was not dependent on the modal operator. It appears, then, that often an S is obligatorily dependent on a modal operator within whose scope it falls.

On the other hand, there are instances where optional dependence of an

[10]Indeed, the extension of command to cases where one node dominates another will permit pronouns within relative clauses to be handled by normal pronominalization. For example, in *the man who thought he was sick*, *he* can be marked coreferential with the entire dominating NP without difficulty. Thus there is no need on this account to

turn to relative clause structures of the form NP⟨NP S⟩; the more traditional NP⟨Det N S⟩ can be retained. Note, however, that this treatment of coreference of relative clauses can be made only in the interpretive theory. In the transformational theory, *he* must be a fully specified NP in deep structure; if it is coreferential with *the man who thought he was sick*, the deep structure will be infinite.

S on a modal operator explains the observed range of interpretations. Consider the readings possible for (7.64e) (*some of the boys built a house*). In section 7.4.4 we mentioned a reading in which each boy built his own house and one in which only one house was built; at that time we discussed only the effect of the modal operator on *a house*. But it is clear that the two readings also differ with respect to the modal condition on the S: the former reading describes several events, while the latter describes a single event resulting from a concerted effort by the boys. Thus we must allow the application of the modal projection rule to the S to be optional in this case.

A more complex example is (7.67):

(7.67) Some of the boys told me a story.

In this example there are three readings. In the first each boy told me a different story; in the second each boy told me the same story; in the third, the boys told me a story in concert. (7.68) represents these three readings.

(7.68)a. the boys, me, some (told, a story)
    b. the boys, me, a story, some (told)
    c. the boys, me, a story, told, some ( )

Again the application of the modal projection rule to the S is optional. The reason there are three readings in (7.67) but only two in (7.64e) is that different people can independently tell the same story, but they cannot independently build the same house; thus the reading of (7.64e) corresponding to (7.68b) is anomalous.

Quantifiers are not the only modal operators which can apply optionally to Ss. (7.69) is an example involving negation.

(7.69) They're fighting about nothing.

On one reading this is synonymous with (7.70a), on the other reading with (7.70b).

(7.70)a. They aren't fighting about anything.
    b. They're fighting without reason.

The (7.70a) reading claims no event to be taking place, so the S must be dependent on negation. In the (7.70b) reading, the event of their fighting is claimed to be taking place, so the S is not dependent on negation. *Not* in the auxiliary apparently requires a dependent S node, producing an unambiguous reading for (7.70a); the scope of *without* does not extend beyond its complement, so (7.70b) is likewise unambiguous.

As can be guessed from the few examples presented, a precise description of the conditions under which modal dependence is optional and when it is obligatory is far from obvious. I will go no farther into the problems it presents.

Before concluding this section, I will show how the extension of modal dependence to Ss as in (7.65) expresses a result discussed in section 7.2: the fact that *a cigar* has only three readings, not four, in *Fred wants a man to ask him for a cigar*. The optionality of the modal projection rule to NPs predicts that *a cigar* can be dependent on *want* or *ask* or both—four readings in all. We showed, however, that the reading in which *a cigar* is dependent on *ask* but not on *want* is anomalous.

Once we extend the modal projection rule to Ss, we observe that the subordinate clause *for a man to ask him for a cigar* is obligatorily dependent on *want*; this is represented by the partial reading (7.71).

(7.71) want (ask)

Given this configuration within the modal structure, there are only three possible positions for *a cigar*:

(7.72)a. want (ask (a cigar))
     b. want (a cigar, ask ( ))
     c. a cigar, want (ask ( ))

But these are precisely the three readings observed for *a cigar*; the fourth reading would require the *ask* clause to be independent of *want*, which is impossible. The ability of the modal structure to express this result forms independent evidence for its validity.

7.6 Questions

Indefinite NPs in *wh*-questions often do not have specific referents:

(7.73)a. Who saw a man walk by?
     b. Who knows the answer to one of these questions?
     c. To which of the boys did Bill give a new book?

These examples are ambiguous, with a nonspecific reading preferred. The specific reading can be forced by the (a) and (b) frames for the coreference condition.

(7.74)a. Who caught a fish? I saw it over there.
     b. Who caught a fish? Who even saw it?
     c. Who caught a fish and ate it?
     d. Who caught a fish? I saw one over there.

These examples suggest that *wh* acts as a modal operator in questions. The meaning of C_{wh} is that the identification of a referent depends on the answer to the question. *Wh* occurs in positions closely parallel to negatives (*who, what, where, when, which* vs. *nobody, nothing, nowhere, never, no* and perhaps *whether* vs. *not*), so it is plausible that its scope is similar to that of negatives, i.e., all commanded material to the right in surface structure (type III). Just as the scope of negation determines the negated part of the sentence, the scope of *wh* determines the questioned part of the sentence.

Given this analysis of *wh*, it is very simple to account for what has always been a somewhat awkward point in the syntax of questions. The problem lies in pairs such as (7.75a, b):

(7.75)a. Bill told Fred whom to see in Paris.
     b. Whom did Bill tell Fred to see in Paris?

Both of these are derived by *wh*-fronting from a deep structure of approximately the form (7.76):

(7.76) Bill past tell Fred [$_s$ for Fred to see *wh*-someone in Paris]$_s$

Now if transformations preserve meaning, something must be added to the deep structure (7.76) so that we can distinguish the obviously nonsynonymous (7.75a) and (7.75b). The usual device employed is a marker Q attached to an S node, indicating that the S is a question and that *wh* should be attracted to it. (7.75a) would have Q attached to the subordinate clause *for Fred to see wh-someone in Paris*, and (7.75b) would have Q attached to the main clause. This is the solution arrived at by Katz and Postal (1964), for example.

Notice, however, that the only syntactic reflex of the marker Q is the eventual surface structure position of the fronted *wh*-word. If an analysis is possible in which the semantic effects of Q can be derived without the need for a syntactic marker, the grammar will obviously be simplified. Further, such a simplification could lead to a simplification of grammatical theory as well, if all place-holding markers such as Q could be eliminated. The elimination of Q is thus significant at two levels.

But in fact it is clear that the treatment of *wh* as a modal operator can accomplish just this goal. It will be the scope of *wh*, determined from the surface structure, which determines what part of the sentence is understood as questioned. Thus (7.75a) and (7.75b) can both be derived from the single deep structure (7.76) without the use of a marker Q. This deep structure expresses the interpretation of *who* as direct object of *see*. *Wh*-fronting will apply optionally either on the subordinate cycle, producing (7.75a), or on the main cycle, producing (7.75b). The difference in interpretation will be purely a function of the difference in modal structure. No extraneous marker Q is necessary, and the necessary semantic mechanisms, complete with statement of scope, are already required by our theory to account for the nonspecificity of (7.73).

This solution to (7.75) raises some interesting questions about complement structures. How is it that certain verbs permit indirect questions in their complements and some do not? For example, *tell* and *know* permit indirect questions, but *believe* and *think* do not:

$$(7.77) \quad \left\{ \begin{array}{l} \text{I told him} \\ \text{He knows} \\ \text{*We believe} \\ \text{*No one thinks} \end{array} \right\} \left\{ \begin{array}{l} \text{where to go} \\ \text{what to do} \\ \text{whom to see} \\ \text{who has left} \end{array} \right\}.$$

In standard analyses, this difference has been expressed as a selectional restriction between the main verb and the presence of Q. In the present analysis, the selection will have to be between the main verb and the modal structure of its complement: *tell* and *know* will allow a modal structure dominated by *wh* in the complement, and *believe* and *think* will not. Selectional restrictions between verbs and the modal structure of their complement, however, are not a great innovation, if it is indeed the case that selectional restrictions are determined on the basis of semantic representation, as argued in section 1.6, rather than on the basis of deep structure, as in the system proposed in Chomsky (1965). The modal structure is as much a part of semantic representation as functional structure, so selectional restrictions on modal structure are to be expected.

The existence of the verb-*wh* selectional restriction immediately brings to mind the fascinating possibility that complementizer selection is based largely on the modal structure. It has been known for a long time that the choice of *that*, *for-to*, and *poss-ing* complementizers is not random, but in part based on certain semantic factors (see for example Kiparsky and Kiparsky 1968). One common verb class, in particular, allows either a *for-to*-complement or a *that*-complement with a modal or a present subjunctive:

7.78)a. I expect $\begin{Bmatrix} \text{that he will go} \\ \text{him to go} \end{Bmatrix}$.

    b. I told him $\begin{Bmatrix} \text{that he should go} \\ \text{to go} \end{Bmatrix}$.

    c. $\begin{Bmatrix} \text{I desire} \\ \text{I order} \\ \text{I recommended} \end{Bmatrix}$ $\begin{Bmatrix} \text{that he go} \\ \text{him to go} \end{Bmatrix}$.

Similar semantic correspondences obtain in relative clauses, where there is a class of relative clauses with *for-to* complementizers, often closely paraphrased by a normal relative clause containing a modal.

7.79)a. Tom is the man $\begin{Bmatrix} \text{to do the job} \\ \text{who can do the job} \end{Bmatrix}$.

    b. I gave Bill a book $\begin{Bmatrix} \text{for you to read} \\ \text{that you} \begin{Bmatrix} \text{should} \\ \text{may} \end{Bmatrix} \text{read} \end{Bmatrix}$.

    c. Can you find a place in which $\begin{Bmatrix} \text{to hide the prize} \\ \text{we can hide the prize} \end{Bmatrix}$?

Having established already that at least some modals are modal operators, the similarity to *for-to* suggests that *for-to* is also a modal operator, and that its selection is in part due to selectional restrictions between main verbs and the modal structures of their complements.

    This suggestion in turn leads to three directions of inquiry. First, one might ask if some of the factors governing application of the rules of the complement system, in particular subject raising, are determined by modal structure. Second, one is led to wonder whether the entire system of tenses and restrictions on sequence of tenses is expressed in the modal structure. The behavior of this aspect of language has been stubbornly recalcitrant to analysis in generative grammar. The appearance of certain elements of this system in the modal structure, for example the modal verbs, strongly suggests that the rest of the system be examined in this light too.

Third, the analysis of questions in terms of modal structure leads to a conjecture that the whole system of illocutionary force—the distinction between declaratives, interrogatives, imperatives, performatives, exclamations, and their variants and nuances—should be analyzed in terms of modal structure. The extension of modal conditions to sentences makes these last two conjectures particularly plausible.

Let us mention briefly two other problems about questions that have been raised and show how they fit into the framework of modal structure. The first, an extension of the case we just discussed, was pointed out by Langacker (1970). He points out that the following question is ambiguous, depending on whether *which book* is to be construed as part of the direct question or part of the indirect question.

(7.80) Who remembers where we bought which book?

On the reading where *which book* is part of the direct question, (7.81) is an answer of the desired form. On the reading where *which book* is part of the indirect question, (7.82) is appropriate.

(7.81) Jack remembers where we bought *Decline and Fall of the Roman Empire*, and Heathcliff remembers where we bought *Nephew of Dracula*.
(7.82) Jack remembers where we bought which book.

Langacker's solution involves introducing a system of indices on Q markers and *wh* words, identity of indices denoting semantic association. However, in the present theory, there is no difficulty, and no new devices need be introduced. There are several possible modal structures for (7.80) (ignoring the S nodes).

(7.83)a. we, who (where (which book))
    b. we, who (where, which book)
    c. we, who (where), which book

Of these three, (7.83c) is probably ill-formed; it seems to indicate that *which book* is not being questioned at all, or that it is somehow part of a different question. (7.83a) and (7.83b) can readily be seen to correspond to the two well-formed readings of (7.80): (7.83a) is the reading with *which book* in the indirect question, and (7.83b) is the reading with *which book* in the direct question. The structure of the data presented in Baker (1970a) indicates that similar ambiguities exist with multiply embedded negatives, but a full account would be too lengthy to give here.

Finally, we recall some examples from section 4.11 whose analysis we left hanging.

(7.84)a. ?During what movie do you cry every time you see it? (= 4.260)
       b. During what movie do you cry every time you get drunk?
            (= 4.261)
(7.85)a. ?Who do you talk about to people that respect his work? (*his* and
            who coreferential) (= 4.262)
       b. Who do you talk about to people that respect Bill's work?
            (= 4.263)

The difficulty in these sentences has to do with the application of pronominalization. In light of the analysis of this chapter, (7.84a) and (7.85a) look suspiciously like violations of the coreference condition. If it were the case that *it* and *his* could not be dependent on the modal operator *wh* in these contexts, such a violation would follow.

As evidence that this is the correct analysis, we can construct similar sentences with other modal operators.

(7.86)a. I want to go to a movie every time I see it advertised.
       b. I want to go to a movie every time I get drunk.
(7.87)a. Three of the girls talked about a friend of mine to people that
            respect his work.
       b. Three of the girls talked about a friend of mine to people that
            respect Bill's work.

In (7.86a), unlike (7.86b), only the specific reading of *a movie* is possible. In (7.87a), all the girls talked about the same friend, but in (7.87b) three different friends may have been talked about. For some reason, the NPs inside the relative clause cannot be subject to modal conditions. Whatever the reason, it generalizes from *wh* to other modal operators, confirming our intuition about (7.84)–(7.85).

7.7 Conclusions

By adopting the rather simple theory of modal structure proposed in section 7.3 and the natural extension proposed in section 7.5, we have been able to achieve an insightful and unified description of a substantial number of grammatical phenomena previously thought to be unrelated. And, as suggested in the last section, we appear merely to have scratched the surface: many other phenomena related to the cases we have discussed cry for attention.

Furthermore, this unification has been accomplished within the bounds of a highly restricted theory whose main innovation is the abandonment of a single-hierarchy theory of semantic representation. If the theory of modal structure is correct, the class of possible grammars it predicts is restricted in a significant and highly interesting way. Thus this theory, like the solutions to problems presented in the previous chapters, is an example of how an innovation in the semantic component of the grammar not only can be more convenient than available syntactic alternatives in treating the immediate problem at hand, but can reveal generalizations that could not have been dreamed of within a purely syntactic approach.

CHAPTER EIGHT

Negation

The previous two chapters have discussed the effect of negation on focus and presupposition and on modal structure. In this chapter we will treat negation in greater depth, concentrating particularly on the interaction of negation with quantifiers and with stress and intonation.[1]

8.1 Klima's Rules for Negation

Edward S. Klima's paper "Negation in English" (1964) presents a comprehensive transformational analysis of negation within a pre-Katz-Postal framework. For the sake of presenting a certain range of data in a systematic fashion, I will first discuss how Klima's rules account for the facts of sentence negation, then proceed to the difficulties this analysis presents for the Katz-Postal Hypothesis when extended to other than sentence negation.

We will use (8.1) as a rough intuitive test for sentence negation.

(8.1) A sentence $[_sX - neg - Y]$ is an instance of sentence negation if there exists a paraphrase (disregarding presuppositions) It is not so that $[_sX - Y]$.

This definition differs from Klima's in that it is based on paraphrase properties rather than on the existence of negative appositive tags such as *not even John* or negative conjoined sentences such as *and neither did Bill*. We will show later how Klima's criteria are related to (8.1).

Klima generates sentence negation in the base as an optional constituent *neg* attached to the main S as a daughter. He then has a sequence of transformations which account for the occurrence of *neg* in a wide variety of surface structure configurations.

The first relevant transformation to apply is the passive. Klima treats this as an optional rule which operates on simple sentences with transitive verbs, taking, for example, *John hit Mary* into *Mary was hit by John.*

---

[1]Parts of this chapter have been published in earlier form in Jackendoff (1969b). Many improvements on the analysis there have been suggested by the discussion in Lasnik (1970), Baker (1970b), and Stockwell, Schachter, and Partee (1969).

The second rule is Indef incorporation, which I will call the *some-any* rule. This rule involves the structural relation *in construction with,* which is defined as follows:

(8.2) A node *A* is in construction with a node *B* if and only if the node *C* directly dominating *B* also dominates *A*.

The rule mentions two different classes of morphemes, affectives and indeterminates. The class affective includes for example *neg, wh* of questions, *reluctant,* and *too* (the degree modifier on adjectives). Indeterminate includes for example *too* (*also*), *once, sometime, somewhere,* and quantifiers like *many* and *some.* The rule says that indeterminate constituents undergo a morphological change to an "indefinite" form when they are in construction with an affective. The morphological change is idiosyncratic for each indeterminate morpheme. The following examples illustrate the rule:

(8.3) John has some money.
      John doesn't have any money.
      (*some* in construction with *neg*)
(8.4) John has been there once.
      Has John ever been there?
      (*once* in construction with *wh*)
(8.5) Irving went to the movies, and Max went too.
      Irving didn't go to the movies, and Max didn't go, either.
      (*too* in construction with *neg*)
(8.6) John was eager to read something about the war.
      John was reluctant to read anything about the war.
      John was too lazy to read anything about the war.
      (*some* in construction with *reluctant, too*)
(8.7) I claim that someone will force John to do some work.
      I'm not claiming that anyone will force John to do any work.
      (*some* changing to *any* in construction with *neg* in a higher sentence)

After Indef incorporation comes the rule that preposes adverbials such as *ever, either, once, somewhere,* and *for two years.* The indefinites among these preposed adverbials will later absorb *neg* to become *never, neither,* etc.

Next comes a set of rules which account for the surface structure placement of sentence negation. The first rule moves the *neg* from its position at the beginning of the sentence to a position directly before the auxiliary, where it remains in the case of infinitival and participial phrases. The second rule is *neg* incorporation into indefinites: if there are any indefinites (the outputs of the *some-any* rule) before the *neg*, then *neg* is obligatorily incorporated into the first of these in the sentence; otherwise *neg* is optionally incorporated into the first following indefinite occurring in the same clause. The third rule, pre-verbal particle placement, moves *neg* to a position after the first element of the auxiliary if it has not been incorporated into an indefinite, and if the auxiliary contains *Tense*.

To illustrate these rules, we first look at the various outputs from the structure

(8.8) *neg* someone once gave John something.

By Indef incorporation this becomes

(8.9) *neg* anyone ever gave John anything.

Neg then moves to the position in front of *gave*, by the first placement rule, then obligatorily incorporates into *anyone*, giving

(8.10) No one ever gave John anything.

On the other hand, if passivization had moved *anything* to the front, so instead of (8.9) we had

(8.11) *neg* anything was ever given to John by anyone,

then *neg* will attach to *anything*, giving

(8.12) Nothing was ever given to John by anyone.

If *ever* preposes in (8.9), it receives the *neg*, giving

(8.13) Never anyone gave John anything,

which by the later rules of subject-aux inversion and *Do*-support becomes

(8.14) Never did anyone give John anything.

Likewise, if *John* is moved to the front by passive, *ever* will receive the *neg*, to give

(8.15) John was never given anything by anyone.

If *ever* is removed from (8.9), and *John* is again moved to the front by passive, we get the intermediate string

(8.16) *neg* John was given anything by anyone.

In (8.16) there is no indefinite before the auxiliary, so we can optionally attach *neg* to *anything*, the first indefinite to the right of the aux, giving

(8.17) John was given nothing by anyone.

If we choose not to attach *neg* to *anything*, then it must attach to the first element of aux to yield

(8.18) John wasn't given anything by anyone.

All the sentences (8.10), (8.12), (8.14), and (8.15) are synonymous and are paraphrases of

(8.19) It is not so that anyone ever gave John anything.

(8.17) and (8.18) are also paraphrases of this, with the exception of the missing adverb *ever*.

Following the rules of *neg* placement, there are two relevant transformations: subject-aux inversion and *Do*-support. We have already seen one instance of their application in the derivation of (8.14). Inversion generalizes to take place either when a constituent containing *wh*- of questions or one containing *neg* is in front of the subject. *Do*-support then operates in either case. In addition, *Do*-support has one other application here. In case there is no element other than *Tense* in the aux, *neg* may end up between *Tense* and the main verb. This prevents *Tense* from attaching to the main verb and so *Do*-support takes place, giving sentences like

(8.20) John didn't see anyone.

To sum up, then, Klima's array of rules looks like this:

(8.21) 1. Passive
   2. Indef incorporation (*some-any*)
   3. Adverb preposing
   4. *Neg* placement rules
   5. Subject-aux inversion
   6. *Do*-support

8.2 Counterexamples to the Katz-Postal Hypothesis

To a certain extent, Klima discusses sentences containing *neg* which are not sentence negation. For example, there are the ambiguous readings of (8.22) and (8.23).

(8.22) They're fighting about nothing.
(8.23) I will force you to marry no one.

One reading of these sentences is synonymous with (8.24) and (8.25), respectively.

(8.24) It is not so that they're fighting about anything.
(8.25) It is not so that I will force you to marry anyone.

But there is another reading for each sentence for which this paraphrase is not available. Klima calls this reading an instance of "constituent negation." In the case of (8.23), the second reading derives from sentence negation in the complement clause, that is, from (8.26).

(8.26) I will force you [$_S$*neg* you marry someone]

If this *neg* is not attached to the object of the complement, it shows up before the verb:

(8.27) I will force you not to marry anyone.

On the other hand, the second reading of (8.22) cannot be derived from an underlying sentence negation, since there is no sentence underlying *nothing*. The *neg* appears to be semantically associated with the NP. Hence we must allow for cases of negation which are not sentence negation.

A more interesting case of nonsentence negation is illustrated by the contrast of (8.28) and (8.29).

(8.28) Not many of the arrows hit the target.
(8.29) Many of the arrows didn't hit the target.

(8.28) can be derived as the ordinary sentence negation of *Many of the arrows hit the target*; it is synonymous with

(8.30) It is not so that many of the arrows hit the target.

In (8.28), *not* is placed before *many* by the obligatory incorporation of *neg* into the first indefinite before the aux. What then of (8.29), which is not synonymous with (8.28) or (8.30)? It could be derived by making the incorporation rule optional (this is Klima's approach). But such a derivation would of course violate the Katz-Postal Hypothesis, since the deep structure would not determine the meaning: (8.28) and (8.29) would have the same deep structure.

Suppose that we try to preserve the Katz-Postal Hypothesis by claiming that (8.28) and (8.29) have different deep structures. One possible difference is in the deep structure position of negation. The *neg* in (8.29) could, for example, be a daughter of VP instead of S. This hypothesis is initially confirmed by the contrast of (8.31) and (8.32).

(8.31) None of the men saw anything.
(8.32) Some of the men didn't see anything.

Again, (8.31) is normal sentence negation. The difference can be produced without altering Klima's transformations by choosing neg^1 in the deep structure (8.33) to get (8.31), and by choosing neg^2 to get (8.32).

(8.33)

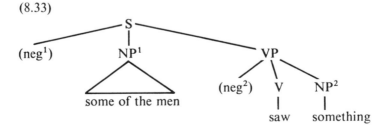

If neg^1 is chosen in (8.33), both NPs are in construction with negation, and so both change to the indefinite form *any*. When *neg* incorporation

applies, the leftmost indefinite will be NP^1, so negation will obligatorily incorporate to form *none* as in (8.31). However, if *neg*^{2} is chosen in the deep structure (8.33), only NP^2 is in construction with negation, and NP^1 remains in the determinate form *some*. Hence when *neg* incorporation applies, there is no indefinite to the left of the auxiliary; the negation either remains in the auxiliary as in (8.32) or incorporates into the indefinite NP^2 to form the synonymous (8.34).

(8.34) Some of the men saw nothing.

(8.29) can be arrived at by a similar derivation. We will refer to sentences of the type (8.29) and (8.32) as instances of VP negation.

Unfortunately, the admission of VP negation as a possible deep structure does not enable us to preserve the Katz-Postal Hypothesis. Surprisingly, sentences such as (8.29) and (8.32) have no synonymous passive. If we form what intuitively looks like the passive of (8.29), we get (8.35), which is also the result we get from passivizing (8.28).

(8.35) The target wasn't hit by many of the arrows.

Thus we predict that (8.35) should be ambiguous. But it is not ambiguous (except with a B accent on *many*—cf. section 8.6); its only reading is synonymous with (8.28). In order to make this clearer, append an additional clause to both (8.28) and (8.29):

(8.36) *Not many of the arrows hit the target, but many of them hit it.
(8.37) Many of the arrows didn't hit the target, but many of them hit it.

(8.36) expresses a contradiction since it asserts both a sentence and its negation. (8.37) is not a contradiction because (8.29), being an instance of VP negation, does not conflict with *many of them hit it*. On the other hand, (8.38), where both clauses are passivized, can be understood only as a contradiction.

(8.38) *The target wasn't hit by many of the arrows, but it was hit by many of them.

This contradiction shows that the only possible reading of the passive (8.34) is the one synonymous with (8.28), the S negation.

There also exist pairs of passive sentences similar to (8.28) and (8.29), for which only one member has a synonymous active:

(8.39) Not many of the demonstrators were arrested by the police.
(8.40) Many of the demonstrators weren't arrested by the police.

Again, (8.39) is an instance of sentence negation and (8.40) is not; only (8.39) is synonymous with

(8.41) It is not so that many of the demonstrators were arrested by the police.

When we form what is intuitively the active of these sentences, we get in both cases

(8.42) The police didn't arrest many of the demonstrators.

However, this sentence has only the reading corresponding to (8.39), the sentence negation case. Again, we can add extra clauses to bring out this fact more clearly.

(8.43) *Not many of the demonstrators were arrested by the police, but many were.
(8.44) Many of the demonstrators weren't arrested by the police, but many were.
(8.45) *The police didn't arrest many of the demonstrators, but they did arrest many of them.

Just as in (8.36)–(8.38), we get a contradiction only when we simultaneously assert both a sentence and its sentence negation; its VP negation does not produce a contradiction.

Under the assumption that transformations do not change meaning, these facts will be very difficult to account for. In order for the *some-any* rule to operate correctly, the *neg* must be in the VP at the time of this rule. If we add a transformation to move *neg* into the VP before the *some-any* rule, this transformation will change meaning only in case there is a quantifier in the subject, as in (8.28) and (8.29). If this transformation is ordered before the passive, then the passive will change meaning only in case it moves a quantifier into or out of the subject. Therefore VP negation cannot be produced by adding a transformation to Klima's system, since this transformation would change meaning.

Let us assume then that the VP negation is generated in the base. Then in order to prevent (8.29) from passivizing, we must add a restriction on the passive to the effect that it is inhibited by VP negation when there is a quantifier in the deep subject. What then is the deep structure of (8.40), the passive VP negation with a quantifier in the derived subject? It would appear that we must make passive obligatory when there is a VP negation and a quantifier in the object, so that we will have no corresponding active for (8.40). Thus we can, with a strange pair of conditions on the passive, create a theory consistent with what we know about VP negation, in which the rules preserve meaning. However, this theory misses the fundamental similarity between the pairs (8.28)–(8.29) and (8.39)–(8.40), namely that VP negation is significant exactly when there is a quantifier in the *derived* subject.

A second approach to the problem is proposed in Fillmore (1966), who suggests that the deep structure difference between (8.28) and (8.29) is in a feature $[\pm \text{specific}]$ associated with the quantifier *many*. In this theory, negation is always associated with the sentence (neg^1 in (8.33)), but it will not change a $[+\text{specific}]$ quantifier to the indefinite form. (8.28) and (8.31) will have nonspecific quantifiers, requiring conversion to indefinite form and the incorporation of *neg*; the specificity of the subject quantifiers in (8.29) and (8.32) will inhibit conversion to indefinite and incorporation.

However, this theory accounts no better for the difficulties of passivization than does the theory of VP negation, if we want to preserve the Katz-Postal Hypothesis. It provides no automatic explanation of why (8.29) has no synonymous passive, or why the passive (8.40) has no synonymous active. We are again forced to resort to an unnatural constraint on the passive: the passive may not take place if there is a specific quantifier in the deep subject, and it must take place if there is a specific quantifier in the deep object.

Still a third approach has been suggested by G. Lakoff (1971) and Carden (1967), using the notion that negation and quantifiers are generated in the base as verbs of higher sentences. We have already met one of the arguments for this position in section 5.7, and showed it to be of less force than claimed. A much more extensive critique of Carden's arguments is presented in Jackendoff (1971b); Partee (1970) points out additional difficulties. According to this approach, the structures of (8.46) and (8.47) are supposed to be (roughly—the details don't matter for this argument) (8.48) and (8.49), respectively.

(8.46) The men didn't come.
(8.47) Many men came.

(8.48)

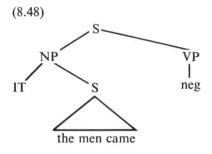

(8.49)

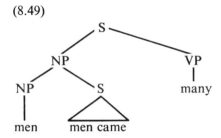

The understood order of quantifiers and negatives in a sentence is supposed to correspond to the hierarchy of upper sentences containing quantifiers and negatives. Thus the difference between (8.28) and (8.29) is reflected in their deep structures, (8.50) and (8.51).

(8.50)

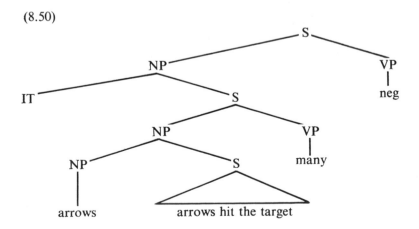

(8.51)

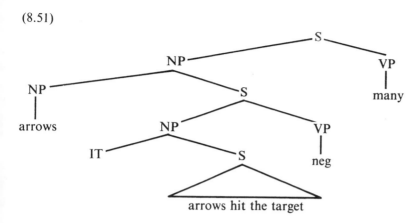

An immediate defect in this formulation is that no such difference in order of quantifiers and negation can be produced when the quantified NP is the *object* of the lowest sentence. For example if the lowest sentence in (8.50) and (8.51) is *John bought arrows* instead of *arrows hit the target* the only possible variants are

(8.52)   John didn't buy many arrows.
(8.53) ?John bought not many arrows.

But these two are synonymous and unambiguous; the negation is interpreted as being outside the quantifier. Therefore we must not allow a quantifier above negation just in case the quantified NP is in the object of its sentence, a very strange restriction.

Next consider what happens when we introduce the passive. The following constraints must hold on its occurrence. If we have a negation and quantifier configuration such as (8.51), the passive may not apply, just in case the quantified NP is a subject, because otherwise the output would be understood the same as (8.50), which has the opposite deep structure order of quantifier and *neg*. If the quantified NP is an object, then the passive *must* apply, giving the difference between (8.39) and (8.40). The single interpretation of the corresponding active shows that this configuration cannot exist without the passive.

Thus the hypothesis that quantifiers and negation are higher verbs fails to explain naturally the facts about VP negation that we have noticed. In fact, the restrictions necessary in this theory are exactly cognate to the restrictions required by the traditional theory that quantifiers and negation are generated as part of the sentence in which they eventually occur.

All of these approaches miss the significant generalization that S and VP negation differ in meaning exactly when there is a quantifier in the derived subject. Since the possibility of difference in meaning is dependent on the derived subject, and not on the underlying subject, a theory which requires that all semantic information be captured in deep structure cannot express this generalization.

If we give up the assumption that transformations do not change meaning and that all semantic information is represented in deep structure, it immediately becomes apparent how to go about explaining the interpretation of VP negation. We simply need a way to relate the understood order of quantifiers and negation to their position in the derived structure. We can do this informally by saying that the understood order is the same as the order in the surface structure. We then get the differences (8.28)–(8.29) and (8.39)–(8.40) because of the difference in surface structure order of *neg* and *many*. On the other hand, in the passive of (8.28)–(8.29) and in the active of (8.39)–(8.40) the quantifier is in the object and so there is no syntactic position to the right of it into which *neg* can fit. Since there is no such position, we cannot produce the expected second reading for the sentence.

If this derived structure theory of negation and quantifiers is correct, we would predict that other transformations that change the relative order of negation and a quantifier may change meaning. And in fact this prediction is borne out. For the first example, consider (8.54)–(8.56).

(8.54) Tom doesn't go to town very often.
(8.55) Not very often does Tom go to town.
(8.56) Very often Tom doesn't go to town.

(8.54) and (8.55) are ordinary sentence negation; they can be paraphrased as *It is not so that Tom goes to town very often.* Under Klima's rules they differ not in deep structure, but only in the optional application of adverb preposing, and the consequent difference in the positioning of *neg*, as illustrated in section 8.1.

But (8.56) then presents a problem. Just as in (8.29), negation has not been incorporated into the leftmost indefinite. Like (8.29), there is a distinct difference in meaning from the sentence negation case. Hence if transformations are not to change meaning, (8.56) must have a different deep structure from the other two. Possible differences in deep structure can be constructed analogous to those proposed for (8.29); but it is clear that by exactly parallel arguments, the difference will ultimately entail a restriction of the adverb preposing transformation, just as (8.28)–(8.29) required a restriction on the passive. Adverb preposing will be obligatory just in case *very often* is marked [+ specific], or is above *neg* in deep structure, or whatever difference is devised. But this approach would miss the generalization that in both the passive and adverb preposing cases, it is the *derived structure order* of negation and the quantifier that determines this aspect of the meaning.

Similarly, consider (8.57)–(8.59).

(8.57) I didn't see many of his friends.
(8.58) Not many of his friends did I see.
(8.59) Many of his friends I didn't see.

(8.58) and (8.59) have both undergone the optional topicalization transformation; they differ in meaning and derivation in exactly the same way as (8.55)–(8.56) do. The same arguments hold: if meaning is determined solely by deep structure, topicalization must be constrained in unnatural ways.

(8.60)–(8.65) show that the same argument obtains for the optional dative shift transformation.

(8.60) I didn't tell many of the stories to any of the men. (S negation)
(8.61) I told many of the stories to none of the men. (non-S negation)
(8.62) I told none of the men many of the stories. (S negation)

(8.63) I didn't tell any of the stories to many of the men. (S negation)
(8.64) I told none of the stories to many of the men. (S negation)
(8.65) I told many of the men none of the stories. (non-S negation)

Again, there is no natural way to constrain the dative shift transformation itself to account for the changes in meaning. If there is a deep structure difference between (8.61) and (8.62), and between (8.64) and (8.65), the dative shift will have to be marked so as not to take place in (8.61), because the result will be either (8.62) or *I didn't tell any of the men many of the stories*, again sentence negation. Likewise, dative shift will have to be marked obligatory for the structure producing (8.65), because otherwise we will get (8.63) or (8.64). This is precisely parallel to the passive case. Again, the clear generalization has to do with the surface order of negation and *many*.

A more complicated case is (8.66)–(8.67).

(8.66) Only then didn't any of my friends arrive on time.
(8.67) Only then did any of my friends not arrive on time.

These sentences differ in meaning: (8.66) could be continued with "Every other time, at least one person has been on time"; (8.67) continues with "Every other time, everyone has been punctual." In Klima's system of rules, both start from the underlying structure (8.68).

(8.68) *neg* some of my friends past arrive on time only then

If adverb preposing is not applied, we get a pair of sentences analogous to (8.31)–(8.32), both differing in meaning from (8.66)–(8.67):

(8.69)   None of my friends arrived on time only then.
(8.70) ??Some of my friends didn't arrive on time only then.

Suppose that *only then* is preposed. *Some* will change to *any* because of the presence of *only*, whether or not *neg* is in construction with the subject. This is shown by (8.71), in which there is no *neg* present at all.

(8.71) Only then did any of my friends agree to arrive on time.

Thus at this stage (8.68) has become (8.72).

(8.72) *neg* only then any of my friends past arrive on time

Now, despite the fact that *some* has changed to *any*, the *neg* must not incorporate into the subject to form *none*; otherwise we would get (8.73):[2]

[2]Fillmore's analysis of (8.28)–(8.29) in terms of the feature [±specific] thus fails for this example. For *some* to become *any* in (8.66)–(8.67), it has to be nonspecific. But since in Fillmore's analysis the only deep structure difference between (8.28) and (8.29) is the specificity of the subject, there is no way to distinguish (8.73) from (8.66)–(8.67) in deep structure.

(8.73) Only then did none of my friends arrive on time.

Neither may it incorporate into the preposed adverbial to form (8.74):

(8.74) Not only then did any of my friends arrive on time.

Rather, after the *neg* placement rules, we must have the string (8.75):

(8.75) only then any of my friends past *neg* arrive on time

   The next relevant rule to apply is the rule that realizes *neg* as *not* or, optionally, the contraction *n't*. When subject-aux inversion applies because of the preposed *only then*, *n't* will be carried along, yielding (8.66), but *not* will stay behind, yielding (8.67).
   The difference in meaning between (8.66) and (8.67), then, hinges solely on the application of the optional *neg* contraction rule. But there is no simple way to constrain *neg* contraction, since the difference in meaning occurs only if subject-aux inversion also takes place: (8.76) and (8.77) are synonymous.

(8.76) Some of my friends didn't arrive on time.
(8.77) Some of my friends did not arrive on time.

Hence any rule that makes contraction take place or not take place on the basis of some underlying difference between (8.66) and (8.67) must know in advance whether inversion will also take place. Inversion itself cannot be constrained, because it is obligatory, and because it takes place in both (8.66) and (8.67).
   The generalization with the other cases is obvious. The difference in meaning stems from the relative order of the negation and the quantifier, no matter what combination of rules applies to produce that order. It is impossible to capture this generalization in the Katz-Postal conception of a grammar; each movement transformation must carry its own restrictions about movement of indeterminates with respect to negation, and these restrictions, as we have seen, are unnatural in any event. In the case involving contraction and inversion, it is not even clear that the restriction can be stated.
   To capture this generalization, we need a system of semantic interpretation rules which mediates directly between the derived structure and the

semantic representation of negation and quantifiers, independent of the deep structure. The modal projection rule of the last chapter, applying to modal operators of scope III, fulfills just such a function. We can thus allow passive, adverb preposing, topicalization, dative shift, *neg* incorporation, and contraction to be optional without restriction; the generality of the examples in this section will be expressed in the derived structure interpretation rules.[3]

Before detailing the application of the modal projection rule to negation, let us clarify the status of *some* and *any* and the negative morphemes within the present framework.

8.3 *Some* and *Any*

Is it really desirable to state the *some-any* alternation as a transformation? If we do state it as a transformation, the rule says that members of a certain class of lexical items are changed in a single feature when in construction with an affective. The changing of this feature initiates a major change in the "phonological spelling" of the lexical item. Some examples of the alterations are

(8.78) some → any
     once → ever
     too → either
     already → yet

The most striking characteristic of this group is its irregularity. We are apparently not dealing with inflectional variants of single lexical items;

[3] G. Lakoff (1970b) introduces the notion of *derivational constraints* to account for examples like these. A derivational constraint, as Lakoff defines it, is a rule of grammar that requires some relation to hold between two (or more) stages of a derivation, independent of the intermediate transformational steps relating them. In this particular case, a derivational constraint rejects any derivation in which the surface order of quantifiers and negation does not correspond to the semantic embedding in the proper way. We will not adopt Lakoff's proposal here for three reasons. First, although the derivational constraint expresses the proper generalization, it does not fit into the derivation in any essential way; it only throws out unsuccessful derivations. In the approach taken here, the generalization follows as a direct result of the rules of interpretation, with no added machinery. Second, the semantic theory of quantifiers assumed by Lakoff has been shown inadequate (section 7.4.4). Third, Chomsky (1970c) shows that the concept of derivational constraint is so general as to lead to an extremely unrestricted class of possible grammars, in conflict with our goal of constraining linguistic theory.

rather, it appears that affective environments permit different sets of lexical items than non-affective environments. This suspicion is substantiated by the fact that there are some "indefinites" for which there is no corresponding form in non-affective environments:

(8.79) any more
    at all
    any good

For these items a "spelling rule" would have to block derivations which end with the nonexistent definite version, not a very pleasant restriction to impose. Since the *some-any* rule clearly violates the Extended Lexical Hypothesis as well, we are led to try to account for the *some-any* alternation by some other means.

In a lexicalist formulation, *some* and *any* will be considered separate lexical items, freely inserted into base trees. The rule conditioning their occurrence will be in the form of a semantic restriction, stating (for the present) that indefinites may occur only when dependent on certain modal operators, the affectives. This approach will immediately eliminate all difficulties in deriving the indefinites in (8.79) as well as the need for "spelling rules" in (8.78). It must be shown, however, that other details can be worked out.

Evidence for the lexicalist *some-any* rule has been presented by Robin Lakoff (1969b). She shows that *some* and *any* must be distinct lexical items, as there are environments where both are possible, but with different meanings.

(8.80) Who wants some beans?
(8.81) Who wants any beans?

(8.82) Do you think those men want to do some work?
(8.83) Do you think those men want to do any work?

(8.84) I wonder if Bill would lend me some money.
(8.85) I wonder if Bill would lend me any money.

(8.86) If you eat some candy, $\begin{cases} \text{?I'll whip you.} \\ \text{I'll give you \$10.} \end{cases}$

(8.87) If you eat any candy, $\begin{cases} \text{I'll whip you.} \\ \text{?I'll give you \$10.} \end{cases}$

(8.88) Unicorns are mythical beasts: if John sees $\left\{ \begin{array}{c} \text{?some} \\ \text{any} \end{array} \right\}$ unicorns out there, I'll eat my hat.

(8.89) If John sees $\left\{ \begin{array}{c} \text{some} \\ \text{?any} \end{array} \right\}$ goldfish in that tank, it's not surprising: there are lots of them in there.

Lakoff explicates the differences in meaning: "The beliefs or expectations of the speaker are reflected in his choice of *some* or *any*, and the meaning of the sentence is correspondingly changed." *Some* appears in questions when the answer is hoped to be or supposed to be positive, and in conditionals when the expectation of the speaker is that the antecedent will be fulfilled; *any* appears when the presupposition is negative or neutral. If we assume the difference in presupposition to be expressed by *some* and *any* themselves, this difference is probably sufficient to explain the fact that, for example, (8.86) is a promise and (8.87) a threat.

An alternative explanation of the meaning of *any* has been offered by Quine (1960, section 29), who claims that *any* is a universal quantifier whose scope is always as wide as possible, that is, including the affective operator that conditions its occurrence. On the other hand, *all* and *every* are taken to be universal quantifiers which take the narrowest possible scope. This approach is rendered most plausible by generic sentences, in which *any* appears to have the value of a universal quantifier:

(8.90) $\left\{ \begin{array}{c} \text{Anyone} \\ \text{Everyone} \end{array} \right\}$ can get in to see *Mary Poppins*.

The difference in induced scope is illustrated by (8.91)–(8.92).

(8.91) I do not know any poem.
(8.92) I do not know every poem.

(8.91) is read by Quine as "It is the case that for every poem, I do not know it"; (8.92) is read as "It is not the case that for every poem, I know it."

Quine's view is not consistent with our hypothesis that dependence of quantifiers and negation on each other is determined by structural considerations, as it claims that relative scope is determined on the basis of lexical, not structural, conditions. Similar claims have been made by generative grammarians, for example Carden (1970a). However, Vendler (1967) presents arguments to show that *any* cannot be a universal quantifier, throwing Quine's theory into doubt. The most convincing example is of the form (8.93).

$$(8.93) \text{ I have here some apples: you may take } \begin{cases} \text{every one} \\ \text{all} \\ \text{any one} \\ \text{any} \end{cases} \text{ of them.}$$

Here *any* is clearly not synonymous with the universal quantifiers, yet there is no logical operator that can provide alternative scopes.

Vendler characterizes *any* in terms which have no equivalent in the predicate calculus, but which seem to provide a more adequate account of *any* in all its uses. The main point of his argument is that *any* presents an offer to the hearer, giving him freedom of choice in picking a referent for the NP containing *any*. As an offer, the decision whether to choose or not is up to the hearer, not the speaker. Hence if a choice is being forced, *any* is not appropriate:

(8.94) *You must take any of them.

Further, the choice must be available; as Vendler says (pp. 80–81),

This is an essential feature; so much so that in situations that exclude such freedom, the use of "any" becomes nonsensical. Suppose you accept my previous offer and take an apple. What can I say now? Well, for sure, I can say things like

He took one.
He took the one he liked.
He took that one.

But I certainly cannot say

He took any one.

even if you acted on my words: "Take any one." Thus, again, the main feature of "any" is not merely indetermination; for "He took one" is indeterminate enough. "Any" calls for a choice, but after it has been made "any" loses its point.

Of the explications of *any* proposed by Lakoff and Vendler, Vendler's seems the more general. On one hand, Lakoff's account cannot explain the difference between (8.93) and (8.94) or between (8.95) and (8.96), while Vendler's can.

(8.95) Someone can get in to see *Mary Poppins*.
(8.96) Anyone can get in to see *Myra Breckinridge*.

In Vendler's terms, *someone* represents an indeterminate person, but *anyone* represents an indeterminate person whose identity is up to the hearer, hence the effect of a universal quantifier in (8.93) and (8.96).

On the other hand, Vendler's account does appear to extend to Lakoff's examples (8.80)–(8.89). In these examples, *some* and *any* are used to specify amounts (of work, money, candy, beans, etc.). *Any* leaves the choice of amount up to the hearer—any amount, no matter how large or small, is guaranteed satisfactory to the speaker. Hence *any* is used when the speaker has a negative expectation: in effect I defy you to find a quantity sufficiently small to satisfy me. For example, *Who wants any beans?* is scornful because it says "No matter how small a quantity of beans you choose, I still want to know who wants them." In (8.85) I am saying, "No matter how large or small an amount of money you choose, I am still not sure Bill will lend it to me."

Some, on the other hand, implies that there is a minimum expected amount below which the speaker will not accept *some X* as appropriate. For example, look again at (8.86)–(8.87).

(8.86) If you eat some candy, I'll give you $10.
(8.87) If you eat any candy, I'll whip you.

In (8.86), you will probably get $10 only if you eat at least a piece or two of candy, but not if you just nibble the corner of one piece. In (8.87), however, you are liable to be whipped even if you take the merest nibble.

The use of *any* in negative contexts is easily explained in Vendler's terms. In (8.97),

(8.97) I didn't buy any beans.

I am saying that whatever amount of beans you choose, no matter how small, I didn't buy that much. On the other hand, (8.98) implies that there was some prearranged quantity of beans I was supposed to buy but didn't; the use of *some* seems to presuppose a minimum acceptable amount.

(8.98) I didn't buy some beans.

Vendler's explanation can be extended to at least some of the other words that occur only in affective contexts. *Ever*, for example, denotes an arbitrary time, to be chosen by the hearer; *at all* represents an arbitrary (or arbitrarily small) degree. Other pairs, such as *already/yet*, do not seem to be immediately susceptible to this analysis. The matter is quite complicated; Baker (1970a) presents a much fuller range of data on this topic. Jackendoff (1972) discusses a further difference between *any* and *every*.

Having shown that *some* and *any* are independent lexical items, we have demonstrated that the *some-any* alternation should be accounted for by a semantic condition rather than by a transformation. In section 8.5 we will integrate this conclusion into a reinterpretation of Klima's analysis within the theory of modal structure.

8.4 The Syntax of Negative Constituents

In Klima's theory of negation, the semantic similarity of (8.99) and (8.100), for example, is accounted for by deriving them from the same deep structure, in which the constituent *neg* is attached to the sentence node.

(8.99) I didn't see anyone.
(8.100) I saw no one.

Rules of *neg* placement then may attach *neg* in various surface positions without affecting meaning.

In section 8.2, however, we showed that the interpretation of negation is dependent at least in part on surface structure considerations. If we make the stronger claim of Chapter 7 that surface structure is the *only* syntactic level relevant to the interpretation of these negative elements, the syntax of negation falls into an entirely different light. For if this is the case, deep structure similarities between (8.99) and (8.100) have no semantic motivation, and we are free to determine the deep structures of negative sentences purely on the grounds of syntactic distribution.

If we are to successfully maintain the Extended Lexical Hypothesis, it is imperative that we choose this approach to the deep structures of negative sentences. Klima's rules of *neg* placement, it will be recalled, require unsystematic and sometimes drastic changes in "spelling":

(8.101) *neg* + any → no (obligatory)

     neg + every → never (obligatory)

     neg + either → neither (obligatory)

     neg + so → not (optional) (as in *I think not*)

     neg + many → few (optional)

     neg + much → little (optional)

     neg + often → seldom (optional)

These are exactly the sort of changes we are trying to eliminate in the Extended Lexical Hypothesis.

The alternative is to claim that each of the words on the right-hand side of (8.101) is a lexical item. Syntactically they will be of various classes: *no*, *few*, and *little* will be quantifiers; *never* and *seldom* will be frequency adverbs; *neither* will be a conjunction. They will however share a semantic marker, the modal operator *neg*. This approach is anticipated in part by Klima in section 41 of his paper, where he introduces the (at that time new) idea of morphemes as bundles of "grammatico-semantic features," and suggests that such negative words as *doubt* and *dislike* can be analyzed as carrying the feature *neg*. We are therefore merely carrying this process to its logical conclusion.

Before adopting this idea too glibly, however, it is important to note one fundamental difference between the negative words in (8.101) and the "inherently negative" words such as *doubt* and *dislike*. Although they are similar in conditioning *some-any* alternations,

(8.102)a. I $\left\{\begin{array}{l} \text{*think} \\ \text{doubt} \end{array}\right\}$ that anyone came.

    b. I $\left\{\begin{array}{l} \text{*like} \\ \text{dislike} \end{array}\right\}$ doing any more than necessary.

the inherently negative words do not pass Klima's tests for sentence negation.

(8.103) I $\left\{\begin{array}{l} \text{don't think} \\ \text{*doubt} \end{array}\right\}$ that anyone came, and neither does John.

(8.104) I $\left\{\begin{array}{l} \text{don't like} \\ \text{*dislike} \end{array}\right\}$ doing any more than necessary, not even a little bit

    more.

Tentatively, then, we will treat as lexical items all those morphemes treated by Klima as combinations of sentence negation with an indefinite. These morphemes are of the same lexical category as the corresponding indefinites; hence their distribution will be the same, ignoring for the moment those aspects of the distribution related to their function as negative particles. It remains to provide a syntactic account of Klima's uncombined negation, which shows up as *not* in surface structure.

The free negative particle *not* occurs in three distinct paradigms: as a conjunction, as an emphatic particle, and as a degree adverb. In the first two of these uses, it is commonly associated with *but*. As a conjunction, we can compare its use with *and*.

(8.105) John $\begin{Bmatrix} \text{, (but) not Bill,} \\ \text{and Bill} \\ \text{, and also Bill,} \end{Bmatrix}$ decided to leave the party.

(8.106) Fred likes Sally, $\begin{Bmatrix} \text{not} \\ \text{and} \end{Bmatrix}$ $\begin{Bmatrix} \text{Bill, Sue.} \\ \text{vice versa.} \end{Bmatrix}$

In the second use, *not* is similar in distribution to the emphatic particle *too*.

(8.107) I mentioned the plot to John, $\begin{Bmatrix} \text{and not to Bill.} \\ \text{but not to Bill.} \\ \text{and to Bill, too.} \end{Bmatrix}$

This use of *not* also occurs in the auxiliary, where it alternates with *too* again. Both occur after the first auxiliary or *do*, and they are mutually exclusive.

(8.108)   Max $\begin{Bmatrix} \text{did} \\ \text{should} \end{Bmatrix}$ $\begin{Bmatrix} \text{TOO} \\ \text{not} \\ \text{n't} \end{Bmatrix}$ perform the *Hammerklavier* as well as Rubinstein does.

(8.109) *Max did $\begin{Bmatrix} \text{TOO not} \\ \text{not TOO} \end{Bmatrix}$ perform *Happy Birthday* as well as Margaret's brother.

Part of this use of *not* is the alternation with *so*, as in I think $\left\{ {so \atop not} \right\}$. Note that *so* also enters into the paradigms (8.108)–(8.109).

The only one of the constructions above for which I will offer an analysis here is the auxiliary position. One obvious way to describe this construction is to introduce the emphatic particles *too*, *so*, and *not* after the auxiliary in the expansion of S:

(8.110) S → NP − Aux − (EmphPrt) − VP

Following the analysis of the auxiliary given in section 3.8, this position in the base will guarantee that the emphatic particle follows the first auxiliary in the surface structure. Alternatively, EmphPrt could be generated in initial position, as in Klima's rules, and moved to post-aux position by a transformation.

In the third use of *not*, it alternates with such degree adverbs as *scarcely*, *nearly*, and *almost*. Examples are

(8.111) $\left\{ {\text{Not all} \atop \text{Nearly all}} \right\}$ of my friends came.

(8.112) The police claim that $\left\{ \begin{array}{l} \text{not one person} \\ \text{scarcely one person} \\ \text{nearly a thousand people} \end{array} \right\}$ broke in last week.

(8.113) $\left\{ \begin{array}{l} \text{Not (just) anybody} \\ \text{Scarcely anybody} \\ \text{Nearly anybody} \end{array} \right\}$ can play Reveille on a garden hose.

(8.114) She's a $\left\{ {\text{not} \atop \text{nearly}} \right\}$ unprincipled woman.

(8.115) He gave $\left\{ {\text{an almost} \atop \text{a not}} \right\}$ completely erroneous answer.

The degree adverbs may also occur in the auxiliary.

(8.116) She $\left\{ {\text{scarcely} \atop \text{almost}} \right\}$ agreed to meet with her lawyer.

However, they have a freedom of occurrence among the auxiliary elements that *not* does not share.

$$(8.117) \text{ The attempt on his life} \begin{cases} \text{nearly could have} \\ \text{scarcely could have} \\ \text{could nearly have} \\ \text{could scarcely have} \\ \text{could have nearly} \\ \text{could have scarcely} \end{cases} \text{succeeded.}$$

In particular, the position before the auxiliary is totally unacceptable for *not*.

(8.118) *The attempt on his life not could have succeeded.

Postauxiliary position of *not* is somewhat acceptable, though awkward.

(8.119) ??The attempt on his life could have not succeeded.

This situation can be described by generating degree adverbs in the post-auxiliary position. A preposing rule which produces preauxiliary position then applies to all degree adverbs but *not*. In addition to (8.110), then, the grammar will contain the base rules (8.120) and (8.121), and the transformation (8.122).

(8.120) Aux → T − (M)
(8.121) VP → (have - en) − (be - ing) − (AdvDeg) − V − . . .
(8.122) (AdvDeg movement)

$$\begin{array}{ccccc} X & - \text{ Aux } - & [_{VP}Y & - \text{ AdvDeg } - & Z] \\ 1 & 2 & 3 & 4 & 5 \end{array}$$

⇒ 1 − 4 − 2 − 3 − 0 − 5

Condition: 4 ≠ *not*

OPTIONAL

Note that (8.121) and (8.122) generalize with the rules for generating adverbs proposed in Chapter 3. There it was argued that the postauxiliary adverb position was necessary in the base to generate certain manner adverbs as well as the class of adverbs including *merely* and *utterly*. AdvDeg movement can also be generalized to this latter class.[4]

It is claimed, then, that *not* in the auxiliary has two sources, as an emphatic particle and, with lower acceptability, as a degree adverb. To further substantiate this claim, observe that a sentence may not contain two degree adverbs in the auxiliary.

$$(8.123) \; ?{*}\text{The attempt} \begin{Bmatrix} \text{scarcely} \\ \text{almost} \end{Bmatrix} \text{could have} \begin{Bmatrix} \text{scarcely} \\ \text{nearly} \\ \text{almost} \\ \text{not} \end{Bmatrix} \text{succeeded.}$$

Likewise, (8.109) shows that there may not be two emphatic particles in the auxiliary.

$$(8.109) \; {*}\text{Max did} \begin{Bmatrix} \text{TOO not} \\ \text{not TOO} \end{Bmatrix} \text{perform } \textit{Happy Birthday} \text{ as well as Margaret's brother.}$$

However, combinations of emphatic particles and degree adverbs are acceptable.

$$(8.124) \; \text{Mike} \begin{Bmatrix} \text{almost did TOO} \\ \text{did TOO almost} \end{Bmatrix} \text{succeed in his attempt to seduce Myra.}$$

Precisely when *not* follows the first auxiliary, i.e. when it could be gen-

---

[4]If the interpretation of adverbs is performed entirely on surface structure, AdvDeg movement can be generalized to all adverbs generated in this position, since the correct interpretation of adverbs depends on whether they are attached to the S or VP node. In fact, given surface interpretation, it would be possible to generate all auxiliary adverbs with the rule (8.121), interpretation depending only on surface constituency and order.

erated as an emphatic particle, it may co-occur with degree adverbs in the auxiliary.

(8.125) Mike $\begin{cases} \text{a. almost didn't} \\ \text{b. ?didn't almost} \end{cases}$ succeed in seducing Myra.

The two possible sources will account also for the occasional occurrence of two *nots* in a single auxiliary:

(8.126) ??Ted can't have not arrived at the party.

The acceptability of (8.126) seems commensurate with that of (8.125b); *almost* and *not* seem to fulfill the same function. We conclude that the dual source of auxiliary *not* is justified.

Finally, lest it seem overly unusual that *not* is both an emphatic particle and a degree adverb, it should be pointed out that *too* and *so* also function in both capacities. Their distribution as degree adverbs is more limited than that of *not*, but the following examples correspond syntactically to (8.111)–(8.115).

(8.127) So many people came that the hall's capacity was exceeded.
        Too many people came to make the effort worthwhile.
(8.128) The police claim that so few people broke in last week that investigation is hardly necessary.
        The police claim that too few people broke in last week to justify an investigation.

(8.129) She's a woman $\begin{cases} \text{so unprincipled that even her husband doesn't trust} \\ \text{her.} \\ \text{too unprincipled to trust.} \end{cases}$

(8.130) He gave an answer $\begin{cases} \text{so completely erroneous as to defy belief.} \\ \text{too completely erroneous to be believed.} \end{cases}$

This correspondence is surprising; I have scanty intuitions as to whether it is of significance in a synchronic description of English. Further research is needed to clarify the issue.

8.5 A Reinterpretation of Klima's Analysis

Let us now recast Klima's analysis of negation in such a way that it will be consistent with the Lexicalist Hypothesis. Following the results of the last two sections, we will treat all the negative morphemes and the members of *some-any* type alternations as independent lexical items rather than as the results of *neg* placement and Indef incorporation transformations. The only syntactic factor in the distribution of these lexical items will be lexical category; the other aspects of distribution observed by Klima will be accounted for by semantic rule.

The semantic device we have at our disposal to explain these phenomena is the modal projection rule developed in Chapter 7. We repeat here the modal projection rule, incorporating the extension to Ss.

(8.131) (Modal projection rule)

Given a lexical item A whose semantic representation contains a modal operator M. If an NP or S is within the scope of A, it is optionally *dependent on* M in the modal structure, that is, subject to C_M. If an NP or S is outside the scope of M, it is not dependent on M.

In Chapter 7 we showed that negation and quantifiers function as modal operators, imposing conditions on the identifiability of referents and the realizability of events. In particular, the modal operator *neg* imposes the condition that there are no identifiable referents for NPs dependent on it and no realizations of Ss dependent on it.

Let us first show why *any* can occur in positions where it is dependent on *neg*. In section 8.3 we presented justification of Vendler's analysis of *any*: *any* presents an offer to the hearer to choose a referent for the NP dominating *any*. Negative contexts are one place where the choice is left open: in negative contexts such as (8.132)–(8.133),

(8.132) No one saw anything.
(8.133) We didn't force anyone to buy anything.

the speaker is claiming that no matter what thing you pick, it is not something that anyone saw or we forced someone to buy. In other words, by using *any* dependent on *neg*, the speaker guarantees that the hearer's every choice of possible intended referent is incorrect, because there is no intended referent. Where *any* is used with a plural or mass NP, such as (8.134)–(8.135),

(8.134) Bill didn't see any unicorns.
(8.135) Mabel didn't eat any mustard.

the inherent arbitrariness of quantity in *any* comes into play as well: the speaker says that no matter how large or small a number of unicorns you may name, that is not the number of unicorns I intend you to understand that Bill has seen. *Any* apparently suppletes *some*, then, because it affords a more sweeping denial of intended reference.

In Klima's analysis, the scope of negation (i.e. the area of the sentence in which *any* can appear) consists of those nodes in construction with the negation. However, in Chapter 7 we claimed that the scope of negation (except in "inherent negatives" such as *doubt*) consists of everything commanded by the negative morpheme and to its right. The difference in definitions stems essentially from the fact that in Klima's analysis, the scope is determined at a point in the derivation when sentence negation is the leftmost daughter of S, whereas in our analysis, the scope of negation must be determined from the surface structure configuration. For example, in (8.136), *any* is not in construction with negation in the surface structure, because *none* is dominated by the subject NP, which does not dominate *any*.

(8.136) [_{NP}None of these examples]_{NP} will convince anyone.

Hence we must replace Klima's structural condition *in construction with* by *command*, which allows *any* in (8.136) to be within the scope of negation, but excludes cases such as (8.137).

(8.137) *The man [_Swho I didn't see]_S bought anything.

Also because the scope of negation is to be determined at the surface, the left-to-right condition must be added in order to distinguish between, for example, (8.138) and (8.139).

(8.138) I told nobody any of my jokes.
(8.139) *I told anybody none of my jokes.

Thus the difference in scope of negation between Klima's analysis and the present one is simply a result of the different nature of the analyses.[5]

Now let us apply the modal projection rule to some of the examples of section 2.

(8.28) Not many of the arrows hit the target.

(8.29) Many of the arrows didn't hit the target.

(8.30) It is not so that many of the arrows hit the target.

(8.31) None of the men saw anything.

(8.32) Some of the men didn't see anything.

(8.34) Some of the men saw nothing.

The modal projection rule assigns these the modal structures (8.140)–(8.145). Recall that dependence on negation, particularly dependence of an S on negation, is very strongly preferred.

(8.140) the arrows, the target, not (many (hit))

(8.141) the arrows, the target, many (not (hit))

(8.142) it, is, the arrows, the target, not (many (hit))

(8.143) the men, none (anything (saw))

(8.144) the men, some (not (anything (see)))

(8.145) the men, some (nothing (saw))

---

[5]Our definition of the scope of negation is consistent with the redefinition of command in section 4.7. There we revised the standard definition to "Node A commands Node B if the lowest node defining a cycle which dominates A also dominates B"; the standard definition has "S node" rather than "node defining a cycle." This was done in order to define properly the application of reflexivization. Note that in exactly those picture-noun cases where we have required an NP cycle for reflexivization, a negation within the picture-noun construction cannot condition *any* outside the picture-noun construction:

  (i)   I gave Bill a picture of himself. (no NP cycle needed)
       I gave pictures of no one to anyone.
 (ii) *I gave Bill Mary's picture of himself. (NP cycle necessary)
       *I gave Mary's pictures of no one to anyone.

Likewise, *wh*, which we have claimed is a modal operator of type III scope, cannot extend its scope outside of a picture-noun construction which requires a cycle:

(iii) Pictures of whom did you give to Bill?
     *Mary's pictures of whom did you give to Bill? (*except as an echo question)

This is further evidence that negation and *wh* are governed by essentially the same semantic rules, as we claimed in the previous chapter.

Note that in (8.143)–(8.145), *saw* in parentheses represents dependence of the S on negation and *any*, so the left-right scope condition is not violated, although *saw* is sometimes to the left of the quantifier (cf. section 7.5, p. 312).

To achieve equivalence with Klima's analysis of negation, it is reasonable to suppose that *none* and *nothing* decompose semantically into the modal structures *not (any (   ))* and *not (anything (   ))*. Under this supposition, (8.143)–(8.145) will be represented more fully as (8.146)–(8.148).

(8.146) the men, not (any (anything (saw)))
(8.147) the men, some (not (anything (see)))
(8.148) the men, some (not (anything (see)))

For more complicated modal structures, consider (8.149)–(8.153).

(8.149)   Only then didn't any of my friends arrive on time. (= 8.66)
(8.150)   Only then did any of my friends not arrive on time. (= 8.67)
(8.151)   None of my friends arrived on time only then. (= 8.69)
(8.152)   ?Some of my friends didn't arrive on time only then. (= 8.70)
(8.153)   Only then did none of my friends arrive on time. (= 8.73)

Since *only* conditions *some-any* alternations, and since the possibility of such alternations is based on modal dependence, it is plausible that *only* is another modal operator. If this is the case, (8.149)–(8.153) receive the modal structures (8.154)–(8.158).

(8.154) then, my friends, only (not (any (arrive)))
(8.155) then, my friends, only (any (not (arrive)))
(8.156) then, my friends, not (any (arrive, only (   )))
(8.157) then, my friends, some (not (arrive, only (   )))
(8.158) then, my friends, only (not (any (arrive)))

In Chapter 7 we claimed that the modal structure represents claims about the identifiability of referents for NPs and realizability of Ss. Paraphrase criteria follow immediately from this analysis. For two sentences to be paraphrases, their truth conditions, including claims made by the modal structure, must be the same. Hence (8.28) and (8.30) are paraphrases because the NP *many of the arrows* is dependent on negation in both; (8.29) has a different reading because *not* is dependent on *many*. Likewise, (8.31) has a different reading than (8.32) and (8.34) because of the subject's dependence on negation in (8.31). Of the five examples (8.149)–(8.153), only the first and last have the same modal structure, and only these two are paraphrases.

The criterion for a sentence S^1 to be a sentence negation of another sentence S^2, in the sense discussed in section 8.1, is clear from the paraphrase criterion. In *it is not so that* S^2, all indeterminates within S^2 will be dependent on negation, as will the node S^2 itself. S^1, in order to be sentence negation, must paraphrase *it is not so that* S^2; hence its modal structure must contain a negation on which all indeterminates in S^1 and S^1 itself are dependent. (8.28), (8.30), and (8.31), but not (8.29), (8.32), and (8.34), thus are instances of sentence negation on these formal grounds, corresponding to our informal descriptions in section 8.2. Intuitively, a sentence is an instance of sentence negation if everything that it is possible to deny is in fact denied. In particular, if it is possible to deny that a noun phrase has an intended referent, by subjecting it to C_{neg}, then it is necessary to do so.

With the grammatical mechanisms and semantic analyses discussed in the last three sections, we have accounted for the essential insights of Klima's analysis. We now turn to certain apparent aberrations in the interpretation of negation and quantifiers, introduced by the use of the pitch accents discussed in Chapter 6.

8.6 Association with Focus Again

The immediate problem is the contrast in meaning between (8.159) and (8.160), produced by a difference in the choice of pitch accent.[6]

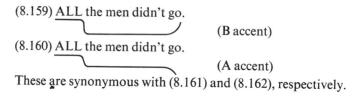

(8.159) ALL the men didn't go.   (B accent)
(8.160) ALL the men didn't go.   (A accent)

These are synonymous with (8.161) and (8.162), respectively.

(8.161) Not all the men went.
(8.162) None of the men went.

[6]Carden (1970a) discusses these examples, claiming that there are dialect differences as to which interpretation of *all the men didn't go* is acceptable. As he does not discuss the intonation contours assigned by his subjects, it is difficult to connect his evidence with the present analysis. The dialect I describe here is probably identical to his AMB dialect.

According to the analysis so far, there is no way to account for this difference, since (8.159) and (8.160) are assigned the same modal structure by the rules of the last section.

One possible solution that comes to mind fairly quickly is that a B accent on a morpheme will have the effect of making that morpheme dependent on negation, if there is negation present. This conjecture is easily destroyed, however, by considering the following pair:

(8.163) The target wasn't hit by many of the ARROWS. (= 8.35)

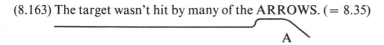

(8.164) The target wasn't HIT by MANY of the arrows.

These are synonymous with (8.165) and (8.166), respectively.

(8.165) Not many of the arrows hit the target. (= 8.28)
(8.166) Many of the arrows didn't hit the target. (= 8.29)

Hence in this case, a B accent has the effect of *removing* the emphasized quantifier from dependence on negation, exactly opposite to the effect observed in (8.159).

In Chapter 6 we developed a general theory of the meaning of the A and B pitch accents and their interaction with negation. We will now see how this theory applies to the examples above and several other well-known examples, accounting for them in a perfectly general way.

Recall the discussion of Chapter 6. The semantic representation of a sentence is divided into focus and presupposition, where a mark F, realized as stress, marks focus constituents. The presupposition is formed by replacing the focus in the semantic interpretation by an appropriate variable, then applying the lambda-operator. The presupposition and assertion are formed from the resulting expression. For example, (8.167) has the presupposition and assertion (8.168).

(8.167) FRED saw John.
(8.168) Presupposition: $\lambda x\,[x$ saw John] is well-formed.
       Assertion: Fred $\in \lambda x\,[x$ saw John]

If there are two foci, the presupposition involves a lambda-function of ordered pairs:

(8.169) Max told SALLY that FRED had left.
   Presupposition: $\lambda(x, y)$ [Max told x that y had left] is well-formed
   Assertion: (Sally, Fred) $\in \lambda(x, y)$ [Max told x that y had left]

When there are two foci, invariably one will receive an A pitch accent (falling) and one will receive a B pitch accent (rising). The A accent denotes a dependent variable; the B accent an independent variable.

   Certain words such as *only*, *even*, and *not* have the property of being able to disassociate themselves from the presupposition if they stand in a particular structural relation to the focus, defined by the *range* of the word. This general process we termed association with focus. The particular case in which negation undergoes association with focus is when there is a single focus with a B accent. Under these conditions the affirmation-negation distinction functions as the dependent variable; hence the negation is not part of the presupposition. On the other hand, if the focus has an A accent, there is no need for a second variable, so the negation remains in the presupposition. The contrast is illustrated by (8.170)–(8.171).

(8.170) FRED didn't see John. (BILL did.)
         B   A
   Presupposition: λx [x saw John] is well-formed
   Assertion: Fred $\notin \lambda x$ [x saw John]
(8.171) (Which one of them didn't see John?)
   FRED didn't see John.
    A
   Presupposition: λx [x didn't see John] is well-formed
   Assertion: Fred $\in \lambda x$ [x didn't see John]

In effect, then, the B accent coupled with negation means that the focus is an incorrect value to satisfy a positive presupposition; the A accent coupled with negation means that the focus is a correct value for a negative presupposition.

   In section 6.6, we discussed the range of a negation in the auxiliary, that is, the part of the surface structure in which the focus must be located in order for the negation to associate with it. The range turned out to be the entire sentence except for material before the subject.[7] But in particular, the subject is in the range of an auxiliary negation, as can be seen from (8.170). Hence the *range* of negation does not coincide with the *scope* of negation, which includes only the material to the right.

The other negative words can also undergo association with focus, for example (leaving the presuppositions in informal form):

(8.172) Buster gave no one a sock in the JAW.
                                          B

       Presupposition: Buster gave $\begin{Bmatrix} \text{someone} \\ \text{people} \end{Bmatrix}$ a sock in some part of the body.

(8.173) Nothing disturbs ME.
                           B

       Presupposition: Some things disturb some people.

(8.174) Alice never gave FRED an indication of her intentions.
                             B

       Presupposition: Alice once gave someone an indication of her intentions.

(8.175) Few people believe that HAROLD has a chance of winning.
                                     B

       Presupposition: Many people believe someone (in particular) to have a chance of winning.

It appears that except in auxiliary position, negation is reluctant to extend its range to material on its left. For instance, (8.176) seems somewhat less acceptable than (8.172).

(8.176) ?BUSTER gave no one a sock in the jaw.
             B

       Presupposition: Someone gave someone a sock in the jaw.

[7]In "Yiddish" dialects some preposed topics are also in the range of negation:

JOHN I didn't see, but BILL I did.
  B   B

This example requires association with focus in the first clause; it sounds somewhat worse to me than if A accents are added on the auxiliaries, making association with focus unnecessary.

More acceptable than (8.176) is (8.177), in which the negation is explicitly used as a second focus, so that it does not have to undergo association with focus.

(8.177) BUSTER gave NO one a sock in the jaw.
        B   A
        Presupposition: Someone gave someone a sock in the jaw.

Note, by the way, that *never* in the auxiliary can undergo association with a focused subject.

(8.178) The boys in IOWA never used to treat your mother that way. (The
                    B
        boys HERE are TERRIBLE to her.)
             B   A

   This disparity in range between auxiliary use and other uses, it should be pointed out, is not unique to negation. We already noted in section 6.5 that *even* displays the same behavior: it admits material to its left into its range only when attached to S in auxiliary position, when it admits the subject but not material before the subject.
   Let us now apply this analysis to the examples from the beginning of the section.

(8.159) ALL the men didn't go.
        B

The B accent will induce association of negation with the focused quantifier, so we get the presupposition and assertion (8.179), exactly parallel to (8.170).

(8.179) Presupposition: λQ [Q of the men went] is well-formed
        Assertion: all $\notin \lambda Q$ [Q of the men went]

In other words, some number of the men went, but *all* is not the correct number. Hence the number that went must be less than *all* (since there is no greater number); thus there is the paraphrase *not all the men went*. On the other hand, (8.160) receives the interpretation (8.180), exactly parallel to (8.171).

(8.160) ALL the men didn't go.
      A

(8.180) Presupposition: λQ [Q of the men didn't go] is well-formed
      Assertion: all $\in \lambda Q$ [Q of the men didn't go]

In other words, some number of the men didn't go, and *all* is that number. Hence the paraphrase with *none of the men went*.

The same effect occurs with *all* in the object.

(8.181) I didn't see ALL of the men.
            B
(8.182) ?I didn't see ALL of the men.[8]
            A

These are paraphrased by (8.183) and (8.184), respectively; their readings are explained in exactly the same way as those of (8.159)–(8.160).

(8.183) I saw not all of the men.
(8.184) I saw none of the men.

Before turning to the examples with *many* (8.163)–(8.164), let us apply this analysis to a number of other interesting examples.

(8.185) Max doesn't beat his wife because he LOVES her.
                          B
(8.186) Max doesn't beat his wife because he LOVES her.
                          A

---

[8] I have no principled explanation of why (8.182) is strange. However, note that the same contrast of acceptability seems to occur with the quantifier at the other extreme end of the scale, *none*:

?I didn't see NONE of the men.
           B
*I didn't see NONE of the men.
           A

This latter constraint has generally been called a "no-double-negative constraint." The generalization with *all* and the dependence on intonation have not been observed before, to my knowledge: otherwise a more appropriate name for the constraint would have been chosen.

With *because he loves her* as focus, (8.185) and (8.186) receive (8.187) and (8.188) as interpretations, derived in exactly the same way as (8.170)–(8.171).

(8.187) Presupposition: λx [Max beats his wife for reason x] is well-formed
Assertion: because he loves her $\notin \lambda x$ [Max beats his wife for reason x]
(8.188) Presupposition: λx [Max doesn't beat his wife for reason x] is well-formed.
Assertion: because he loves her $\in \lambda x$ [Max doesn't beat his wife for reason x]

Hence (8.185) is correctly predicted to have the presupposition that Max beats his wife, and (8.186) that he doesn't beat her.

Two other variants of this example are

(8.189) Max doesn't beat his WIFE(,) because he LOVES her.
$\qquad\qquad\qquad\qquad$ B $\qquad\qquad\qquad\qquad$ A
(8.190) Because he LOVES her, Max doesn't beat his WIFE.
$\qquad\qquad$ B $\qquad\qquad\qquad\qquad\qquad\qquad$ A

The emphasis on *wife* produces a second focus which includes either the VP *doesn't beat his wife* or the whole main clause *Max doesn't beat his wife*. The presupposition is thus reduced to causal connection between the two clauses and, if the VP is focused, the subject: (8.191) is the interpretation of VP focus and (8.192) the interpretation of S focus in both examples.

(8.191) Presupposition: $\lambda(x, y)$ [Max's reason for doing x is y] is well-formed.
Assertion: (not beating his wife, because he loves her) $\in \lambda(x, y)$ [Max's reason for doing x is y]
(8.192) Presupposition: $\lambda(x, y)$ [the reason for x is y] is well-formed.
Assertion: (Max doesn't beat his wife, he loves her) $\in \lambda(x, y)$ [the reason for x is y]

(8.189) and (8.190) differ only in the order in which the variables are chosen: the B accent in each case indicates the independent variable. But in neither one is the negation disassociated from the *beat* clause as it is in

(8.185); hence in each case it is understood that Max doesn't beat his wife. Thus only one of the four intonation patterns (8.185)–(8.186), (8.189)–(8.190) has an apparent reversal of quantifier order, a striking asymmetry predicted by our rules.

The next examples involve a focused conjunction. (These examples were brought to my attention by Barbara Partee.)

(8.193) Both John AND Bill didn't go.
                    B
(8.194) Both John AND Bill didn't go.
                    A

(8.193) means that one or the other, but not both, went; (8.194) means that neither went. Applying the rules for focus assignment, we get the interpretations (8.195) and (8.196), respectively.

(8.195) Presupposition: λconj [John conj Bill went] is well-formed.
        Assertion: both-and $\notin \lambda$conj [John conj Bill went]
(8.196) Presupposition: λconj [John conj Bill didn't go] is well-formed.
        Assertion: both-and $\in \lambda$conj [John conj Bill didn't go]

The variable *conj* inserted in these expressions ranges over different combinations of the conjuncts: *both-and, either-or,* and *neither-nor.* (8.195) says that some combination of John and Bill went, but *both-and* is not the correct combination. (8.196) says that some combination of John and Bill didn't go, and that *both-and* is that combination. Hence the interpretations observed for (8.193)–(8.194), hardly obvious at first glance, are accounted for by our analysis.

Finally, let us deal with the example left over from the beginning of this section. We observed that quantifiers receive a specific interpretation in contexts like (8.197)–(8.198).

(8.197) The target wasn't HIT by MANY of the arrows. (= 8.164)
                           A   B
(8.198) I didn't get to SEE THREE of my friends.
                        A   B

These examples pose a problem for the analysis of focus assignment we have given so far, since we have only allowed complete constituents as foci.

However, the only complete constituents available for the focus with an A accent in (8.197)–(8.198) are the accented verbs themselves, since the next constituent up, the VP, includes the other focus. But it is semantically quite unlikely that the verbs *hit* and *see* could serve as foci, since the possible contrasts occur only in rather improbable assertions such as (8.199).

(8.199) ?The target wasn't HIT by MANY of the arrows, and it wasn't
                            A   B
        MISSED by many OTHERS.
          A   B

A more likely presupposition for (8.197) is that various things happened to certain of the arrows, or possibly that various things happened to certain of the arrows with respect to the target. Hence the A accent must identify a focus on the nonconstituent string *(the target) wasn't hit*. Since focus assignment as formulated in Chapter 6 does not generate this interpretation, we must modify the rule somehow.

   Let us put off for a moment the question of how to derive this presupposition and focus for (8.197) and first see how such an interpretation would force a specific reading on the quantifier. Assume then that the A accent marks as focus *the target wasn't hit*. The representation of (8.197) will then be crudely representable as (8.200).

(8.200) Presupposition: $\lambda(x, Q)$ [x happened to Q of the arrows] is well-
        formed.
        Assertion: (the target wasn't hit by, many) $\in \lambda(x, Q)$ [x happened to
        Q of the arrows]

Now observe that there is no negation in the presupposition. This means that the variable Q in the presupposition is not subject to C_{neg}, and hence it ranges over only specific quantifier readings. Therefore whatever quantifier is given in the assertion as the correct value of Q, it must carry a specific reading, since this quantifier must be chosen from the semantic domain defined by the variable Q. If we can derive the correct reading (8.200) for (8.197), then, the specific reading for the quantifier follows automatically.

   Here is one possible way of deriving the reading (8.200). We have proposed that a focused constituent is identified by a marker F on its topmost node. We have not, however, discussed the interpretation of surface structures in which one F marker is dominated by another. There is nothing in our formalism so far which excludes such cases. (8.201) is a structure of this form.

(8.201)

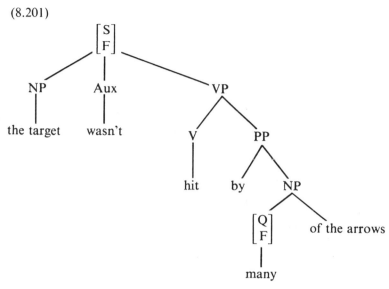

There are no principled syntactic reasons for excluding a structure like (8.201), since F may generally be assigned freely. In the semantic component, we could either choose to rule it out, on the principle that one focus may not be embedded in another, or we could modify the focus assignment rule to give (8.201) the reading (8.200). One such modification would be to mark as a focus all the material dominated by the F marker that is not in construction with another F marker. The stress rule of course would also require modifications. I will not pursue these modifications here. I merely point out that they provide a way of accounting for the interpretation of (8.197) without a drastic reevaluation of the derivation of focus and presupposition: we can without too much difficulty derive the correct interpretation from a surface structure that we otherwise would have to find an ad hoc way to get rid of.

We have shown in this section that the strict application of the rules for focus and presupposition of Chapter 6 interact with the behavior of negation to predict a rather wide range of data, much of which looks at first contradictory. The ability of the approach taken here to account for these apparent irregularities on perfectly general principles is strong evidence for its correctness.

8.7 *Neither*-Tags

Now let us consider *neither*-tags, for example in sentences like (8.202)–(8.203).

(8.202) Prudence doesn't ever swim at Peter's, and neither does Charity.
(8.203) Jimmy didn't paint much of the boathouse, and neither did John.

Two points are of interest in these examples. First, one of Klima's criteria for sentence negation is the existence of a *neither*-tag; we would like to show how this criterion follows from our analysis. Second, the nonspecific readings of *ever* and *much* are carried over as nonspecifics in the interpretation of the *neither*-tag; we must see that our rules will derive these interpretations.

In sections 6.8–9 we discussed how rules such as VP-anaphora create interpretations for empty nodes by copying over partial interpretations in examples such as *I like to swim at Peter's whenever Brigitte does*. Clearly, examples with *neither*-tags are interpreted by the same rule. This rule constructs an interpretation for an empty VP node (designated as Δ) on the basis of the interpretation of the surface structure of the VP of the first clause.

The use of *neither*, however, puts a special requirement on the form of the first clause: the readings of the two clauses must have parallel instances of negation. Since the position of *neither* in the second clause will make the entire S dependent on negation in modal structure, the first clause must exhibit a similar modal structure. Thus the parallelism requirement rules out sentences such as (8.204), in which the first negation governs only a subordinate clause.

(8.204) *The man who didn't know Jimmy painted the boathouse, and neither did John.

It also rules out examples with verbs of "inherent negation" such as *doubt*, since these likewise govern only a subordinate clause (as shown in section 7.4.3):

(8.205) *Jimmy doubts that anyone painted the boathouse, and neither does John.

Notice that (8.206), apparently synonymous with (8.205), is acceptable because the negation is realized as *not*, which can govern the main clause:

(8.206) Jimmy doesn't think that anyone painted the boathouse, and neither does John.

Furthermore, because *neither* is at the beginning of the tag, it will be the outermost modal operator in the modal structure of the tag. Hence negation must be the outermost modal operator in the first clause as well; it cannot be dependent on a quantifier, for example, as in (8.207).

(8.207) ??Many of the arrows didn't hit the target, and neither did many of the javelins.

Rather, the clauses must be given parallel modal structures, either by using *not many* in the first clause as in (8.208), or by using an *either*-tag, which puts negation in the auxiliary, as in (8.209).

(8.208) Not many of the arrows hit the target, and neither did many of the titanium-alloy bullets.

(8.209) Many of the rockets didn't hit the moon, and many of the cannon-balls didn't, either.

Thus the parallelism requirement imposed by *neither* automatically requires sentence negation of the sort described in section 5, confirming Klima's use of it as a test for sentence negation.

However, there are certain cases of sentence negation which cannot take a *neither*-tag, so the existence of a *neither*-tag is a sufficient but not a necessary condition for sentence negation. The examples in question contain a sentence negation in the VP: compare (8.210) with (8.211).

(8.210) ?Bill saw nothing, and neither did Fred.
(8.211) Bill didn't see anything, and neither did Fred.

The difficulty in (8.210) comes about through the operation of VP-anaphora. VP-anaphora carries over the interpretation of all elements in the VP of the first clause as the interpretation of the VP of the tag. In particular, it carries over the negation and assigns it a parallel place in the modal structure, that is, as sentence negation. But *neither* explicitly represents sentence negation in the second clause, so the interpretation of the second clause has two negations instead of the single one required for parallelism. Notice that if *neither* is replaced by *so*, leaving only one negation in the second clause, the result is satisfactory:

(8.212) Bill saw nothing, and so did Fred.

Implicit in our account of *neither*-tags has been the unsurprising assumption that the rule of VP-anaphora carries over not only parallel functional structure and coreference relations, as demonstrated in section 6.8, but parallel modal structure as well. But this assumption of parallelism predicts the nonspecificity of quantifiers in the interpretation of *neither*-tags, observed in (8.202)–(8.203): if a quantifier is dependent on negation in the first VP, it must be dependent on it in the interpretation of the second as well. Thus general considerations about VP-anaphora and the particularly stringent parallelism required by *neither* suffice to explain the behavior of these tags.

8.8 Preposed Negatives and Inversions

We conclude this chapter with a problem for which I cannot find a satisfying solution but which is of sufficient interest to warrant inclusion here. (The examples of this section are predominantly from Klima 1964, pp. 305–307. (8.219) and (8.231) are due to Charles Bird.)

We observed in section 8.1 that a preposed *never* conditions subject-aux inversion, for example in *Never* $\left\{ \begin{array}{l} did\ anyone\ give \\ *anyone\ gave \end{array} \right\}$ *John anything.* A variety of other preposed negatives likewise can cause inversion.

(8.213) Nothing could I find.
(8.214) At no time may Bill enter this room without John's permission.
(8.215) In none of those years will Christmas fall on Sunday.
(8.216) Not until you agree to come along will Bill be willing to face the boss.
(8.217) Not for more than five minutes did he hesitate.
(8.218) Not even ten years ago could you get away with that.
(8.219) In no clothes does Mary look attractive.

Let us call these preposed constituents "inverting negatives."

In all of these examples, negation governs the entire sentence, since *any* and *ever* occur freely outside the preposed constituent.

(8.220) Nothing could I find anywhere.

(8.221) At no time may anyone enter this room.

(8.222) In none of these years will there ever be more than two Friday the thirteenths.

(8.223) Not until then will Bill ever consider doing anything about that.

(8.224) Not for more than five minutes did anyone hesitate.

(8.225) Not even ten years ago could anyone ever get away with that.

One additional point we notice is that the most natural intonation of the inverting negative contains an A pitch accent, in contrast with the B accent usually found in preposed constituents.

There is also a class of preposed negative constituents ("noninverting negatives") which do not induce inversion. This class partially overlaps with the class of inverting negatives.

(8.226) Not long ago $\left\{ \begin{array}{l} \text{there was} \\ \text{*was there} \end{array} \right\}$ a rainstorm.

(8.227) Not even ten years ago, you could get away with that.

(8.228) In not many years, Christmas will fall on a Sunday.

(8.229) In no time at all $\left\{ \begin{array}{l} \text{they had} \\ \text{*had they} \end{array} \right\}$ routed the enemy.

(8.230) Not much later $\left\{ \begin{array}{l} \text{they arrived} \\ \text{*did they arrive} \end{array} \right\}$.

(8.231) In no clothes, Mary looks attractive.

Negation in these examples does not govern the entire sentence, since *any* and *ever* do not occur outside the preposed constituent.

(8.232) *Not long ago there was a rainstorm anywhere in that valley.

(8.233) *Not even ten years ago, anyone could ever get away with that.

(8.234) *In not many years, anything unpleasant will happen.

(8.235) *In no time at all they had finished anything.

(8.236) *Not much later anyone had arrived.

Notice that the noninverting negatives are most natural with a B pitch accent.

The problem posed by these examples is finding a syntactic environment which conditions subject-aux inversion. There is a clear semantic difference between the two classes of preposed constituents; but the fact that *not even ten years ago*, *in not many years*, and *in no clothes* belong to both classes makes it difficult to imagine a syntactic difference.

One might try to claim that there is a syntactic difference between the two classes at the time of subject-aux inversion which disappears by the time the surface structure is reached. In Klima's analysis, the inverting negatives have a deep structure with *neg* attached to the main S node, and the noninverting negatives have a deep structure with *neg* contained in the constituent to be preposed. One might think, then, that Klima's analysis could provide exactly the difference we need to condition inversion. Unfortunately, this turns out not to be the case. In the ordering of rules required by Klima's system (and listed at the end of section 8.1), the sentence negation must be incorporated into preposed constituents before inversion, so that it can be in front of the subject and thus cause inversion. But if the sentence negation is incorporated into the preposed constituent, it is syntactically indistinguishable from constituent negation at the time of inversion. Hence Klima's rules do not provide a correct environment for inversion. Without introducing obvious artificialities into the syntactic rules for negation, it seems impossible to find a purely syntactic environment for inversion.

If inversion is not purely syntactically conditioned, we must incorporate semantic factors into a description of when inversion takes place. There are two possible approaches to this problem. In the first approach, we could claim that subject-aux inversion mentions semantic factors, in particular the scope of negation, in its structural description. This solution contains a fundamental innovation in our theory; we have so far been able to maintain that, although semantic interpretation is in part dependent on the output of transformations, the application of transformations is independent of semantic interpretation. Thus we accept this solution to the problem of inversion only at greatest peril to the hitherto restricted power of our linguistic theory. Nevertheless, for the sake of argument we will state this version of subject-aux inversion as (8.237).

(8.237) (Subject-aux inversion, version 1)

$$\begin{Bmatrix} NP \\ PP \\ Adv \end{Bmatrix} - NP - Aux - VP$$

$$1 \qquad 2 \quad 3 \quad 4 \Rightarrow 1 - 3 - 2 - \emptyset - 4$$

Condition: 1 contains a negation whose scope is the entire S.
OBLIGATORY

Alternatively, we could claim that inversion itself makes no reference to meaning, but that it has an effect on the semantic interpretation which is compatible with sentence negation and incompatible with constituent negation. This claim entails that the conditions on inversion are broken into three components: an optional inversion transformation, a projection rule describing the semantic effect of inversion, and a well-formedness condition relating the semantic effect of inversion to the presence of sentence negation. (8.238)–(8.240) represent these rules. The semantic rules are necessarily in crude descriptive form because we have not made clear what inversion could possibly mean. Presumably, the semantic marker X bears some relationship to *any*, as condition (8.240) is clearly similar to the condition for occurrence of *any*.

(8.238) (Subject-aux inversion, version 2)

$$\left\{ \begin{matrix} NP \\ PP \\ Adv \end{matrix} \right\} - NP - Aux - VP$$

$$\quad 1 \qquad 2 \quad 3 \qquad 4 \Rightarrow 1 - 3 - 2 - \theta - 4$$

OPTIONAL

(8.239) (Projection rule for inverted Ss)

A sentence containing the configuration Aux $-$ NP $-$ VP receives the semantic marker X in its semantic interpretation (presumably in the modal structure).

OBLIGATORY

(8.240) (Well-formedness condition for inverted Ss)

A sentence containing a preposed negative whose scope is the entire sentence must have the semantic marker X in order to be semantically well-formed. Conversely, X may only occur in the scope of an affective.

In this system of rules, inversion is based only on the presence of a preposed constituent. If a preposed constituent contains a sentence negation but inversion does not take place, or if a preposed constituent does not contain a sentence negation but inversion does take place, the well-formedness condition will be violated.

One would hope of course that (8.239)–(8.240) could be presented in a more general form. In section 3.10 we presented some evidence that similar well-formedness conditions obtain between certain sentence adverbs and subject-aux inversion. This fact is at least further evidence for the existence of the projection rule (8.239) and well-formedness conditions similar to (8.240).

We are presented, then, with a difficult choice in accounting for the inversion problem. One solution is mechanically fairly simple, but it involves an important break with the linguistic theory we have been otherwise able to maintain. The other solution remains within the bounds of our theory but is more complex, though we have some evidence that this solution is independently necessary.

I will present one more argument that favors the solution (8.238)–(8.240) over the solution (8.237). Consider the behavior of preposed constituents in *that*-complements. Most preposed constituents, including noninverting negatives, are possible in *that*-complements.

(8.241) Ralph tried to convince Bill that, aside from Jack, no one could beat Schwarz at Chinese checkers.

(8.242) The primary reason for Bill's getting angry is that(,) at noon today(,) Myra walked out on him.

(8.243) ?Phil is prone to forget that BEANS(,) he has a hard time
$$\text{B}$$
DIGESTING.
$$\text{A}$$

(8.244) It is hard to believe that, in not too many years, Christmas will fall on a Sunday.

(8.245) The girl acknowledged that not long ago she had walked out on Bill.

However, preposed inverting negatives are much less satisfactory in these contexts, either with or without inversion.

(8.246)   Ralph tried to convince Bill that at no time $\left\{\begin{array}{l}??\text{had he}\\ *\text{he had}\end{array}\right\}$ beat Schwarz.

(8.247)   The primary reason for Bill's getting angry is that not for more than five minutes $\left\{\begin{array}{l}?*\text{had Fred}\\ *\text{Fred had}\end{array}\right\}$ hesitated.

(8.248)   Phil is prone to forget that nobody $\left\{\begin{array}{l}?*\text{could you}\\ *\text{you could}\end{array}\right\}$ find.

(8.249) ?*It is hard to believe that in not too many years will Christmas fall on a Sunday.

How can (8.246)–(8.249) be ruled out? It is well known that inversion must be restricted to main clauses. Accordingly, we can add the simple condition "This is a main clause" to the two versions of the inversion rule, (8.237) and (8.238). Now if (8.237) encounters a preposed inverting negative in a subordinate clause, the structural description of the transformation will not be met and no inversion will be performed. (8.237) therefore predicts the ungrammaticality of the inverted examples in (8.246)–(8.249); but it provides no way of eliminating the uninverted alternatives, since a transformation cannot rule out sentences that do not meet its structural description.

In the system of rules (8.238)–(8.240), preposed inverting negatives in subordinate clauses will also fail to trigger inversion, since inversion is restricted to main clauses. But if inversion does not take place, the projection rule (8.239) cannot assign the feature X to the subordinate clause, so the well-formedness condition (8.240) is not met. Hence examples like (8.246)–(8.249) are caught on the horns of a dilemma: if they undergo inversion, they are ungrammatical for violating the structural description of a transformation; if they do not undergo inversion, they are ungrammatical for failing a semantic well-formedness condition.

We conclude, then, that of the two possible solutions to the inversion problem, the more complex, but also more theoretically orthodox, is more adequate on independent empirical grounds. It remains for future research to clarify the nature of the necessary semantic rules.[9]

[9] I have not considered here the generalization of inversion to direct and indirect questions, which differs from its behavior with inverting negatives. Labov's data, cited in G. Lakoff (1970b), concerning dialects in which inversion can take place under certain conditions, may be of interest in this connection.

CHAPTER NINE

Consequences for the Transformational Cycle

Under the Lexicalist Hypothesis, nominalization transformations have been discarded in favor of a lexicon containing both verbs and nominalizations, with redundancy rules expressing the relationships between them. The elimination of nominalization transformations enables us to clarify and improve the conventions governing application of the transformational cycle.

In section 4.5, we mentioned an argument by Ross (1967a) that the transformations particle movement, extraposition, and extraposition from NP are last-cyclic, because they must take place after nominalization transformations. We will show that the acceptance of this position leads to some rather embarrassing results, and that an alternative is possible which simultaneously eliminates these difficulties and permits a strong constraint on the application of transformations in the cycle.

First, if Ross's argument is correct, we must conclude that dative shift is last-cyclic as well, by the following argument: If nominalizations are derived transformationally, and dative shift is cyclic, dative shift can take place before the nominalization transformations, which must apply on a later cycle. We then incorrectly predict that both (9.1) and (9.2) are acceptable derivations.

(9.1) We are happy to acknowledge your giving $500 to the fund.
    $\Rightarrow$ We are happy to acknowledge your gift of $500 to the fund.
    nom.
(9.2) We are happy to acknowledge your giving $500 to the fund.
    $\Rightarrow$ we are happy to acknowledge your giving the fund $500.
    dative
    $\Rightarrow$ *we are happy to acknowledge your gift (of) the fund (of) $500.
    nom.
    (*?Your gift to the fund of $500* arises from complex NP shift, parallel
    to *?you gave to the fund $500*, so it is irrelevant here.)

But if dative shift is last-cyclic and applies only in sentences, not in nominalizations, the derivation (9.2) will not take place.

Unfortunately, an independent argument seems to show dative shift to be cyclic. The standard case of cyclic application of transformations is exhibited by derivations with sequences of subject-raising and passive:

(9.3) $[_{s1}$ Bill believes $[_{s2}$ Max expects $[_{s3}$ Joe will slice the salami$]]]$.

   $\Rightarrow$ Bill believes Max expects the salami will be sliced by Joe.
passive in S³

   $\Rightarrow$ Bill believes Max expects the salami to be sliced by Joe.
subj. raising in S²

   $\Rightarrow$ Bill believes the salami is expected by Max to be sliced by Joe.
passive in S²

   $\Rightarrow$ Bill believes the salami to be expected by Max to be sliced by Joe.
subj. raising in S¹

   $\Rightarrow$ The salami is believed by Bill to be expected by Max to be
passive in S¹

      sliced by Joe.

But similar derivations can be constructed in which the noun phrase being successively raised and moved into subject position achieves that status through the application of dative shift:

(9.4) Bill believes Max expects Joe will give the salami to Fred.

   $\Rightarrow$ Bill believes Max expects Joe will give Fred the salami.
dative shift

   $\Rightarrow$ Bill believes Max expects Fred will be given the salami by Joe.
passive

   $\Rightarrow$ Fred is believed by Bill to be expected by Max to be given the salami
as in (9.3)

      by Joe.

Hence dative shift, by this argument, is in the cycle, in contradiction to the previous argument. If nominalization is a lexical process, however, we can resolve the contradiction. Dative shift, applying cyclically, will then never take place before nominalization, so restricting it to sentences will produce exactly the correct results.

    The hypothesis that such rules as dative shift, particle movement, extraposition, and extraposition from NP are last-cyclic leads to other difficulties as well. If these rules are last-cyclic, they must be able to apply to deeply embedded clauses as in the following examples:

(9.5) Max forced Tim to acknowledge that
$$\begin{cases} \text{Bob had given Fred the book.} \\ \text{Jill had looked the answer up.} \\ \text{it bothered Sue that Fred} \\ \quad \text{was sick.} \\ \text{a man had come in who was} \\ \quad \text{from Philadelphia.} \end{cases}$$

(9.6) John doesn't think that the fact that $\left\{\begin{array}{l}\text{Bob gave Fred the book} \\ \text{Jill looked the answer up} \\ \text{it bothered Sue that Fred was} \\ \quad\text{sick} \\ \text{a man came in who was from} \\ \quad\text{Philadelphia}\end{array}\right\}$

will faze your uncle.

But serious ordering problems arise if it is in general the case that, on a particular cycle, transformations may apply to clauses subordinate to the main clause of that cycle, that is, if transformations may contain *end variables* in the sense of Postal (1971, Chapter 13). For example, consider a derivation that starts as (9.7).

(9.7) John said that Bill gave the salami to Fred.

Suppose that on the first cycle the passive applies, yielding (9.8).

(9.8) John said that the salami was given to Fred by Bill.

Now on the second cycle, the subordinate clause of (9.8) meets the structural description for the passive again: there is a PP directly following the verb, whose NP can passivize under ordinary circumstances. But it is obvious that the passive cannot take place a second time to form (9.9).

(9.9) *John said that Fred was been given to by the salami by Bill.

It is true that suitable restrictions could be placed on the passive to prevent (9.9) from being formed. But in the simplest statement of the rule, if passive may operate on subordinate clauses, there is nothing to prevent (9.9). If we add restrictions, then, we are implying that the grammar of English would be simpler if (9.9) were grammatical, which is certainly incorrect.

Similarly, consider a derivation that begins with the underlying structure (9.10).

(9.10) $[_{S1}$John said $[_{S2}$that $[_{S3}$to show $[_{S4}$that $2 + 2 = 5]_{S4}]_{S3}$ is tougher than $[_{S5}$ to show that deep structure is slimy$]_{S5}]_{S2}]_{S1}$.

On the S^2 cycle, extraposition of S^3, followed by some comparative reduction rules, will yield (9.11).

(9.11) $[_{S1}$John said $[_{S2}$that it is tougher $[_{S3}$to show $[_{S4}$that $2 + 2 = 5]_{S4}]_{S5}$
than that deep structures are slimy$]_{S2}]_{S1}$.

Now *Tough* movement can apply to the NP dominating S^4, to yield (9.12).

(9.12) $[_{S1}$John said $[_{S2}$that $[_{S4}$that $2 + 2 = 5]$ is tougher to show than that
deep structures are slimy$]_{S2}]_{S1}$.

(9.12) as it stands is ungrammatical only because of the two *thats* in a row.
Removal of one of them makes the sentence reasonably acceptable:

(9.13) ?John said that $2 + 2 = 5$ is tougher to show than that deep structures are slimy.

However, if extraposition may operate on totally embedded clauses, its
structural description is met on the S^1 cycle by S^2, even though it already
has extraposed S^3 in the S^2 cycle to form (9.11). We then might expect S^4
to extrapose to form the totally unacceptable (9.14).

(9.14) *John said that it is tougher to show than that deep structures are
slimy that $2 + 2 = 5$.

If we try to avoid this conclusion by making extraposition last-cyclic, so
that it can only apply once in S^2, we are then unable to account for cases
like (9.15), in which extraposition and *Tough* movement must precede rules
applying on earlier cycles.

(9.15) Bill believes Max expects [[to please Joe] is tough].
⇒ Bill believes Max expects it is tough to please Joe
extraposition
⇒ Bill believes Max expects Joe to be tough to please
Tough movement
⇒ Joe is believed by Bill to be expected by Max to be tough to please
subj. raising and passive,
cyclically, as in (9.3)

These difficulties can be eliminated if we place the following constraint
on transformations:

(9.16) (Analyzability convention).

For a transformation to be applied correctly, the main clause (relative to the present cycle) must play an essential part in its application.

The constraint (9.16) can be divided into four cases, at least one of which must be met in applying a transformation:

(9.17)a. The transformation deletes, inserts, or moves a constituent of the main clause.

b. The transformation moves a constituent of a lower clause into the main clause.

c. The transformation performs some operation on a subordinate clause under direction of a rule feature on some element of the main clause.[1]

d. The transformation performs some operation involving elements of two disjoint subordinate clauses.

Adoption of this constraint will prevent the passive from applying to the subordinate clause on the second cycle of (9.8), and it will prevent extraposition from applying to the subordinate clause on the final cycle of (9.13).

If particle movement, dative shift, and the two extraposition rules were last-cyclic, constraint (9.16) could not be imposed on the theory, since (9.5) and (9.6) would be counterexamples. If they are cyclic, as in the present theory, there is no difficulty. As I know of no other derivations requiring

---

[1]The only examples of case (c) that come to mind immediately are complementizer deletion rules, such as the deletion of *to* after *see*: *I saw him* (**to*) *leave* but *He was seen* $\begin{Bmatrix} to \\ *0 \end{Bmatrix}$ *leave*. There may be a reanalysis of these constructions that eliminates these cases. There are to my knowledge no examples of case (d), in the present theory. However, the semantic rules of coreference and anaphor interpretation (for example *do so*) will often refer only to elements of two disjoint subordinate clauses, as in the interpretation of the pronoun in (i) or the *do so* in (ii).

(i) The man who met Mary yesterday claims that he has already seduced her.
(ii) His merely claiming that he seduced Mary does not convince me that he really did so.

Of course, in a transformational theory of these rules, the corresponding transformations will satisfy case (d).

violation of (9.16), and as it is a strong constraint on possible derivations, I suggest that (9.16) is a universal convention on applicability of transformations. (Related, even stronger, constraints have been proposed for independent reasons in Chomsky 1971.)

It appears also that no necessary flexibility is lost if the cyclic semantic rules of coreference also obey (9.16). This suggests that (9.16) is a more general condition on analyzability of structural descriptions. Whether it can be made to apply to the entire system of semantic rules proposed here (perhaps by making them all cyclic) remains an open question. Note that the noncoreferentiality rule, which must refer to potentially deeply embedded pairs of NPs, need not be an exception to (9.16), since it need have no syntactic conditions on its application—it can operate correctly, referring only to the functional structure and the table of coreference.

If (9.16) is correct, the scope of last-cyclic transformations is vastly restricted: a last-cyclic transformation must essentially involve the main clause. Thus the distinction between cyclic and last-cyclic transformations is coextensional with (and replaceable by) the distinction between transformations that apply in any clause and transformations which apply only in main clauses. This is in turn has important implications for Emonds's (1970) theory of constraints on transformations.

In Chapter 1 we briefly mentioned Emonds's hypothesis that transformations fall into two basic groups: root transformations and structure-preserving transformations. Root transformations may induce relatively drastic deformations on sentences, but they may occur only in root sentences—main clauses and a certain small class of other cases such as direct quotes. Structure-preserving transformations may operate in any clause, but they may perform only operations that result in a derived structure all of whose nodes are generable by the base rules, though perhaps with different semantic significance. Thus, for example, the passive, a structure-preserving rule, moves the direct object into subject position, a position provided for in the base, and the subject into a prepositional phrase, a position also provided for in the base. Emonds's hypothesis is a strong limitation on possible grammars; the present theory, with its rich base component and lack of transformations which create new structures (such as quantifier lowering), makes the hypothesis far more attractive than does a theory with an impoverished base and a rich transformational component, as advocated by the followers of Katz and Postal.

What is interesting in the present context is that Emonds's class of root

transformations will fall into our class of last-cyclic, or main clause, transformations. One might speculate that the two classes coincide, that is, that
all last-cyclic transformations perform the deformations characteristic of
root transformations, and that all structure-preserving transformations are
cyclic. If this were true, the cyclic or last-cyclic nature of a transformation
could be predicted simply on the basis of its structural change, further
constraining the theory.

CHAPTER TEN

Conclusions and Hypotheses

10.1 The Organization of the Grammar

According to the results of this study, a generative grammar consists of five major components: the lexicon, the base component, the transformational component, the phonological component, and the semantic component.

The *lexicon* contains a list of the formatives of the language and their syntactic, phonological, and semantic properties. It also contains a set of (probably unordered) redundancy rules which express morphological and semantic relationships among lexical items.

The *base component* contains a context-free phrase structure grammar, consisting of a set of unordered rules which collectively expand the symbol S into phrase markers whose preterminal strings are lexical category symbols. The base also contains a set of lexical insertion rules, which freely insert lexical items by category into the preterminal strings to form *deep structures*. The form we have suggested here for lexical insertion rules differs from that of *Aspects of the Theory of Syntax* in two important respects. First, lexical insertion is always optional, as we need to allow deep structures to contain empty (nonlexicalized) nodes (cf. sections 5.2 and 6.8). Second, we have claimed that the enforcement of strict subcategorization and selectional restrictions is a function of the semantic component; hence the mechanisms of *Aspects* for constraining lexical insertion according to these conditions, including the notion *complex symbol*, are not present in our conception of the base component.

The *transformational component* consists of a set of transformations which collectively map deep structures into a second set of phrase-markers called *surface structures*. The transformations are ordered with respect to each other, and their operation is governed according to the principle of the transformational cycle. In all these respects our conception of transformations is identical to that of *Aspects*. One important refinement was discussed in Chapter 9; several more will appear in section 10.2.

The *phonological component* maps surface structures into phonetic representations, as proposed in Chomsky and Halle (1968). We have made one addition to the system of rules developed there: in Chapter 6 we showed that the phonological component must contain rules which phonetically realize syntactic markers of focus and focus type as emphatic stress and intonation contour.

The *semantic component* consists of at least four subcomponents, corresponding to the four aspects of semantic interpretation we have discussed: functional structure, modal structure, coreference relations, and focus and presupposition. One subcomponent, corresponding to the type 1 projection rules of Katz and Postal (1964), derives the functional structure from deep structure grammatical relations and the functional semantic properties of lexical items. A second subcomponent develops the modal structure from lexical properties of modal operators and the structural configurations of both deep and surface (or perhaps end-of-cycle) structures, the choice being determined in a highly constrained fashion. A third subcomponent constructs a table of coreference from the structural configurations at the end of each transformational cycle. Finally, the focus and presupposition are derived on the basis of surface structure. In addition, there are rules that construct readings for empty nodes; these rules are probably allied to the coreference system, but they depend on the output of all the subcomponents.

The general nature of the rules of the semantic component is rather different from the rules in the transformational and phonological components. The latter two components take as input a labeled bracketing and convert it by a sequence of operations into another labeled bracketing. The intermediate stages of the derivation are likewise labeled bracketings. Semantic rules, on the other hand, construct a semantic interpretation by a process of accretion, each rule adding more information on the basis of syntactic structure at some level of derivation and (in some cases) the portion of the semantic interpretation already derived. Although there is an ordering among the subcomponents of the semantic component, induced by the levels of syntactic derivation at which they operate, we have found no evidence that the semantic rules are extrinsically ordered within subcomponents.

In addition to the five "generative" components of the grammar, there are at least two sets of well-formedness conditions on levels of derivation. The first is the system of *surface-structure constraints* proposed by Perlmutter (1970b, 1971). These constraints act as a filter on permissible derivations, rejecting derivations in which the surface structure does not fulfill some particular syntactic form, independent of what it means or how it has been derived. So far surface structure constraints have been applied most convincingly to problems of clitic ordering; Emonds (1970) points out that the constraints discovered by Perlmutter can be expressed by a phrase-structure grammar. Whether all surface structure constraints will be of this form is a matter of speculation.

We have made extensive use here of well-formedness conditions on semantic representations. Most of these appear to be expressions of a need for conceptual consistency, for example selectional restrictions and the Consistency Condition on the table of coreference. On the other hand, certain of these conditions, such as the Thematic Hierarchy Conditions on reflexivization and the passive, seem to be purely formal requirements on semantic representations. One would hope that these cases can eventually be shown to have conceptual rather than formal force.

We have given reason to believe that an adequate theory of grammar with an interpretive semantic component must include the concept of syntactic nodes as complexes of distinctive features. We have used the syntactic and semantic similarity of noun phrases to sentences essentially in our analysis of reflexivization, complement subject interpretation, and modal structure. In the analysis of adverbs we have crucially used the relation between adjectives and adverbs and their place in the syntactic structure of noun phrases and sentences respectively.

One particularly interesting revision of earlier theory that has been suggested by syntactic distinctive features is the extension of the transformational cycle to complex noun phrases. Concomitantly, the definition of the structural relation *command* has been revised to be dependent on any node that governs a cycle, rather than only S nodes.

10.2 Constraints on Possible Grammars

In Chapter 1 it was emphasized that the goal of a theory of grammar is to provide a maximally constrained concept of "possible human language." In this section we will propose some hypotheses about the nature of universal grammar that are suggested by the results of this study.

First consider the nature of semantic representation. If we are to preserve the idea of the universality of semantic representation, we must claim that all languages have semantic representations containing the same four aspects we have discovered in English: functional structure, modal structure, a table of coreference, and focus and presupposition. Furthermore, it is clear that those well-formedness conditions we have found in English with conceptual force must be universal, as we claim they follow immediately from the nature of human perception of the world.

A more interesting claim we could make is that the organization of the semantic component is universal. That is, the functional structure is derived from deep phrase-markers, the table of coreference from end-of-cycle phrase-markers, focus and presupposition from surface structures, and modal structure from both deep and surface structures. Further, we have seen that each subcomponent in English consists of a highly restricted type of rule. The rules building functional structure either attach additional semantic markers to a constant or function (attribution rules, e.g. P_{manner}) or replace variable arguments of functions with constants (e.g. $P_{speaker}$ and the rules of Chapter 2). The rules building modal structure assign modal conditions to noun phrases and Ss within the scope of modal operators. The rules of coreference add entries to the table of coreference. The rules of focus and presupposition form a presupposition by replacing the focus in the semantic representation with a variable. It would be an extremely powerful constraint on the class of possible grammars if the forms of these rules were universal. In fact, such a constraint is more powerful than the Katz-Postal Hypothesis, because it specifies much more precisely the form of possible semantic rules and their interactions.

This is not to say that the rules of semantic interpretation are universal, any more than the base or transformations are. It is clear, for example, that focus and presupposition are not realized with the same syntactic and phonological devices in all languages, and that reflexivization does not universally obey the constraints of English. What is claimed, rather, is that any device used to mark focus and presupposition, be it stress, syntactic position, or a focus morpheme, will be interpreted at the surface structure, conditioning a rule which performs the same operations upon semantic interpretation; whatever the structural conditions on reflexivization, if there is reflexivization in a language, they will be operative at the end of cycles, conditioning a rule making an entry in the table of coreference. Similarly, one might guess that certain aspects of the environment for pronominalization and reflexivization are universal; it might turn out that there are only a small number of possible options available.

Thus we have introduced a highly structured semantic component and made a very strong hypothesis about its universal limitations. If there were no concomitant reduction in the power of transformations, of course we would end up with a theory of grammar not significantly more constrained than that predicted by the Katz-Postal Hypothesis. Still, we would have shown that the theory proposed here captures a large number of generalizations inexpressible within the framework of the Katz-Postal Hypothesis; on these grounds alone the present theory is preferable.

However, it appears that some important reductions in the power of the transformational component are possible within our theory. First consider the simple problem of ordering. If there are transformations performing pronominalization, reflexivization, adverb lowering, quantifier lowering, focus marking, negative placement, and so forth, human grammars can presumably differ in how these transformations are ordered with respect to each other and with respect to other transformations. If, on the other hand, these aspects of language are accounted for as part of the highly structured semantic component we have proposed here, no question ever can arise as to their ordering—it is fixed by the structure of the semantic component and its relation to the transformational component. Hence the class of possible grammars is reduced by the elimination of a large number of combinatorial possibilities.

More significantly, the partial removal of the burden of interpretation from the deep structure permits a much less abstract conception of deep structure than necessary under the Katz-Postal Hypothesis; therefore the work the transformational component has to do to produce surface structures is reduced in important ways. To see this, let us go through the repertoire of operations transformations can perform, in the order (i) insertions, (ii) deletions, (iii) movements.

We have retained the traditional transformations that insert constants, for example *Do*-support, the insertion of *of* in nominalizations such as *the destruction of the city*, the pleonastic *it* of extraposition, and possibly the *by* of the passive. On the other hand, we have succeeded in severely reducing the need for insertion transformations to alter the morphological form of lexical items. The rules producing the phonological forms of nominalizations, adverbs, anaphoric expressions of all kinds, and complex modal forms such as *nothing* have been shown to be more adequately stated as part of the lexicon than as transformations inserting morphological material to replace or alter formatives in a phrase-marker. Hence the class of possible insertion operations is considerably reduced, if the Extended Lexical Hypothesis can be maintained.

There is strong syntactic motivation for certain transformations that delete constants, for example the deletion of the complementizer *that*, deletion of the complementizer *for* in the absence of a lexical subject, deletion of prepositions before complementizers, and deletion of some form of *be* in constructions like *the child sleeping in the alley*.[1] However, two important kinds of deletion operations appear to be eliminable under the present theory. The first is the large class of transformations proposed by generative semanticists which delete a main clause of some sort, often lowering some formative into a complement sentence: such transformations as adverb lowering, quantifier lowering, negative lowering, and performative deletion are replaced in our theory by semantic rules. Hence there is no need ever for a transformation to delete a main clause of any sort.

Furthermore, we have given reason to believe that many regularities expressed in earlier theories as transformations which delete constituents under conditions of identity with some other constituent can be expressed in our theory as semantic rules which provide interpretations for proforms generated in the base or empty nodes. It would be a highly significant restriction of linguistic theory if *all* deletions under identity could be eliminated. In section 6.8, an argument was presented showing that the interpretive theory of coreference predicts this restriction of linguistic theory, in that it is inconsistent with a theory which allows deletion of, for example, verb phrases containing pronouns under conditions of identity. We have sketched an approach to some of the simpler of these rules, but much further work is needed. It remains to be shown, in particular, that the interpretive approach can successfully account for those rules leaving a fairly complex syntactic residue, such as the comparative construction and Ross's (1969b) rule of Sluicing (producing sentences like *Some of the people left,*

but I don't know $\begin{Bmatrix} who \\ how\ many\ of\ them \end{Bmatrix}$. A revealing account of these con-

structions in interpretive terms would be strong confirmation of the ap-

---

[1]The paradigms seem to indicate that the deleted form is *being*: note *the people having seen the most*, **the child being sleeping in the alley*. *The people doing the most work* is ambiguous between *the people who* $\begin{Bmatrix} do \\ are\ doing \end{Bmatrix}$ *the most work*, which is explained by the deletion of the progressive *being* on one reading. *Be* occurs in present participial constructions only in the sense of a progressive passive, when there are two *bes* in the underlying form: *the house being built over there*. This contrasts with a nonprogressive present participial construction, in which the present participle of the passive auxiliary is deleted, leaving only a past participle at the surface: *the house built on that lot*. This argument was pointed out to me independently by Joseph Emonds and David Vetter.

proach, as it would eliminate a very important and powerful class of transformations.

The elimination of lowering transformations also permits a heavier constraint on movement transformations, namely, that transformations cannot move material from a higher clause into a lower clause. (This constraint was first suggested in Chomsky 1965.) The parenthetical transformation, an exception to the generalization that transformations move only constituents, has been eliminated (section 3.12). This leaves only the following three kinds of possible movement transformations: movement of constituents within a clause (e.g. passive, dative shift, subject-auxiliary inversion), upward movement of constituents over exactly one sentence boundary (e.g. subject raising, *Tough* movement), and upward movement of constituents over an essential variable (e.g. *wh*-fronting, topicalization, *Though* movement). Movements over a variable are further constrained by the complex NP constraint and the coordinate structure constraint (Ross 1967a), and if Ross's conjecture is correct, they may move constituents only to the left. Thus the class of movement transformations is relatively limited.

Various results of this study contribute to a simplification of the theory of syntactic exceptions proposed by G. Lakoff (1971). A significant number of transformations he used as evidence for his theory are treated in the present theory as lexical redundancy rules, for example, various nominalization processes, adverb formation, and his rule FLIP (= Postal's Psych Movement). Other generalizations he discusses are not captured in our theory by transformations, but by rules of semantic interpretation, for example interpretation of quantifiers and so-called *Not*-transportation (see the discussion of *Not*-transportation in Jackendoff 1971b). Other phenomena which Lakoff treats as syntactic irregularity have been accounted for by semantic processes of a much more restricted nature. For example, many verbs that do not undergo the passive can be restricted by the Thematic Hierarchy Condition on the passive. Likewise, the apparently irregular behavior of certain verbs with respect to complement subject deletion (or interpretation) is accounted for (Chapter 5) with the highly restricted devices of networks of coreference and assignment of responsibility, which were shown to have independent semantic justification. The work of Kiparsky and Kiparsky (1968) has shown some apparent irregularities in complement *It*-deletion to be motivated on semantic and structural grounds. Hence there remain many fewer cases of what can be called genuine syntactic irregularity, and in particular the notion of absolute exception seems to be dispensable. As it is precisely the use of absolute exceptions that permits the introduction of abstract lexical items, the elimination of this device is a clear reduction in the power of linguistic theory.

We see, then, that the research on English grammar presented here tends toward a picture of universal grammar as a relatively rigid, highly structured affair, with fewer options for the language learner than the variety of rule types seems initially to indicate. The degree to which such limitation can be carried out while maintaining fundamental generalizations is an important measure of the success of the investigation.

10.3 Why Are There Transformations?

In a search for deeper explanations of grammatical phenomena, one is led to ask why there should be transformations at all. More precisely, why should there be two syntactic levels in the grammar, deep and surface structure, related by transformations?

Although an absolute answer to this question is of course impossible, various hypotheses have been suggested, for example, by Yngve (1961) and Miller and Chomsky (1963). These hypotheses, interpreted in our framework, hinge on the assumption that the functional structure is mapped into a syntactic structure that preserves the embedding of the functional structure, and that the mapping is provided by the projection rules that interpret deep structures. Furthermore, it is supposed that one step in producing and interpreting sentences is passing them at some level of representation through a short-term memory of extremely limited capability. Transformations, it is suggested, alter deep structure in such a way as to eliminate structural complexities which are beyond the capability of short-term memory. These hypotheses differ primarily in what particular kinds of structural complexity are alleged to be of difficulty to the short-term memory. Yngve claims that excessive left-branching is a source of difficulty; Miller and Chomsky discuss the particular difficulty of self-embedded constructions, and more generally, difficulty in handling constructions with a high node-to-terminal ratio.

Many transformations, it is pointed out, have the property of eliminating these difficult structures and in general flattening out the embedding that must be present in deep structure to represent the functional structure adequately. Katz and Postal, under the assumption that all semantic information can be represented in functional structure, use this property of transformations as an argument that deep structure is the source of all semantic information (pp. 40 ff.). They argue that the flattening out of deep structures can represent only a loss of structural information; hence it is logical that interpretation should take place where the most information is available, at the level of deep structure.

The results of this investigation suggest another reason why there is a distinction between deep structure and surface structure. We have found that the semantic interpretation of a sentence contains at least four independent factors; functional structure, modal structure, table of coreference, and focus and presupposition. If these factors are to be relatively independent of each other, it may be in general difficult to represent all four consistently in a single syntactic phrase-marker. A particular choice of functional structure determines an associated phrase-marker fairly rigidly. If the other semantic factors, especially the modal structure, had to be represented in the same phrase-marker, conflicts would inevitably arise; a single phrase-marker does not provide sufficient information-carrying capability to represent four independent factors (especially two independent hierarchical structures), given the available types of projection rules. The use of two phrase-markers (deep structure and surface or end-of-cycle structure) in forming the interpretation of a clause provides a great deal more flexibility and independence of the semantic factors. For an extreme case, recall the examples of section 8.2:

(10.1) Only then didn't any of my friends arrive on time.   (= 8.66)
(10.2) Only then did any of my friends not arrive on time.   (= 8.67)
(10.3) None of my friends arrived on time only then.   (= 8.69)
(10.4) Not only then did any of my friends arrive on time.   (= 8.74)

These examples have the same functional structure but differ in modal structure and presupposition. Without a grammar involving two levels of interpretation, such variation would be impossible.

It seems plausible, then, that the function of transformations is to mediate between the various phrase-markers required for semantic interpretation, so that the phrase-markers can be identified as representations of the same sentence. If this hypothesis is correct, we would expect transformations not to preserve meaning, but rather to create new semantic possibilities or eliminate ambiguities. And in general this seems to be the case with those movement transformations we have had occasion to mention. The deformation of phrase-markers under transformations, in particular the reduction of embedding, does not then constitute a reduction in information content in the phrase-marker, as Katz and Postal claim, but rather a gain in the ability of the syntactic component to carry multidimensional semantic information.

It is important to observe that this conjecture is on a different level of inquiry than the rest of our investigation. Up until this point, we have been asking questions of the form: If we open up a human being, what do we find inside? The answers have been of the form: We find a four-chambered heart, a spine, some intestines, and a transformational grammar with two or more syntactic levels. The question of this section has been: What function do the things we have found serve? Why do they have the structure they have as opposed to any other? For example, why wouldn't a two-chambered heart do as well? To be sure, some questions of this sort may be unanswerable (for example, Why does the speed of light have the particular value it does as opposed to some other?), but this fact does not make the general line of inquiry useless.

Of course, our conjecture about the function of a two-level syntax only scratches the surface. We are immediately led to ask what it is about the mechanisms of human language capability that makes ordered rules and the transformational cycle essential parts of an accurate description, or even more basic, why language should be processed in terms describable by phrase-markers as opposed to any other formalism. At present, though, we are so far from being able to attack these questions intelligently that it is not even clear what would constitute a possible answer.

חזק

Akmajian, Adrian (1970a). On Deriving Cleft Sentences from Pseudo-Cleft Sentences. *Linguistic Inquiry* 1:2, 149–168.

——— (1970b). Aspects of the Grammar of Focus in English. Unpublished doctoral dissertation, Massachusetts Institute of Technology.

———, and Ray S. **Jackendoff** (1970). Coreferentiality and Stress. *Linguistic Inquiry* 1:1, 124–126.

Anderson, Stephen (1968a). Pro-Sentential Forms and Their Implications for English Sentence Structure. In **Kuno** (1968), VI:1–43.

——— (1968b). On the Linguistic Status of the Performative/Constative Distinction. Unpublished paper, Massachusetts Institute of Technology.

——— (1969). On How to Get *Even*. Unpublished paper, Massachusetts Institute of Technology.

——— (1970). Two Notes on Split Antecedents. *Linguistic Inquiry* 1:4, 545–547.

Austin, J. L. (1956–1957). A Plea for Excuses. *Proceedings of the Aristotelian Society,* 1956–1957. Reprinted in J. O. Urmson and G. J. Warnock, eds., *John L. Austin's Philosophical Papers,* New York: Oxford University Press, 1961.

——— (1962). *How To Do Things with Words,* ed. by J. O. Urmson. New York: Oxford University Press.

Bach, Emmon (1968). Nouns and Noun Phrases. In Bach and Harms (1968), pp. 91–124.

——— (1970). Problominalization. *Linguistic Inquiry* 1:1, 121–122.

———, and Robert T. **Harms,** eds. (1968). *Universals in Linguistic Theory.* New York: Holt, Rinehart, and Winston.

Baker, C. Leroy (1966). Definiteness and Indefiniteness in English. Unpublished master's thesis, University of Illinois.

——— (1970a). Double Negatives. *Linguistic Inquiry* 1:2, 169–186.

——— (1970b). A Note on Scope of Quantifiers and Negation. *Linguistic Inquiry* 1:1, 136–138.

Bever, Thomas (1970). The Cognitive Basis for Linguistic Structures. In J. R. Hayes, ed., *Cognition and Language Learning.* New York: Wiley.

Bierwisch, Manfred (1967). Semantic Universals of German Adjectivals. *Foundations of Language* 3:1, 1–36.

Binnick, R. I., A. **Davidson,** G. **Green,** and J. **Morgan,** eds. (1969). *Papers from the Fifth Regional Meeting of the Chicago Linguistic Society.* Chicago: University of Chicago, Department of Linguistics.

Bolinger, Dwight (1965a). The Atomization of Meaning. *Language* 41:555–573.

——— (1965b). *Forms of English: Accent, Morpheme, Order.* Edited by I. Abe and T. Kanekiyo. Cambridge: Harvard University Press.

——— (1970). The Meaning of *Do So. Linguistic Inquiry* 1:1, 140–144.

Bowers, John S. (1968). Some Adjectival Nominalizations in English. Unpublished paper, Massachusetts Institute of Technology.

——— (1969a). Adjectives and Adverbs in English. Bloomington: Indiana University Linguistics Club.

——— (1969b). Surface Structure Interpretation in English Superlatives. Unpublished paper, Massachusetts Institute of Technology.

Bresnan, Joan (1969). On Instrumental Adverbs and the Concept of Deep Structure. *MIT Quarterly Progress Report* No. 92 (15 January 1969), pp. 365–375.

Carden, Guy (1967). English Quantifiers. Unpublished master's thesis, Harvard University.

——— (1968). English Quantifiers. In Kuno (1968), IX:1–45.

——— (1970a). A Note on Conflicting Idiolects. *Linguistic Inquiry* 1:3, 281–290.

——— (1970b). Logical Predicates and Idiolect Variation in English. *Mathematical Linguistics and Automatic Translation*, Report NSF-25, Harvard Computation Laboratory.

Carnap, Rudolf (1956). *Meaning and Necessity: A Study in Semantics and Modal Logic.* Chicago: University of Chicago Press.

Chapin, Paul (1967). *On the Syntax of Word-Derivation in English.* Unpublished doctoral dissertation, Massachusetts Institute of Technology.

Chomsky, Noam A. (1957). *Syntactic Structures.* The Hague: Mouton.

——— (1964). Degrees of Grammaticalness. In Fodor and Katz (1964), pp. 384–389.

——— (1965). *Aspects of the Theory of Syntax.* Cambridge: MIT Press.

——— (1970a). Remarks on Nominalizations. In Jacobs and Rosenbaum (1970), pp. 184–221.

——— (1970b). Deep Structure, Surface Structure, and Semantic Interpretation. In Jakobson and Kawamoto (1970). Also in Steinberg and Jakobovits (1971), pp. 183–216.

——— (1970c). Some Empirical Issues in the Theory of Transformational Grammar. In Peters (to appear).

——— (1971). Constraints on Transformations. In S. Anderson and P. Kiparsky, eds., *Festschrift for Morris Halle.* New York: Holt, Rinehart and Winston.

———, and Morris **Halle** (1968). *The Sound Pattern of English.* New York: Harper & Row.

Culicover, Peter (1970). Syntactic and Semantic Investigations. Unpublished doctoral dissertation, Massachusetts Institute of Technology.

Darden, B., C.-J. **Bailey,** and A. **Davison,** eds. (1968). *Papers from the Fourth Meeting of the Chicago Linguistic Society.* Chicago: University of Chicago, Department of Linguistics.

Dean, Janet (1968). (= Janet Fodor) Nonspecific Noun Phrases in English. In Kuno (1968), VII:1–43.

Dougherty, Ray C. (1969). An Interpretive Theory of Pronominal Reference. *Foundations of Language* 5:4, 488–519.

——— (1970). A Grammar of Coordinate Conjoined Structures: I. *Language* 46:4, 850–898.

——— (1971). A Grammar of Coordinate Conjoined Structures: II. *Language* 47:2, 298–339.

Emonds, Joseph E. (1969). A Structure-Preserving Constraint on NP Movement Transformations. In Binnick et al. (1969), pp. 60–65.

———— (1970). *Root and Structure-Preserving Transformations.* Doctoral dissertation, Massachusetts Institute of Technology. Bloomington: Indiana University Linguistics Club.

Fillmore, Charles (1966). On the syntax of preverbs. Unpublished paper, Ohio State University.

———— (1968). The Case for Case. In Bach and Harms (1968), pp. 1–90.

———— (1971). Verbs of Judging: An Exercise in Semantic Description. In Fillmore and Langendoen (1971), pp. 273–290.

Fillmore, Charles, and D. T. **Langendoen,** eds. (1971). *Studies in Linguistic Semantics.* New York: Holt, Rinehart, and Winston.

Fischer, Susan D. (1968). Cleft Sentences and Contrastive Stress. Unpublished paper, Massachusetts Institute of Technology.

————, and Byron **Marshall** (1969). The Examination and Abandonment of the Theory of Begin of D. M. Perlmutter as Carried Out by Two of the Inmates of Room Twenty-E-Two-Fifteen, under the Direction of Divine Providence. Bloomington: Indiana University Linguistics Club.

Fodor, Janet Dean (1970). *The Linguistic Description of Opaque Contexts.* Unpublished doctoral dissertation, Massachusetts Institute of Technology.

Fodor, Jerry (1970). Three Reasons for Not Deriving "Kill" from "Cause to Die." *Linguistic Inquiry* 1:4, 429–438.

————, and Merrill **Garrett** (1966). Some Reflections on Competence and Performance. In J. Lyons and R. J. Wales, eds., *Psycholinguistics Papers.* Edinburgh: Edinburgh University Press.

————, and **Garrett** (1967). Some Syntactic Determinants of Sentential Complexity. *Perception and Psychophysics,* Vol. 2, pp. 289–296.

————, and Jerrold J. **Katz,** eds. (1964). *The Structure of Language.* Englewood Cliffs: Prentice-Hall.

Fraser, J. Bruce (1965). *An Examination of the Verb-Particle Construction in English.* Unpublished doctoral dissertation, Massachusetts Institute of Technology.

———— (1969). An Analysis of Concessive Conditionals. In Binnick et al. (1969), pp. 66–75.

———— (1970). A Reply to "On Declarative Sentences." In Kuno (1970), pp. 305–322.

Gleitman, Lila (1965). Coordination Conjunctions in English. *Language* 41:260–293. Reprinted in Reibel and Schane (1969).

Gruber, Jeffrey S. (1965). *Studies in Lexical Relations.* Doctoral dissertation, Massachusetts Institute of Technology. Bloomington: Indiana University Linguistics Club.
———— (1967a). Look and See. *Language* 43:937–947.

———— (1967b). *Functions of the Lexicon in Formal Descriptive Grammar.* Santa Monica: Systems Development Corporation, TM-3770/000/00.

Halliday, M. A. K. (1967). Notes on Transitivity and Theme in English. *Journal of Linguistics* 3:2, 199–244.

Heringer, James (1969). Indefinite Noun Phrases and Referential Opacity. In Binnick et al. (1969), pp. 89–97.

Horn, Laurence R. (1969). A Presuppositional Analysis of *Only* and *Even.* In Binnick et al. (1969), pp. 98–107.

Jackendoff, Ray S. (1966a). A Note on Selectional Restrictions. Unpublished paper, Massachusetts Institute of Technology.

———— (1966b). The Erased NP in Relatives and Complements. Unpublished paper, Massachusetts Institute of Technology.

———— (1968a). Quantifiers in English. *Foundations of Language* 4:4, 422–442.

———— (1968b). An Interpretive Theory of Pronouns and Reflexives. Bloomington: Indiana University Linguistics Club.

———— (1968c). Speculations on Presentences and Determiners. Bloomington: Indiana University Linguistics Club.

———— (1969a). *Some Rules of Semantic Interpretation for English.* Unpublished doctoral dissertation, Massachusetts Institute of Technology.

———— (1969b). An Interpretive Theory of Negation. *Foundations of Language* 5:2, 218–241.

———— (1971a). Gapping and Related Rules. *Linguistic Inquiry* 2:1, 21–36.

———— (1971b). On Some Questionable Arguments about Quantifiers and Negation. *Language* 47:2, 282–297.

———— (1971c). Review of Beverly Robbins, *The Definite Article in English Transformations. Foundations of Language* 7:1, pp. 138–142.

———— (1972). *Any* vs. *Every. Linguistic Inquiry* 3:1, 119–120.

———— (to appear). Morphological and Semantic Regularities in the Lexicon.

Jacobs, R., and P. **Rosenbaum,** eds. (1970). *Readings in Transformational Grammar.* Waltham, Mass.: Blaisdell.

Jakobson, Roman, and S. **Kawamoto,** eds. (1970). *Studies in General and Oriental Linguistics.* Tokyo: T.E.C. Corporation.

Karttunen, Lauri (1968). *What do Referential Indices Refer To?* Santa Monica: RAND Corporation, P–3854.

———— (1969). Discourse Referents. Bloomington: Indiana University Linguistics Club.

———— (1970). Implicative Verbs. Unpublished paper, University of Texas.

Katz, Jerrold J. (1966). *The Philosophy of Language.* New York: Harper & Row.

———— (1967). Recent Issues in Semantic Theory. *Foundations of Language* 3:2, 124–194.

————, and Jerry **Fodor** (1963). The Structure of a Semantic Theory. *Language* 39:2, 170–210. Reprinted in Fodor and Katz (1964).

————, and Paul M. **Postal** (1964). *An Integrated Theory of Linguistic Descriptions.* Cambridge: MIT Press.

Keyser, Samuel Jay (1968). Review of Sven Jacobson, *Adverbial Positions in English. Language* 44:357–374.

King, Harold (1970). On Blocking the Rules for Contraction in English. *Linguistic Inquiry* 1:1, 134–136.

Kingdon, Roger (1958). *The Groundwork of English Intonation.* London: Longmans, Green.

Kiparsky, Paul (1968). How Abstract is Phonology? Bloomington: Indiana University Linguistics Club.

———, and Carol **Kiparsky** (1968). Fact. In Steinberg and Jakobovits (1971), pp. 345–369.

Klima, Edward S. (1964). Negation in English. In Fodor and Katz (1964), pp. 246–323.

——— (1965). *Studies in Diachronic Syntax.* Unpublished doctoral dissertation, Harvard University.

——— (1966). Unpublished lectures, Massachusetts Institute of Technology.

Köhler, Wolfgang (1956). *The Mentality of Apes.* New York: Vintage Books.

Kuno, Susumu, ed. (1968). *Mathematical Linguistics and Automatic Translation,* Report NSF–20, Harvard Computation Laboratory.

———, ed. (1970). *Mathematical Linguistics and Automatic Translation,* Report NSF–24, Harvard Computation Laboratory.

Kuroda, S.-Y. (1968). Remarks on English Manner Adverbials. In Jakobson & Kawamoto (1970).

——— (1969). Attachment Transformations. In Reibel and Schane (1969), pp. 331–351.

Lakoff, George (1966). Deep and Surface Grammar. Bloomington: Indiana University Linguistics Club.

——— (1968a). Instrumental Adverbs and the Concept of Deep Structure. *Foundations of Language* 4:1, 4–29.

——— (1968b). Pronouns and Reference. Bloomington: Indiana University Linguistics Club.

——— (1969). On Derivational Constraints. In Binnick et al. (1969), pp. 117–139.

——— (1970a). Pronominalization, Negation, and the Analysis of Adverbs. In Jacobs and Rosenbaum (1970), pp. 145–165.

——— (1970b). On Generative Semantics. In Steinberg and Jakobovits (1971).

——— (1970c). Repartee, or a Reply to "Negation, Conjunction, and Quantifiers." *Foundations of Language* 6:3, 389–422.

——— (1971). *On Syntactic Irregularity.* New York: Holt, Rinehart, and Winston.

———, and P. S. **Peters** (1969). Phrasal Conjunction and Symmetric Predicates. In Reibel and Schane (1969), pp. 113–142.

———, and John Robert **Ross** (1966). A Criterion for Verb Phrase Constituency. In *Mathematical Linguistics and Automatic Translation,* Report NSF–17, Harvard Computation Laboratory, pp. II:1–11.

Lakoff, Robin T. (1968). *Abstract Syntax and Latin Complementation.* Cambridge: MIT Press.

——— (1969a). A Syntactic Argument for Negative Transportation. In Binnick et al. (1969), pp. 140–147.

——— (1969b). Some Reasons Why There Can't Be Any *Some-Any* Rule. Language 45:3, 608–615.

Langacker, Ronald (1969). Pronominalization and the Chain of Command. In Reibel and Schane (1969), pp. 160–186.

———— (1970). An Analysis of English Questions. Unpublished paper, University of California, San Diego.

Langendoen, D. T., and H. **Savin** (1971). The Projection Problem for Presuppositions. In Fillmore and Langendoen (1971), pp. 55–62.

Lasnik, Howard (1970). The Scope of Negation. Unpublished paper, Massachusetts Institute of Technology.

Lees, Robert B. (1960). *The Grammar of English Nominalizations.* The Hague: Mouton.

————, and Edward S. **Klima** (1963). Rules for English Pronominalization. *Language* 39:1, 17–28. Reprinted in Reibel and Schane (1969).

Lindholm, James (1969). Negative-Raising and Sentence Pronominalization. In Binnick et al. (1969), pp. 148–158.

McCawley, James D. (1968a). The Role of Semantics in a Grammar. In Bach and Harms (1968), pp. 125–170.

———— (1968b). Lexical Insertion in a Transformational Grammar without Deep Structure. In Darden et al. (1968), pp. 71–80.

———— (1970). Where Do Noun Phrases Come From? In Jacobs and Rosenbaum (1970), pp. 166–183.

Matthews, G. H. (1968). Le cas echéant. Unpublished paper, Massachusetts Institute of Technology.

Miller, George, and Noam **Chomsky** (1963). Finitary Models of Language Users. In R. D. Luce, R. Bush, and E. Galanter, eds., *Handbook of Mathematical Psychology,* vol. 2, pp. 419–492. New York: John Wiley and Sons.

Newmeyer, Frederick J. (1970). The "Root Modal": Can It Be Transitive? In *Festschrift for Robert B. Lees,* Linguistic Research, Inc.

Partee, Barbara Hall (1970). Negation, Conjunction, and Quantifiers: Syntax vs. Semantics. *Foundations of Language* 6:2, 153–165.

Perlmutter, David M. (1970a). On the Article in English. In M. Bierwisch and K. E. Heidolph, eds., *Progress in Linguistics.* The Hague: Mouton, pp. 233–248.

———— (1970b). Surface Structure Constraints in Syntax. *Linguistic Inquiry* 1:2, 187–256.

———— (1970c). The two verbs *begin.* In Jacobs and Rosenbaum (1970), pp. 107–119.

———— (1971). *Deep and Surface Structure Constraints in Syntax.* New York: Holt, Rinehart, and Winston.

Peters, P. S. (to appear). *Goals of Linguistic Theory.* Englewood Cliffs: Prentice-Hall.

Pope, Emily (1971). Answers to Yes-No Questions. *Linguistic Inquiry* 2:1, 69–82.

Postal, Paul M. (1967). Restrictive Relatives and Other Matters. Unpublished mimeo, IBM Corporation, Yorktown Heights.

———— (1970a). On the Surface Verb "Remind." *Linguistic Inquiry* 1:1, 37–120.

———— (1970b). On Coreferential Complement Subject Deletion. *Linguistic Inquiry* 1:4, 439–500.

———— (1970c). A Global Constraint on Pronominalization. Yorktown Heights: IBM Thomas J. Watson Research Center. Also in *Linguistic Inquiry* 3:1, 35–60.

———— (1971). *Crossover Phenomena.* New York: Holt, Rinehart, and Winston.

———— (to appear). The Best Grammar. In Peters (to appear).

Quang Phuc Dong (1969). Phrases anglaises sans sujet grammatical apparent. *Langages* 14:44–51.

Quine, W. V. O. (1960). *Word and Object.* Cambridge: MIT Press.

Rardin, Robert (1968). Sentence-Raising and Sentence-Shift. Unpublished paper, Massachusetts Institute of Technology.

Reibel, David, and Sanford **Schane,** eds. (1969). *Modern Studies in English.* Englewood Cliffs: Prentice-Hall.

Rosenbaum, Peter S. (1967). *The Grammar of English Predicate Complement Constructions.* Cambridge: MIT Press.

Ross, John Robert (1967a). *Constraints on Variables in Syntax.* Doctoral dissertation, Massachusetts Institute of Technology. Bloomington: Indiana University Linguistics Club.

———— (1967b). On the Cyclic Nature of English Pronominalization. In *To Honor Roman Jakobson,* The Hague: Mouton, pp. 1669–1682.

———— (1967c). Gapping and the Order of Constituents. Bloomington: Indiana University Linguistics Club.

———— (1967d). Auxiliaries as Main Verbs. Unpublished mimeo, Massachusetts Institute of Technology.

———— (1969a). Adjectives as Noun Phrases. In Reibel and Schane (1969), pp. 352–360.

———— (1969b). Guess Who? In Binnick et al. (1969), pp. 252–286.

———— (1970). On Declarative Sentences. In Jacobs and Rosenbaum (1970), pp. 222–272.

Ruwet, Nicolas (1968). Adverbs: A Note on the Question: Where Do they Come From? Unpublished paper, Massachusetts Institute of Technology.

Smith, Carlota (1969). Ambiguous Sentences with "And." In Reibel and Schane (1969), pp. 75–79.

Staal, J. F. (1965). Review of Katz and Postal (1964). *Foundations of Language* 1:133–154.

Steinberg, D., and L. **Jakobovits** (1971). *Semantics: An Interdisciplinary Reader in Philosophy, Linguistics, and Psychology.* New York: Cambridge University Press.

Stockwell, Robert P. (1960). The Place of Intonation in a Generative Grammar of English. *Language* 36:3, 360–367.

————, Paul **Schachter,** and Barbara **Partee** (1969). *Integration of Transformational Theories on English Syntax.* Department of Linguistics, University of California, Los Angeles.

Vendler, Zeno (1967). Each and Every, Any and All. In Vendler, *Linguistics in Philosophy.* Ithaca: Cornell University Press.

Warshawsky, Florence (1965). Reflexivization I, II. Unpublished paper, Massachusetts Institute of Technology.

Weinreich, Uriel (1966). Explorations in Semantic Theory. In T. Sebeok, ed., *Current Trends in Linguistics,* Vol. III. The Hague: Mouton.

Williams, George (1968). Why do you *Do So* like you Do Do Do? Unpublished paper, Massachusetts Institute of Technology.

Wittgenstein, Ludwig (1958). *The Blue and Brown Books.* New York: Harper and Row.

Yngve, Victor (1961). The Depth Hypothesis. In Roman Jakobson, ed., *Proceedings of the Twelfth Symposium in Applied Mathematics.* Providence: American Mathematical Society.

INDEX OF RULES MENTIONED

See Index for page numbers
* denotes a rule not in the grammar proposed here
? denotes a rule whose existence is questionable
# denotes a rule whose proper component has been left open

Base Component
Base rules for Aux, $\bar{\text{N}}$, PP, S, VP
Lexical insertion rules
Lexicon redundancy rules
Transportability

Phonological Component
Compound Rule
Emphatic Stress Rule
Main Stress Rule
Nuclear Stress Rule

Transformational Component

Constant insertions
* Attachment transformations
Do-support
Number agreement
Of-insertion
Possessive insertion
There-insertion

Constant deletions
By someone deletion
It-deletion
* Performative deletion
Preposition deletion before *that* and *for*
Relative clause reduction
With-deletion (instrumentals)

Clause-internal movements
About movement
? Adverb movement transformations
AdvDeg movement
Adverb(ial) preposing
Affix attachment
Complex NP shift
* Conjunct movement
Dative shifts (*to* and *for*)
* *Each*-movement
* *Even*-movement
Extraposition
Extraposition from NP
Have-be raising
? *Have* raising

Negative constituent preposing
Neg-contraction
* *Neg*-placement rules
Particle movement
Passive
PP preposing
* Psych movement
Subject-aux inversion
There-insertion
Transportability

Movements over clause boundaries
Adj-N ← N which is Adj
* Adverb lowering rules
* Cleft sentence formation
Complement subject raising (*It*-replacement)
* Focus transformation (Cleft → stress)
How exclamation fronting
* *Neg* lowering
* *Not*-transportation
* NP creating transformations
* Parenthetical transformation
* Quantifier lowering
So-Adv preposing
Though movement
Topicalization (Y movement)
Tough movement
Wh-preposing

* *Deletions under identity*
# Comparative reductions
* Complement subject (Equi-NP)
  deletion
Conjunction reduction
* *Do So, Do It*
* Gapping
* Late reflexivization
* Pronominalization
* Prosententialization
* Reflexivization
* Sluicing
* *Too-enough* NP deletion
* VP deletion